In this brilliant, definitive study, Père de Vaux has collected, sifted and organized a tremendous amount of information about the society and institutions of ancient Israel. His work is vast in scope, covering every aspect of Israelite life in Old Testament times, and will be an indispensable reference book for scholars. But it was primarily written for the non-specialist, giving him a fascinating and readable account of the society that was ancient Israel.

Father Roland de Vaux, O.P., is the director of the renowned Ecole Biblique in Jerusalem (Jordan) and was for fifteen years editor of its famous Revue Biblique. He is also a distinguished field archaeologist and a specialist in Biblical scripts and languages. In 1964-65 he was guest professor at Harvard Divinity School.

Volume 1: Social Institutions contains the Introduction and Parts I through III of the original one-volume edition.

Volume 2: Religious Institutions contains Part IV of the original edition.

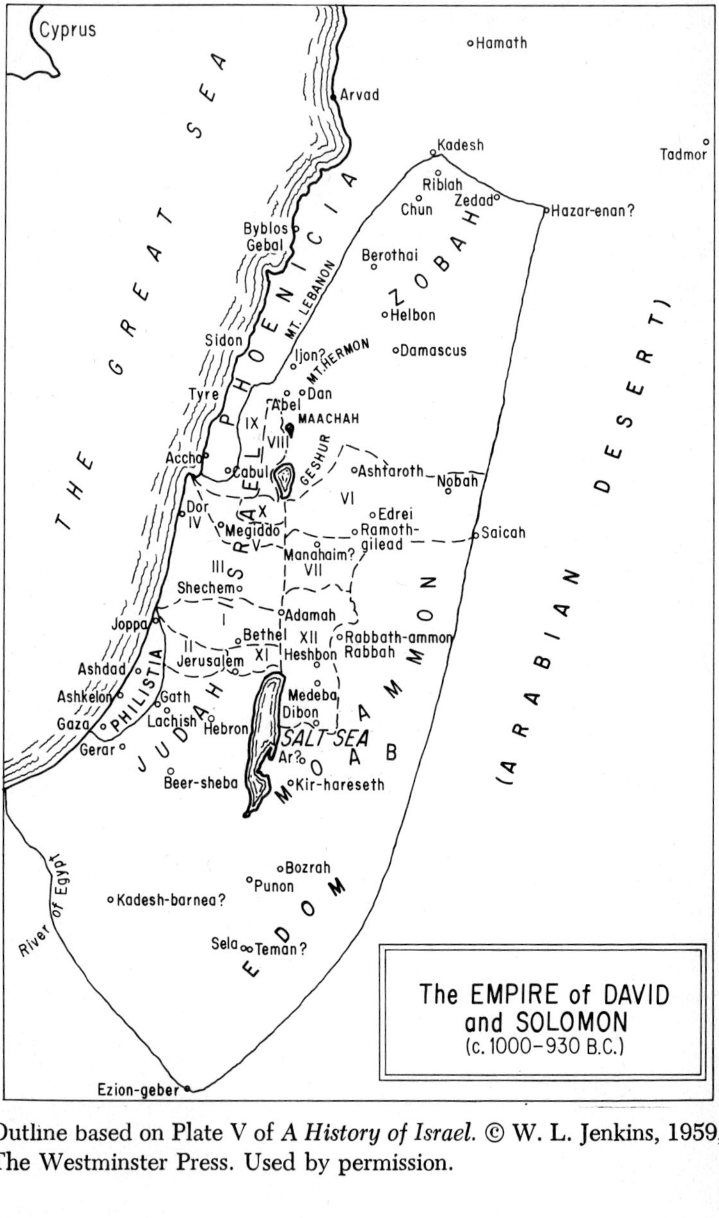

Outline based on Plate V of *A History of Israel.* © W. L. Jenkins, 1959, The Westminster Press. Used by permission.

Ancient Israel

Roland de Vaux

Volume 2

Religious Institutions

McGraw-Hill Book Company
New York Toronto

First McGraw-Hill Paperback Edition, 1965
1213141516171 MUMU 8987654321
ISBN 07-016600-5

Library of Congress Catalog Card No: 61-12360
Originally published in France under the title of
Les Institutions de L'Ancien Testament
by Les Editions du Cerf

First published in the United States by McGraw-Hill, Inc. in 1961

McGraw-Hill Paperbacks

Nihil obstat: Joannes M. T. Barton, S.T.D., L.S.S., Censor deputatus. Imprimatur: E. Morrogh Bernard, Vic. Gen., Westmonasterii, die 8a Februarii, 1961. The Nihil obstat and Imprimatur are a declaration that a book or pamphlet is considered to be free from doctrinal or moral error. It is not implied that those who have granted the Nihil obstat and Imprimatur agree with the contents, opinions or statements expressed.

Printed in the United States of America

TO THE STUDENTS OF THE ÉCOLE BIBLIQUE

WITH WHOM I HAVE LEARNED

WHAT THIS BOOK CONTAINS

TRANSLATOR'S NOTE

THIS book is a translation of *Les Institutions de l'Ancien Testament*, published in two volumes by *Les Editions du Cerf*, Paris; the first volume was published in 1958, the second in 1960. The translation has been made from this first edition of the French original, but it incorporates a number of additions and corrections which Fr de Vaux wishes to see inserted in the text; he has also brought the entire bibliography up to date to the beginning of 1961. The principal additions will be found on pp. 37, 58, 82, 130 and 208, and the main corrections on pp. 147, 183 and 203.

The spelling of proper names follows that to be adopted in the forthcoming *Jerusalem Bible*,[1] the English edition of the *Bible de Jérusalem*,[2] but biblical names have been registered in the index under the spelling given in the Authorized Version as well. Biblical references are in every instance to the original text (Hebrew, Greek or Aramaic); where the numeration of verses differs among the various translations, it would have been cumbersome to refer to all the numerations in both Catholic and non-Catholic versions. The references have therefore been left as they stand, but they can always be found by referring to the *Bible de Jérusalem*. The index has been rearranged and expanded; in particular, the longer entries (*e.g.* Abraham) have been broken down into sub-headings, and the main references have been given first.

It only remains for me to thank Fr de Vaux for the interest he has taken in this translation, for the promptness with which he has answered all my queries, and for enabling us to include so much new material, especially in the Bibliography.

Ushaw College, Durham
Easter, 1961

1. London: Darton, Longman & Todd Ltd; New York: Doubleday & Co. Inc.
2. Paris: Les Editions du Cerf.

NOTE ON NOMENCLATURE OF SOME BOOKS OF THE BIBLE AND APOCRYPHA

FOR the convenience of readers who are not familiar with the nomenclature adopted in this book, the lists below show the equivalents in the Authorized/King James Version, and in Douai-Challoner and Knox, where differences occur.

A.V./K.J.	*In this book*	*D-C., Knox*
Joshua	Josue	Josue
1 Samuel	1 Samuel (1 S)	1 Kings
2 Samuel	2 Samuel (2 S)	2 Kings
1 Kings	1 Kings (1 K)	3 Kings
2 Kings	2 Kings (2 K)	4 Kings
1 Chronicles	1 Chronicles (1 Ch)	1 Paralipomena
2 Chronicles	2 Chronicles (2 Ch)	2 Paralipomena
Ezra	Esdras (Esd)	1 Esdras
Nehemiah	Nehemias (Ne)	2 Esdras
1 Esdras	3 Esdras	——
2 Esdras	4 Esdras	——
Tobit	Tobias	Tobias
Ecclesiastes	Qoheleth (Qo)	Ecclesiastes
Ecclesiastes	Sirach (Si)	Ecclesiasticus
Solomon	Canticle (Ct)	Canticle of Canticles (D-C.) Song of Songs (Knox)
Hosea	Osee (Os)	Osee
Obadiah	Abdias (Abd)	Abdias
Micah	Michaeas	Michaeas
Zephaniah	Sophonias (So)	Sophonias
Haggai	Aggaeus	Aggaeus
Revelation	Apocalypse (Ap)	Apocalypse

CONTENTS VOLUME II

PART IV

RELIGIOUS INSTITUTIONS

IV

RELIGIOUS INSTITUTIONS

INTRODUCTORY

THOUGH this section has been entitled 'Religious Institutions', to keep the parallel with the three previous sections, the title is not meant to indicate a rigid distinction, for religion penetrated the entire social life of the nation. Circumcision had a religious significance; in the sense defined above, the monarchy was a religious institution; war itself, at least at the beginning of Israel's history, was a religious act; and Israelite law, even where it concerned profane matters, remained a religious law, and allowed for the possibility of an appeal to the judgment of God. In this section, however, we shall discuss those institutions which are directly concerned with the external worship of God.

By 'cult' we mean all those acts by which communities or individuals give outward expression to their religious life, by which they seek and achieve contact with God. But since God, as Creator, necessarily takes precedence of every creature, man's action in cultic worship is basically the response of a creature to his Creator. Lastly, cultic worship is essentially a social phenomenon: even when an individual offers such worship, he does so in accordance with fixed rules, as far as possible in fixed places, and generally at fixed times. If we take cult in this, its strict sense, it cannot exist without ritual.

The usual Hebrew word for the cult is *'abodah*: it is a 'service', like the service given to the king (1 Ch 26: 30). The primary meaning of 'serving' God is giving him outward worship (Ex 3: 12; 9: 1, 13, etc.). The Bible speaks of the 'service' of Yahweh (Jos 22: 27), of the 'service' of the Tent (Ex 30: 16, etc.), of the Dwelling (Ex 27: 19, etc.) and of the Temple (Ez 44: 14, etc.). The same word is used for a particular act of cultic worship (Ex 12: 25-26; 13: 5).

By 'rites' we mean the outward forms which this service takes. Israelite ritual may be similar to the rituals of other religions, or even borrowed from them; but its important feature lies in the new meaning which these rites received, a meaning which was determined by the religious ideas of Israel's faith. Without trespassing into the domain of biblical theology, we must underline the characteristics of the Israelite cult, and see what distinguishes it from other Oriental cults, even when the rites are the same.

(1) The Israelites worshipped a God who was the only God. From the first settlement in Canaan almost to the end of the monarchy, this did not prevent them from worshipping in several sanctuaries, but it did mean that in all these sanctuaries the same God was adored, and that any worship offered to gods

other than Yahweh was condemned, as in the first of the Ten Commandments (Ex 20: 3; Dt 5: 7) and in Dt 6: 13: 'Thou shalt fear Yahweh thy God, and shalt "serve" none but Him'. In particular, this faith precluded belief in any female deity as consort of Yahweh, and thereby excluded all those sensual rites which stemmed from belief in wedded divinities. For Israel there was only one God, a holy God, before whom man became conscious of his uncleanness and his sins: hence one of the purposes of Israelite cult was purification and expiation, though the precise degree to which this idea was present depended on the particular act of worship and the stage of religious development at the time.

(2) The Israelites worshipped a personal God who intervened in history: Yahweh was the God of the Covenant. Their cult was not the re-enacting of myths about the origin of the world, as in Mesopotamia, nor of nature-myths, as in Canaan. It commemorated, strengthened or restored that Covenant which Yahweh had made with his people at a certain moment in history. Israel was the first nation to reject extra-temporal myths and to replace them by a history of salvation, and all the echoes of ancient myths which can be perceived in certain passages of the Old Testament do not lessen the originality of this idea. To-day, when some writers would hold that even in Israel, ritual was the expression of myth, it is important to stress that the Israelite cult was connected with history, not with myth.

(3) The Israelites had no images in their cult. Both versions of the Decalogue contain the prohibition of images (Ex 20: 4 and Dt 5: 8), and the prohibition certainly dates back to the age of Moses. This prohibition was a primitive and characteristic feature of Yahwism, and the reason for it was that Yahweh was a God who could not be seen, and who therefore could not be represented. Yahweh spoke from the height of heaven (Ex 20: 22-23), and the Israelites saw nothing when Yahweh spoke to them out of the fire on Sinai (Dt 4: 15-18): the two texts draw the same conclusion, that men must not fashion cultic images. This does not mean that Yahweh was thought of, from the very beginning, as a purely spiritual being, for such words would have meant nothing to the Hebrew mind; but it does mean that any image of God would be inadequate. In other words, the prohibition of images is an implicit recognition that God is transcendent; it was left to later ages to define him as a spiritual being. From the very beginning, the prohibition of images safeguarded the religion of Israel from copying foreign systems of worship, where gods were represented like men, with bodily and sensual needs demanding satisfaction. The consequences of this were important. In spite of modern arguments to the contrary, there was never any image of Yahweh in the Ark. There was never any such image at Shiloh or in the Temple of Solomon, and Jeroboam's 'golden calves' were originally only the supports of the invisible godhead. The Holy of Holies, where Yahweh made himself present, was not open to the faithful; and the altar of Yahweh, unlike other

altars, had no statue or divine symbol connected with it. Rather, Israelite sacrifices rose in smoke to the heaven where Yahweh dwelt.

The study of cultic institutions is therefore bound up with biblical theology. But it is connected also with the history of religions, where it looks for analogies, for the explanation and perhaps even the origin of rites. In the present work, however, we are not concerned to describe how in fact the Israelites practised their religion, for they were, especially at certain periods, allured to a syncretist, or even to a purely pagan, cult. Such deviations will be touched on only indirectly in the following chapters. Our aim is rather to describe those cultic institutions which the Old Testament presents as legitimate institutions of true Yahwism. We shall describe first, the places of cultic worship, secondly, the persons involved in it, then the acts prescribed (especially sacrifice, the main act), and lastly, the religious calendar and its feasts.

CHAPTER ONE

SEMITIC SANCTUARIES

CULT is the outward homage paid to a god. Since the god is thought of as receiving this homage and listening to the prayer of his suppliant in the place where this worship is offered, the god is considered to be present there in some way or other, at least while the act of worship is being performed. This notion is common to all religions, and our present purpose is to see how it was expressed among the Semites, and, more particularly, among the Canaanites and Israelites.

1. *Sacred territory*

It seems to be a characteristic of Semitic religion that the holy place is not merely the precise spot, an altar of sanctuary, where worship is performed; it includes also a certain space around the temple or altar. Of course, this is not something exclusively Semitic: the larger Greek Temples were surrounded by a *temenos*, enclosed by a *peribole*: the area inside was the sacred precinct. Among the Semites, however, this sacred precinct seems to have had a special importance.

At Khafajeh in central Mesopotamia, there was from 3000 B.C. onwards a temple which had a large forecourt and which was surrounded by an oval precinct of 100 by 70 yards. There may have been a similar sanctuary at the same epoch in northern Mesopotamia, at El-'Obeid. At Uqair the temple stood on a broad esplanade, but occupied less than half of it. Though this type of temple did not survive, the great Babylonian temples generally had a large forecourt; the strictly Assyrian temples, however, did not, but their plans show evidence of non-Semitic influence. Inside big towns, the temples with their courts were grouped together in a sacred quarter. Under the Third Dynasty of Ur, the ziggurat and the buildings connected with the cult were enclosed in a precinct measuring 200 yards square; it was repaired time and time again, and even enlarged in the neo-Babylonian period. At Babylon, the ziggurat of Etemenanki stood inside an enclosure 400 yards square, with religious buildings along its sides. At Mareb in Arabia, in the first millennium B.C., there was a sanctuary of the moon-god Ilumqah, to which later tradition gave the name *Mahram Bilqis*, the 'sacred territory of Bilqis', the Arabic name for the queen of Sheba: its shape was oval, its size 100 by 70 yards, and it was flanked by a large peristyle entry.

In Phoenicia and in Syria, the oldest temples which have been well preserved date back only to the Hellenistic period, but they certainly carry on the tradition of a more ancient style. The most impressive is the sanctuary of Bel at Palmyra, which stands in the centre of an esplanade 225 yards square. Similarly, the sanctuary of Betotece, near Tartus, is a little Ionic temple in a courtyard of 140 by 90 yards; Amrit and Umm el-'Amed could also be mentioned.

Solomon's temple in Jerusalem followed this tradition: it too was surrounded by a courtyard. This court was enlarged by Herod until it became an esplanade 300 yards broad and nearly 500 yards long. Indeed, even in the desert sanctuary, according to Ex 27: 9-19, the Tent stood in an enclosure of 100 by 50 cubits, and Ezechiel visualized the future temple as standing in a court 500 cubits square 'to separate the sacred from the profane' (Ez 42: 20).

Where public worship was conducted in the open air outside the cities, the sacred space could be marked off by a line of stones, like those which nowadays surround certain Moslem *welis* or which mark a place of prayer in the desert. If any of these crude installations have survived from antiquity, it is impossible to distinguish them from enclosures of a much later period. But one biblical text throws light on them. The first halt of the Israelites after crossing the Jordan was *ha-Gilgal*, 'the Gilgal'. Here they camped (Jos 4: 19; 5: 10; 9: 6; 10: 6, etc.), were circumcised (Jos 5: 9), and celebrated the Passover (Jos 5: 10). Under Saul, sacrifices were offered there 'before Yahweh' (1 S 10: 8; 11: 15; 13: 7f.; 15: 21, 33). Later, however, the prophets condemned the sacrifices at Gilgal, along with those offered at Bethel (Os 12: 12; Am 4: 4). Gilgal, then, was a place of public worship, which retained its importance for several centuries, but there is no mention of a temple built there. (The Beth-ha-Gilgal of Ne 12: 29 refers to another place.) Now the word *gilgal* means a 'circle' (of stones)—cf. *galgal*, 'a wheel'—and Jos 4: 20 says that Josue there set up twelve stones taken from the bed of the river Jordan. These stones, then, probably marked the boundaries of the sacred enclosure: they may have been placed there by the Israelites when they selected their first place of worship in the Promised Land; or it may be that they marked the site of an older Canaanite sanctuary, and that their presence was explained later by a reference to the history of Israel.

The 'holy place' might be a vast stretch of land or even an entire mountain. Mecca is surrounded by sacred territory, the *haram*: it takes several hours to walk through it, and, in days gone by, its boundaries were only vaguely indicated by a number of stones (*anṣab*). The whole of mount Hermon was sacred, as its name (a cognate of *ḥaram*) implies. Indeed, just before the great theophany of Sinai, Moses was commanded by Yahweh to mark out the circumference of the mountain: no one was to climb it, or even to touch its base (Ex 19: 12).

2. *The sacred character of places of cultic worship*

A place of worship was sacred, *i.e.* withdrawn from profane use: this is the ultimate meaning of 'sacred'. The 500 cubits around the temple of Ezechiel were there 'to separate the sacred from the profane' (Ez 42: 20). There were two possible reasons for setting apart a space which was held to be sacred: men may have decided to cut off a definite portion of land from their own territory in order to consecrate it to God, as a kind of tithe on the earth; by paying this tithe, they could then make free use of the rest; alternatively, they may have put a stop to profane activity because the mysterious and fearful presence of a divinity in his sanctuary radiated around the place of worship, and this second reason is more in conformity with the texts, the rites and the spirit of Semitic religion. But whichever view be correct, the consequences are the same: the sacred territory was reserved, and characterized by certain prohibitions and privileges. Throughout the whole of Mecca's *ḥaram*, hunting, cutting down trees and even cutting grass are forbidden, apart from a few exceptions which the skill of casuists has devised. Before entering it, everyone must perform certain sacral rites, and put on special clothes; at least one part of this territory is a place of asylum.

It was exactly the same in Israel. The interdict concerning Sinai has already been mentioned (Ex 19: 12). After his dream at Bethel, Jacob cried out: 'How fearsome is this place!' (Gn 28: 17). God said to Moses at the burning bush: 'Do not come near this place. Take off thy sandals from thy feet, for the place where thou art standing is holy ground' (Ex 3: 5). The Israelites were forbidden to go near the Tent (Nb 18: 22). In the Temple at Jerusalem, notices protecting the sanctuary were posted up, and the admonitions became more and more severe as one approached the sanctuary itself. Gentiles were not allowed into the court of Israel, and notices reminded them that the penalty for infringing this precept was death. The liturgy itself did not take place in the Holy of Holies; the high priest alone could enter there, and then but once a year, and alone, on the great Day of Atonement (Lv 16: 15; He 9: 7). The Temple was also a place of asylum (1 K 1: 50-53; 2: 28-31). The six cities of refuge, which also enjoyed this privilege of asylum (Jos 20: 1-6), had inherited it from ancient sanctuaries in the same place.[1]

3. *The choice of places of cultic worship*

The choice of places where the cult might be practised was not left to man's discretion. In such a place, the worshipper could meet his god: the place had to be indicated, therefore, by a manifestation of the god's presence or by his activity. This could happen in two ways: by an explicit manifestation, *e.g.* when the deity appeared, or gave a command, or a sign; or by an

1. Cf. p. 163.

implicit manifestation, when natural effects were ascribed to the power of a god.

(a) *Theophanies.* We shall see later[1] how divine apparitions determined the places where the patriarchs worshipped. Under the Judges, the sanctuary of Ophra was founded by Gideon on the spot where, according to one tradition (Jg 6: 24), the Angel of Yahweh appeared to him or, according to another tradition (Jg 6: 25-26), where he received the command of Yahweh in a dream. The Temple of Jerusalem was built on the spot where the Angel of Yahweh had stood and where David had set up an altar (2 S 24: 16-25). In Ex 20: 24 (the text needs no correction), God promises to accept the sacrifices offered in any place where he may 'call to mind his Name', *i.e.* wherever he may manifest his presence.

There is nothing quite like this anywhere else in the Semitic world, presumably because we do not happen to have sufficiently explicit texts about the first foundation of sanctuaries. In Mesopotamia, however, the deity intervenes when his temple has to be restored. Akkadian ritual prescribes that when a temple is in danger of falling down, it may be demolished and rebuilt only if favourable omens can be obtained. Marduk gave Nabopolassar the order to restore the ziggurat of Babylon, the Etemenanki. Under Nabonidus, Marduk is said to have stirred up the winds which uncovered the foundations of the temple which the king was to restore. Again, Nabonidus saw Marduk and Sin in a dream, ordering him to restore the temple of Sin at Haran. But the most explicit example of all is the dream of Gudea at Lagash, about 2000 B.C.: the god Ningirsu appeared to him and commanded him to restore his temple, the Eninnu, according to a plan which he showed him. If the gods intervened in this way to have their sanctuaries restored, they must have done the same when they were first built and when the site itself was selected.

(b) *Sacred waters.* The nature-religion of Canaan saw a manifestation of divine presence or action in the springs which made the earth fruitful, in the wells which provided water for flocks, in the trees which bore witness to this fertility, and in the high places where the clouds gathered to give their longed-for rain. The Israelites and their ancestors were shepherds and peasants, and they too shared this mentality.

If, however, we set aside all ideas and myths concerning the sacredness of waters, rivers and the sea, and fix our attention on places of worship connected with water, we are struck by the relative scarcity of such places. In Syria, there is a spring at Palmyra and the pool of Hierapolis; in Phoenicia, there is the spring of Afqa and a few others. Monuments and texts provide no evidence of any public worship in these places before the Hellenistic epoch, but the cult practised at that time was a Syrian or Phoenician cult in a Greek disguise, and the cult had probably been in vogue in earlier ages.

1. Cf. p. 288 ff.

In Palestine, during the Graeco-Roman epoch, there was a sanctuary dedicated to Pan near one of the sources of the Jordan: it must have taken the place of an earlier sanctuary of a Canaanite divinity. A few place-names in the Bible, taken in their immediate context, probably point to the existence of sanctuaries near a spring or well: Qadesh, whose name marks it out as a 'holy' place, is also called (Gn 14: 7) the Spring of Judgment or of the Oracle—En-Mishpat. On the road from Jerusalem to Jericho, there was a Spring of the Sun—En-Shemesh (Jos 15: 7; 18: 17); in Jerusalem there was a Dragon's Spring—En-ha-Tannin (Ne 2: 13); a village in the Negeb was called Baalath-Beer, which may mean 'Lady of the Well' (Jos 19: 8); all these names are evidence of a cult, or at least of a religious legend. The well of Lahai-Roi, 'of the Living One who sees', preserved the memory of the divine apparition to Hagar (Gn 16: 13-14), and Isaac lived there (Gn 24: 62; 25: 11). According to 1 K 1: 33-40, Solomon was consecrated king at the spring of Gihon in Jerusalem, and there seems to have been a sanctuary there (perhaps for the Ark) before the Temple was built.[1] Best known of all are the wells of Beer-sheba, where Abraham called upon Yahweh (Gn 21: 31), and where Isaac set up an altar to Yahweh who had appeared to him there (Gn 26: 23-25).

(c) *Sacred trees*. Throughout the ancient Near East, certain trees were acknowledged to have a religious character. Sacred trees are especially frequent in Mesopotamian iconography. They are shown as a symbol of fertility or as closely associated with the fertility gods, but it is questionable whether the tree itself ever represented the gods: the tree was incidental to the cult, and, strictly speaking, was not itself worshipped. All our information from Phoenicia is of late date, and affected by Greek influence, but the association of trees with the cult of female divinities must not be forgotten. The cypress in particular was consecrated to Astarte.

In modern Palestine, an isolated tree or a group of trees often marks the site of a Moslem *wely*. The tradition is age-old. The prophets condemned those Israelites who went to sacrifice on the tops of hills in the shade of trees (Os 4: 13-14), or near terebinths (Is 1: 29; 57: 5). Deuteronomy, and the texts which stem from it, condemn the places of worship set up 'on the hills, under every verdant tree' (Dt 12: 2; 1 K 14: 23; 2 K 16: 4; 17: 10; cf. Jr 2: 20; 3: 6; 17: 2; Ez 6: 13; 20: 28 and also Is 57: 5). But here too it must be noted that not one of these texts speaks of any worship paid to these trees: they merely mark the place of worship.

In ancient Israel, legitimate places of cultic worship could also be marked by a tree but one must beware of applying this principle to all the trees mentioned in the Old Testament. There is no sign whatever of a sanctuary in the Valley of the Terebinth (1 S 17: 2), and the Oak of Thabor (1 S 10: 3) may be nothing more than a topographical reference. The Palm-tree of Deborah, on the other hand, between Ramah and Bethel, where the prophetess used to

1. Cf. p. 102.

settle disputes between Israelites, probably did have a religious significance (Jg 4: 5): and it is clearly a different tree from the Oak of Tears, which stood below Bethel and marked the grave of a different Deborah, who was Rachel's nurse (Gn 35: 8). It is still more certain that the Oak near Shechem, where Jacob buried his family's idols (Gn 35: 4), belonged to a place of worship. This is apparently the tree which stood 'in the sanctuary of Yahweh' at Shechem, beneath which Josue set up a big stone (Jos 24: 26); hence we may identify it with the 'Terebinth of the stele which stands at Shechem' (Jg 9: 6, correcting the text), which marked a place of worship where Abimelek was proclaimed king. The same tree is also called the Oak of Moreh, *i.e.* the 'Oak of the Teacher' or 'of the Soothsayer': it is called the *maqôm*, *i.e.* the holy place, of Shechem in Gn 12: 6, and must be the same as the Oak of the Soothsayers near Shechem (Jg 9: 37). Near Hebron, there stood the Oak of Mambre, where Abraham set up an altar (Gn 13: 18), and under which he received the three mysterious visitors (Gn 18: 4, 8); it was venerated until the Byzantine epoch.[1] In describing the foundation of the place of worship at Beersheba, Gn 21: 33 says that Abraham 'planted a terebinth'.

The translations 'oak' and 'terebinth' are inspired by the ancient versions of the Bible, and are only approximate. The two Hebrew words seem to be synonymous and to mean simply any large tree.

(d) *Heights.* Since the mountains reached up to heaven, they were considered as the dwelling-place of the gods. Babylonian mythology placed the birth of the great gods on the Mountain of the World. East of this mountain, they believed there was a Mountain of the East where the sun arose, and where the gods assembled on New Year's day, to fix the destinies of the universe. In the Epic of Gilgamesh, too, the Mountain of Cedars was a dwelling-place of the gods.

The poems of Ras Shamra mention a holy mountain called Saphon. On the crests, or peaks, or slopes of Saphon, the gods met together; there Anath built a temple for Baal, and Baal had his throne. Because of his connection with this mountain, Baal was called Baal Saphon, and Phoenician sailors carried his worship, under this name, to Pelusium and probably as far as Corfu. Traces of this mythology can be found in the Bible. The fallen tyrant of Is 14: 13-15 who wanted to be equal to God had said: 'I shall take my seat on the mountain of the assembly, on the slopes of Saphon, I shall climb to the very top of the black clouds, and I shall be like Elyon'. In Ez 28: 14-16, the king of Tyre, identified with Melqart, the god-king of his city, stood on the 'holy mountain of God' before being cast down from it.

Devotion and cult alike demanded that this holy mountain should be fixed in a definite spot on earth. Concrete reality and the pure ideal, cult and myth were inseparable: Olympus was both the home of the gods and a mountain in Greece. In the same way, Saphon was both the home of Baal and Jebel

1. Cf. pp. 292–293.

al-Aqra', lying on the northern horizon from Ras Shamra: in Graeco-Roman times it was called Mount Casios, and Zeus Casios was venerated there: he was the heir of Baal.

There were other holy mountains in the land of Canaan. Lebanon and Siryon (another name for Hermon, Dt 3: 9) are mentioned in lists of gods given in Hittite treaties of the second millennium B.C. Several centuries later, an inscription from Cyprus records that a Phoenician invoked the Baal of Lebanon. It has already been stated that the very name of Hermon indicates that it was a holy mountain,[1] and the slopes and peaks of this massif are even to-day covered with the ruins of several sanctuaries, which were still in use in the fourth century A.D. There was a place in the neighbourhood called Baal Hermon, according to 1 Ch 5: 23, and the apocalyptic Book of Henoch states that the angels who sought to have relations with women came down on to Hermon.

Thabor, too, was a place of worship. In the blessings of Zabulon (Dt 33: 19), the mountain where the peoples come to offer sacrifices is very probably Thabor, which stood on the frontier of this tribe: the lawfulness of this worship is not questioned in this text, but Os 5: 1 accuses the priests, the king and the leaders of Israel of having been 'a snare set on Thabor', *i.e.* of having paved the way for the ruin of the people through an unholy cult. On the other hand, quite a plausible case can be made out for a slight textual correction which would include Thabor among the sacred mountains of the Phoenicians listed by Philo of Byblos: it would then stand together with Saphon, the Lebanon and Hermon. In the text of Osee just quoted, the Greek version translated Thabor by Itabyrion, which, together with Atabyrion, is its name in Greek authors. Now Rhodes had a sanctuary dedicated to Zeus Atabyrios; in all likelihood, the cult was brought to Rhodes from abroad, and did in fact represent a Baal of Thabor. Christian tradition eventually fixed upon Thabor as the site of the unnamed mountain where the Transfiguration took place (cf. Mt 17: 1).

Carmel, too, had a long history as a place of worship. The Sacred Cape, *rôsh qadôsh*, mentioned in Egyptian geographical lists from Thutmoses III onwards, is probably Carmel. In the fourth century B.C., the Periplus of Scylax calls Carmel a holy mountain of Zeus. Tacitus says it is the name both of a mountain and of a god: there was an altar on the top, where Vespasian offered sacrifice, but no temple or statue. The god was the Baal of the mountain, the manifestation of a great Oriental god, now identified as Baalshamem or, more probably, as Melqart, the patron of Tyre. Just as the Phoenicians and the Israelites disputed over the possession of the mountain, so the cult of the Tyrian Baal was a rival to that of Yahweh: Yahweh's exclusive rights were finally established by the miraculous triumph of Elias over the prophets of Baal (1 K 18: 20-48).

1. Cf. p. 275.

This is but one example of how Yahweh appropriated the mountains formerly consecrated to the old gods. He made the Lebanon and Siryon leap like young calves (Ps 29: 6); he created Saphon and the 'South' (the word must have replaced the name of another mountain); Thabor and Hermon sing for joy to his name (Ps 89: 13). And yet the Old Testament expressly teaches that Yahweh had only two holy mountains, Sinai where he had revealed himself, and Sion where he lived. Sinai-Horeb is called the 'mountain of God' in the stories of the Exodus (Ex 3: 1; 4: 27; 18: 5; 24: 13), and of Elias' pilgrimage (1 K 19: 8). Yahweh came from Sinai (Dt 33: 2, and the obscure text in Ps 68: 18), and made his home in the Temple of Jerusalem (1 K 8: 10–13). The mountain of Bashan (does this mean the massif of Hauran? or Hermon, which overlooks that region from the north?) was a 'mountain of God'; why, then, did it despise Sion, the little mountain Yahweh had chosen for his home (Ps 68: 16–17)? Mount Sion is the 'holy mountain' of the Psalms (Ps 2: 6; 3: 5; 15: 1; 43: 3; 99: 9) and of the later prophetical texts (Is 27 :13; 56: 7; 57: 13; 65: 11; 66: 20; Jr 31: 23; Ez 20: 40; Dn 9: 16, 20; Ab 16; Jl 2: 1; 4: 17; So 3: 11). The true 'slope of Saphon' was mount Sion, the dwelling place of Yahweh, the great king (Ps 48: 2–3). In days yet to come, mount Sion would be raised still higher, 'set upon the peak of the mountains, raised high above the hills, and peoples would come to the "mountain of Yahweh"' (Is 2: 2–3 = Mi 4: 1–2). The future temple of Ez 40: 2 stood 'on a very high mountain', where an ideal Jerusalem was built (cf. Za 14: 10).

4. *Ziggurats*

The feeling that divinity revealed itself on the mountains led men to build high sanctuaries not only where there was already a mountain, but even in the low-lying plains. Some of the oldest temples of Mesopotamia are built on top of a high terrace (*e.g.* Uruk, Khafajeh, El-'Obeid, Uqair, etc.). The artificial base upon which the temple stood was built as a series of terraces, and was shaped like a pyramid; and eventually it became the principal element in the structure, giving birth to a type of religious architecture which is characteristic of Babylonia and of the regions which came under its influence: the many-storeyed tower, or ziggurat.

The thickest concentration of ziggurats is in Lower Mesopotamia, but they are found in Assyria too, on the Syrian side of the Euphrates at Mari, and at Susa in Persia. At Tchoga-Zanbil in Persia an enormous ziggurat has recently been discovered, 114 yards square at its base, and over 165 feet high. These vast constructions were merely sub-structures: texts and monuments alike make it clear that there was a sanctuary on top, and excavations have proved that there was another sanctuary at the base. There are two possible explanations for this fact: either the god was held to live in the sanctuary at the top, and to come down to make his presence known in the lower sanctuary, or the upper sanctuary was thought of as a kind of rest-house for the god on his way down to earth, as if he stopped there on his way to the lower sanctuary, which was his permanent residence on earth. Whichever explanation is right, it certainly seems to be true that the ziggurat was built as a kind of 'mountain' where the god could meet his devotees, a giant stairway which the god could go down, and the devotee go up, to meet each other.

The ziggurat in Babylon was called *E-temen-an-ki*, the 'temple of the foundation of heaven and earth'. Its base was 100 yards square, and we learn from a cuneiform tablet and from Herodotus that it was at least as high. The earliest references to it are in the 7th century B.C., but it must have been in existence long before this date: it was several times destroyed and restored. The biblical tradition about the Tower of Babel (Gn 11: 1-9) must refer to this, or to some other ruined tower of Babylon. The idea in building it was to bring their god closer to them, but the Tower fell down, and the theological mind of the biblical author interpreted this disaster as a divine chastisement of men whose pride had sought to climb into heaven.

5. *Temples*

A temple may be defined as a building in which public worship is performed, erected on a 'holy place'. The older Semitic languages have no special word for a temple. In Akkadian, it is called simply the 'house' (*bitu*) or the 'palace' (*ekallu*: from the Sumerian E-KAL, meaning 'Big House') of the god; another Akkadian word is *ekurru*, which is also borrowed from the Sumerian E-KUR, meaning 'House of the Mountain'. In Phoenician, the Ras Shamra texts give us the words *bt* (house) and *hkl* (palace: from the Akkadian *ekallu*): both are equally common. In Hebrew too, the temple is a 'house' (*beth*) or a 'palace' (*hekal*, from the Akkadian, via the Phoenician). In the later books of the Bible, especially Ezechiel, the Temple is often called *miqdash*, which, strictly speaking, means a 'holy place or sanctuary', and not a building which is used as a temple. In older texts, the word stands parallel with 'high places' (Is 16: 12; Am 7: 9), and it is used for the open-air sanctuary under the Oak of Shechem (Jos 24: 26).

In Akkadian, Phoenician and Hebrew, then, the same words are used for the 'house' or 'palace' of a god and for the 'house' or 'palace' of a king. And in fact, every temple was built as a home for a divinity. Mesopotamian temples usually followed the same plan as a large house or palace; and the god, represented by his statue, was held to dwell there. But the plans of Assyrian temples are not the same as those in Babylonia, except where Babylonian influence was felt; and the reason is that the two nations built their houses in different ways. In Babylonia, the worshippers entered a courtyard flanked by buildings to pray in front of the rooms where the service was conducted: they were not allowed into these rooms, but a door in the middle gave them a straight view of the divine image which stood in the *cella* at the back. Those Assyrian temples which were untouched by Babylonian influence had no courtyard; instead, an open door led into one of the longer sides of the temple, and you had to turn to see the statue, which stood at the back of the room where the services were held: the statue stood where the fireplace was in ordinary houses. Thus the approach to the divinity was both closer and more mysterious than in Babylonia, and this fact corresponds to a difference of religious feeling between the two peoples.

It has also been debated whether some of the buildings in Syria-Palestine were religious buildings or not (*e.g.* the 'palace' or 'temple' at Ai); this is in itself sufficient proof that the house of a god was built on the plan of the king's palace. In the third millennium B.C. the temples discovered at Jericho, Megiddo and the (northern) Tell el-Farah, and the building at Ai, all have an indirect entry on the longer side, like the old Assyrian temples. In the second millennium, the plan was modified (as were presumably, the plans of the royal residences): the buildings became much more elaborate. A *cella* (sometimes raised), and a portico or a vestibule were added; these stood one behind the other, and worshippers entered on the shorter side of the building. This plan is followed in a sanctuary built about 1400 B.C. which has recently been discovered at Hazor, and in the little temple at Tell Tainat in Syria, *ca.* 1000 B.C. It is also the plan which Solomon adopted for his Temple in Jerusalem.

We have more information about Mesopotamian temples than any others, and in them the daily routine of the god was the same as the king's: the statue was first dressed, then had meals served to it, and was taken for walks with a sumptuous escort. This daily ritual meant that the temple had to be surrounded with a great many dependent buildings, such as lodgings for the priests and the servants, stores, kitchens and stables, all of which emphasized still more the similarity between the god's temple and the king's palace.

Even in Mesopotamia, however, the god did not live only in the temple, in the sense that his presence and his activity were restricted to this building. Some of his devotees may have thought so, but this was not the real meaning of their religion. The statue or sacred symbol was not the god himself, but only a visible sign and tangible embodiment of his presence. The temple was, of course, his dwelling-place, but he could have several temples in the same country, or even in the same town, and the great gods, whether their name was Marduk or Assur or Baal, could act throughout the length and breadth of the universe. The purpose of ziggurats was, as we have seen, to meet the god half-way when he was coming down from heaven to his temple.

When we come to discuss the Temple at Jerusalem, we shall see how these same ideas are found, in a purified form, in the religion of Israel. Though the lawful worship of Yahweh forbade images, the Temple was still referred to as the 'house of Yahweh' and the place of which he had said: 'My Name shall be there' (1 K 8: 29).

6. *'High places'*

(a) *The name.* The Bible often refers to Canaanite sanctuaries, and to those Israelite sanctuaries which were imitations of them, as *bamôth,* which the Vulgate translates as *excelsa,* and modern versions as 'high places'. This rendering is not exact, and calls at least for clarification.

We do not know the verbal root from which the noun *bamah* is derived, and the noun itself may be pre-Semitic. The cognate word in Ugaritic means the 'back' or 'trunk' of an animal, and the corresponding word in Akkadian has this meaning too, though it can also denote any elevated ground, such as the crest of a hill or a height. In the Bible, apart from the cultic references and some obscure texts, *bamah* can mean the 'back' of one's enemies (Dt 33: 29), 'heights' (used of ground, without further precision, Dt 32: 13; Is 58: 14; Mi 1: 3; Am 4: 13; Ha 3: 19; Ps 18: 34), the 'back' of clouds (Is 14: 14) or the 'waves' of the sea (Jb 9: 8). The idea which the word expresses, therefore, is something which stands out in relief from its background, but the idea of a mountain or hill is not contained in the word itself.

(b) *The situation of the 'high places'.* The last statement is confirmed by the information given in the Bible about the place of the *bamôth.* It is quite true that some, perhaps many, of them, stood on the heights of Palestine: men 'went up' to the neighbouring *bamah* from Samuel's home-town (1 S 9: 13, 14, 19), and 'came down' from it (1 S 9: 25). In Ez 20: 28–29, the word *bamah* is interpreted, by a play on words, as the name of the lofty hill where men went to offer sacrifice, and the worship conducted in the *bamôth* is set alongside worship on the hills (in 2 K 16: 4; 17: 9–10). Solomon built a *bamah* for Kemosh and Milkom on the mountain east of Jerusalem (1 K 11: 7). The fact that high hills seemed to be places destined for worship is a sufficient explanation of these texts. But not all the *bamôth* were on uninhabited hills: there were *bamôth* in the towns (1 K 13: 32; 2 K 17: 29; 23: 5), and even at the gate of Jerusalem (2 K 23: 8). In Ez 6: 3, Yahweh, tells not only the mountains and hills, but even the ravines and valleys, that he is going to destroy their *bamôth.* The *bamah* of Topheth stood in the valley of Ben-Hinnom at Jerusalem (Jr 7: 31; 32: 35). Clearly, the rendering 'high places' will not fit these last texts. The one and only meaning which suits all the references is 'a mound or knoll' for purposes of cultic worship. They may have used, sometimes, a prominent rock, but it would seem that this mound was usually artificial: this would make sense of the texts which speak of *bamôth* being 'built' (1 K 11: 7; 14: 23; 2 K 17: 9; 21: 3; Jr 19: 5), 'torn down' and 'destroyed' (2 K 23: 8; Ez 6: 3).

(c) *The evidence of archaeology.* Recent discoveries throw light on this explanation of *bamôth.* A large oval platform, 8 by 10 yards across, has been uncovered at Megiddo: it stood approximately 6 feet above the surrounding ground. It was built of big stones, had a flight of steps leading up to the platform, and had a rectangular wall around it. It was built about the middle of the third millennium B.C., and remained in use for several centuries. It is quite certain that sacrifice was offered there, and temples were later built beside it. At Nahariyah, near Haifa, there is a little sanctuary whose foundation is dated in the eighteenth or seventeenth century B.C., and beside it a heap of stones, roughly circular in form, which was originally 6 yards in diameter, and later widened to 14 yards. A similar platform has been unearthed at Hazor in a thirteenth century sanctuary. South-east of Jerusalem, on the crest of a hill near Malhah, there is a series of artificial mounds, two of which have been excavated. The one which is better preserved is 25 yards in diameter, and is made of earth and stones held in position by a polygonal wall: a flight of man-made steps led to the top. The pottery associated with this level belongs to the seventh and sixth centuries B.C.

There is no need for hesitation: these installations were *bamôth*. Their dates range from the old Canaanite epoch to the end of the monarchy in Judah, *i.e.* the first ones were places of worship for the Canaanites, and the last ones for the Israelites. Sometimes they stand in a town (as at Megiddo), sometimes near a town (as at Nahariyah, where the site of the ancient town has been discovered close by), and sometimes in the open country, on a natural height (as at Malhah): here, then, are three examples from the Bible of the different places in which *bamôth* were found.

(d) *Cultic installations.* Since the 'high place' was a place of worship, each one had to have its altar. The knoll itself, from which the name *bamah* comes, could serve as an altar, but an altar could also be built on it, and some biblical texts do in fact mention an altar as part of the 'high place' (2 K 21: 3; 2 Ch 14: 2, 4; Ez 6: 6).

The most characteristic adornments of a *bamah*, however, were the *maṣṣebah* and the *'asherah*, mentioned in connection with 'high places' in 1 K 14: 23; 2 K 18: 4; 23: 13–14; 2 Ch 14: 2, 4. To these must be added texts which, though not expressly mentioning any *bamah*, certainly have the same type of worship in mind: Ex 34: 13; Dt 7: 5; 12: 3; 16: 21–22; Mi 5: 12–13. On the other hand, such furnishings are not found only in *bamôth*: Achab installed an *'asherah* according to 1 K 16: 33, and a *maṣṣebah* according to 2 K 3: 2, in the temple of Baal at Samaria.

A *maṣṣebah* is a stone standing upright, a commemorative stele. It stood as the sign of an alliance or an undertaking (Gn 31: 45, 51–52; Ex 24: 4; Is 19: 19–20): compare with these texts the 'stone' set up by Josue in the sanctuary at Shechem (Jos 24: 26–27); alternatively it might be a monument in honour of the dead (Gn 35: 20; 2 S 18: 18). As an object of cult, it recalled a manifestation of a god, and was the sign of the divine presence. Jacob, after his vision at Bethel, set up the stone he had used for a pillow as a *maṣṣebah*, and declared that this was a *beth El*, a 'house of God' (Gn 28: 18; cf. Gn 31: 13 and the parallel tradition in 35: 14). It was a short step from this reasoning to accepting the stone itself as a representation of the divinity, and there was no need for the stone to be hewn into the form of a statue: even in its crude, natural shape, it was a symbol of the divinity. This explains why the *maṣṣebôth*, which older texts regard as legitimate signs of the divine presence, are, in later texts, condemned, along with all the other panoply of Canaanite worship. (Note that in some of these texts, *maṣṣebah* stands close beside *pesel*, 'a sculptured idol': Lv 26: 1; Dt 7: 5; 12: 3; Mi 5: 12.)

A *maṣṣebah* was the symbol of a male deity (2 K 3: 2 mentions the *maṣṣebah* of Baal: and cf. 2 K 10: 26-27, though the text is here uncertain). The female divinities were represented by an *'asherah*, a name which stands both for the goddess and for her cultic symbol. The Ras Shamra texts mention the goddess Asherah as the consort of the god El, and in the Bible she is the consort of Baal (Jg 3: 7; 2 K 23: 4). The *'asherah* itself was made of wood (Jg 6: 26), cut into shape by man (Ex 34: 13; Jg 6: 25), and could be burned (Dt 12: 3; 2 K 23: 6, 15). Apparently, it could also be a living tree planted by man (Dt 16: 21) and uprooted by him (Mi 5: 13; 2 K 23: 14); but, far more commonly, it was a wooden object made by man (1 K 14: 15; 16: 33; 2 K 17: 16; 21: 3; Is 17: 8), erected like the *maṣṣebôth* (2 K 17: 10), and standing upright (2 K 13: 6; Is 27: 9)—which means it must have been a kind of post or stake. It is impossible to be more precise about its appearance, and there is no proof that the post was carved to look like a goddess.

Some texts include among the appurtenances of the *bamôth* the *ḥammanîm* (Lv 26: 30; 2 Ch 14: 4; 34: 4, 7; Ez 6: 4, 6). The word is never found outside *bamôth* except when it is with an *'asherah* (Is 17: 8), or with an altar and an *'asherah* (Is 27: 9). These *hammanîm* could not have been very large, for, according to 2 Ch 34: 4, they could be placed on an altar. For a long time, they were thought to be 'pillars of the sun', but Nabatean and Palmyra inscriptions leave no doubt that the correct translation is 'altars for incense'. None of the texts which contain the word is earlier than the Exile, and Ez 6: 4, 6 appears to be the oldest. (Is 17: 7-8 is commonly considered as an addition.) Now some excavations in Palestine, especially those at Lakish, have yielded small stone objects, cubic or elongated in shape, which date from post-Exilic times: the upper part is hollowed out like a cup, and bears traces of fire; it is a reasonable theory to identify them as *ḥammanîm*. Possibly the name and this particular type of perfume-brazier were introduced into Palestine at a rather late date, but incense-offerings (with no mention of *ḥammanîm*) are connected with the cult of *bamôth* in the Deuteronomic redaction of the Books of Kings (1 K 3: 3; 22: 44; 2 K 12: 4, etc.); Jr 19: 13 and 32: 29 tells us that incense was offered on the roof-tops, and Os 4: 13 records these offerings as an element of the cult practised on the heights. Perhaps in those earlier days, the incense-offerings were offered on something larger than the *ḥammanîm* of Lakish: excavations have yielded perfume-braziers of baked clay from the Canaanite period, and little stone altars from the period of the Israelite monarchy have been discovered at Megiddo and at Shechem: all of these may be called 'altars for incense'.[1]

The Bible speaks time and time again of the 'high places' set in the shade, 'under every verdant tree',[2] which proves that they were open-air sanctuaries: but buildings were sometimes attached to them. When it simply says that a 'high place' was 'built', it may mean, as we have seen, merely that the artificial mound, the *bamah*, was constructed. But other texts presuppose that roofed buildings also existed there. According to 1 S 9: 22, in the town where Samuel lived the high place had a 'room' which could hold thirty guests. At the great high place of Gibeon where Solomon spent the night and had a vision of Yahweh in a dream (1 K 3: 5), there was probably a building for him to sleep in. Several texts refer to the 'houses', the temples in the *bamôth*, like the one Jeroboam built at Bethel (1 K 12: 31) or those in which the Samaritan colonists installed their idols (2 K 17: 29) and conducted their services (2 K 17: 32), which were demolished by Josias (2 K 23: 19).

(e) *'High places' and funeral services.* Apparently, the *bamôth* were also used for funeral services. It has already been stated that a stele, a *maṣṣebah*, could mark the place of a grave (Gn 35: 20) or stand as a monument to the dead (2 S 18: 18). On the other hand, a heap of stones was sometimes piled over a tomb, *e.g.* Akan's (Jos 7: 26), the king of Ai's (Jos 8: 29), and Absalom's (2 S 18: 17). These funeral mounds looked exactly the same as the mounds used for worship, the *bamôth*, in the sense defined at the beginning of this section. This throws light on a number of texts. The Qumran manuscript of Isaias allows us to translate Is 53: 9 as: 'They set his grave among the wicked, and his *bamah* with the rich (or, the wicked, or, demons)'. A simple change of the vowels makes the meaningless text of Jb 27: 15 read: 'those who survive them will be buried in *bamôth*, and their widows will shed no tears for them'. Ez 43: 7 needs no correction, and reads: 'They shall no longer defile my holy name by their prostitution, and by the funeral pillars of their kings in their *bamôth*' (cf. v. 9). The word translated 'funeral pillar' is *peger*, which in the Bible usually means 'a corpse': but in the Ras Shamra texts it means 'monument, stele'. It is therefore a synonym for *maṣṣebah*, and it recurs in connection with the 'high places' in Lv 26: 30: this verse can therefore be translated: 'I shall destroy your high places (*bamôth*), reduce your altars of incense (*ḥammanîm*) to dust, and heap your steles (*peger*) on the steles (*peger*) of your false gods'. Archaeology confirms these statements: there was a line of steles on what has been rightly called the 'high place' of Gezer, and a Canaanite sanctuary with several upright steles has recently been discovered at Hazor: both of these must have been memorials to deceased of some rank. These conclusions are very reasonable, but they must not be pressed too far: the 'high places' were destined for general purposes of worship, and funeral rites were merely one element in this worship.

1. On the altar of perfumes in the Temple, cf. p. 411. 2. Cf. pp. 278–279.

(f) *The lawfulness of 'high places'*. These places of worship were not at first condemned by Israel's religion. Samuel offered a sacrifice in the high place of his home-town (1 S 9: 12f.); Gibeon had 'the biggest high place' where Solomon offered sacrifice and was favoured with a divine message (1 K 3: 4f.). The Israelites flocked to these sanctuaries right to the end of the monarchical period. Ezechias, of course, wanted to destroy them in the first attempt to centralize worship (2 K 18: 4), but Manasseh brought them back into service (2 K 21: 3), and they stayed in use until Josias' reform (2 K 23, which makes it quite clear that they were sanctuaries of Yahweh[1]).

They did, however, keep alive Canaanite traditions, often on the very same spot; and there was a strong temptation to practise a syncretist cult, to place beside the altar of Yahweh the stele of Baal and the sacred stake of 'Ashera, and to introduce the immoral practices of the Canaanites, and their funeral rites. This is what the prophets so often reacted against, and when they explicitly attack the *bamôth* by name (Os 10: 8; Am 7: 9; Jr 7: 31; cf. 19: 5; 32: 35), it is precisely because of the sins against true worship which were being committed there. The abuses continued, and the movement to centralize worship led to the condemnation of all 'high places' without discrimination: so the word *bamôth* became a synonym for pagan sanctuaries, or, at the very least, for unlawful sanctuaries. The Deuteronomic editor of the Books of Kings takes the word *bamôth* in this sense of 'illegitimate sanctuaries' and condemns all the kings of Israel and of Judah, except Ezechias and Josias, for not suppressing them: and the same censure is found in the later texts of the Pentateuch.

1. Cf. p. 337.

Chapter Two

THE FIRST ISRAELITE SANCTUARIES

1. *The places where the Patriarchs worshipped*

THE Israelites attributed the foundation of certain sanctuaries to the Patriarchs. Obviously, the historian of to-day cannot verify this assertion, but he must acknowledge that the tradition is in perfect agreement with two proven facts: first, the places in question all stand along the line of demarcation between arable land and the zone where shepherds and goat-herds pastured their flocks; and this corresponds perfectly with the social position of the Patriarchs, who were semi-nomads. Secondly, these sanctuaries were not the most popular ones in the period of the Judges and under the monarchy, as they would have been if the tradition had been invented at a later date to provide an illustrious origin for certain places of worship. (Bethel is an exception, but it owed its importance under the king of Israel to political reasons.) From the time of the monarchy all these patriarchal sanctuaries became, apparently, suspect to orthodox Yahwists: they were certainly very old even in those days.

The last chapter described the rules which governed the choice of a place for worship, and the patriarchal sanctuaries were founded in accordance with these principles. Sanctuaries were erected where nature manifested the presence of the God of Abraham, Isaac and Jacob—near a tree, for example, or on a natural height, or by a water-source: but they were erected principally in places where God had shown himself in a theophany. Sanctuaries of this kind are found all along the route the patriarchs travelled.

(a) *Shechem*. According to Gn 12: 6-7 (Yahwistic tradition), Abraham's first stop in Canaan was at Shechem. He stopped at the *maqôm*, *i.e.* at the holy place where the Oak of Moreh stood: it was also called the 'Oak of the Teacher' or 'of the Soothsayer', and must therefore have been a tree where oracles were sought. It was in fact a Canaanite sanctuary, as the text itself recognizes by adding the explanation: 'the Canaanites were living in the country at the time'. But Yahweh appeared there to Abraham and promised the country to his descendants. So Abraham built him an altar there. Here, in skeleton form, is a typical story about the foundation of a sanctuary: theophany, divine message, beginning of the cult.

The origins of this sanctuary, however, have deeper roots in the Elohistic tradition, in its stories about Jacob and his sons. When Jacob was returning from Mesopotamia, he camped just outside Shechem, bought the piece of land where his tent stood from the sons of Hamor and set up an altar there (some critics prefer to read: a *maṣṣebah*), which he called 'El, God of Israel' (Gn 33: 18-20). After the agreement with the Shechemites had been broken by the treacherous attack of Simeon and Levi, Jacob left Shechem for Bethel (Gn 35: 1-4): it was a pilgrimage from one sanctuary to the other, for which he and his followers purified themselves and changed their clothes. The idols belonging to Jacob's family were buried 'under the Oak near Shechem', *i.e.* the Oak which is called, in the story of Abraham, the Oak of Moreh. Several theories have been advanced about the original significance of this ritual act of burying the idols: and yet there is no doubt what the Bible takes it to mean. It was an abandoning of pagan practices, parallel to the rejection of foreign gods which Josue demanded of the Israelites at Shechem because they had chosen to serve Yahweh (Jos 24: 21-24). One last memory of patriarchal times was connected with Shechem: Joseph's bones were said to have been taken there from Egypt, and in later ages his tomb was shown to visitors (Jos 24: 32). We have already discussed, under 'high places',[1] how tombs and funeral monuments were connected in this way with places of worship.

The pact which bound the tribes together and bound them all to Yahweh was concluded at Shechem, and Josue erected 'under the oak in the sanctuary at Yahweh' (*i.e.* the tree mentioned in the stories about Abraham and Jacob), a 'large stone', *i.e.* a *maṣṣebah* (Jos 24: 25-28). It was under this tree (called the tree of the *maṣṣebah*, if we accept a commonly received correction of the text) that Abimelek was proclaimed king (Jg 9: 6). This, too, was evidently the sanctuary where Roboam met the northern tribes when they were going to recognize him as king, and where his own clumsy behaviour destroyed all prospects of ending the political schism (1 K 12: 1-19).

Shechem was eclipsed by Shiloh during the period of the Judges, and by Bethel after the schism. It is possible, however, that the Deuteronomic redactors of the canonical books drew a veil over the survival of a sanctuary where the worship, to them, seemed stained by pagan practices. We have mentioned that they did not dare to call the 'great stone' of Jos 24: 26 a *maṣṣebah*, and probably they or their copyists suppressed the *maṣṣebah* of Jg 9: 6. In the book of Deuteronomy itself, the name of Shechem is not even mentioned, but the book does order large stones, with the Law written on them, to be set up on mount Ebal, and commands that an altar be built there: curses and blessings for the breaking and keeping of the Law are then to be pronounced on the two mountains, Ebal and Garizim (Dt 27). The same command is given more briefly in Dt 11: 26-32, with a mention of the Oak of Moreh in a retouched context. The Deuteronomic redaction of Jos 8: 30-35 relates, with important nuances, how this command was executed. Now Shechem stands between Ebal and Garizim, and there is certainly some con-

1. Cf. p. 287.

nection between these texts and that of Jos 24: 25-28, which relates how the inter-tribal pact was sealed at Shechem.[1] Lastly, Dt 31: 10-13 prescribes that the Law should be read periodically, during a feast. It is a tenable hypothesis, therefore, that the texts just mentioned may preserve the memory of a ritual for the renovation of the Covenant, celebrated at Shechem.

(b) *Bethel.* The Yahwistic tradition says that Abraham erected a second altar in Canaan, at his second camping station, between Bethel and Ai (cf. the short note in Gn 12: 8). Yet Gn 28: 10-22, which is much more detailed, and which combines both Yahwistic and Elohistic traditions, attributes the founding of this sanctuary to Jacob (cf. the analogous stories about Shechem). According to this text, when Jacob was on his way to Haran, he stopped for the night in a holy place, a *maqôm*. He had a dream in which he saw a 'ladder' (better, a stairway or a ramp) between heaven and earth. Thereupon he recognized that this was a *beth-El*, a 'house of God', and the gate of heaven: here we meet the same religious thought which gave rise to the building of ziggurats in Mesopotamia.[2] Jacob set up the stone he had used for a pillow as a *maṣṣebah*, and anointed it with oil. He made a vow that if he returned safe and sound, he would build a sanctuary there to which he would pay a tithe of all his possessions: so far the Elohistic narrative. The Yahwistic tradition adds an account of an apparition of Yahweh, who reaffirmed in Jacob's favour the promises made to Abraham. On his return from Mesopotamia, Jacob went on pilgrimage from Shechem to Bethel and set up there an altar and a stele (Gn 35: 1-9, 14-15: Elohistic tradition): this is presented as the fulfilment of his vow in Gn 28: 20-22, but it is also a doublet, for the erection of the stele and the explanation of the name Bethel in 35: 14-15 are a repetition of Gn 28: 18-19.

The actions of the founder constituted a ritual which was perpetuated by the faithful: there was, then, at Bethel a sanctuary which was said to have been founded by the patriarchs: the faithful went on pilgrimage there, poured oil on a stele and paid tithes. The pilgrimage is attested by 1 S 10: 3, the tithe by Am 4: 4. The tradition enshrined in Jg 20: 18, 26-28; 21: 2 told how men gathered before Yahweh at Bethel, offered him sacrifices, and consulted him: even the Ark was kept there for a time.

After the political schism, Jeroboam chose Bethel as the site for a place of worship to rival Jerusalem. We shall treat of the later history of the sanctuary elsewhere,[3] and content ourselves here with the story of its origin. It seems that at Bethel the cult of Yahweh had ousted that of a Canaanite divinity as it had done at Shechem. Jacob stopped in 'the *maqôm*', took one of the stones of the *maqôm* for his pillow, and slept in 'this *maqôm*' (Gn 28: 11): when he awoke after his dream, he cried out: 'How fearful is this *maqôm*!' (Gn 28: 17). The repetition of the word suggests that in the context it means—as it can—more than just 'place' or 'spot', and denotes rather a 'place of worship'.

1. Cf. pp. 143, 147, 148. 2. Cf. pp. 281-282. 3. Cf. pp. 333-335.

According to Gn 28: 19; 35: 7, Jacob gave the place the name Bethel or El-Bethel. Now El was the principal god in the Canaanite pantheon, and Bethel was for many centuries a divine name in the popular religion of Israel (cf. the documents from the Jewish colony at Elephantine and also two biblical references, Am 5: 4 and, clearer still, Jr 48: 13). The revelation which Jacob received was that it was his own God who was showing himself in this place.

(c) *Mambre*. Gn 13: 18 says that Abraham erected an altar under the Oak of Mambre. This is the only text in Genesis which refers to Mambre as a place of worship: elsewhere it is mentioned as the residence of Abraham, Isaac and Jacob (Gn 14: 13; 18: 1; 35: 27), or to help locate the cave of Macpelah 'facing Mambre', where the Patriarchs and their wives were buried (Gn 23: 17 and 19; 25: 9; 49: 30; 50: 13). Yet Abraham was sitting by the Oak of Mambre when he welcomed the three mysterious guests among whom Yahweh concealed himself (Gn 18), and Mambre is the best site for the scene of the Covenant in Gn 15, if we retain that scene in its present context. These two theophanies, and the presence of an altar and a tree, indicate that there was a sanctuary there.

Mambre is never mentioned in the Bible outside Genesis, but later texts prove that it continued to be a place of worship, and many legends grew up about the sacred tree. According to Josephus (*B.J.*, IV, ix, 7 and *Ant.*, I, x, 4), Abraham's Oak had existed from the creation of the world and was called Ogyges: in Greek mythology, Ogyges was the founder of Eleusis and was connected, therefore, with mystery-religion. The Book of Jubilees (XIV, 11) explicitly locates the nocturnal scene of Gn 15 in Mambre, and other apocryphal books interpret it as a revelation of mysteries: Abraham, it is said, there saw the future Jerusalem and learnt the secrets of the end of time. In the first centuries A.D., Mambre was a pilgrimage centre, and the tree of Abraham was greatly venerated: every year a big fair was held where, according to Sozomenus (*Hist. Eccl.*, II, iv), Jews, Christians and pagans transacted business and performed their devotions, each in his own way. This was the final chapter in a long history: the Roman and Byzantine ruins of Mambre are still to be found at Ramath el-Khalil, 2 miles north of Hebron, and beneath these later sanctuaries traces of Israelite occupation have been found.

In all probability, a syncretist cult was practised there, and was regarded with disfavour by orthodox Yahwism. This would explain why Mambre was ostracized, and why it is never mentioned in the Bible outside Genesis; in Genesis itself, the text seems to have been deliberately obscured whenever Mambre is mentioned. In Gn 13: 18; 14: 13; 18: 1, the Hebrew text speaks of the Oaks of Mambre in the plural, while the better ancient versions read the singular (which is in fact demanded by the story of Gn 18: 4 and 8): the idea was to water down the superstitious veneration of a particular tree, and the Jewish commentators went a step further by substituting the word 'plain of'

Mambre. Again, the editors of Genesis try to do away with the independence of the sanctuary by misleading the reader about its position: 'the Oaks of Mambre which are at Hebron' (Gn 13: 18), and 'Macpelah, facing Mambre' in the five texts cited above, when in fact the tomb of the Patriarchs faced ancient Hebron. In the end, Mambre was simply identified with Hebron in Gn 23: 19: 'Macpelah, facing Mambre, *i.e.* Hebron', and Gn 35: 27: 'at Mambre, Qiryath-Arba, *i.e.* Hebron'. All these texts were edited at a later period. It is no doubt possible that the sole aim of the redactors was to put side by side a tomb and a sanctuary which were both venerated, as when the nearby tomb of Rachel is mentioned in connection with Bethel (Gn 35: 8), but it seems far more probable that they were trying to minimize the religious importance of Mambre.

(d) *Beersheba.* Beersheba stands at the southern extremity of the Holy Land: its name was interpreted as meaning the Well of the Oath or the Well of the Seven (Gn 21: 22-31; cf. 26: 33). The memory of Isaac was particularly cherished there. Yahweh had there appeared to him one night and confirmed the promise made to Abraham: there Isaac had set up an altar and had called on the name of Yahweh (Gn 26: 23-25). There Jacob offered a sacrifice to the God of his father Isaac, and was favoured with a vision (Gn 46: 1-4). In the end, however, the foundation of the sanctuary was attributed to Abraham: Gn 21: 33, which has all the marks of an addition, says that Abraham planted a tamarisk at Beersheba and there called on the name of Yahweh El-'Olam, Yahweh El of Eternity. This divine name, which is never mentioned elsewhere, must be the name of the Canaanite divinity whom Yahweh replaced. There is a good parallel to this divine title in the Phoenician inscription of Karatepe, where we find a Shamash 'Olam, and perhaps, too, in the Elath-'Olam inscribed on an amulet originating from Arslan-Tash.

According to 1 S 8: 1-2, Samuel made his sons judges at Beersheba; this presupposes there was a sanctuary there, as at Bethel, Gilgal, Mispah and Ramah, where Samuel himself had judged Israel (1 S 7: 16-17). Under the monarchy, the northern Israelites went there on pilgrimage (Am 5: 5), and took oaths by the Dod, the Darling, of Beersheba (Am 8: 14: corrected, but perhaps the Hebrew text should be retained: 'by the Way of Beersheba'). These lasting links between Beersheba and the northern tribes are interesting precisely because they confirm the antiquity of the sanctuary. In the context, the prophet is condemning this place of worship along with Gilgal, Bethel, Dan and Samaria.

(e) *Conclusion.* The study of the patriarchal sanctuaries leads to a paradoxical conclusion: on the one hand, the links which connected Shechem, Bethel, Mambre and Beersheba with Abraham, Isaac and Jacob were multiplied as time went on: on the other hand, all these sanctuaries were condemned by the spokesmen of Yahwism—Bethel and Beersheba explicitly, Shechem and Mambre implicitly. This odd conclusion cannot be explained by a centralization of worship, for Amos was not aiming at that. It must mean that Yahwism eventually rejected the very cult which was celebrated there. What probably happened was that these places were Canaanite sanctuaries adopted by the Israelites when they settled in Palestine: the new immigrants continued the kind of cult which was celebrated when they arrived, without anyone's taking offence at it. Twice the divinity to whom these sanctuaries belonged is named: El-Bethel at Bethel, and El-'Olam at Beersheba. It is tempting to attach El-Shaddai to Mambre, for the name occurs for the first time in Gn 17: 1 (Priestly tradition, and a doublet both of the account of the Covenant in Gn 15, which probably took place at Mambre, and of the story in Gn 18, which is explicitly placed at Mambre). We may reasonably suggest that at Shechem, where covenants were concluded and renewed, there was an El-Berith (cf. also Jg 9: 46), an El of the Covenant, parallel to the Baal-Berith who had, and who retained, a temple at Shechem (Jg 9: 4): in later times, the Deuteronomic redactor condemned the Israelites for 'taking Baal-Berith as god' (Jg 8: 33).

El-Bethel, El-'Olam, El-Shaddai and El-Berith, were not, however, different local deities: they were all manifestations of the supreme god El, whose exalted and universal aspect is better known to us now through the the texts of Ras Shamra. For this stage in revelation, it was sufficient for the ancestors of the Israelites to recognize the El venerated in these ancient sanctuaries as their one and only God, author and guarantor of the promises made to their race. The altar set up by Jacob at Shechem was called 'El, God of Israel' (Gn 33: 20): it was 'El, the God of thy father' who appeared to Jacob at Beersheba (Gn 46: 3), and Ex 6: 3 says that God first revealed himself to Abraham, Isaac and Jacob under the name of El-Shaddai. In the following period, Yahwistic revelation became more exigent. Yahweh assumed the place and the most exalted attributes of El; the new centres of the Yahwistic cult eclipsed the old sanctuaries, though the populace still remained attached to them. The transition, however, was peaceful, without any of the struggles which ensued where the worship of Yahweh came face to face with that of Baal.

2. *The desert sanctuary: the Tent*

Before passing on to Israel's own sanctuaries in the Promised Land, we must study another set of traditions about the first beginnings of the cult of Yahweh. The Bible tells us that in the desert, the Israelites had a tent as a sanctuary, which has become known in Christian literature, through the influence of the Vulgate, as the Tabernacle. This Tent is called in Hebrew the *'ohel mô'ed*, the Tent of Re-union, or, of Meeting, or, of Rendezvous. In fact, it was the place where Yahweh talked with Moses 'face to face' (Ex 33: 11), or 'mouth to mouth' (Nb 12: 8). These texts belong to the oldest tradition, which stresses the rôle of the Tent in oracles: everyone who wanted 'to consult Yahweh' went to the Tent, where Moses acted as his spokesman before God (Ex 33: 7). The Priestly tradition kept the name, with the same meaning: the Tent of Re-union was the place where Yahweh 'met' Moses and the people of Israel (Ex 29: 42-43; 30: 36). This tradition, however, prefers to call it the Dwelling, or Abode, *mishkan*, which seems to be a term originally used for the temporary dwelling of a nomad (cf. the very old text in Nb 24: 5, and the corresponding verb in Jg 8: 11; cf. also 2 S 7: 6), *i.e.* a tent. The Priestly tradition chose this archaic word to express the way in which the God who resides in heaven dwells on earth. By doing so, they were preparing the ground for the Jewish doctrine about the Shekinah, and St John too remembered how 'the Word . . . pitched a tent among us' (Jn 1: 14).

Nevertheless, in the Priestly tradition, the divine presence in the Tent appears to be more stable than it was in the old Elohistic tradition. The latter tells how the presence of Yahweh revealed itself by the descent of a cloud which covered the entrance of the Tent, and Moses spoke with God inside the cloud (Ex 33: 9): again (Nb 12: 4-10), it says that the cloud came down over the Tent when Yahweh was arriving, and left it when he was departing: both of these accounts suggest visits rather than a permanent abode. According to the Priestly tradition, the cloud covered the Dwelling as soon as it was erected, for Yahweh was taking possession of his sanctuary (Ex 40: 34-35); afterwards, it apparently stayed over the Dwelling all the time, doing duty for the pillar of cloud and the pillar of fire which had guided the Israelites during the Exodus: it indicated where and for how long they were to set up camp, and when the moment had come to strike camp (Nb 9: 15-23; cf. Ex 40: 36-38). The two traditions do not agree about the position of the Tent: according to Ex 33: 7-11 and Nb 11: 24-30 (Elohistic), it stood outside the camp, while Nb 2: 2, 17 says it stood in the middle of the camp. Ex 25: 8 adds that Yahweh lives there in the middle of his people, and Nb 5: 3 gives this as the reason why the Israelites must keep careful watch over the purity of their camp (Priestly texts).

The most ancient texts give no indication what this Tent looked like, how it was set up, or what its furnishings were. The Priestly tradition, on the other hand, gives a lengthy description of the Dwelling when Yahweh orders it to be built (Ex 26) and when Moses carries out the order (Ex 36: 8-38). This description is very difficult to understand, and it is hard to see how the various elements it mentions can be combined. The Dwelling was made of wooden frames which were put together and made a rectangular building of 30 by 10 cubits, and 10 cubits high: it stood open on the eastern side. The building seems then to have been covered with bands of fine-woven material, sewn together to make two big pieces, which were then fastened together with hooks and clips: they were embroidered with figures of cherubim. Next, goat-skin bands were stretched 'like a tent over the Dwelling': they were a little wider and a little longer than the first material, and fell down over the sides of the Dwelling. Lastly, the whole construction was covered with the skins of rams, dyed red, and then by very light leather hides. There was a curtain over the entry to the Dwelling, and a costly veil drawn across the innermost ten cubits marked the division between the Holy Place and the Holy of Holies. Behind the veil, in the Holy of Holies, stood the Ark: in the Holy Place, there stood the candle-stick and the table of shewbread. The altar, with the basin for washing, stood outside the entrance of the Tent (Ex 40: 30). Around the Dwelling there was an open court of 100 by 50 cubits, the edge of which was indicated by a barrier of bronze posts and silver curtain-rods from which linen curtains fell down to the ground (Ex 27: 9-19).

It is only too obvious that much of this description is merely an idealization: the desert sanctuary is conceived as a collapsible temple, exactly half as big as the Temple of Jerusalem, which served as the model for this reconstruction. However, not everything in the description is made up, and the notion of a 'prefabricated' sanctuary clashes with the idea—so firmly rooted in tradition that the authors of this description could not wholly remove it—that the dwelling was a Tent.

This tradition fits in excellently with Arab usage, ancient and modern. Bedouin tribes have a little tent, a sort of palanquin or litter, which they call *'uṭfa*, *merkab*, or *abu-Dhur*. When the tribe is moving camp, they always take it with them and it is the last object they pick up when leaving. It is carried on a camel. In combat, the sheikh's daughter or another beautiful young girl used to ride in it to spur on the fighting men. It is considered to be blessed with supernatural power, and sometimes a sacrifice is offered to the *'uṭfa* or to the divinity who is thought to dwell in it. There is an evident analogy with the Ark of the Covenant and its rôle in the early wars of Israel,[1] and also with the Tent, the travelling sanctuary of the desert years. From the thirteenth century onwards, caravans making the pilgrimage to Mecca from Damascus or Cairo were led by a camel carrying a *maḥmal*, a little cubic tent containing a copy of the Koran. In spite of the apparent resemblances, however, it is not altogether certain that the *maḥmal* was related to the *'uṭfa* of Bedouin tribes: and on the other hand, it is quite certain that the modern *'uṭfa* is a continuation of a pre-Islamite institution, the *qubba*. This was a little sacred tent of red leather in which the stone idols belonging to the tribe were carried. It was carried on camel-back in religious processions and in combat, and young women looked after it. In camp, it was set up beside the sheikh's tent, and men came there to seek oracles. Here we perceive the rôle of the desert Tent in the giving of oracles (Ex 33: 7), and even the colour, red, of the ram-skins which covered it (Ex 26: 14). Indeed, the very women who looked after the *qubba* recall the women who 'were in service' at the entrance to the Tent of Re-union, according to the somewhat enigmatical text of Ex 38: 8.

1. Cf. p. 259.

This *qubba* of the pre-Islamic Arabs itself had Semitic antecedents. Diodorus (XX, 65, 1) tells us that in a Carthaginian camp a sacred tent was set up near the chief's tent. Little statues of baked earth originating from Syria represent women (*i.e.* goddesses or assistants in the cult) riding on camel-back in a litter covered by a pavilion. A bas-relief from Palmyra, of the first century A.D., shows a religious procession in which a camel is carrying a little tent still bearing traces of red paint, and there are other Palmyra texts which contain the word *qubba*. In the Bible, the word *qubbah* occurs once only, in Nb 25: 8, and it may mean a tent, or part of a tent: the Tent of Re-union is mentioned in the same passage (verse 6), but it is not clear what connection if any, it has with this *qubbah*.

It is reasonable then to suggest an hypothesis which fits the evidence of the texts and to assert that the ancestors of the Israelites, during their nomad life, had a portable sanctuary, and that this sanctuary was a tent, like their own dwelling-places. It would be quite in order for this sanctuary to disappear when they settled in Canaan. The Tent of Re-union was set up in the Plains of Moab, the last station before the entry into the Promised Land (Nb 25: 6), and this is the last indisputable mention of it. The tradition which speaks of the Tent's being at Shiloh under Josue (Jos 18: 1; 19: 51) is late, and in Ps 78: 60 (a late psalm) the *mishkan* and the Tent of Shiloh are poetic expressions. Moreover, the sanctuary which housed the Ark at Shiloh towards the end of the period of the Judges was a building (1 S 1: 7, 9; 3: 15). The tent under which David is said to have put the Ark in Jerusalem (2 S 6: 17) is evidently meant to recall the desert sanctuary, but it is no longer the Tent of Re-union, though it is so called by a glossator in 1 K 8: 4. The same anxiety to connect the new worship with the old inspired the Chronicler when he pretended that the Tent of Re-union stood on the high place of Gibeon under David and Solomon (1 Ch 16: 39; 21: 29; 2 Ch 1: 3-6).

3. *The Ark of the Covenant*

Ex 26: 33 and 40: 21 state that the Tent was designed to house the Ark of the Testimony (*'arôn ha-'edûth*). This 'Testimony' or 'Solemn Law' means the two 'tablets of the Testimony', *i.e.* the stone tablets on which the Law was inscribed: God had given them to Moses (Ex 31: 18) and he put them inside the Ark (Ex 25: 16; 40: 20). That is why the Tent containing the Ark was called the Tent of the Testimony (Nb 9: 15; 17: 22; 18: 2). The Ark is described in Ex 25: 10-22; 37: 1-9. It was a chest made of acacia wood, about 4 feet long, $2\frac{1}{2}$ feet wide and $2\frac{1}{2}$ feet high: it was covered with gold plates and had rings attached, through which the poles used for carrying it could be passed. Over the Ark was a plate of gold, of the same size as the Ark, and called the *kapporeth*, which is sometimes translated 'propitiatory' or 'mercy-seat', in accordance with the meaning of the verbal root and the rôle the *kapporeth* played on the Day of Atonement (*Yôm ha-kippurim*: Lv 16). Two cherubim stood at the end of the *kapporeth* and covered it with their wings.

According to Dt 10: 1-5, Moses built an Ark of acacia wood at Yahweh's command, and put inside it the two stone tablets on which Yahweh had written the Ten Commandments. Dt 10: 8 says that the honour of carrying this chest was entrusted to the Levites, and that it was called the Ark of the Covenant (*'arôn habb'rith*) because it contained the 'tablets of the Covenant' which Yahweh had made with his people (Dt 9: 9). The 'second Law' of Deuteronomy was eventually itself placed 'beside the Ark of the Covenant of Yahweh' (Dt 31: 9, 26).

Nb 10: 33-36 says that when the Israelites left Sinai, the Ark of the Covenant went before them, and signalled the halts. When it was leaving, they cried: 'Arise, Yahweh, and let thy enemies be scattered . . .', and when it came to rest: 'Return, Yahweh, to the countless thousands of Israel'. And Nb 14: 44 adds that when the Israelites, disobeying Moses' orders, attacked the Canaanites and were defeated, the Ark of the Covenant did not leave the camp.

These are the only explicit details about the Ark of the Covenant mentioned in the Pentateuch, and it is obvious that they stem from different traditions. The texts from Exodus belong to the Priestly tradition, and, like the description of the Tent, they are influenced by the memory of the Temple of Solomon, where the Ark stood in the Holy of Holies, overshadowed by the Cherubim (1 K 8: 6). The Deuteronomic tradition gives no description of the Ark, and does not connect it with the Tent. It has therefore been suggested that it was a cultic object adopted by the Israelites (from the Canaanites!) only after the settlement in Palestine, and later attributed to the years in the desert by the authors of the Priestly traditions. Two considerations are fatal to this theory: first, the passage in Nb 10: 33-36 (except verse 34, an interpolation) is quite certainly a very old text and it too connects the Ark with the journeying through the desert; secondly, the Ark plays the same rôle of guide in the traditions about the entry into the Promised Land (Jos 3-6), where its part in the story cannot be suppressed.

The Ark, then, like the Tent, was part and parcel of the worship in the desert, but it had a longer history than the Tent. The Ark, without the Tent, stood in the camp at Gilgal (Jos 7: 6), and when Jg 2: 1-5 says that the Angel of Yahweh went up from Gilgal to Bokim, near Bethel, we should of course take it to mean that the Ark was transferred. In fact, it is next mentioned at Bethel (Jg 20: 27). (True, Jos 8: 33 notes that it was at Shechem, but the passage is part of the Deuteronomic redaction of the book.) We are on much firmer ground when the Ark is said to be kept at Shiloh, during Samuel's young days (1 S 3: 3). From Shiloh it was taken to the battle of Apheq (1 S 4: 3f.), where it was captured by the Philistines (1 S 4: 11). After its travels from Ashdod to Gath, and from Gath to Eqron, it was given back to the Israelites at Beth-Shemesh and housed for a while at Qiryath-Yearim (1 S 5: 5-7: 1), until David brought it to Jerusalem and installed it in a tent (2 S 6). Solomon built his Temple to house the Ark in its holiest place (1 K 6: 19; 8: 1-9). From this time onwards, the historical books do not mention it again, but it probably shared the fate of the Temple, and disappeared only when the Temple itself was destroyed in 587 B.C. (cf. Jr 3: 16, which is later than 587). An apocryphal tradition used in 2 M 2: 4f. says that before the final ruin of Jerusalem, Jeremias had hidden the Ark, along with the Tent (!) and the altar of incense in a cave on mount Nebo.

What, then, was the religious significance of the Ark? The texts concerning it allow us to glimpse two notions which, according to many critics, are irreconcilable: the Ark is presented as the throne of God and as a receptacle for the Law.

In the very detailed passages of 1 S 4-6; 2 S 6 and 1 K 8, the Ark is the visible sign of the presence of God. When it arrives in the Israelite camp, the Philistines say: 'God has come into their camp!' (1 S 4: 7), and the capture of the Ark is taken as the loss of God's presence: the 'glory' has been taken away from Israel (1 S 4: 22). Similarly, in the very old text of Nb 10: 35, when the Ark leaves, it is Yahweh who is arising. Psalm 132: 8 sings of the transfer of the Ark by David (2 S 6) in similar terms: 'Arise, Yahweh, into thy rest, thou and the Ark of thy strength!' When the Ark is brought into the Temple of Jerusalem, the 'glory of Yahweh' takes possession of the sanctuary (1 K 8: 11), as it had once filled the Tent in the desert when the Ark was put there (cf. Ex 40: 34-35). In the desert wanderings (Nb 10: 33-36) and in the holy wars (1 S 4; 2 S 11: 11), the Ark was the palladium of Israel.[1] Since it was the symbol of Yahweh's presence, its power was formidable: the Philistines felt its effect (1 S 5), and seventy men from Beth-Shemesh were struck down for not rejoicing when the Ark appeared (1 S 6: 19); Uzzah was struck dead for touching it (2 S 6: 7), and according to the Priestly Code, the Levites approached it only when it had been veiled by the priests (Nb 4: 5, 15), and carried it by poles which were never taken off it (Ex 25: 15; cf. 1 K 8: 8).

In the account of the Philistine war, the Ark is called 'the Ark of Yahweh Sabaoth who sits above the cherubim' (1 S 4: 4), and this epithet, which was presumably applied to the Ark from the time of its stay at Shiloh, continued to be used in later days (2 S 6: 2; 2 K 19: 15=Is 37: 16). In 1 Ch 28: 2, the Ark is the 'foot-stool' of God, and it is clearly the Ark which is meant by the same expression in Ps 99: 5; 132: 7; Lm 2: 1. When Is 66: 1 says: 'Heaven is my throne, and the earth my foot-stool! What kind of a house could you build for me?', the protest is certainly directed against the Temple, which the Jews wished to rebuild when they returned from the Exile, but it refers directly to the sacred furniture of the old Temple, *i.e.* to the Ark, which was considered as the 'throne' or the 'foot-stool' of God: the text is, as it were,

1. Cf. p. 259.

an echo of Jr 3: 16–17. Ez 43: 7 should be taken in the same way: Yahweh, returning to his Temple, says: 'Here is the place of my throne, the place where I put the sole of my feet'. It has been suggested that we should make a distinction between the foot-stool and the throne, *i.e.* between the Ark, and a throne which was attached to it during its stay at Shiloh, and which was later transferred, along with the Ark, to the Debir of the Temple. There seems little foundation for this theory: in the prose texts, the throne is never mentioned as an object distinct from the Ark, and there is no evidence that there was anything other than the Ark and the Cherubim inside the Debir. When Jr 3: 16–17 offers some consolation for the disappearance of the Ark by foretelling that in a future age all Jerusalem will be called 'the throne of Yahweh', it assumes that the Ark could be considered either as the throne or as the foot-stool of God. More precisely, the Ark, with the Cherubim, could be said to represent both the foot-stool and the throne of Yahweh. Since the religion of Israel forbade all images, the throne was empty, but even this is not without parallels. Oriental and Greek religions had among their sacred furniture empty thrones, or thrones on which only a symbol of the god was set: some of them, originating from Syria, are flanked by winged sphinxes which remind one of the Cherubim. It is pointless to ask how the Cherubim and the Ark could be both a throne and a foot-stool: it is like asking how Yahweh could actually sit down there, and the question would have seemed as absurd to the Israelites as it does to us: both Cherubim and Ark were the all-too-inadequate symbol of the divine presence, the 'seat' of this presence. When the idea became an image, in the minds of visionaries, it took on various shapes which had nothing to do with the Ark: it is called a throne by Isaias (Is 6: 1), and a chariot by Ezechiel (Ez 10; cf. Ez 1).

According to the Priestly tradition about the desert cult, Yahweh 'met' Moses and spoke to him from above the *kapporeth*, from between the Cherubim (Ex 25: 22; cf. 30: 6; Nb 7: 89). This *kapporeth* stood on top of the Ark but was distinct from it (Ex 35: 12); it is described at length and seems to have been more important than the Ark itself (cf. Ex 25: 17–22; 37: 6–9). In the ritual for the Day of Atonement, which stems from the same tradition, the high priest sprinkled blood on the mercy-seat, and in front of it (Lv 16: 14–15); this makes us suspect that the mercy-seat was something more than the simple gold plate which, in the description given of the desert worship by the same tradition, covered the Ark; moreover, there is no suggestion of any rôle for the Ark or for the Cherubim in this ritual of Lv 16. It is justifiable to conclude that the *kapporeth* was a substitute for the Ark in the post-Exilic tradition, for no new Ark was ever made (cf. Jr 3: 16); this would be confirmed by 1 Ch 28: 11, where the 'room of the *kapporeth*' stands for the Holy of Holies. This *kapporeth* fulfilled the rôle formerly ascribed to the Ark: it was the seat of the divine presence (Lv 16: 2, 13 and the texts cited at the beginning of this paragraph). In the end, it too disappeared: Josephus (*Bell.*, V, v, 5) tells us that in Herod's Temple there was nothing in the Holy of Holies at all.

Leaving aside the *kapporeth* then, it seems probable that the Ark and the Cherubim represented the throne of God in the sanctuaries of Shiloh and Jerusalem. But can we say the same of the simple Ark of the desert period, in which there were neither Cherubim nor *kapporeth* below them? It is possible to do so, for the oldest tradition of the Pentateuch, in Nb 10: 35-36, which links the Ark with the movements of Yahweh, seems to look upon the Ark as the support of the invisible godhead, a pedestal rather than throne—if the distinction is of importance: but the religious idea was the same.

Yet there is a second interpretation of the Ark's significance to be considered. According to Dt 10: 1-5 (cf. 1 K 8: 9), the Ark appears to be nothing more than a small chest containing the tablets on which the Ten Commandments were written: from this it takes its name as 'the Ark of the Covenant' (*b'rith*). The idea is not limited to the schools of Deuteronomy, for the Priestly tradition uses a synonymous expression, 'the Ark of the Testimony' (*'eduth*), and in this tradition *'eduth* is the name used for the Law which was kept in the Ark (Ex 25: 16; 40: 20). However, as extra-biblical documents show, there is no contradiction involved in the vivid contrast presented by the notions of the Ark as a pedestal or throne and of the Ark as a receptacle. A rubric of the Egyptian Book of the Dead (ch. LXIV) reads: 'This chapter was found at Khmun on an alabaster brick, under the feet of the Majesty of this venerable place (the god Thot), and it was written by the god himself': the comparison with the tablets of the Law, written by God's own finger and placed in the Ark which was his foot-stool, is obvious. The finding of the Book of the Dead under the feet of Thot is no doubt a legendary detail, but it fits in with a custom attested by historical documents. Hittite treaties stipulate that the text shall be placed in a temple at the foot of an image of a god. A letter from Ramses II about his treaty with Hattusil is most explicit: 'The writing of the oath (pact) which I have made to the Great King, the king of Hattu, lies beneath the feet of the god Teshup: the great gods are witnesses of it. The writing of the oath which the Great King, the king of Hattu, has made to me, lies beneath the feet of the god Ra: the great gods are witnesses of it'. In the same way, the Decalogue was the official instrument of the pact between Yahweh and his people, and was put into the Ark, under the feet of Yahweh.

We still have to clarify the connection between the Ark and the Tent. If we look at the Pentateuchal traditions in the probable order in which they were committed to writing, it is noticeable that the oldest tradition speaks of the Tent (Ex 33: 7-11) and of the Ark (Nb 10: 33-36; 14: 44) but never connects the two. Again, Deuteronomy knows of the Ark (Dt 10: 1-5; 31: 25-26) and mentions the Tent (Dt 31: 14-15) apart from the Ark. Later the Priestly tradition describes both the Ark and the Tent as things connected with worship in the desert: the Tent houses the Ark which contains the Testimony, and the

Tent is the Dwelling of Yahweh who reveals himself above the Ark (Ex 25-26; 36-40).

We have tried to prove above that both the Ark and the Tent existed in the desert; if this is admitted, how can one explain that the oldest traditions never connect the two? Perhaps this is an indication that the two objects belonged to different groups among the ancestors of Israel. The Priestly tradition, taking its inspiration from the Temple of Solomon, combined the two objects of worship in its literature, just as the two groups who had each possessed one of the objects had combined together in history. But it is more probable that the Ark and the Tent were in fact originally connected with each other. If the oldest tradition does not mention this connection explicitly, that is because the final redactors of the Pentateuch have preserved only fragments of this tradition, and have omitted what was described well enough in a later tradition. And in fact the old texts referring to the Ark and the Tent seem rather out of place in the middle of a Priestly tradition. There is one text about the Tent (Ex 33: 7) which may even contain the proof that it has been torn from a context which also mentioned the Ark: 'Moses took the Tent and set it up for him (*or*, for it) outside the camp'. The pronoun *him* may refer to Moses or to Yahweh, but it can also be translated *it*, and might then refer to the Ark, which is masculine in Hebrew and which, originally, might have been mentioned immediately before. This interpretation is accepted by some distinguished exegetes, and it would mean that in the oldest traditions the Ark and the Tent were related in exactly the same way as in the Priestly description. But even without relying on this text, we may call on one argument of a general nature: the Ark needed to be sheltered, and the normal shelter in the desert is a tent. Conversely, the Tent itself must have covered something: we have compared it with the *qubba* of the pre-Islamic Arabs, which contained divine symbols. It would appear, then, that we ought not to separate the Ark and the Tent, and that the Priestly description of the desert sanctuary—however deeply influenced by Solomon's Temple and even (for the *kapporeth*) by the post-Exilic temple—did preserve an authentic tradition.

4. *The sanctuaries in the land of Israel before the building of the Temple*

We have seen[1] that the places of worship whose foundation was attributed to the Patriarchs are scarcely mentioned in the Bible once Israel is settled in Canaan. But from this time onwards other sanctuaries are brought to the fore.

(a) *Gilgal.* There are in the Old Testament various scattered references to Gilgal, a place whose precise location once occasioned some dispute among critics. Modern scholars, however, claim that all the texts refer to a site in the neighbourhood of Jericho, which raises a difficulty over the Gilgal mentioned in the story of Elias (2 K 2: 1; 4: 38): this one seems rather to lie in the hill-

1. Cf. p. 289.

country of Ephraim. But in Jos 4: 19 the sanctuary called Gilgal in the early days of Israel is situated east of Jericho, *i.e.* between Jericho and the Jordan, in a spot which cannot be located more precisely. The place of worship was marked by a circle of stones (Jos 4: 20), from which it took its name.[1] This name, which is here mentioned for the first time and without comment, seems to be pre-Israelite and to indicate a sanctuary which was already in existence; the explanation of the name in Jos 5: 9 is evidently secondary. In Jos 5: 13-15, the 'leader of the army of Yahweh' appears to Josue and orders him to take off his shoes, for 'the place is holy': if this episode is to be placed at Gilgal itself, we should here have the usual theophany for the foundation of a sanctuary. It may be so, but this episode is only a fragment of an independent tradition, and is connected with Jericho, not Gilgal. But it is quite certain that Gilgal was an important sanctuary immediately after the conquest, for tradition recorded that the Ark had come to rest there after the crossing of the Jordan (Jos 4: 19; 7: 6); there the people had circumcised themselves (Jos 5: 2-9), and there they celebrated the first Passover in Canaan: there the manna had ceased to fall (Jos 5: 10-12). It was the place, then, where they kept alive the memory of the entry into the Promised Land, of the end of desert wanderings, and of the first stages of the conquest (Jos 2-10). The Gibeonites came to Gilgal to seek an alliance with the Israelites (Jos 9: 6), and the oath by Yahweh's name which confirmed this pact must have been made at this sanctuary (Jos 9: 19).

Samuel came to Gilgal to judge Israel because there was a sanctuary there, as at Bethel and Mispah (1 S 7: 16), and the story of Saul's life underlines its importance: one of the traditions about the institution of the monarchy (1 S 11: 15) says that Saul was proclaimed king 'before Yahweh' at Gilgal, and that sacrifices were offered there. Both traditions agree in placing the rejection of Saul by Samuel at Gilgal (1 S 13: 7-15; cf. 10: 8 and 1 S 15: 12-33), and both of them place this rejection in a cultic context: Saul offered sacrifice, and Samuel cut the throat of Agag 'before Yahweh'. Lastly, Judah came out to Gilgal to meet David on his return from Transjordan, and Israel and Judah quarrelled whose king he was near the sanctuary where Saul had been proclaimed the first king of Israel (2 S 19: 16, 41).

Although Gilgal is not mentioned after this in the historical narratives, people continued to attend the sanctuary. We have no details about the kind of cult which was conducted at the time, but the prophets condemn Gilgal along with Bethel (Os 4: 15; Am 4: 4; 5: 5; cf. Os 12: 12). In Os 9: 15, the 'wickedness' of Gilgal seems to lie in the fact that Saul was there proclaimed king, and the reason seems to lie in Osee's hostility to the monarchy (cf. Os 8: 4). Perhaps there is a veiled censure of Gilgal as early as Jg 3: 19, 26: the 'idols near Gilgal' might mean the *maṣṣebôth* of the sanctuary, which had been the focus of a suspect cult.

1. Cf. p. 275.

(b) *Shiloh.* During the period of the Judges Gilgal was eclipsed by Shiloh, which became the central sanctuary of the tribal federation at that time. Its origins are obscure. The book of Josue makes Shiloh a meeting-place for the tribes (Jos 18: 1; 21: 2; 22: 9, 12), and says that the territory of seven tribes was there apportioned by lot (Jos 18: 8), and even adds that the Tent of Re-union was set up there (Jos 18: 1; 19: 51). It is very questionable whether the Tent was ever at Shiloh,[1] but there was certainly a sanctuary there from very early times. Every year there was a pilgrimage to Shiloh, a *ḥag*, during which groups of young girls used to dance in the vineyards (Jg 21: 19-21). Elqanah, the father of Samuel, went there every year to offer a sacrifice to Yahweh Sabaoth (1 S 1: 3). During these years the cult centred round a building, a 'house of Yahweh' (1 S 1: 7, 24; 3: 15), a *hêkal* or 'palace' of Yahweh (1 S 3: 3), a 'house of God' (Jg 18: 31): in a word, it was the first temple of Yahweh, and the Ark was kept there (1 S 3: 3).

It was at Shiloh, apparently, that Yahweh was first called 'Sabaoth, who sits above the Cherubim'. The first mention of Yahweh Sabaoth is in 1 S 1: 3, and the first mention of 'who sits above the Cherubim' is in the story of how, during the Philistine war, the Ark was taken from Shiloh to the battle-front (1 S 4: 4). Could there have been, in pre-Israelite times, a deity called Sabaoth who was represented as carried by Cherubim? It is not impossible, but it cannot be proved. In any case, the application of this title to Yahweh underlined his majesty and his supreme dominion, for whatever be the exact meaning of Sabaoth, the word certainly includes the idea of power.

We have only scattered allusions to the sanctuary at Shiloh until the time of Samuel, and just when we are beginning to know more about it, its end is near: the Philistines captured the Ark at Apheq (1 S 4: 1-11), and their victory probably opened up the road to Shiloh, and the town was sacked. Excavations at Seilun, the modern name of the site, show that the town was destroyed in the middle of the eleventh century, and that it was unoccupied, or at least in decline, for a long period afterwards. Jeremias sees in the ruins a lesson for the people of Jerusalem, who are rather too confident that God will not abandon their Temple (Jr 7: 12-14; 26: 6, 9), and the echo of his words can be heard in Ps 78: 60. The destruction of Shiloh must have taken place around 1050 B.C., but half a century later David recovered the Ark and Jerusalem became the successor of Shiloh.

(c) *Mispah in Benjamin.* In the story of the crime of Gibeah, the Israelites assemble before Yahweh at Mispah and there take a solemn oath (Jg 20: 1, 3; 21: 1, 5, 8). Mispah was clearly a sanctuary. It is next mentioned in the stories of Samuel and Saul: the Israelites meet together at Mispah, call on the name of Yahweh there, pour out water in supplication and offer sacrifice to Yahweh (1 S 7: 5-12). Samuel judged Israel at Mispah (1 S 7: 16), as he did in the sanctuaries of Bethel and Gilgal. Lastly, the tradition of 1 S 10: 17-24 tells

1. Cf. p. 297.

how Saul was chosen king when the sacred lots were drawn 'before Yahweh' at Mispah. After that, Mispah is not mentioned as a religious centre until the time of the Maccabees: the Jews gathered there, fasted, prayed and consulted the Law 'for in former times there was a place of prayer for Israel at Mispah' (1 M 3: 46–54).

This last text is evidently inspired by the passages in Jg and 1 S cited in the last paragraph: hence it is not an independent witness to what actually happened in ancient times. But even the value of the texts from Jg and 1 S has been questioned: in Jg 20–21, Bethel, where the Ark was kept at the time, seems to be a serious rival to Mispah (Jg 20: 18, 26–28; 21: 2); the portrait of Samuel as judge and liberator in 1 S 7 is not based on an ancient document and is an introduction to the anti-monarchist account of the institution of kingship; 1 S 10: 17–24 also belongs to this tradition, but the monarchist version places the proclamation of Saul as king (1 S 11: 15) at Gilgal. Some authors, however, have rushed to the conclusion that these texts are trying to heighten the importance of Mispah because immediately after the fall of Jerusalem, under the aegis of Godolias, it became the centre of the Jewish community (Jr 40–41). To this we may reply that the texts in question belong to the Deuteronomic redaction of the historical books, and must therefore represent an older tradition, memories concerning an old sanctuary, like those about Bethel and Gilgal. If we could use Os 5: 1 without qualms, we should be on surer ground, for it accuses the priests and leaders of Israel of having been 'a snare' for the people 'at Mispah'. Unfortunately, it may refer to a Mispah in Gilead, and even if it does refer to Mispah in Benjamin, Osee is probably thinking only of the choice of Saul as king in this sanctuary (cf. 1 S 10). But this would at least confirm the antiquity of this tradition.

Once we admit that there was a sanctuary at Mispah, another problem arises. The Mispah of Godolias, which is also the Mispah of 1 K 15: 22, is generally identified as Tell-en-Nasbeh north of Jerusalem. Extensive excavations on this site have shown that it was not densely populated until after the time of Solomon: this tempts us to look elsewhere (though still, of course, in Benjamin) for the site of the Mispah which is mentioned under the Judges and Samuel. The name was originally a common noun, meaning 'The Watch-post', and the Bible mentions several Mispah or Mispeh. Yet it would be unwise to over-estimate the negative argument from excavations: a sanctuary can be an important religious centre without necessarily being connected with a large town, and Tell-en-Nasbeh may have been a place of worship before the town developed.

(d) *Gibeon*. If we take it that the Mispah of the Judges was not the same place as the Mispah of the monarchical period, the former may be the same place as the high place of Gibeon which, under Solomon, was 'the greatest high place'.[1]

1. Cf. p. 288.

The popularity of Gibeon implied in this title cannot be explained unless the sanctuary had a long history behind it, even though it is never mentioned earlier in the Bible. Now if this 'high place' of Gibeon stood, as is probable, on the height nowadays called Nabi-Samwil, the site would well deserve the name of 'The Watch-post' (Mispah), and the connection with Samuel which the Arabic name records would fit in well with the traditions of 1 S 7 and 10.

The story about the descendants of Saul whom David handed over to the Gibeonites for vengeance (2 S 21: 1-14) is clearly connected with this sanctuary. According to the Hebrew text (verse 6), the victims were dismembered before Yahweh 'at Gibeah of Saul, the chosen one of Yahweh', but the text should certainly be corrected to read, with the Greek, 'at Gibeon, on the mountain of Yahweh' (cf. verse 9). The ritual brings to mind the Canaanite practices and presupposes that the cult of Yahweh had there replaced an older form of worship. Lastly, that clause of the pact with the Gibeonites which obliged them to cut wood and to carry water for the house of God and to do service for the altar of Yahweh would presumably first be put into practice in this sanctuary (Jos 9: 23, 27).

(e) *Ophra*. While the origins of Mispah and Gibeon are unknown, we have information about the foundation of two other sanctuaries in the period of the Judges, Ophra and Dan.

There are two accounts of the foundation of Ophra. In the first (Jg 6: 11-24), the Angel of Yahweh appeared under a tree which belongs to Yoash, the father of Gideon, near a rock where Gideon was treading corn. Gideon was then charged to save Israel from the Midianite oppressors. Gideon had prepared a meal before he knew who was speaking to him, and Yahweh accepted it as a sacrifice upon the rock. Gideon thereupon built an altar which he called Yahweh-Shalom, 'Yahweh-Peace'. This story is close akin to the tales of the patriarchal period and contains all the elements of a *hieros logos*, *i.e.* of a narrative which sets the seal on the authenticity of a sanctuary: it mentions a sacred tree, a theophany, a message of salvation, the inauguration of worship on an altar of rock, and finally the building of an altar.

A second account follows immediately (Jg 6: 25-32): Yahweh spoke to Gideon in a dream, and ordered him to destroy the altar of Baal which belonged to his father Yoash, to cut in pieces the *'asherah*, to build an altar to Yahweh on the hill and there to offer sacrifice with the wood of the *'asherah*. When Gideon carried out this command, the townspeople were angry, but Yoash stood by his son: 'Let Baal defend his own rights if he is god' (a tendentious explanation of the name Yerubbaal, a second name of Gideon). This second account brings to mind the story of Elias on Carmel: the theme of it is that the worship of Yahweh replaced the worship of Baal because the latter was powerless to defend his rights.

It is not suggested that there were two different sanctuaries at Ophra: the big tree of the first account means that it was already a place of worship, and the tree belongs to Yoash, as does the altar in the second account. It was a private sanctuary, if the term may be used, but a private sanctuary such as the Patriarchs had: it was the sanctuary of the clan which Yoash represented. But there were two traditions about the origin of the worship of Yahweh in Ophra: one told how it had replaced a previous worship without any trouble, and the other told how it had forcibly ousted the cult of Baal. The first tradition seems to be the older, and would show how the people did not at once realize that the cult of Yahweh was incompatible with worship of Baal. (Note that Yoash, the patron of Baal's altar, has a Yahwistic name, and that Gideon's second name, Yerubbaal, means 'May Baal defend (the bearer of his name)'.) The second tradition reflects the struggle which eventually took place against the worship of Baal.

These two aspects are found also in the one and only episode which can be related to the sanctuary at Ophrah: after his victory over the Midianites, Gideon used part of the booty to make an ephod.[1] Here the ephod is a cultic object which formed part of the furnishings of a sanctuary, as it did with the Canaanites (cf. Jg 17: 5). Gideon, who had just refused supreme power because Yahweh alone ought to reign over Israel, meant this ephod for the cult of Yahweh, but the redactor condemns it as an idolatrous object: 'All Israel prostituted itself there' (Jg 8: 22-27). This local sanctuary is never again mentioned in the Old Testament.

(f) *Dan*. The sanctuary of Dan had a longer history. Its foundation is connected with the migration of the tribe of Dan described in Jg 17-18. We shall return to this account later, when we study the priesthood in Israel[2]; here we shall concern ourselves only with the facts about the sanctuary, or, rather, about the two successive sanctuaries at Dan: the domestic chapel of Mikah and the tribal sanctuary of Dan.

Its origin was, you could say, just about as unlawful as possible: Mikah had stolen some silver from his mother, and given it back to her; with some of this silver she had an idol made. Mikah put it in a sanctuary, a 'house of God', with an ephod and some teraphim. He installed his son as priest, and later hired a wandering Levite. Then a passing clan of Danites stole all the sacred furniture during their migration northwards, and easily talked the Levite into going with them: the Levite found it far more advantageous to be priest to a group than to a private individual. Mikah bewailed the fact that he had at one blow lost both his god and his priest. When the Danites reach Laish, they massacred a peaceful population, changed the name of the place to Dan and set up Mikah's idol there.

There is nothing here in the least like any of the accounts of the foundation of patriarchal sanctuaries or of Ophrah. It is not God, but men, who take the initiative, and the men are not very likeable. There is an accumulation of faults which the Law and the Prophets will condemn: an image they call a

1. Cf. p. 350, 351. 2. Cf. pp. 361, 362.

'god', a highly-suspect ephod, teraphim and a priest who is not a Levite. This tale is certainly not the account of a foundation, a *hieros logos* destined to show the legitimacy of a sanctuary. A Jewish reader of the book would draw quite the contrary conclusion: it is a false sanctuary served by a false priest—which is exactly the impression the redactor wanted to produce by telling this story. His plea is that the first sanctuary of Dan was worthless, and was a fitting predecessor of the sanctuary into which Jeroboam brought the second golden calf (1 K 12: 29-30): it was to be condemned along with Bethel (2 K 10: 29).

Yet the account is really concerned with a sanctuary of Yahweh: Mikah's mother consecrated the stolen silver to Yahweh, and Mikah was blessed by Yahweh for returning it to its owner. Mikah was at first content to have his son as priest, but he was glad to replace him by a Levite because that would bring Yahweh's blessing upon him: the spies from the tribe of Dan consulted God through Mikah's ephod, and received a reply: and the sanctuary where the idol stood was served by Jonathan, a grandson of Moses.

Neither the hypothesis of two literary sources for Jg 17-18 nor the suggestion that the document is full of long interpolations explains away the fact that here we have a sanctuary of Yahweh set up in defiance of all the rules of Yahwism.

The account does reproduce an old tradition of which the Danites must have been proud, but the story contains many elements which astonish us in the same way as they shocked the redactor of the book: it is a story from the time when 'there was no king in Israel and everyone did as he pleased' (Jg 17: 6, cf. 18: 1). This story shows us, even better than the story about Ophra, the great danger which Yahwism encountered when Israel first came into contact with the settled population of Canaan.

According to Jg 18: 30, Jonathan's descendants continued as the priests of the sanctuary of Dan until the Assyrian conquest. The following verse (Jg 18: 31) adds that Mikah's idol stayed there 'all the time that the house of God in Shiloh stood', which may mean that it disappeared when Shiloh was destroyed by the Philistines or that this idolatrous cult continued all the time that the true 'house of God', *i.e.* Shiloh, lasted. The second period of the history of the sanctuary at Dan, from the schism of Jeroboam, will be discussed when we deal with the sanctuaries which were rivals to Jerusalem.[1]

(g) *Jerusalem.* Jerusalem was the last of all the sanctuaries founded in the first period of Israel's history. Its foundation under David comprised two stages: the installation of the Ark, and the erection of an altar on the site of the future Temple.

After his conquest of Jerusalem and his first victories over the Philistines, David had deprived the Philistines of the control they could still exercise over the Ark at Qiryath-Yearim: he then went to bring it back (2 S 6). It was brought back in a religious procession, with shouts of joy, and the noise of

1. Cf. pp. 334–336.

trumpets, with David himself offering sacrifice and dancing before the Ark. Its transference was marked with incidents which revealed the holiness, beneficent and yet awesome, of the sacred object: the death of Uzzah, its stay with Obed-Edom and the subsequent blessing of his house, the punishment of Mikal. At length the Ark was laid at rest in its *maqôm*, its 'holy place', under the tent which had been specially prepared for it. Ps 24: 7-10 and 132 should be compared with this account: they were sung on the anniversary of this entry of Yahweh Sabaoth into Sion where he had chosen to dwell, and this feast probably influenced the cultic aspect of the account in 2 S 6. The most questionable conclusions have been deduced from these texts. It has been suggested that this liturgy of the Ark coincided with the crowning of David as king of Jerusalem in the Canaanite fashion, that it was repeated at the crowning or on the coronation anniversaries of the kings of Judah, or even that it formed part of a feast for the enthronement of Yahweh. This seems to be reading far too much into the texts.

Nevertheless, it is quite certain that David's action had important consequences. From the political point of view, the capital was his own personal conquest, and did not belong to the territory of any of the Twelve Tribes: in it he had installed the Ark, which all the tribes venerated and which had formerly been the focal point of their common worship; he thereby increased his power over the various parts of the nation and ensured national unity around his own throne. But the religious aspect was even more important: the restoration of a sanctuary for the Ark meant that Jerusalem was the heir to the sanctuary of Shiloh and to the Tent in the desert. The installation of the Ark in Jerusalem meant that the religious traditions of the Twelve Tribes were centred there, and Jerusalem became the focal point of that history of salvation which stretched from the Exodus from Egypt to the conquest of the Holy Land: the continuity of Yahwism was assured. By the transfer of the Ark, Jerusalem became the Holy City, and its religious significance was destined to eclipse its political importance: as a religious centre it would survive the break-up of David's empire, and even the total destruction of national independence.

The second step was taken when David set up an altar in the place where Solomon's Temple would stand. The story in 2 S 24: 16-25 may perhaps combine two traditions which the parallel passage in 1 Ch 21: 15-22: 1 harmonizes and explains. It is a foundation-story, with all the essential elements we have met so often before: a theophany—the appearance of the Angel of Yahweh to David near the threshing-floor of Araunah the Jebusite; a message of salvation—the arresting of the plague; the inauguration of worship—the setting up of an altar on the site of the apparition, and the first sacrifices.

We have seen how the patriarchal sanctuaries and some of those which date from the period of the Judges had perpetuated or replaced previous places of worship. The texts so far examined do not justify similar conclusions about Jerusalem, but there are some others which should be taken into consideration. In Ps 110: 4, the king of Israel is called a priest after the manner of Melchisedech.[1] The only other text which mentions Melchisedech is Gn 14: 18-20, which tells the story of his meeting Abraham. Melchisedech was king of Shalem, *i.e.* Jerusalem (Ps 76: 3), and also a priest of El-'Elyon. He blessed Abraham by his god and Abraham paid him a tithe. By linking Abraham with the future capital of David, the text is trying to justify Israel's very ancient connections with Jerusalem, and the rights which the king and the priesthood of Jerusalem held over Israel; but at the same time we learn from this text the name of the pre-Israelite god who was venerated there. El-'Elyon was a Canaanite god. According to Philo of Byblos, the Phoenician pantheon included an 'Eliun called the Most High', who was the father of Ouranos (heaven) and of Gé (earth); now, in Gen 14: 19, the name El-'Elyon is followed by the epithet 'Creator of heaven and earth'. We may also compare the Phoenician inscription from Karatepe and a Neo-Punic inscription from Leptis Magna where the 'Creator of the earth' is invoked: the same epithet is attached to the name El in an inscription and on potsherds from Palmyra, and in the Hittite translation of a Canaanite myth the name and epithet are transcribed El-Kunirsha. An Aramaic treaty from Sfire includes among the gods who guarantee it 'El *and* 'Elyon', which some writers have interpreted as two distinct divinities. But El *and* 'Elyon may mean, as in Gn 14, 'El who is 'Elyon'. Thus the title represents another form in which the supreme god reveals himself, like the El-Bethel, El-'Olam and El-Shaddai we met when discussing the sanctuaries of the Patriarchs. And, as in the previous instances, Yahweh replaced the former divinity and assumed his titles: he is 'the God of heaven and the God of earth' in Gn 24: 3. 'Elyon became an epithet of Yahweh (Ps 47: 3), and is employed as a parallel for Yahweh (Ps 18: 14), for he alone is "Elyon over all the earth, most high above all the gods' (Ps 97: 9).

Some writers have tried to go further, but the ground becomes very unsure. It has been said that just as Yahweh replaced 'Elyon, so he usurped his sanctuary. But the text does not say so, and in fact suggests the contrary: in Gn 14 there is no mention of a sanctuary of El-'Elyon, though of course there must have been one, because his priest was present and Abraham gave a tithe. The narratives in the books of Samuel stress that David put up a special tent to house the Ark (2 S 6: 17; cf. 7: 2) and that he set up his altar in a place which had previously been profane ground: it was a barn for threshing corn which belonged to a private individual (2 S 24: 18-10). Yet it could be objected that the silence of Gn 14 and the insistence of 2 S were deliberately meant to conceal the fact that the Temple of Jerusalem had been built on the site of a pagan sanctuary. It is easier to put the objection than to answer it; but any answer must recognize the fact that there was a genuine tradition of a tent

1. Cf. pp. 109, 114.

over the Ark, and that this Tent remained the centre of Yahwistic worship until the Temple was built, for it is almost certainly the 'tent' where Solomon was anointed (1 K 1: 39), and the 'tent of Yahweh' where Joab sought refuge (1 K 2: 28f.). This question, moreover, is tied up with another one: did Yahweh inherit the priesthood of El-'Elyon? Under David, another line of priests, that of Sadoq, makes its appearance in Jerusalem itself. Its origins are obscure, and some authors have maintained Sadoq was the priest of 'Elyon at the time of the conquest, and that he was subsequently engaged by David for the service of Yahweh. This problem will be treated when we discuss the priesthood,[1] but it is already obvious that unless some link can be establishad between the sanctuary of Yahweh and that of 'Elyon, the principal argument in favour of a Canaanite origin for the priesthood of Sadoq falls to the ground, for Sadoq is never mentioned except in connection with the Ark and the tent of Yahweh (2 S 15: 25; 1 K 1: 39).

Whatever be the answer to these questions,. it was under David that the Ark, the symbol of the divine presence, was brought to Jerusalem, and that the city acquired a site for worship which was chosen by Yahweh himself. Everything was set for the work of Solomon.

1. Cf. pp. 373-374.

CHAPTER THREE

THE TEMPLE AT JERUSALEM

DAVID'S purpose in transferring the Ark to his new capital was to make Jerusalem the religious centre of Israel, but the Ark had to be kept in a tent, for there was no building to house it. According to 2 S 7: 1-7, David thought of building a 'house' for Yahweh, but was dissuaded by a divine command which Nathan brought him. The text of this prophecy, however, contains an addition (2 S 7: 13), according to which Yahweh was reserving the honour of building such a sanctuary for the son and successor of David. The Deuteronomic redaction of the book of Kings tells us that Solomon recalled this promise and presented himself as the executor of a plan which his father had conceived but had failed to carry out because he was too preoccupied by his wars (1 K 5: 17-19; 8: 15-21). The Chronicler, however, assigns a far more important rôle to David: David did not build the Temple because he was a man of war and had shed blood, whereas Solomon was predestined for this task by his name, which means the 'peaceful' king (1 Ch 22: 8-10; 28: 3). David, however, had prepared everything; he was responsible for the plans of the Temple and the inventory of its furnishings; he collected the materials for the building and the gold ingots which were to be used for the sacred objects; he assembled the teams of workmen, and fixed the classes and functions of the clergy (1 Ch 22-28). The theological ideas expressed in these different traditions will be discussed at the end of the chapter: for the moment, we are concerned only with what they have in common, namely, that David first thought of having a Temple, and that Solomon actually built it.

1. *Solomon's Temple*

The building of the Temple occupied Solomon from the fourth to the eleventh year of his reign (1 K 6: 37-38; cf. 6: 1). He made a contract with Hiram, king of Tyre, for the timber to be brought from the Lebanon (1 K 5: 15-26), while the stone was quarried near Jerusalem (1 K 5: 29, 31). The Israelites were conscripted to provide the bulk of the labour force (1 K 5: 20, 23, 27-30), but the skilled workmen (*i.e.* the lumbermen in the Lebanon, the sailors who transported the wood, the carpenters and the stonemasons in Jerusalem) were Phoenicians (1 K 5: 20, 32). Hiram, who cast the two pillars and the other bronzes in the Jordan valley, was also a Phoenician, though his mother was an Israelite (1 K 7: 13-47).

There is a description of the Temple and its furnishings in 1 K 6-7, of which 2 Ch 3-4 is a summary, with some variations. This description certainly goes back to a document which was almost contemporary with the building, and the final editor had seen the Temple still standing; but the description is very hard to interpret. The editor did not have the interests of an architect or an archaeologist and he has omitted details which would be essential for a reconstruction (*e.g.* the thickness of the walls, the layout of the façade, the way in which it was roofed). Moreover, the text is full of technical terms, and has been disfigured by scribes who understood it no better than we do; and it has been loaded with glosses meant to enhance the splendour of the building. Lastly, not a stone of this glorious building is to be seen to-day. Our only guides are the texts, where the exegesis is often uncertain, and the comparisons which can be drawn from the archaeology of Palestine and of the neighbouring countries. It is not surprising that the reconstructions which have been attempted differ considerably from each other, and the interpretation presented here makes no claim to be definitive.

(a) *The buildings.* The Temple was a long building, open on one of its shorter sides. The interior was divided into three parts: a vestibule, called the Ulam (from a root meaning 'to be in front of'), a room for worship called the Hekal (which has the double meaning of 'palace' and 'temple' in both Hebrew and Phoenician),[1] and which was later called the 'Holy Place', and lastly the Debir (roughly, the 'back room') which was later called the 'Holy of Holies': this was the part reserved to Yahweh, and the Ark of the Covenant stood there.

The measurements given in the Bible do not include the thickness of the walls. The Temple was 20 cubits wide: the Ulam was 10 cubits long, the Hekal 40 cubits and the Debir 20 cubits. There is no mention of walls which partitioned it inside, and yet there certainly was one between the Ulam and the Hekal, though we do not know whether there was one between the Hekal and the Debir. The Hekal and the Debir are in fact treated as one whole (1 K 6: 2): properly speaking they formed the 'house', the Temple, and together they were 60 cubits long: it is only later in the description that we are told the Debir was 20 cubits long, and the Hekal 40 cubits (1 K 6: 16-17). If there had been a real wall separating them, the total length would have been 60 cubits plus the thickness of the wall. Moreover, the details given about the Debir seem to confirm this conclusion: though the text has been tampered with, a very slight correction gives an excellent sense (1 K 6: 16): Solomon 'used cedar planks to build the twenty cubits from the back of the Temple, from the ground to the rafters, and (these twenty cubits) "were set apart" from the Temple for the Debir'. These planks are not the wooden

1. Cf. p. 282.

panelling on the main walls, which was mentioned in the preceding verse and which was found both in the Hekal and in the Debir: they seem to be a partition-wall in front of the Debir. Later texts lend support to this hypothesis: in the Tent of desert days, the description of which is inspired by the Temple at Jerusalem,[1] the Holy of Holies was separated from the Holy Place by nothing more than a veil (Ex 26: 33): Ezechiel's Temple has only a comparatively thin wall at this point (Ez 41: 3); the Mishnah, treating of Herod's Temple, records only curtains between the Holy Place and the Holy of Holies, and Josephus, whose description is more trustworthy, speaks only of a veil (*B.J.*, V, v, 5).

In ancient Oriental temples, the *cella* stood somewhat higher than the level of the room, or, failing this, the symbol of worship itself stood on a raised platform or podium. Though the Bible does not mention it, at Jerusalem too the Debir seems to have been on a higher level than the Hekal. The measurements given in 1 K 6: 20 make the Debir a perfect cube with a 20-cubit side, but the Hekal was 30 cubits high according to the Hebrew, 25 according to the ancient Greek version and the Lucianic recension (1 K 6: 2). To explain this difference of 10 or 5 cubits in height, it has been suggested that the roof of the Debir was lower than that of the Hekal, as was the *cella* of some Egyptian temples, or that there was a room over the Debir. Both these solutions are improbable, and it is better to say that the floor of the Debir stood higher than the floor of the Hekal, and that it was approached by a flight of stairs. The Hebrew text makes this podium 10 cubits high, which is higher than any other examples we know of, but according to the Greek text it would be only 5 cubits higher, which is quite reasonable.

Two bronze pillars stood before the vestibule (1 K 7: 15-22; 41-42). They were 18 cubits high, and were crowned by capitals, also in bronze, 5 cubits high. They were not, apparently, supports for the lintel of the vestibule; on the contrary, they stood upright in front of it, on each side of the entrance. It has recently been suggested that they were enormous cressets or pillars on top of which lights could be burnt, but it is far more probable that they were traditional steles or *maṣṣebôth*, which had always had their place in the old Canaanite sanctuaries. There is no lack of Phoenician analogies, and one may compare also the two pillars of Heliopolis mentioned by Lucian, *De Dea Syria* § 28, the two steles of Heracles' Temple at Tyre mentioned by Herodotus II 44, and the two pillars which decorate a relief from the neighbourhood of Tyre; for a period nearer to that of Solomon's Temple, one can point to a model, in baked clay, of a sanctuary (from Idalion in Cyprus), and to two similar models recently discovered in Transjordan and at Tell el-Farah near Nablus. The names of the two columns, *Yakîn* and *Bo'az*, are still a riddle: they have been explained as meaning 'he will establish with strength', or as the opening words of royal oracles, with the following phrase understood

1. Cf. p. 296.

('Yahweh will establish . . .; In the strength of Yahweh . . .'), or as dynastic names (*Bo'az* would represent the husband of Ruth, David's forefather, and *Yakîn*, it has been suggested, might be an ancestor of Bathsheba). The two words are never found again, and there is no guarantee that they were engraved on the pillars. It has been suggested that they were so named by the Tyrian artist who made and erected them, and perhaps they merely express his satisfaction on seeing his masterpieces completed: *Yakîn* (or, better, *Yakûn*, the Phoenician form preserved in the Greek version) meaning 'It is solid!', and *Bo'az* (perhaps with a Phoenician vocalization) 'With strength!'

1 K 6: 5-10 describes a construction which surrounded the Temple on three sides. It seems to have been a building in three very slight storeys, erected against the walls of the Debir and the Hekal, but leaving the surrounds of the Ulam quite clear. It is sometimes called *yaṣia'*, in the singular, and sometimes *ṣᵉla'ôth*, a plural, the singular of which denotes one of three storeys. The two words are not synonyms, and seem to indicate that our present text is combining information about two successive stages in the form of this building. The *yaṣia'*, to judge by etymology, was a low construction, a bottom storey which surrounded the Temple on three sides. It was only 5 cubits high, and was like the low rooms which flanked certain temples in Egypt and Mesopotamia: like the latter, it was an adjunct to the sanctuary and was used as a store-place for offerings. It was built at the same time as the Temple, and was closely connected with it (1 K 6: 10). Later on, this building proved too small for its purpose, so it was raised by storeys, either at the same or at different times. The name *yaṣia'*, which meant a low building, was no longer appropriate, and so the whole structure was then called *ṣᵉlaôth*, the singular of which means primarily a man's rib, and then the side of an object or of a building: here it means each of the storeys which flanked the Temple. Since the upper two storeys of this building were added later, they were not part of the plan of the Temple like the *yaṣia'*; but their joists rested on the already existing recesses in the wall: consequently, each storey was a cubit wider than the lower one (1 K 6: 6). The entrance to the *yaṣia'* was at the right corner of the Temple, obviously from outside. When the upper storeys were added, *lûlim* were put in. The ancient versions and many modern translations take this term to mean spiral staircases; but the meaning of the word in Rabbinical Hebrew makes it more likely that they were merely trap-doors connecting the different storeys, for they all had low ceilings and were used as store-places.

The description of the side-building shows that the wall of the Temple receded one cubit at three points. There was a technical reason for these recesses: the higher parts of the wall were not so heavy, and the wall was thus more stable. The upper parts of buildings excavated in Syria and Palestine have all been destroyed, so that we cannot point to archaeological confirmation, but clay models of sanctuaries, found at Beisan, clearly indicate the same kind of recess. The Egyptians obtained the same result by giving a pronounced batter to the surface of high walls.

How was it built? There is one piece of information about the walls of the Temple courts and of the Palace (1 K 6: 36; 7: 12) which is most useful: they had three courses of dressed stones, and one course of cedar-timber. The Temple walls were probably built in the same way, for when it was to be rebuilt after the Exile, Cyrus' edict gave orders for it to have three courses of stones and one of timber (Esd 6: 4). Excavations in the Near East have unearthed many parallels which show that these timbers formed a series of wooden ties to hold the wall together. Sometimes these wooden joists are found in a wall built entirely of stones; alternatively, the joist-framing sometimes begins above a stone footing and locks together a brick superstructure. There is good evidence of this at Troy, and it seems to have been followed in the Solomonian buildings at Megiddo: we shall see later that it is also found in the sanctuaries which are most similar to Solomon's Temple. It may be, then, that the Temple had stone foundations, on top of which was a brick superstructure: the walls would have been panelled with cedar (1 K 6: 15) to hide the brickwork: and there are several parallels for this, too.

A text about the Palace may perhaps give the technical name for this framework of wooden ties which held the bricks locked together. 1 K 7: 9 says that all the royal buildings were built of magnificent stones 'from the foundation to the *ṭ'paḥôth*'. The ancient versions translated the word anyhow, and modern commentators have guessed at its meaning, suggesting a crenellated balcony or wall-brackets for the ceiling joists. But it is quite certain that the word is only a metaphorical use of *ṭepaḥ*, meaning 'the palm of the hand'. Now the Assyrian equivalent, *ṭappu*, means both 'the sole of the foot' and 'plank' or 'joist'. Three letters from El-Amarna contain this phrase: 'The brick may slip from under its *ṭappati*, but I shall never slip from under the feet of the king, my master'. *Ṭappati* has been translated 'companions', but its sense seems clear: the puppet kings of Canaan are protesting that they will never stir under the feet of Pharaoh, not even as much as the bricks of a wall may move under the wood which locks them together. *Ṭappati* then, in these letters, stands for the whole framework, like the *ṭ'paḥôth* of 1 K 7: 9, and this text would mean that the walls were of splendid stonework up to the wooden framework which held together the brick superstructure: it would be the equivalent of the three courses of stones crowned by one of cedar timber in 1 K 6: 36; 7: 12; Esd 6: 4.

The Temple, like other Semitic sanctuaries,[1] stood in the middle of a courtyard called the inner court (1 K 6: 36), by contrast with the great court (1 K 7: 12), which included both the Temple and the Palace. The Palace, too, had an inner court (1 K 7: 8), the northern wall of which was common to the inner court of the Temple. You passed straight from the king's domain into

1. Cf. pp. 274–275.

the domain of God, and this close proximity later aroused the indignation of Ezechiel: 'The house of Israel, they and their kings, shall no longer defile my sanctuary . . . by building a wall common to them and to me' says God (Ez 43: 7-8).

The inner court of the Temple was later divided, or extended, at the expense of the great court. 2 Ch 20: 5 speaks of a 'new court' under Josaphat, and we are told that Manasseh set up altars 'in the two courts of the house of Yahweh' (2 K 21: 5); Jr 36: 10 mentions an 'upper court', apparently the top of the esplanade on which the Temple stood, by contrast with a lower court. Thus the divisions of Herod's sanctuary are already beginning to appear: the court of Israel, the court of the women, and the court of the Gentiles.

(b) *Analogies and influences.* It was once customary to see Egyptian influence in Solomon's Temple. But its architectural concept was entirely different from that of Egyptian temples. The latter were spreadeagled over a large area, behind a broad façade, with a network of buildings surrounding the *cella* of the god, while Solomon's Temple consisted of three rooms one behind the other, with a narrow front. Other writers have thought of Assyrian influence, and the plans of certain sanctuaries are in fact quite similar; but differences still remain, and above all, Palestine and Assyria were too far from each other, and had no contacts at this period. We must look for comparisons closer to Jerusalem.

The threefold division into Ulam, Hekal and Debir, found in Solomon's Temple, is very common. It is found, for example, in the Ditch temple at Tell ed-Duweir, which belongs to the pre-Israelite period, and again in the little sanctuaries of Beisan, which are not quite so old. On the other hand, this division is quite natural: what is characteristic of the Jerusalem Temple is rather that the three rooms stand one behind the other in a straight line, and that the building is the same width all along its length. Several recently discovered sanctuaries follow the same plan: at Alalakh (Tell Atchana) in northern Syria, a badly preserved temple of the thirteenth century B.C.; at Hazor in Palestine, a temple, somewhat better preserved, from the same period; at Tell Tainat, not far from Tell Atchana, a temple of the ninth century B.C. The similarity extends even to methods of building. The method we described for the building of the Temple in Jerusalem was followed in these temples: they had brick walls locked together by a framework of wooden ties, which, at least at Alalakh and at Hazor, stood on a stone footing; at Alalakh and perhaps at Hazor too, the brick walls were faced with woodwork.

These parallels fall within the same chronological framework as the Temple of Solomon, and all come from the Syro-Phoenician region where we must certainly look for the model Solomon copied. We have already stated that the skilled workmen he employed on the Temple were Phoenicians, and that the bronze-work was cast by a Tyrian artist. It is quite likely that the architect responsible for the plan and for its building was also a

Phoenician, and it is tempting to identify him with the superintendent of the king's major works, the master of conscripted labour, Adoram, who has a Phoenician name (1 K 5: 28).

(c) *The site of the Temple*. David set up an altar on the threshing-floor of Arauna (2 S 24: 18-25), and according to 1 Ch 22: 1 he destined the place to be the 'house of Yahweh', and the altar to be 'the altar of holocausts for Israel'. Solomon built his Temple on this 'place prepared by David' (2 Ch 3: 1). The general position is unquestionable: it is the rocky ridge which overlooks Ophel, the site of the original town, from the north. The temple of Zorobabel and that of Herod were later built in the same place, and the Herodian enclosure is to-day the esplanade of the Mosque of Omar, the Haram esh-Sherif. Similarly, there is no doubt about the orientation of Solomon's Temple: like Ezechiel's (Ez 47: 1) and Herod's, its entrance faced east (cf. also 1 K 7: 39).

To place it exactly is more difficult. Towards the centre of the Haram esh-Sherif, at its highest point, the dome of Omar to-day rises above a rocky protuberance called the '*Sakhra*' or the 'Rock', beneath which there is a cave. The Temple must certainly be closely connected with this rock which has remained the object of such great veneration. But two hypotheses here confront each other. The more common opinion to-day is that the rock which is still visible was the foundation-mass of the altar of holocausts, which stood in front of the Temple: the Temple would therefore lie to the west of the sacred rock. It is claimed that traces of the altar's supports can be distinguished in the rock, that the cave underneath was the place where the ashes and the refuse of sacrifices were thrown, and that a canal running north was used to get rid of the blood and the water used for cleansing. Following the tradition of 1 Ch 22: 1, it is claimed that the altar of holocausts was erected on the very site of David's altar, and it is assumed that David's altar stood on the highest point of the rock. None of the arguments brought forward is self-evident, and if the Temple stood to the west of the rock, then it stood where the hill slopes away very rapidly: the Debir would then have been supported by enormous substructures, and this seems rather odd. There is another objection to this location if we look at it from the east: in Herod's Temple, the steps leading from the court of Israel to the court of the women would not correspond to any irregularity in the rock, while a sharp difference of level would have cut across the court of the women.

These reasons have led a number of authors to come back to an old theory which held that the sacred rock was the foundation of the Debir, of the Holy of Holies. The area of the rock is larger than that covered by the Debir, but this is no difficulty, for the Debir was built on the rock, not around it, and it would be quite in order for the rock to be somewhat higher than the rest of the ground if, as we have said, the Debir was higher than the Hekal. If this hypothesis is accepted, then there is no longer any need for substructures supporting the Debir, the steps of Herod's Temple would be found where one would expect them, at the edge of the upper terrace, and there would be no shelf cutting across the court of the women. This theory, too, has its disadvantages: it is hard to see how the walls of the Debir could have been built on top of the rock; it gives no explanation of the cave and the canal; lastly, in Herod's Temple, that part of the court of the Gentiles which stood directly in front of the Temple would be reduced almost to nothing, whereas the area to the north and the south would have been very large.

Both theories present good arguments, and both run up against serious difficulties. All things considered, the second seems the more acceptable. There is a kind of confirmation of it in the rabbinical tradition that the surface of a rock broke through in the Holy of Holies: it was called *'eben sh'tiyyah*, the 'foundation stone', and was considered as the foundation stone of heaven and earth. Could it perhaps be that when Jesus told Peter: 'Thou art Peter, and upon this rock I shall build my church' (Mt 16: 18), he was alluding to this rock upon which the sanctuary of the Old Covenant was built?

(d) *Furnishings of the Temple.* The Ark of the Covenant, which has already been studied,[1] stood in the Debir. Above it were two great wooden figures of cherubim, plated with gold, which stretched right across the width of the Debir and reached half-way to the ceiling (1 K 6: 23-28; 2 Ch 3: 10-13; cf. 1 K 8: 6-7; 2 Ch 5: 7-8). The cherubim were winged animals with human heads, like the winged sphinxes of Syro-Phoenician iconography. Their name, however, *K'rûb*, comes from the Akkadian, in which the word *karibu* or *kuribu* means a genie who was the adviser to the great gods and an advocate for the faithful. In the Temple, the cherubim, together with the Ark, represented the throne of Yahweh,[2] just as, in 2 S 22: 11=Ps 18: 11, they served as his steeds, and according to the visions of Ez 1 and 10, drew his chariot.

In the Hekal there stood the altar of incense (also called the altar of cedar in 1 K 6: 20-21, and the altar of gold in 1 K 7: 48), the table of shewbread and ten candlesticks (1 K 7: 48-49). The altar of sacrifices is not mentioned, but this is merely an oversight, for it is spoken of later on: it is the altar of bronze (1 K 8: 64), which Solomon set up (1 K 9: 25). It was a metal structure, which according to 2 K 16: 14, stood in front of the Temple, outside the building, like the altar in Herod's Temple.

In the court, south-east of the temple, there stood also the 'Sea' of bronze, an enormous basin supported by twelve statues of bulls (1 K 7: 23-26). The best parallel is the stone basin from Amathonte in Cyprus, but one could also compare the reservoir (?) called *apsû* which is found in some Mesopotamian temples. There were also ten wheeled pedestals, each supporting a bronze basin, five to the right and five to the left of the entrance (1 K 7: 27-29). There are parallels, though much smaller models, in Cyprus and at Megiddo. We

1. Cf. pp. 297-302. 2. Cf. p. 299-300.

shall discuss the symbolism of all this material later, but its practical use is clear: 2 Ch 4: 6 says that the Sea was used for the priests to purify themselves (cf. Ex 30: 18-21), and that the basins were used to wash the victims.

(e) *The Temple as a national sanctuary.* The Temple was only one of a group of buildings which included the Palace and its dependencies. Elsewhere in the East, temple and palace are often connected, but not always in the same way. In Egypt, the temple occupied more space and the palace annexed to it was not the usual residence of the Pharaoh: he merely stayed there when he came to visit the temple and to perform ceremonies: clearly, it was not so in Jerusalem. In Syria and Mesopotamia, on the other hand, the temple was a mere annexe to the palace, a royal chapel, more or less, where the king and his court could perform their devotions. This is particularly true of the temple of Tainat, which has already been compared with that of Jerusalem.

Consequently, many exegetes hold that Solomon's Temple was a palace chapel, the private temple of the king and his household. It stood side by side with the Palace, which occupied much more ground; it was built by Solomon on ground bought by David, at the public expense; it was endowed by the king and dedicated by him. His successors, too, made gifts to the Temple (1 K 15: 15; 2 K 12: 19), but withdrew funds from its treasury just as freely as they did from the Palace treasury (1 K 15: 18; 2 K 12: 19; 16: 8; 18: 15). They undertook work on it, repairing and modifying the Temple buildings and its furnishings (2 K 15: 35; 16: 10-18; 18: 16; 23: 4f.). They had their own dais set up in the court (2 K 11: 14; 16: 18; 23: 3).[1] Joas ordered his civil servants to look after the collection and distribution of the offerings of the faithful (2 K 12: 5-17; 22: 3-7). In short, the Temple at Jerusalem, was, like that at Bethel, a 'royal sanctuary' (Am 10: 13).

This is all perfectly true, but it does not mean that the Temple was nothing more than a chapel attached to the Palace. The intervention of the king was quite justified by his right of patronage, to which he was entitled as founder or benefactor, and by the privileges he inherited by reason of his sacral character and his lawful rôle in worship.[2] But the Temple was not a private chapel; like the sanctuary at Bethel (Am 10: 13), it was a 'temple of the kingdom', a national sanctuary where both king and people offered public worship to the national God. Nor did the Temple at Jerusalem gradually acquire this character over the years: it had it from the time of its foundation. When Jeroboam began the worship at Bethel, immediately after Solomon's death, he was openly trying to prevent his subjects from going to the Temple at Jerusalem (1 K 12: 26-33), and he wanted to have a sanctuary for his people inside his own domains; Jerusalem had been precisely such a sanctuary for the United Kingdom, and, in Jeroboam's mind, was obviously going to continue as a national sanctuary for the kingdom of Judah. When David brought the Ark to Jerusalem, his intention was not to confiscate it for his own private

1. Cf. pp. 102-103. 2. Cf. pp. 113-114.

chapel, but to make it the centre of worship for all the tribes, and when he first thought of building a temple, it was to give Yahweh a 'house' where he could be at home (2 S 7: 1-2). This was the 'house' which Solomon built and consecrated with 'all Israel' (1 K 8: 1-5, 13, 62-66). There were, of course, political, as well as religious, advantages in the idea: the Temple and the Palace stood next door to each other, as if Yahweh and the king chosen by him to rule his people lived next door to each other, and this fact expressed the theocratic ideal of Israel.

2. *The history of Solomon's Temple*

Since the Temple of Jerusalem was the national sanctuary in the capital city, and the religious centre of the nation, its destiny was of course closely bound up with the political and religious history of the nation. It remained standing for four centuries after its foundation, until the kingdom itself ceased to exist. Throughout this long period its structure was never altered, and its buildings were only slightly modified. We argued above[1] that the upper two storeys of the side building were not part of the original structure; if this is true, then Asa may have been responsible for this additional construction when he wanted somewhere to put the offerings he made to the Temple (1 K 15: 15). According to 2 Ch 20: 5, a new court was laid out under Josaphat, lower than the original court, which then became the upper court of Jr 36: 10. The two courtyards were connected by a gate built by Yotham (according to 2 K 15: 35), which would be the Upper Gate of Jr 26: 10; 36: 10.

The rising against Athaliah, the proclamation and sacring of Joas, which are recounted in detail in 2 K 11, took place in the Temple court: there too, all the kings of Judah after Solomon were anointed. The maintenance of the buildings was a permanent source of anxiety, and the biblical account of Joas' reign gives some details about it. The king had at first ordered the priests to take from the Temple income the amount necessary for repairs (2 K 12: 5-6). Since they did not do so, Joas issued a new order transferring the matter to the civil power: a chest would be placed near the entrance to the Temple for the offerings of the faithful, and would be emptied by the royal secretary, who would give the money to the foremen attached to the Temple (2 K 12: 7-17). This arrangement was still in force in the reign of Josias, for his secretary learnt of the discovery of the Book of the Law when he went to empty the money-chest (2 K 22: 3-10).

On the other hand, the kings always kept a tight control over the Temple, and their own religious attitude or political considerations guided their conduct towards the building. Achaz removed the bronze altar erected by Solomon and had a new altar built like the one he had seen at Damascus (2 K 16: 10-16). He dismantled the wheeled pedestals and took away the

1. Cf. p. 315.

bulls underneath the Sea: in all probability, he had no intention of changing the form of worship, but merely wanted some ready cash to pay the tribute he owed to Tiglath-Pileser (2 K 16: 17): similarly, when he had the royal dais and entrance removed from the Temple, he was only trying to please his suzerain by doing away with the symbols of independence. The irreligious king Manasseh erected altars to false gods and an idol of Ashera in the Temple (2 K 21: 4-5, 7).

The pious kings, on the other hand, made away with these defilements of the sanctuary. Ezechias removed the Nehushtan, an idolatrous object venerated by the Israelites as the bronze serpent of desert days (2 K 18: 4). But it was above all Josias who, after the discovery of the Law, swept out of the Temple 'all the cultic objects which had been made for Baal, for Asherah and for all the hosts of heaven' and the very detail is astounding: the sacred post, the house of male prostitutes where women wove veils for Asherah, the horses and the chariot of the sun dedicated by the kings of Judah, the altars which the kings of Judah had set up on the terrace, and those which Manasseh had built in the two courtyards (2 K 23: 4-12). His reform, however, was short-lived: Ez 8 describes the rites practised, with official approval, in the Temple on the eve of its ruin. The Temple mirrored the religious life of the nation, and these deviations in worship, which were accepted, or at least tolerated, in the official sanctuary of Yahwism, show how permanent a danger syncretism was. They also provide a partial explanation of why some genuinely faithful Israelites looked unfavourably on the Temple: we shall return to this subject later.[1]

The king had control of the Temple treasury,[2] but conquerors too turned covetous eyes on it: immediately after Solomon's death, Shesonq emptied it (1 K 14: 26), and even a king of Israel, Joas, was not afraid to pillage the house of Yahweh after his victory over Amasias (2 K 14: 14). Pillaging sanctuaries was just another custom of war in ancient times: the post-exilic Temple was sacked by Antiochus Epiphanes, and Herod's Temple by the soldiers of Titus.

This, too, was how Solomon's Temple came to an end. After the first invasion of Nabuchodonosor, in 597, the Temple treasury was pillaged along with the royal exchequer (2 K 24: 13). After the second attack, in 587, the Temple shared the fate of the city of David and Solomon. Everything was carried away, even the two great pillars and the Sea of Bronze, which were broken up so that the metal could be sent to Babylon (2 K 25: 13-17; Jr 52: 17-23). Such was the end of the Temple which had been the pride of Israel.

3. *The post-exilic Temple*

Ezechiel, in the land of Exile, had a vision of a new Temple in a restored and idealized Jerusalem. His long description of the buildings (Ez 40: 1-44: 9)

1. Cf. pp. 329-330. 2. Cf. pp. 139 and 320.

is only of indirect interest to us, for this Temple was never built. The prophet however, had himself seen Solomon's Temple while it was still standing, and he arranged his idealized sanctuary in essentially the same way: moreover, these chapters seem to have inspired the later reconstructions of the Temple: this is perhaps true of Zorobabel's reconstruction, and can be affirmed with greater certainty of the Temple of Herod.

More important, however, was the mentality which gave birth to this vision: a reformer was there planning how to give concrete expression to those ideas of holiness, purity and spirituality which were the soul of his preaching. The stains which had defiled the former sanctuary were to disappear (cf. especially Ez 43: 1-12; 44: 4-9). The Temple would stand in a sacred square, cut off from profane land, and encircled by two walls, the gates of which would be guarded to prevent any foreigner from entering. Ezechiel does not mention any cultic installations except the altar of holocausts in front of the Temple: this altar is like a miniature ziggurat with three storeys whose names, interpreted in the light of cognate Akkadian words, have a cosmic symbolism (Ez 43: 13-17). Otherwise the only cultic object he mentions is a 'kind of altar' in the Hekal: it was to be made of wood, and is called 'the table before Yahweh' (Ez 41: 21-22), *i.e.* the former table of shewbread. In the Debir, which he calls explicitly the Holy of Holies (Ez 41: 3-4), there would no longer be any Ark of the Covenant, but the glory of Yahweh would fill the sanctuary (Ez 44: 4), where he would make his dwelling among the children of Israel (Ez 43: 7) as he had once done in the desert days (Ex 25: 8). The Temple would be the centre of a restored theocracy (Ez 37: 23-28). These theological ideas had a deeper influence on the thought of Judaism than his description had on the buildings of after-time.

In 538 B.C. Cyrus authorized the Jews to return to Jerusalem and to rebuild their Temple there at the expense of the royal exchequer; he also returned to them the gold and silver furnishings which Nabuchodonosor had carried off as booty. This decree of Cyrus has been preserved in two forms: one is in Aramaic, as cited in the decree of Darius of which we shall speak soon (Esd 6: 3-5), and one in Hebrew (Esd 1: 2-4). The authenticity of the Aramaic decree is well founded, but many writers will not allow that the Hebrew text is authentic: this latter is probably a free composition of the Chronicler, who knew that there had been such a document and reconstructed its text. Other scholars, however, have argued in favour of its authenticity, suggesting that there were in fact two official acts: an Aramaic memorandum destined for the royal exchequer (which was afterwards kept in the archives), and a proclamation in Hebrew addressed to the Jews.

The first exiles to return to Palestine erected an altar on the site of the old one (Esd 3: 2-6), and, under the direction of Sheshbassar, began work on the Temple (Esd 5: 16). Apparently, they merely cleared the rubble away from the line of the old walls and did some levelling: work was then interrupted, because of Samaritan obstruction, according to Esd 4: 1-5, because of the lack of interest among the Jews, according to Ag 1: 2. In the second year of Darius, 520 B.C., the task was again taken in hand, under the direction of Zorobabel and of Josue, and with the encouragement of the two prophets, Aggaeus and Zacharias (Esd 4: 24—5: 2; Ag 1: 1-2, 9; Za 4: 7-10). Tattenai, the satrap of Transeuphrates, was worried by this activity, and asked Darius for instructions: the emperor, when he had read the memorandum left by Cyrus, ordered him to honour its terms and to allow the Jews to continue their work. It was finished in 515 B.C.

We know very little about this Temple. Cyrus' decree laid down its measurements (Esd 6: 3: unfortunately, the text is corrupt) and the way in which it was to be built: three courses of stone and one course of wood (Esd 6: 4; cf. 5: 8), as in Solomon's buildings.[1] It is quite certain that it followed the plan of the former Temple, and it is highly probable that it was exactly the same size. The books of Esdras and Nehemias show that some dependent buildings were attached to it: the rooms for the offerings Esdras brought (Esd 8: 29) remind us of the side-building of Solomon's Temple (1 K 6: 5-10), and of the side-cells or rooms of Ez 41: 5-11; 42: 1-14. Tobiyyah was given a lodging in these rooms, until he was evicted by Nehemias (Ne 13: 4-9).

Esd 3: 12-13 and Ag 2:3 say that the older generation, which had seen the former Temple, wept at the sight of this new one, which was 'like nothing' in comparison. It had been deduced, all too hastily, that the Second Temple was a poverty-stricken building, but the two texts cited refer to the very beginning of the work and not to the completed building; and Esdras' text is inspired by that of Aggaeus. It is quite possible that the payments Cyrus had allowed from the royal exchequer, and Darius from the taxes of Trans-euphrates (Esd 6: 4 and 8), were not paid in full, and that the Jews had to revert to raising the money locally, among men of no great means; but Tattenai's report implies that the work was solid and carefully executed (Esd 5: 8), and even if the result did not achieve the legendary splendour of Solomon's Temple, it must have been quite suitable for worship. Aggaeus, to encourage the builders, had promised that the treasures of the Gentiles would flow there, and that the glory of the new sanctuary would surpass that of the old one (Ag 2: 7-9).

At the turn of the fourth century B.C., Hecataeus of Abdera, cited by Josephus in *c. Apionem*, I, xxii, wrote that the Temple was a large building encircled by a wall: near it stood an altar of stones, which was the same size as the altar of Solomon, according to 2 Ch 4: 1, and as the altar of Ezechiel (Ez 43: 13-17). Inside the building was an altar and a golden chandelier, the flame of which was kept continually alight. A century later, the Letter of Aristeas, a piece of Jewish propaganda writing, stresses, in its description, the splendour of the sanctuary, the three walls marking off the courts, the curtain hanging

1. Cf. p. 316.

before its door, the altar and the ramp which led up to it. Josephus, in *Ant.*, XII, iii, 4, has preserved an order of Antiochus III from the same epoch: its authenticity has been defended recently by strong arguments. Like the inscriptions which later stood on the barrier separating the court of the Gentiles in Herod's Temple, it forbade any foreigner to enter the precincts of the sanctuary. Antiochus' order may have been hung or engraved at a similar place in the Temple of Zorobabel, perhaps on that 'wall of the inner court of the sanctuary' which Alkimus, who had forced his way to the high priesthood, wanted demolished, to please the Greeks (1 M 9: 54).

The books of Maccabees give us some details about the Temple when relating how Antiochus Epiphanes pillaged it in 169 B.C.: he took away the golden altar, the chandelier, the table of offerings, the veil, the gold plating, the precious vessels and the treasures (1 M 1: 21-24; 2 M 5: 15-16). Like the story of Heliodorus (2 M 3), this presupposes that the Temple was rich. In 167, the Temple, already pillaged, was profaned, when the lawful sacrifices were suppressed and the worship of Zeus Olympios was introduced there (1 M 1:44-49; 2 M 6: 1-6): this indeed was the 'abomination of desolation' (Dn 9: 27; 11: 31). Three years later, in 164, Judas Maccabee purified and repaired the Temple, built a new altar, and put back in the sanctuary the candelabra, the altar of perfumes, the table and the curtains: worship was restored and this feast of the new dedication was thereafter celebrated every year (1 M 4: 36-59).

A hundred years later, when Pompey took Jerusalem, he entered the Temple, but respected the sanctuary and did not touch the treasury, which was then estimated at 2,000 talents. In 20-19 B.C. Herod began to rebuild the entire Temple, and all the essential work was finished in ten years. But Herod's Temple is not one of the institutions of the Old Testament.

4. *The theology of the Temple*

Solomon's Temple was the religious centre of Israel, and it remained so even after the separation of the two kingdoms, and this in spite of Jeroboam's building a rival sanctuary at Bethel. When Ahiyyah, a prophet from Shiloh in Israel, foretold the political schism, he still spoke of Jerusalem as the city which Yahweh had chosen (1 K 11: 32), and the faithful in the Northern Kingdom never ceased to look towards Jerusalem: even after the fall of the city, pilgrims from Shechem, from Shiloh and from Samaria brought their offerings to the ruined Temple (Jr 41: 5). If Jerusalem was regarded as the Holy City, the reason lay in its possession of the Temple. We must therefore try to define the religious significance of the Temple.

(a) *The Temple as the seat of the divine presence*. The Temple was the 'house of God'.[1] When the Ark was taken there, God took possession of his house,

1. Cf. pp. 282-283.

and the Temple was filled by a cloud (1 K 8: 10), that cloud which, in the stories of the desert, was the sign of Yahweh's presence in the Tent of Re-union (Ex 33: 9; 40: 34-35; Nb 12: 4-10).[1] In the short poem which he read aloud on the occasion of the dedication, Solomon says he has built Yahweh 'a dwelling-place, a home where he will live for ever' (1 K 8: 13), and the darkness of the Debir, where Yahweh was enthroned above the Ark and the cherubim, recalled the cloud (1 K 8: 12). This belief in Yahweh's presence in his Temple was the whole reason for the worship celebrated there and for the pious customs of the faithful. Ezechias' action provides a most striking example: when he received Sennacherib's threatening letter, 'he went up to the Temple of Yahweh and spread it out before Yahweh' (2 K 19: 14). The connection of the Psalms with worship and the Temple is evident: they often speak of devotion to the 'house of Yahweh' or to the 'courts of Yahweh', and they do so because of the writers' confidence that God lived in the Temple (*e.g.* Ps 27: 4; 42: 5; 76: 3; 84; 122: 1-4; 132: 13-14; 134, etc.).

The Prophets share the same belief, in spite of their reservations about the worship practised there. 'Yahweh roars from Sion, and from Jerusalem he makes his voice heard' (Am 1: 2). Isaias was called to take up the office of a prophet when he was in the Temple; he had a vision of Yahweh seated on his throne, and of a cloud filling the sanctuary as on the day of its dedication (Is 6: 1-4). The Temple was built on the 'mountain of Yahweh' (Is 2: 2-3) and especially from the time of Isaias onwards the name Sion takes on a religious meaning.[2] For Jeremias, too, the throne of Yahweh's glory is in Sion (Jr 14: 21). This presence of God amid his people, however, was a grace, and would be withdrawn if the people were unfaithful. It was in the Temple itself that Jeremias preached against the Temple, and against that blind confidence in the building which was unaccompanied by the desire to reform one's life (Jr 7: 1-15; 26: 1-15). Ezechiel, too, saw the glory of Yahweh leave the Temple, which had been defiled by Israel's sins (Ez 8-10); but God would come back to the new Temple, which would be the place of his throne, where he would live forever among the children of Israel (Ez 43: 1-12). The name of Jerusalem would then be 'Yahweh-is-there!' (Ez 48: 35). Again, after the Return, the Prophets encourage the rebuilding of the Temple: and the reason is that God must come back to live in Jerusalem (Ag 1: 9; Za 2: 14; 8: 3). The Temple, the holy Dwelling-place, still remained the very centre of Jewish piety.

This same period saw an evolution in the notion of the divine presence in the Temple. If God dwelt in this 'house', if he made his voice heard from Sion (Am 1: 2; Is 2: 3; Mi 4: 2), if he acted from his sanctuary (Ps 20: 3; 134: 3), was there not a risk of limiting, or at least of binding, his presence to the material temple? Theological thought was conscious of the tension between the transcendence of Yahweh, who from the beginning had been

1. Cf. pp. 294-295. 2. Cf. the texts cited on p. 281.

recognized as master of the universe, and his historical and human proximity to Israel. The Deuteronomic redactor of the books of Kings asks and answers the question in the prayer he ascribes to Solomon for the dedication of the Temple: 'But is God really to dwell with men on earth? The heavens, even the highest heavens, cannot contain him, much less this house which I have built' (1 K 8: 27). The solution is given in the following verses: the faithful pray at the Temple, and Yahweh hears their prayer from heaven, where he dwells (1 K 8: 30-40). To avoid too crude a concept of the divine presence, they said it was the Name of Yahweh which dwelt there (1 K 8: 17, 29), following the usage of Deuteronomy (Dt 12: 5, 11, etc.). To the Semitic mind, the name expressed and represented the person: God was present in a special way wherever the 'Name of Yahweh' was. The last development of this theology came when Judaism evolved the notion of the Shekinah, 'the dwelling', which is an attempt to express the gracious presence of God amid Israel without taking anything away from his transcendence.

(b) *The Temple as the sign of election.* This presence, we have just asserted, was a grace. God himself chose to live among his own, and he chose to live in *this* city and in *this* Temple. Before ever it was built, the site was marked out by a theophany (2 S 24: 16; 2 Ch 3: 1). Yahweh chose Sion as his home (Ps 132: 13); Sion was the mountain God chose for his residence (Ps 68: 17; cf. 76: 3; 78: 68). Deuteronomy stresses, even more than it stresses the choice of the people, the fact that Yahweh selected this place among all the tribes, that his Name might be there, and might dwell there (Dt 12: 5): the formula occurs, complete or in shortened forms, no less than twenty times in the book. The 'place' itself is never identified by name, but later ages recognized it as Jerusalem and the Temple there, where Josias would centralize the nation's worship.[1] The idea itself, however, dates back to the time before Josias. It was a consequence of Yahweh's choice of David, and of the promise that his dynasty would endure in Jerusalem (cf. 1 K 8: 16 (Greek) and 2 Ch 6: 5-6; 1 K 11: 13, 32). In the end, the people became utterly convinced of this as a result of an historical event, namely, the deliverance of Jerusalem, under Ezechias, from Sennacherib's siege. Yahweh had kept his promise: 'I shall protect this city and save it, for my own sake, and for the sake of my servant David' (2 K 19: 34; Is 37: 35). The formula of Deuteronomy was perhaps coined at this time, and there is an echo of it in 1 K 8: 44, 48; 11: 13, 32, 36; 14: 21; 2 K 21: 7; 23: 27, and their parallels in Chronicles.

The saving of the Temple in 701 was the visible sign of divine election, and the memory of this miraculous deliverance gave rise to a confidence that the Temple would always afford unfailing protection. The Israelites went on repeating 'This is the sanctuary of Yahweh, the sanctuary of Yahweh, the sanctuary of Yahweh!' and thought they were safe against the world (Jr 7: 4). The destruction of the same Temple in 587 was an agonizing trial for

1. Cf. pp. 336-339.

Israel's faith, but all was not lost, for the election would be renewed: after the return from the exile, Zacharias proclaimed that Yahweh would once more make Jerusalem his choice (Za 1: 17; 2: 16; 3: 2), and Nehemias, taking up the formula of Deuteronomy, reminded God that he had promised to reassemble the exiles in the place which he had chosen as the home for his Name (Ne 1: 9).

(c) *Symbolism of the Temple?* Jewish thought, especially in certain apocryphal works, and Hellenistic thought also, in Josephus and Philo, endeavoured to find in the Temple a cosmic symbolism; the Temple hill was for them the centre of the world. Similar speculations can be found in the Fathers of the Church and in medieval theologians, and some modern writers have tried to justify a symbolic interpretation by seeking analogies among the religious concepts of the Ancient East.

In the Bible there is very feeble support for these theories. The idea of the Temple hill as the centre of the world is nowhere explicitly affirmed, and the most one can say is that the ground is prepared for the theory when Mount Sion is exalted as the 'holy mountain', or when in poetry, it is identified with Saphon, the home of the gods.[1] But there is not a single text which suggests that the Temple itself ever had a cosmic significance. A late psalm reads: 'He built his sanctuary like the heights of heaven, like the earth which he made firm for ever' (Ps 78: 69), but all this verse means is that God's choice of Sion as his dwelling-place, and of David as his servant (cf. vv. 68 and 70), is definitive, and as enduring as the heavens and the earth. This statement adds nothing to what we have already said about the Temple as the sign of God's election. Only one point seems to have been established: the cosmic symbolism of Ezechiel's altar can be deduced from the names which he gives to its various parts. But Ezechiel was a visionary, borrowing his images from the foreign background in which he lived, and describing the ideal altar of a Temple which was never built.

If we keep to the real Temple, that of Solomon, the reader will remember that its plan and decoration were of foreign inspiration and that they were executed by foreign craftsmen. We do not know what symbolism these foreigners gave to this plan or decoration, nor do we know whether the Israelites accepted this symbolism. It is quite arbitrary to suppose that the three parts of the Temple represented the three parts of the world: the Debir certainly was symbolic, but what it signified is explained in the text and it is not a cosmic symbolism: it stands for the cloud in which God concealed himself (1 K 8: 12). It is most improbable—to cite a few examples current to-day—that the two bronze pillars represented the sun and the moon, or summer and winter, or that the ten candelabra represented the five planets twice over, or that the wheeled pedestals stood for clouds charged with rain. There is less certainty, however, in saying that the 'Sea' of bronze does not represent the

1. Cf. pp. 279-280 and 281.

primordial waters. It has been said that this 'Sea' is the equivalent of the *apsû* in Mesopotamian temples, a name which also denotes the ocean under the earth. But we are ill informed as to what precisely this *apsû* in the temples was, and we have no information whatever about its symbolic value. And the 'Sea' of Solomon's Temple is called in Hebrew *yam*, a word which stands for the sea, or a lake, or a large river (*e.g.* the Euphrates or the Nile), but which in later Hebrew also means a 'basin' or 'vat'.

If the Temple and its furnishings had had a cosmic significance, the theological problem of how God dwelt there, which we examined above, would have presented itself in quite a different way. Moreover, the solution of the problem would have emerged: God, the master of the universe, would have dwelt in the Temple which was an image of the universe. But Israelite thought did not move in these patterns: right to the end of the monarchy, the Israelites were confronted with the paradox that here was a man-made house in which there dwelt that God whom the heavens could not contain (1 K 8: 27); consequently, they distinguished between the Temple, where men prayed, and heaven, where God dwelt (1 K 8: 30, etc.). They did not think of the Temple as representing the universe, and ideas of cosmic symbolism emerged only long afterwards.

If the Temple did not have a symbolic value, then we ought to look for the key to it not in myths nor in cosmology, but in Israel's history, for the religion of Israel is not a religion of myths nor a nature religion, but an historical one. Just as the great liturgical feasts recalled the different events of the Exodus, and the Ark of the Covenant recalled God's pact with his chosen people, so the Temple recalled and signified Yahweh's choice of Jerusalem and of David's dynasty, and then the subsequent protection afforded to this city and this dynasty.

(d) *Opposition to the Temple.* We have stressed the importance of the Temple in the religious life of Israel, and the positive attitude which the Prophets themselves adopted towards it, even when they condemned the abuses which had crept in there. Yet there was opposition to the Temple itself. When David wanted to build a Temple, Nathan took him a message from Yahweh: David will not build a 'house' for Yahweh, rather Yahweh will make a 'house' (a dynasty) for David. Yahweh had never had a house since he had brought the Israelites out of Egypt, and had never asked for one (2 S 7: 5-7). This does not mean that Yahweh was refusing to accept David's temple but would accept Solomon's when the time comes, as the glossator of 2 S 7: 13 understood it (also the redactor of 1 K 5: 19 and the Chronicler, 1 Ch 17: 12; 22: 10; 28: 6; 2 Ch 6: 8-9). What it does mean is that Yahweh did not want a temple built at all, but that he wanted the desert customs maintained. Nathan's prophecy deliberately omits all mention of the fact that there had previously been a temple built at Shiloh. It would seem then, that certain Israelites viewed the building of a 'house' for Yahweh as an act of infidelity, as a concession to the influence of Baal's religion, the 'established' religion of Canaan, and we know for certain that the institution of the Temple brought with it the danger of syncretism, and that this danger was not always avoided, as we have seen.

This school of thought which disliked the Temple continued in existence, though it is rarely mentioned. The Rekabites, that group of Yahwistic reactionaries who lived in tents and never built a house for themselves (Jr 35), saw no need to have a house for their God, and when they fled to Jerusalem to seek refuge, they did not attend the Temple services until Jeremias persuaded them to after he had 'talked with them' (Jr 35: 2). When the Temple was rebuilt after the Exile, a prophet protested: 'Thus says Yahweh: Heaven is my throne, and the earth is my foot-stool! What kind of a house would you build for me, and where is the spot that would be the place of my rest?' (Is 66: 1). The question asked in 1 K 8: 27 here receives a different answer from the one in Deuteronomy: Yahweh has no need of any Temple.

Stephen the deacon, referring to Nathan's prophecy and citing explicitly Is 66: 1, will later affirm in front of the Jews that 'the Most High does not dwell in buildings made by human hands' (Ac 7: 48). Jesus himself is accused of having said: 'Destroy this temple, and within three days I shall build another not made by human hands' (Mk 14: 58), and in fact, according to Jn 2: 19, he did say: 'Destroy this sanctuary; within three days I shall raise it up again'. But the Evangelist explains that 'he was speaking of the sanctuary which was his body'. The old economy came to an end because it was superseded: the privileges of the material Temple, seat of the divine presence and sign of election, were transferred to the body of the Word made flesh, who from that time onward becomes the 'place' where we encounter the Presence and the Salvation of God.

CHAPTER FOUR

THE CENTRALIZATION OF THE CULT

IN the course of time, the Temple of Jerusalem became the only place where sacrificial worship could legally be performed; it was destroyed in 70 A.D., and since then Judaism has been deprived of both altar and sacrifice. But the Temple did not attain this unique position in a day; first came long years of hard struggle against rival sanctuaries, and against a trend which favoured decentralization.

1. *Central sanctuary or sole sanctuary?*

In the period of the Judges and in the early days of the monarchy, there were numerous sanctuaries in Palestine,[1] and even the 'high places' were recognized as lawful institutions[2]; but this does not mean that these various places of worship were all of equal importance. The federation of tribes was held together by a religious bond, and when all the tribes took part in a common cult at a central sanctuary, their presence was a witness to, and a confirmation of, this religious bond. In early days these meetings were almost certainly held at Shechem, for that was where the tribes had made their pact of confederation.[3] But the place of worship was changed when the Ark was moved, for the Ark was the symbol of God's presence among his people. The Deuteronomic redactor of Jos 8: 33 mentions the presence of the ark at Shechem, but in the time of the Judges it was certainly kept at Shiloh, in a building; indeed, by then it must have been at Shiloh for some time, because the tribes met there and went on pilgrimage there from very early times.[4] Since the place where the Ark was kept was the central sanctuary for the tribes, a serious religious problem had to be faced when the Philistines captured the Ark and dismantled the temple at Shiloh: where should Israel go to pray in common 'before Yahweh'? During these troubled years, Gibeon seems to have taken the place of Shiloh. According to 2 S 21: 6 (corrected in accordance with the Greek version), the sanctuary of Gibeon stood on the 'mountain of Yahweh', and it is significant that at the beginning of his reign Solomon first went to Gibeon to offer sacrifice there; there he was favoured with a divine message and in the same text

1. Cf. pp. 289-294 and 302-310. 2. Cf. p. 288. 3. Cf. pp. 289-291.
4. Cf. the texts cited on p. 304.

Gibeon is referred to as 'the greatest high place' (1 K 3: 4-15). And if, as has been suggested, the high place of Gibeon is identified with the sanctuary of Mispah in Benjamin,[1] then we may note that it was an important place under Samuel and Saul (1 S 7: 5f. and 10: 17), *i.e.* after the ruin of Shiloh. Lastly, 1 Ch 16: 39; 21: 29; 2 Ch 1: 3 all assert that the Tent of Reunion was kept at Gibeon; is this perhaps a distorted tradition of the years when Gibeon was for a short time the central sanctuary of Israel?

The central sanctuary of the tribes was not, however, the only sanctuary. There is evidence in the historical books that the cult of Yahweh was practised at one and the same time in various places. In Chapter II we discussed only the more important of these sanctuaries, or those about which we have the most information, but if all the evidence available in the Old Testament had been used, a far longer list, still not complete, could have been drawn up. After the conquest the Israelites installed their national God in several Canaanite sanctuaries; and though the number of these old sanctuaries may have contributed to the multiplication of sanctuaries in Israel, it does not provide the ultimate explanation. This is to be found in the progressive development of society. After the settlement, tribal bonds were weakened, the clan became more important, and small autonomous groups fixed themselves permanently on the land they cultivated; this process affected the cult also, which became a concern of the village or the city. Provincialism in politics led to provincialism in religion, and the latter proved a counter-balance to the movement which sought to gather the tribes around a common centre of cultic worship.

The Book of the Covenant, which was the law of the tribal federation, recognized that it was quite lawful to have several sanctuaries. This collection opens with a law about altars (Ex 20: 24-26) which allows that sacrifice may be offered, and the divine blessing thus obtained 'in every place, says Yahweh, where I shall remind men of my Name'. This does not authorize anarchy in public worship; the altars, and therefore the sanctuaries too, are not to be erected in places chosen arbitrarily, but only where God makes his presence known in some way; thus we return to the foundation-stories discussed above. Yet the fact remains that there could be as many sanctuaries as there were places where the divine presence was recognized.

2. *Solomon's Temple and rival sanctuaries*

(a) *The attraction of Jerusalem.* David's altar in Jerusalem is in harmony with this law; it was erected on the spot where the Angel of Yahweh appeared (2 S 24: 16-25). But David had also transferred to Jerusalem the Ark of the Covenant, the sacred cultic object which was venerated by all the tribes. He thus restored the tradition which had been broken while the Ark

1. Cf. p. 305.

was in the hands of the Philistines, and in his mind Jerusalem was to succeed Shiloh as the central sanctuary of Israel.[1] This objective, however, was not attained during David's lifetime; even after his death Gibeon remained the 'greatest high place', and Solomon visited it even before he offered sacrifices beside the Ark of Covenant (1 K 3: 4-15).

Jerusalem did not become an Israelite city until long after Israel had settled in Canaan. David's conquest and David's personality made it the political capital, and the presence of the Ark made it, in the eyes of the tribes, the lawful capital. Yet it remained the king's private domain, and only when Solomon built his Temple for the Ark did Jerusalem become the centre of the nation's public worship. Solomon summoned the elders of Israel for the dedication of the new sanctuary (1 K 8: 1) and visitors came from the furthest parts of his kingdom 'from the Pass of Hamath to the Brook of Egypt' (1 K 8: 65); from that time onwards crowds of pilgrims made their way to Jerusalem, drawn there by the splendour of the cult in that magnificent building which was the pride of the nation.

(b) *The religious schism of Jeroboam.* The attraction of Jerusalem as a religious centre meant that in practice there was some centralization of the cult, but it had another consequence also: it strengthened the political unity of the kingdom. Hence the political division which took place when the Northern tribes seceded after the death of Solomon was followed and perpetuated by a religious schism. The motive which led to this schism is given in the words ascribed to Jeroboam: 'If this people continues to go up to the Temple of Yahweh in Jerusalem to offer sacrifices, the people's heart will turn back to their lord Roboam, king of Judah' (1 K 12: 27). It was to arrest this trend that 'he made two golden calves and told the people: "You have gone up to Jerusalem for long enough! Here is thy God, Israel, who led thee up from the land of Egypt." He set up one of them at Bethel . . . and the people went in procession before the other as far as Dan' (1 K 12: 28-30).

Yet this was not a change of religion: the God Jeroboam asked his subjects to adore was Yahweh who had brought Israel out of Egypt. The novelty lies in the cultic symbol, the 'golden calves'. But the word *'egel*, which certainly can mean 'calf', can also mean a young bull, and this is its sense here. They were wooden statues covered with gold plate. It seems certain that these statues were not thought of, originally, as representations of Yahweh. In the primitive religions of Asia Minor, Mesopotamia and Egypt, the sacred animal is not the god and is not confused with the god; it merely embodies his attributes, is an ornament of his throne or a support for it, or a footstool for his use. There are several examples extant of gods riding on the animal which is their symbol. The Temple of Jerusalem had the Ark, and the Cherubim above it formed the throne of Yahweh;

1. Cf. pp. 308-309.

Jeroboam needed something similar for the sanctuaries he founded and he made the 'golden calves' as the throne for the invisible godhead. Perhaps, too, he was giving a new lease of life to an old tradition of the Northern tribes: there is clearly some connection between the step taken by Jeroboam and the story of the golden calf at Sinai (Ex 32). It has often been presumed that the story in Exodus was made up to support attacks on the cult of the Northern kingdom by ascribing to Moses and to God himself a condemnation of such worship; but it is possible that the story in Exodus preserves an ancient tradition which was later distorted by hostile elements in Judah. Perhaps certain groups which claimed descent from Aaron[1] had with them a bull which was a sign of the divine presence, to guide them in their wanderings (Ex 32: 1, 4; 1 K 12: 28), just as the groups which belonged to Moses had the Ark to go before them and to indicate the stages of their journey (Nb 10: 33-36).

That Jeroboam's measures did not imply any abandonment of Yahwism is proved by the fact that the oldest texts are not at all hostile to them; Elias and Jehu fought strenuously against paganism in Israel, yet neither of them ever spoke a word against the golden calves (cf. 2 K 10: 29). Amos, too, who preached in the temple of Bethel, does not say a word against the statue which was there in front of him, though he condemns the religious moral faults of Israel. And yet the choice of the bull, even if it were understood as a mere pedestal for the invisible presence of Yahweh, had its dangers. The bull was the animal which symbolized the great Canaanite god Baal, and the discoveries at Ras Shamra are most instructive on this point. Whatever may be true of the more educated classes, the mass of the people were bound to confuse the bull of Yahweh and the bull of Baal; they would also confuse Yahweh with the cultic statue which symbolized his presence; the door was thus opened to syncretism and idolatry. Hence the reaction of the loyal Yahwists: tradition tells how Ahiyyah, a prophet in Shiloh contemporary with Jeroboam, condemned these 'molten idols' (1 K 14: 9). Osee, living at the same time as Amos, says that the 'calf of Samaria' is not a god but a man-made idol (Os 8: 5-6; cf. 10: 5), that men blow kisses to calves as tokens of adoration (Os 13: 2), as others do to the statues of Baal (cf. 1 K 19: 18). The Deuteronomic redactor of the Book of Kings makes the same judgment; he says that the Israelites offered sacrifices to the bulls of Dan and Bethel as if they were gods (1 K 12: 32), and Jeroboam's great sin, shared by all his successors (cf. especially 2 K 10: 29) and by all the people (2 K 17: 22), consisted in setting up these statues.

(c) *Dan and Bethel.* Jeroboam merely wanted to set up two rival sanctuaries to Jerusalem, and his choice of Dan and Bethel was shrewd. The two towns stood at the northern and southern extremities of his kingdom. Dan, near one of the sources of the Jordan, would cater for the most northerly

1. Cf. p. 395.

tribes, who were always tempted to keep to themselves, and Bethel, close to the southern frontier, would draw off the pilgrims who were on the road to Jerusalem. Moreover, both Dan and Bethel had, in Israelite tradition, older titles to respect than Jerusalem. Dan was a sanctuary dating back to the period of the Judges, and was still served by the descendants of Moses[1]; as a place of cult, Bethel could trace its origins back to Abraham,[2] and Aaron's grandson had there kept watch over the Ark of the Covenant (Jg 20: 28).

Although we know that one of the golden calves was put in the sanctuary, we have no further details about the organization of the cult at Dan under Jeroboam, nor about the later history of the sanctuary. Amos condemns Dan along with Samaria and Beersheba, and the redactor of Jg 18: 30 says that a priesthood of Mosaic origin continued there 'up to the deportation of the country'; the inhabitants of Dan were exiled after the conquest of Galilee by Tiglath-Pileser III in 733-732 (cf. 2 K 15: 29), but by that time Dan, apparently, had long lost its importance as an official sanctuary of the kingdom.

We are somewhat better informed about Bethel. The site was hallowed by the memory of Abraham and Jacob,[3] before ever Jeroboam established a sanctuary, a *beth bamôth*, there. (*Beth bamôth* means literally a 'temple of the high places', the plural form being no more extraordinary than in the place-name Beth-Bamoth which is mentioned in the stele of Mesha.) It is tempting to look for the site of the temple some distance outside the town, at Borj Beitin, where a Byzantine church was built on the ruins of a pagan *temenos* of the second century A.D. There was, of course, an altar in the sanctuary (1 K 13: 1f.; 2 K 23: 15f.) and the oracle in Am 9: 1, first delivered at Bethel, suggests that this altar stood in front of a door or a portico with columns. Like Solomon's temple at Jerusalem, Jeroboam's sanctuary was built by the king; he staffed it with priests and he controlled the cult (1 K 12: 31-32)[4]; it was a state temple, a 'royal sanctuary', in which Amos preached (Am 7: 10f.). This building survived the destruction of the Northern kingdom, for, according to 2 K 17: 28, one of the deported priests was sent home by the king of Assyria to instruct the new immigrants in the worship of Yahweh, and he settled at Bethel. The altar of Bethel and the 'high place' built by Jeroboam were dismantled by Josias during his great reform (2 K 23: 15).

(d) *Other sanctuaries*. Neither Dan nor Bethel, the official sanctuaries of the kingdom of Israel, nor Jerusalem, the official sanctuary of the king of Judah, ever replaced the other centres of worship. Everyone continued to attend the 'high place' of his own town, and the ancient sanctuaries of the pre-monarchic period continued to attract pilgrims. This we know not only from the Deuteronomic redaction of the Book of Kings, where the introductory notes to each reign in Israel and Judah repeat the refrain that

1. Cf. p. 308. 2. Cf. pp. 291-292. 3. Cf. pp. 291-292. 4. Cf. p. 320.

'the high places did not disappear', but also from the Prophets who accuse the Israelites of still going to Beersheba (Am 5: 5; 8: 14) and to Gilgal (Os 4: 15; Am 4: 4; 5: 5). From Am 7: 9 to Ez 7: 24 the Prophets raise their voices against 'the sanctuaries' of Israel.

3. *Reforms aiming at centralization*

Nevertheless, even when confronted with these many places of worship, the Temple at Jerusalem always retained a place of pre-eminence. As the official state sanctuary in the capital, it was always the religious centre of the kingdom of Judah, and in spite of the rivalry of an official temple at Bethel, it continued to attract the faithful from the kingdom of Israel; even when it lay in ruins, pilgrims came from the North to make offerings on the site (Jr 41: 5).

Two kings of Judah tried to make Jerusalem's Temple not merely the central sanctuary of the nation but the one and only sanctuary in which public cult could be performed. The Books of Kings praises Ezechias for having suppressed the high places (2 K 18: 4), and in the speech which they place on the lips of Sennacherib's Lord Chamberlain, they say that Ezechias 'has done away with the high places and the altars, and told the people of Judah and Jerusalem: "You must worship before this altar, at Jerusalem"' (2 K 18: 22; Is. 36: 7). There is no reason to doubt this information: Ezechias had learnt a lesson from the destruction of the Northern Kingdom, and wanted to strengthen and to unite the nation by a return to traditional ways; the centralization of the cult at Jerusalem, under his own eyes, was one element in this policy. The Chronicler develops the history of this reform in three chapters (2 Ch 29-31), and gives more space to it than to the reform of Josias, though his narrative is inspired by the latter. According to him, Ezechias cleansed the Temple, celebrated a solemn Passover and reorganized the clergy; the historical information afforded by the Books of Kings, that he did away with the high places, is almost lost in the length of this description (2 Ch 31: 1). The work of Ezechias, however, died with him, and his immediate successor, Manasseh, re-established the high places (2 K 21: 3).

The second attempt to centralize the cult at Jerusalem came under Josias, and it too formed part of a great movement of religious reform (2 K 23); historically there is more evidence for this reform than for that attributed to Ezechias by the Chronicler. When the empire of Assurbanipal was in the process of disintegration, Josias shook off the yoke of Assyria and tried to make Judah independent once again. The nationalist movement brought with it the rejection of religious customs borrowed from Assyria, and indeed the rejection of all those foreign cults, of Baal and Astarte and the rest, which were contaminating the cult of the national God, Yahweh. To secure the centralization of Yahwistic cult, Josias recalled to Jerusalem all the Priests in Judah 'from Geba to Beersheba' and suppressed the local sanctuaries, *i.e.* the 'high places' (2 K 23: 5, 8–9: the text shows quite clearly that it refers to sanctuaries and to priests of Yahweh, for they are called to join their 'brothers' in Jerusalem).[1] The reform covered the territory of the former Northern kingdom, too: the sanctuary at Bethel was certainly dismantled, but the details given in 2 K 23: 15–20 are clearly inspired by the prophetical midrash which was inserted in the story of Jeroboam in 1 K 13. The conclusion of the reform was celebrated by a solemn Passover, attended by the entire nation, at Jerusalem; it was a natural consequence of the centralization of worship (2 K 23: 21–23). This was the Passover of the year 621. Unfortunately, the reform was quickly compromised: after the death of Josias at Megiddo in 609, the country once again fell under foreign domination, first Egyptian, then Babylonian. The old errors returned—syncretism in the Temple, foreign cults, and a new lease of life for the country sanctuaries (Jr 7: 1–20; 13: 27 and elsewhere). In the interval between the two sieges of Jerusalem, Ezechiel foretold the chastisement of the mountains of Israel and the destruction of their high places (Ez 6: 1–6, 13). The situation in Judah, it seems, scarcely changed during the Exile: shortly after the return, a prophet of the school of Isaias condemned his contemporaries along with those ancestors of theirs who had burnt perfume on the mountains (Is 65: 7). From 586 onwards, the Temple lay in ruins, and although pilgrims still paid visits to the site (cf. Jr 41: 4–5) and presumably offered sacrifices there, historical circumstances seemed to have put an end to the reforms of Josias. But his ideas triumphed in the end, for the community which returned from exile never had any sanctuary in Judah except the rebuilt Temple in Jerusalem. The reason was that the reform was based on a written law which survived longer than the men who opposed it: it was the Book of Deuteronomy.

4. *Deuteronomy*

According to the Books of Kings, Josias' reform was the result of the discovery in the Temple of a 'Book of the Law', the prescriptions of which were put into practice by the king (2 K 22: 1—23: 3; cf. 23: 21). According to Chronicles (2 Ch 34–35) the reform had begun in the twelfth year of Josias' reign, and the discovery of the Law in the eighteenth year marked only the second stage. This additional precision given by Chronicles deserves credence; the obvious time for Josias to begin his attack on foreign cults was when he threw off the Assyrian domination, and it is probable that he rose in revolt just before, or just after, the death of Assurbanipal in 627–626 B.C. But the suppression of the high places where Yahweh was

1. For further details on this episode see the history of the priesthood, p. 363.

worshipped and the centralization of the clergy and of the cult at Jerusalem were evidently inspired by Deuteronomy which is, basically, that 'Book of the Law' found in the Temple in 621.

For a long time critics favoured the idea that this 'discovery' was a pious fraud and that Deuteronomy was written to show the lawfulness of Josias' reform; to-day this opinion has long been abandoned. It is quite certain that the work belongs to an older age, and recent studies seem to have proved that it is a collection of Levitical traditions which originated in the Northern kingdom and which were brought to Judah after the fall of Samaria; this assertion, however, is not necessarily true of each and every one of its prescriptions, and the law insisting on one sanctuary needs to be examined on its own. It is given in chapter 12, where a change in style enables us to recognize two parts. The first part (12: 1-12) is in the plural and states a general law: the Israelites must suppress all the places of cult in Canaan and must perform their own strictly cultic acts only 'in the place chosen by Yahweh, your God, for his Name to dwell there'. The second part (12: 13-31) is in the singular, and gives a series of particular injunctions: 'Beware of offering holocausts in every sacred place thou shalt see; only in the chosen place of Yahweh in one of thy tribes shalt thou offer holocausts' (vv. 13-14); similar injunctions are then given for tithes and offerings.

The second section, which is in the singular, debars the Israelites from attending Canaanite sanctuaries, but the first part, in the plural, adds to this the obligation of destroying such places of worship; this first section seems to have been edited at a later date. Apart from this distinction, the law expressed in the two sections is basically the same: Israel has only one God, and it is to have only one sanctuary and one altar. This is a new idea, as can be seen by comparing v. 8 with the Book of the Covenant, which authorized the erection of an altar wherever the divine presence made itself known (Ex 20: 24), or with the ancient custom that regarded slaughtering an animal as always equivalent to sacrifice (and therefore needing an altar, cf. 1 S 14: 32-35). Since there was to be henceforth only one altar, the same law of Deuteronomy authorized the slaughtering of beasts for food without any religious rites, retaining only the prohibition against eating the blood (Dt 12: 15-16, 20-25).

The sole sanctuary was to stand 'in the place which Yahweh has chosen for his Name to dwell there', and, apart from Dt. 12, the formula recurs frequently throughout the rest of Deuteronomy. At the time of Josias' reform and in those later writings which stem from Deuteronomy, this 'place' was evidently Jerusalem. But the place is never explicitly named: the reason may be that since the book was presented as spoken by Moses. Jerusalem could not be mentioned by name. But there is another possibility: perhaps the formula referred originally to a central sanctuary in the Northern kingdom (where Deuteronomy originated), such as Shechem or Bethel, whose servants wanted to make it the only sanctuary in Israel. It is hard to decide, and both solutions are attractive. There are two alternatives: either the reform of Ezechias (2 K 18: 4) derived some stimulus from this law, already formulated in the North by Levites and brought by them to Jerusalem after 721; if so, then Dt 12: 1-12, which insists on the abolition of other places of worship, must have been added after this reform. Alternatively, the law prescribing that there should be only one sanctuary is, in general, a reflection of the reform of Ezechias, and was added, during his reign, to the traditions originating in the North and compiled by the King's command (like certain collection of proverbs, cf. Pr 25: 1); if this be so, then the 'place chosen by Yahweh' always referred to Jerusalem, and the section which is in the plural (Dt 12: 1-12) would point only to a later redaction, possibly connected with the reform of Josias. In support of the second solution, three arguments may be noted. First, the story of Ezechias' reform makes no reference to any previous law, whereas the account of Josias' reform does; secondly, if this hypothesis is accepted, there is no need to postulate, for Ezechias' reform, anything more than a royal policy of establishing a strong and united kingdom; thirdly, the formula 'the place chosen by Yahweh for his Name shall dwell here' seems to be connected with the theology of the Temple in Jerusalem.[1]

The Book of Deuteronomy was put together in some form or other under Ezechias, but was forgotten, lost or hidden during the syncretist reaction of Manasseh, and re-discovered under Josias; and this discovery either set in motion (Kings) or gave the support of tradition to (Chronicles) the great reform.

5. *Later sanctuaries outside Jerusalem*

The influence of Deuteronomy lasted longer than the reform it inspired, and its precepts dictated the religious attitude of the deportees in Babylon. The exiles never built a sanctuary in that foreign land, and their thoughts and their hopes were still turned towards Jerusalem (Ps 137). The episode recorded in Esd 8: 15-20 has sometimes been interpreted as indicating the existence of a place of cult in Babylonia, and the argument runs as follows: when Esdras assembled his caravan he found he had both priests and layfolk, but no Levites; he asked Iddo, who lived with his brothers at Kesiphya, for some Levites, and was given a whole contingent. From this some authors conclude that this region, peopled by Levites, was a place of cult. But the mere fact that Kesiphya is called a *maqôm* is not enough to prove that it was a 'holy place',[2] and the great number of Levites there may be explained by the fact that the exiles lived in family groups, and according to their place of origin; we are not told that priests came from Kesiphya.

1. Cf. p. 327. 2. Cf. p. 291.

Similarly, the post-exilic community of Palestine had no sanctuary except Jerusalem, but we do know that during this period there were two sanctuaries of Yahweh outside Palestine, one at Elephantine and the other at Leontopolis; in addition, there was, in Palestine itself, outside the district of Judaea, the temple of the dissident Samaritans.

(a) *The Temple at Elephantine.* At Elephantine, on the southern frontier of Egypt, there was a military colony in which Jewish mercenaries were stationed at some unknown date, probably in the sixth century B.C. Our information about them comes from certain papyri, dating over the whole of the fifth century, from which we know that they spoke Aramaic, not Hebrew, and that they practised a syncretist religion which the Prophets had condemned. The only point of interest to us at the moment is their sanctuary. They had a temple of Yaho (Yahweh), which was in existence before the invasion of Cambyses in 525 B.C. The precise spot in Elephantine where it stood is not known for certain, and we hardly know anything about its design. It was called in Aramaic *egora* a word borrowed from the Akkadian *ekurru*, meaning 'temple'. In 410 B.C. an Egyptian priest of the god Khnum, the ram-god who was patron of Elephantine, took advantage of the absence of the satrap on a visit to the court of Persia to persuade the local governor to destroy the temple of Yaho. The Jews asked Bagoas, the govenor of Judaea, and Yohanan, the high priest in Jerusalem (cf. Ne 12:22-23), to intervene in their favour, but received no answer to their request. Three years later, they again approached Bagoas and wrote also to the two sons of Sanballat, who was governor of Samaria while Nehemias was governor of Judaea. This time they received an answer, which took the form of a memorandum entrusted to a messenger: the messenger was to request the satrap of Egypt for permission to rebuild the temple and to present offerings and incense there. This document, however, makes no reference to holocausts, which the Jews had specifically mentioned in their request. The temple was in fact restored, and is mentioned in a document dated 402 B.C. Some years later, and shortly after the end of Persian rule over Egypt, the Jewish colonists at Elephantine were scattered, and the temple disappeared.

It is clear that these Jews were either unaware of, or paid no attention to, the law of Deuteronomy forbidding sanctuaries outside Jerusalem. Various explanations have been put forward. Some say that the community originated from the Northern kingdom, before the reform of Josias: this date seems, for other reasons, far too early, and it does not explain why they called themselves Jews, that is, 'Judaeans', or why they sent their first appeal to the governor of Judaea and to the high priest in Jerusalem. One recent suggestion is that they came from a Judaean enclave in the North of Syria—to be precise, near Ya'udi = Senjirli—where Solomon established an outpost of his empire; the existence of this outpost is known from cuneiform inscriptions. In spite of certain historical difficulties, this hypothesis could, at a pinch, explain the name 'Judaeans', but it does not explain why they should have appealed to the governor of Judaea. The only solution left is that the group came from Judaea itself; they must have left when the recently promulgated prescriptions of Deuteronomy had once more become a dead letter after the failure of Josias' reform. These Jews practised the popular religion as described and denounced by Jeremias and Ezechiel at the time of the fall of Jerusalem, and during the Exile. They were unaware of the changes which had taken place since the return from Babylon and so sent the high priest a request which they considered quite in order, but which the clergy of Jerusalem, applying the Law of Deuteronomy, could not countenance.

(b) *The temple at Leontopolis.* From texts in Josephus and from a passage in the Mishnah, we learn of another temple of Yahweh in Egypt, at a later date. Josephus' information is sometimes self-contradictory, but he states that after the murder of the high priest Onias III (cf. 2 M 4: 33-34), his son Onias sought refuge in Egypt and commanded a Jewish contingent in the service of Ptolemy VI Philometor and of Cleopatra. This Onias was commander of the Jewish military colony stationed at Leontopolis, probably Tell el-Yahudiyeh, and he obtained permission from the monarchs to build a temple for the Jews on the site of an abandoned Egyptian temple; there he could exercise the functions of high priest which were his by birth (Josephus, *Ant.* XIII iii 1-2[1]). The temple, built on the model of the Temple at Jerusalem, was smaller and less magnificent than its original, according to *Ant.*, XIII, iii, 3, and was different in its plan and its furnishings, according to *Bell.*, VII, x, 3. It was served by a lawful priesthood, and Onias, to justify his action, had invoked the prophecy of Is 19: 19 which foretold that there would be an altar in the centre of Egypt as a witness to Yahweh Sabaoth. Though this prophecy is post-exilic, it was not made up in Maccabean times to justify the step Onias had taken. This temple was founded about 160 B.C. and remained standing until 73 A.D., when it was pulled down by the Romans because Leontopolis, which was still called 'the region named after Onias', had become a centre of Jewish nationalism (*Bell.*, VII, x, 2-4).

This temple was regarded with disfavour by the Jews. Josephus accuses Onias of bad faith, and the Mishnah (*Menahoth*, XIII, 10) questions the validity of the sacrifices offered and of vows fulfilled in the temple of Onias. Nevertheless, it is strange that the rabbis did not condemn it more severely, by virtue of the law prohibiting sanctuaries other than the one at Jerusalem. Perhaps they were restrained by the undoubted legitimacy of its priesthood, or impressed by the text of Isaias and by the memory of the altar of the Transjordanian tribes which, according to Jos 22: 26-28, 34, had been authorized to remain as a 'witness' of Yahweh; perhaps they even considered that the law of Deuteronomy did not apply so strictly outside

1. Cf. p. 401.

Palestine, for it was only in the Holy Land that Dt 12: 14 spoke of 'the place chosen by Yahweh in one of the tribes' (note that this would excuse the Jews of Elephantine also). But the simplest solution of all is that the temple on Leontopolis owed its existence solely to the vanity of Onias and the political schemes of Ptolemy, and that it never had any real attraction, even for the Egyptian Diaspora; it was not considered of any great importance, and the rabbis merely took it as a rather curious phenomenon on which they could exercise their casuistic ingenuity.

(c) *The Temple at Garizim.* The Samaritans claimed that they possessed the 'place chosen by Yahweh' in Palestine itself; it was, they said, mount Garizim, where they built a temple. No one knows the precise date at which it was built. Samaritan tradition says that it was founded by Josue, destroyed by Nabuchodonosor and restored by Sanballat after the return from the Exile; its history, then, is modelled on that of the Temple in Jerusalem, but Sanballat lived long after the return, for he was a contemporary of Nehemias. Josephus, curiously enough, assigns the construction of the temple on Garizim to the period of a certain Sanballat, but this one is said to have lived a century later than Nehemias. He says (*Ant.*, XI, vii, 2 to viii, 4) that Sanballat's daughter married Manasses, whose brother was high priest in Jerusalem, and that Manasses fled to his father-in-law to get away from the criticisms of his brother and the elders in Jerusalem. Sanballat promised to build him a temple on Garizim if he could obtain the consent of the king, Darius. During these negotiations, however, Darius was defeated by Alexander the Great; Sanballat abandoned the cause of the Persians and rushed to make his submission to Alexander, who was then besieging Tyre. He returned thence armed with the authorization of the conqueror, and quickly built his temple and appointed Manasses as its priest. Thus we should be able to date its foundation exactly, in 332 B.C.

In spite of the efforts of certain historians to justify this claim, there is nothing in this story which is worthy of credence: in placing the foundation during the lifetime of Alexander, it contradicts what Ne 13: 28 tells us about one of the sons of Yoyada, the high priest, who became the son-in-law of Sanballat and was expelled by Nehemias. On the other hand, if we reject the story of Josephus, it is arbitrary to retain, as some authors do, the date presupposed by this story for the foundation of the temple on Garizim. It may have existed before Alexander, or only after his days, and there is no need to connect its foundation with the definitive break between the Samaritans and the Jews, the date of which is itself disputed. All one can say for certain is that the temple was in existence in 167-166 B.C. when Antiochus Epiphanes dedicated it to Zeus Xenios (according to 2 M 6: 2), or to Zeus Hellenios (according to Josephus, *Ant.*, XIII, v, 5). It was destroyed by John Hyrcanus after the death of Antiochus VII Sidetes in 129 B.C. (again according to Josephus, *Ant.*, XIII, ix, 1). There is no mention in any later text of its having been rebuilt, or even of its existence, but the conversation of Jesus with the Samaritan woman (Jn 4: 20–21) implies that the sanctuary remained in existence at least until the first century A.D.

6. *The origin of synagogues*

Synagogues were buildings erected not for sacrifice, but for prayer, reading of the Law and instruction: they first came into existence when Judaism was finally organized, and they were soon found throughout Palestine, in the Diaspora and even in Jerusalem itself, alongside the Temple. The origin of the synagogues (and it is only with their origin that we are here concerned) is shrouded in mystery. The predominant opinion to-day is that they originated in Babylonia during the Exile as a substitute for the Temple services, and that they were introduced into Palestine by Esdras. Others, however, think they first came into existence in Palestine itself after the time of Esdras and Nehemias, or even after the end of the Persian period. A few scholars consider them an institution of Palestinian origin, and pre-exilic; they would then be a result of the reform of Josias. Their idea is that when the country people were deprived of their local sanctuaries, and of their sacrifices, too (apart from those rare occasions on which they could go off to Jerusalem for the big feasts), they began to meet on certain days for public worship, but without offering sacrifice.

The reason for this variety of hypotheses is that there is nothing really explicit in ancient texts. Inscriptions and papyri show that there were 'places of prayer' (προσευχή) in Egypt from the middle of the third century B.C., and Josephus (*Bell.*, VIII, iii, 3) says that there was a synagogue at Antioch under the successors of Antiochus Epiphanes; this is the earliest evidence we possess. None of the biblical texts (not even Ez 11: 16 or Esd 8: 15–20) which are usually cited prove the existence of common places of prayer in Babylonia during the Exile, and Ps 137 seems to prove the contrary. The mention of 'meeting houses' in the apocryphal Book of Henoch (46: 8) is usually brought forward to support the theory that there were synagogues in Palestine, but its testimony refers, at the earliest, to the time of Maccabees. There remains Ps 74: 7–8: 'They have burnt thy sanctuary . . . they have burnt every meeting-place of God throughout the land'. Many critics assign this psalm to the Maccabean period, but this seems too late, and the passage cited is much easier to explain if we take it to refer to the destruction of the Temple in 587; the other meeting-places could have been the predecessors of the synagogues. Nevertheless, it is not easy to connect these institutions with the reform of Josias, for we have seen that the local sanctuaries were closed only for a short period. Could not these 'meeting-places' be the same local sanctuaries which were once more functioning at the time of the fall of Jerusalem? The hortatory character of certain passages in the Book of Jeremias does not necessarily mean that these texts were written to be read in synagogues.

There is, then, no way of deciding for certain when synagogues came into existence. The institution probably came into being gradually, under the pressure of two factors, which played a great part in post-exilic Judaism. The first was the application of the law insisting on one sole sanctuary; once this was admitted, it seemed not merely lawful but necessary to have places of prayer (without sacrificial worship) outside Jerusalem. Secondly—and perhaps this was the more important factor—the Law became more prominent, and this meant that it had to be read and taught in the communities; and in the synagogues teaching was at least as important as prayer. These factors were at work in Palestine as well as in Diaspora, and it is mere chance that the first synagogue we know of happens to be in Egypt. 2 Ch 17: 7-9, in its account of the reign of Josaphat, tells how layfolk, Levites and priests were sent out with the book of the Law to teach the people throughout the towns of Judah. This information seems to be modelled on the reform of the judiciary by the same king (2 Ch 19: 4-7), and though it is certainly not true of the reign of Josaphat, it may reflect a practice in vogue at the time of the Chronicler; and there must have been buildings in which they could give this teaching. But wherever we turn, we are still in the realm of hypothesis, and it is not until the beginning of the Christian era that we are fully informed about synagogues; these synagogues, however, are no longer institutions of the Old Testament.

Chapter Five

THE PRIESTLY OFFICE

THERE was no official priesthood in the time of the Patriarchs; acts of public worship (especially sacrifice, the central act) were performed by the head of the family (Gn 22; 31: 54; 46: 1). The Patriarchs themselves, who were nomads, offered their sacrifices in the sanctuaries they visited, and the Book of Genesis never mentions priests except in reference to foreign nations, which were not nomadic (*e.g.* the Egyptian priests referred to in Gn 41: 45; 47: 22, and Melchisedech, the king-priest of Salem in Gn 14: 18). There are only two texts which imply the existence of a sanctuary served by regular attendants. Gn 25: 22 says that Rebecca went 'to consult Yahweh' about the twins, Esau and Jacob, whom she was soon to bear: the normal meaning of this expression is that she went to a holy place to ask for an oracle from a man of God. Secondly, in Gn 28: 22, Jacob promises to pay tithes to the sanctuary he had founded at Bethel—which implies that it was a sanctuary administered by a group of clergy (cf. Gn 14: 20); but this, too, is an act attributed to the founder of a sanctuary to justify a later custom (cf. Am 4: 4). The priesthood properly so called did not appear until the social organization of the community had developed considerably; then certain members of the community were entrusted with the special tasks of looking after the sanctuaries and of performing rites which were becoming ever more and more complicated.

1. *The Name*

The only name by which the Old Testament ever refers to priests of Yahweh is *kohen*; the same word is used for priests of foreign gods, whether Egyptian (Gn 41: 45; 47: 22), Phoenician (2 K 10: 19; 11: 18), Philistine (1 S 5: 5; 6: 2), Moabite (Jr 48: 7) or Ammonite (Jr 49: 3). The word has the same form in both Hebrew and Phoenician, and is frequently found in Nabatean also. There is another noun, however, derived from the root *kmr*, which was used from about 2000 B.C. in the Assyrian colonies of Cappadocia, then in ancient Aramaic, and later on in the dialect of Palmyra and in Syriac. The corresponding Hebrew word, always in the plural *k^emarîm*, occurs only three times in the Bible and always refers to priests of false gods (2 K 23: 5; Os 10: 5; So 1: 4).

The etymology of *kohen* is not known. It has been suggested that it is related to the Akkadian verb *kanu*, from the root *k'n*, which, in the Shaphel, means 'to bend down, to do homage'. It is more common, though, to connect it with the root *kwn* meaning 'to stand upright'; the priest would then be a man who stands before God (cf. Dt 10: 8) like a servant. But all this is still uncertain.

2. *The installation of priests*

In Israel, the priesthood was not a vocation but an office. The texts speak of a man being called or chosen by God to be a king or a prophet, but they never use the term of a priest. True, in 2 Ch 24: 20, the Spirit of God descends on Zachary, a priest's son, but it is to make him a prophet, not to raise him to priesthood. Again, tradition told how Yahweh had chosen the tribe of Levi for the service of his sanctuary, but this did not involve any particular charisma for the individual members of the tribe. In fact, according to the older documents, priests were appointed by men without any divine intervention: Mikah chose first one of his sons (Jg 17: 5) and then a Levite (Jg 17: 10) for his private sanctuary; the men of Qiryath-Yearim chose Eleazar to keep watch over the Ark (1 S 7: 1), and the kings nominated and dismissed the servants in their official sanctuaries (1 K 2: 27; 12: 31). Later on, a man was sufficiently qualified for the priesthood if he was of priestly descent, unless he suffered from some physical disability which constituted an impediment (Lv 21: 16-24).

The oldest and most explicit text about a priest's assuming office is Jg 17: 5-12, which uses the term 'filling his hand' for 'appointing him'. The phrase is found again in Ex 32: 29; 1 K 13: 33 and then in a number of texts belonging to the Priestly tradition (Ex 28: 41; 29 *passim*; Lv 8: 33; Nb 3: 3); in the end the literal meaning of the word was forgotten and it came to mean, in Ez 43: 26, inaugurating an altar. As a result, the cognate noun *millu'îm*, literally 'a filling' (of the hand), means 'investing' a priest in Ex 29: 22-34; Lv 8: 22-33. The original meaning of the expression is debated. One explanation is found in Lv 8: 27-28 and Ex 29: 24-25; Moses puts into the hands of Aaron and his sons parts of the victims which are to be placed on the altar, makes the gesture of presentation along with them, and then takes the offerings from their hands and burns them on the altar: 'it was the sacrifice of *millu'îm*'. By so performing, for the first time, the ritual gesture of a minister of the altar, the man was invested with priestly power. Unfortunately, these are late texts which are trying to give an explanation of a phrase whose original meaning had been forgotten. Alternatives have been suggested: some authors hold that the phrase originally referred to the salary the priest received, and that he was given a first instalment at the beginning of his ministry; the hypothesis can claim support from Jg 17: 10; 18: 4, in which the Levite whom Mikah engages 'had his hand filled' and 'was engaged' for ten silver shekels per annum, plus food and clothing. Another suggestion is that the phrase is connected with the Akkadian expression 'to fill someone's hand', which means 'to put a man in charge of something', to give him a task to perform. Lastly, the archives of Mari have yielded texts from the time of Hammurabi concerning the distribution of booty, part of which, was assigned, as of right, to certain types of officers; it is called 'filling the hand'; perhaps this is the closest parallel, and then the Hebrew phrase would mean that the priest was given the right to a part of the revenues accruing to the sanctuary and to a share of the offerings made there. This would be 'the priest's right' mentioned in 1 S 2: 13, and later defined in greater detail by the Priestly laws. But whatever be the truth of the matter, the precise meaning of this ancient phrase had been lost by the time the Israelites began to use it; it does not describe a rite of ordination.

Similarly, in Nb 8: 10, the Israelites lay hands upon the Levites, but this is not a rite of investiture either: it is a gesture of offering[1] whereby the Levites are offered to Yahweh as substitutes for the first-born.[2] The *s'mikah* or imposition of hands is not mentioned in the post-exilic ritual for the investiture of priests (Ex 29; Lv 8), and in post-biblical times it was never practised by the Jews except for the installation of Doctors. These later Jews based their practice on the text which states that Moses laid his hands on Josue (Nb 27: 15-23), and they presumed that he had done the same for the seventy elders of Israel (Nb 11: 16-17).

According to the post-exilic ritual, the high priest was anointed (Ex 29: 7; Lv 8: 12, etc.) and the last redaction of the Pentateuch added that in fact all priests were anointed (Ex 40: 12-15, etc.).[3] But it seems quite certain that this rite did not exist before the Exile and that it was in fact the transference of a royal prerogative to the high priest insomuch as he was head of the new community.[4]

Consequently, priests in ancient Israel were not 'ordained': they began their work without any religious rite conferring on them grace, or special powers. And yet a priest was made holy and sacred by virtue of his work. 1 S 7: 1 does not use the technical phrase 'to fill the hands' but says instead that Eleazar was 'sanctified' (*qiddesh*) for the services of the Ark. Priests were 'sanctified' (Lv 21: 6), and the high priest had to wear on his forehead a golden flower on which was engraved 'sanctified for Yahweh' (Ex 28: 36). This means that the priest no longer belonged to the profane world, but, like the territory around the sanctuary and the offerings presented there, he was 'set apart'; according to Nb 8: 14; Dt 10: 8, the Levites were 'set apart' for the service of God, and according to 1 Ch 23: 13, Aaron was

1. Cf. p. 416.
2. Cf. p. 360.
3. The texts were quoted and discussed on p. 105.
4. Cf. *ibid.* and also below, pp. 399-400.

'set apart' to consecrate the most holy things. The priest, therefore, had quitted the profane world, and entered into a sacred realm. He could therefore move around on sacred ground without sacrilege, enter into the sanctuary, handle sacred objects, eat gifts offered in sacrifice, and so forth. But he had to remain detached from profane things, and was subject to certain prohibitions and special rules concerning purity. In their daily life, priests were forbidden to take part in funerals; an exception was made for the funeral of a close blood-relative, but even then, they were bound to abstain from certain practices (Lv 21: 1-6). They were forbidden to marry a woman who had been a prostitute, or a woman who had been divorced by her husband (Lv 21: 7). When they were performing their duties, every care was taken to avoid any confusion between the sacred and the profane: they had to put on special vestments to enter the sanctuary (Ex 28: 43), to wash their clothes (Nb 8: 7), to purify themselves in special ways (Ex 30: 17-21; 40: 31-32; Lv 8: 6) and to abstain from wine and alcohol (Lv 10: 8-11).

This transference into the order of things sacred conferred a real dignity on the priest. When Mikah engaged the Levite he said 'Be a father and a priest to me' (Jg 17: 10), even though the Levite was only a young man (cf, vv. 7 and 10) the significance of this remark is that the priest had inherited those religious prerogatives which, in the patriarchal period, had belonged to the head of the family.

3. *The priest and the sanctuary*

Every priest was chosen and installed to serve in a sanctuary. The ruling was universally acknowledged particularly by the Arabs in the days before Islam. The priest was for them essentially a *sadin*, a 'guardian' of the temple; he looked after the sanctuary, received visitors and took charge of their gifts. Indeed, the bond tying him to the sanctuary was so strong that when a tribe emigrated, the *sadin* stayed behind and continued to exercise his office among strangers. His sons would then take his place, so that the various sanctuaries were always administered by priestly families. The same was true of Israel. In the stories about the wanderings in the desert, the Levites camped around the Tent (Nb 1: 53); each clan had its appointed place (Nb 3: 23, 29, 35), and Aaron's sons were posted in front of the Tent to prevent layfolk entering it (Nb 3: 38). The word used for this office is 'the guard' (Nb 1: 53; 3: 28, 32, etc.). In Israel, however, the Tent was a movable sanctuary; the priests moved with it and carried it (Nb 4: 5f.; Dt 10: 8). Ezechiel, when he was describing the partition of the Holy Land, drew his inspiration from this ideal of the desert and assigned to the priests the sacred ground around the Temple (Ez 45: 4).

Consequently, it is impossible to imagine a sanctuary without any priest to look after it. In the time of the Judges, Mikah built a private domestic sanctuary, but he appointed a priest at once; at first he installed his own son, but later replaced him when a Levite happened to pass by (Jg 17). This same Levite joined the men of Dan when they were migrating to the North, and took charge of the new sanctuary at Laish-Dan (Jg 18: 30). The temple where the Ark was kept at Shiloh was entrusted to the family of Eli (1 S 1-2). And when the Ark was laid at rest in Qiryath-Yearim, on its way home from Philistia, a priest was at once consecrated (*i.e.* set apart) to look after it (1 S 7: 1).

The destinies of the priesthood in Israel were therefore bound up with the fate of the sanctuaries. Under David, Sadoq and Ebyathar were in charge of the Ark (2 S 15: 24-29), but under Solomon, Ebyathar was dismissed (1 K 2: 26-27) and Sadoq alone was left in charge of the Temple; later, he was succeeded by his son (1 K 2: 35; 4: 1). When Jeroboam founded the sanctuary at Bethel, he at once installed priests there (1 K 12: 31). But just as the Temple in Jerusalem far outshone all the other places of public worship, so the priesthood of Jerusalem was far more important than the priests who looked after the smaller sanctuaries in the provinces; and, naturally enough, the attempts made to centralize cultic worship were accompanied by a regrouping of the clergy (2 K 23: 8). However, we have detailed information only about the priests of the Temple, and we shall have occasion to discuss them in later chapters.[1]

4. *Priests and divine oracles*

In ancient Israel men went to a sanctuary 'to consult Yahweh', and the priest gave oracles. It is noteworthy that in Dt 33: 8-10 the rôle played by the sons of Levi in giving oracles is mentioned even before the teaching of the Torah and their service of the altar. In the desert, the Israelites turned to Moses 'to consult God' (Ex 18: 15), and although, on Jethro's advice, Moses accepted help from others in the administration of justice, he kept for himself the task of taking the people's quarrels before God (Ex 18: 19). Anyone who wanted 'to consult Yahweh' went to the Tent; Moses then went inside, alone, and conversed face to face with Yahweh (Ex 33: 7-11). This last action, however, was a personal privilege of Moses (Nb 12: 6-8) which the priests did not share (cf. Nb 27: 21). They used to consult God by means of the ephod and of the Urim and Thummin. What exactly is meant by these procedures is a most intricate and obscure question.

(a) *The ephod.* The texts in which the Bible mentions the ephod (*'ephôd*) can be classified under three headings:

(1) Some texts refer to a linen ephod (*'ephôd bad*), which in the oldest historical texts is one of the priest's vestments. Samuel wore one as a boy in the temple of Shiloh (1 S 2: 18); the priests of Nob wore it (1 S 22: 18)

1. Cf. pp. 372 ff.

and so did David when he danced in front of the Ark (2 S 6: 14). It was worn around the waist (1 S 2: 18; 2 S 6: 14) but did not cover much of the body (cf. 2 S 6: 20); hence it must have been a kind of loin-cloth such as Egyptian priests wore, which may originally have been the only clothing worn by the priests in performing their offices.

(2) Other texts refer to an ephod which was a special part of the clothing of the high priest; it was part of his outer clothing, worn over the tunic and the cloak (Ex 29: 5; Lv 8: 7). It is described in Ex 28: 6–14; 39: 2–7, but the description is overburdened with later additions reflecting the changes in the high priest's robes during the post-exilic period. The earliest edition of the text, dating from the Exile, may well preserve information dating from the end of the monarchy. The ephod is there presented as a wide band of material woven out of golden and linen thread, and of variously coloured wools; this strip of material was lined with a belt, with which it was fastened around the body. (The mention of braces in conjunction with the ephod seems to be a later addition.)

The *ḥoshen* or 'breast-plate' was distinct from the ephod, but attached to it (Ex 28: 15–30; 39: 8–21). It was woven out of the same material as the ephod, and was shaped like a small (?) square bag in which were kept the Urim and Thummim; in Ex 28: 15, 30 it is called *ḥoshen hammishpaṭ*, 'the breast-plate of the (oracular) decision'.

(3) Yet other texts refer to an ephod which was an object of cultic worship. Mikah had one made for his sanctuary (Jg 17: 5; 18: 14, 17, 20); Gideon too made one with the gold he captured from the Midianites and kept it in his home-town (Jg 8: 27). It was a portable object (1 S 2: 28; 14: 3), and could even be held in the hand (1 S 23: 6); it could be 'brought out' or 'put away' (1 S 23: 9; 30: 7). In the sanctuary at Nob, Goliath's sword was kept behind the ephod (1 S 21: 10). Lastly, the ephod was left in the care of the priests and was used for consulting Yahweh (1 S 23: 10; 30: 8).

The original meaning of the word—a subject of long dispute in the past—is no longer in doubt: *'epd* is the word used for the robe of the goddess Anath in a poem of Ras Shamra, and *epattu* (plural: *epadatu*) means 'rich vestment' in the ancient Assyrian tablets from Cappadòcia. Now priestly vestments easily come to perpetuate archaic customs, and the *'ephôd bad* would be a traditional garment still worn by the priests, of which the high priest's ephod was a later and more luxurious form; in the intervening years, however, what had once been the sole vestment of a priest had become a large piece of material worn on top of all the other priestly vestments.

At first sight, this meaning does not seem to suit the third series of texts mentioned above, in which the ephod is spoken of as a cultic object used for consulting Yahweh: the texts do not give us to understand that it was anything like an article of clothing, but rather that it was something solid which could be carried, brought out, put away or put down. As a result, many scholars have refused to see any connection between this ephod and that worn by the priests and the high priest. Some of them prefer to correct the text and to read instead of *'ephôd* the word *'arôn* (ark) or, in other passages, *'abbir* (bull). Others, less radical in their views, presume that the word *'ephôd* stands sometimes for a statue of a god; and there are some who understand it as a small-scale model of the desert Tent where oracles were delivered, or a little box in which the sacred lots were kept.

Yet the difficulty remains: why should one and the same word, in the same cultic context, at the same period, be used both for a priestly vestment and for a box? The use of these words in biblical and other Semitic texts makes it quite certain that the ephod worn by the priests and the high priest was a garment; it is only reasonable to try to find some similar meaning for the ephod used in delivering oracles. Various suggestions have been made. First, we know that statues of gods were sometimes clothed in a richly decorated garment; the ephod, it is suggested, was at first a vestment used to decorate the statute of a god; later it became the distinguishing mark of a priest who gave oracles in the name of a god, and finally it became the official dress of the high priest.

In contrast to this, a very recent opinion maintains that the primary meaning of the ephod as one of the high priest's vestments lies behind its use in connection with the oracles. This apron or loincloth, it is said, was very stiff by reason of the thread of gold in it, and kept its shape when put down; hence the sword of Goliath could be hidden behind it, it could be carried by hand and brought out when needed: and the *ḥoshen*, the pocket containing the Urim and Thummim, was attached to it, so that the ephod itself was brought out when oracles were needed. A third opinion suggests that the ephod for oracles was different from the ordinary ephod worn by the priests and from that worn by the high priest, too, but was still a vestment or outer covering for a statue of a god (cf. the cognate word *'apuddah* in Is 30: 22); it is suggested that, though Israel did not have any statues of its god, it kept an ephod for some time as an instrument for giving oracles. This would explain why the priests carried it or brought it out, but never put it on, and why Gideon's ephod weighed 1,700 shekels and was condemned by the redactor of Jg 8: 26–27; it would also explain why Os 3: 4 groups the ephod with the teraphim, domestic idols from which men sought oracles (Ez 21: 26; Za 10: 2).

None of these hypotheses is absolutely convincing. The last interpretation seems the least improbable, but it could go further. Since the Israelites refused to have statues of their God, they could not use the ephod except for oracles; in some way or other, the ephod was a receptacle for sacred lots. There is an old proverb which may not refer directly to the ephod but which does at least indicate how a vestment could be used for drawing lots:

'From the pocket (*i.e.* the fold of the vestment: *ḥeq*) men draw lots, but the decision (*mishpaṭ*) always comes from Yahweh' (Pr 16: 33). This reminds us of the *ḥosen hammishpaṭ*, the pocket of the oracle's reply; this pocket contained Urim and Thummim, and it was attached to the ephod of the high priest (Ex 28: 30).

(b) *Urim and Thummim.* These were the sacred lots. The etymology and the meaning of the words is unknown, and modern attempts to explain them are not much better than the arbitrary translations of the ancient versions. The names must have been borrowed, like the things, from the pre-Israelite civilization of Canaan, and the plural form is just a singular which has retained its primitive mimation.

Nor have we any idea what they looked like. Small pebbles or dice have been suggested, and, more often, little sticks (cf. Os 4: 12?); they were picked out of the pocket of the ephod. Some authors see a parallel in the ancient Arab custom called *istiqsam*, *i.e.* divining by means of small sticks or arrows, similar to that practised by the king of Babylon in Ez 21: 26–27; but according to the term used by Ezechiel, this was a practice of diviners (the *qᵉsamîm*), and may well have nothing to do with the Urim and Thummim used by the priests.

According to Nb 27: 21, these lots were entrusted to the priest Eleazar: Dt 33: 8 says they were entrusted to the tribe of Levi. The way in which the oracle worked is shown in 1 S 14: 41–42 (corrected in accordance with the Greek). 'Saul then said: "If I or my son Jonathan should be to blame, Yahweh, God of Israel, give *urim*; if thy people Israel is to blame, give *tummim.*" Saul and Jonathan were picked out and the people escaped. Saul said: "Cast lots between me and my son Jonathan", and Jonathan was picked out'. Verse 36 presumes that the priest had a rôle to play. Now this text does not prove that Thummim was the favourable object, and Urim the unfavourable one; on the contrary, it implies that, like our 'heads or tails', the two objects had a purely conventional meaning, which was fixed each time by the parties; this is itself a warning against trying to find a meaning for the words. The answer of the oracle lies in producing one rather than the other. Its answer, then, was always 'Yes' or 'No', and it proceeded by elimination or by becoming more precise (cf. also 1 S 23: 9–12). Hence the procedure could go on for a long time; in 1 S 14: 18–19 (corrected in accordance with the Greek) Saul wants to know whether he should attack the Philistine camp, but as the questioning of the oracle takes longer and longer, Saul, seeing the excitement in the enemy camp increasing, tells the priest to 'withdraw his hand'. Thus he interrupts the consultation of Yahweh and goes into action. Sometimes, too, the oracle refused to give an answer (1 S 14: 37; 28: 6), presumably because nothing came out of the pocket, or because both came out together.

(c) *The decreasing importance of oracles given by priests.* After the reign of

David, there is no evidence that the ephod, with the Urim and Thummim, was ever used for oracles. If Pr 16: 33, cited above, does in fact refer to the ephod, this would give us a slightly later date, and Os 3: 4 seems to say that the ephod was used in the Northern kingdom down to the fall of Samaria; but Osee groups the ephod with teraphim and *maṣṣebôth*, which are forbidden by the law of Yahwism. Whatever be the truth on this matter, Achab and Joram of Israel and the kings of Judah contemporary with them (1 K 20: 13–14; 22: 6; 2 K 3: 11) consult Yahweh through prophets, in circumstances where Saul and David used to consult him by the ephod. Under Josias, the head of the priesthood in Jerusalem goes in person to ask guidance from the prophetess Huldah (2 K 22: 14; cf. also Jr 21: 1–2, under Sedecias). If the description of the ephod and of the 'breast-plate' of the high priest in Ex 28: 6–30 comes (basically) from the last years of the monarchy, it was no longer an instrument for giving oracles; it is significant that the Urim and Thummim are mentioned there, but not described in minute detail, as all the other ornaments of the high priest are; they are probably mentioned to give an archaic touch, and the writer himself probably did not know exactly what they were. There is a perceptible development in the last edition of the text: stones engraved with the names of the tribes of Israel were fixed on the ephod and on the breast-plate, and their purpose is merely to remind Yahweh of his people (Ex 28: 12 and 29).

Esd 2: 63 = Ne 7: 65 says that after the Exile there was no priest to handle the Urim and Thummim; this is confirmed by the Jewish tradition which often repeats that there was neither Urim nor Thummim in the second Temple. One text of the Talmud (*Sota* 48a) even asserts that there had been no Urim and Thummim since the death of the 'first prophets', *i.e.* Samuel, David and Solomon. It is possible, however, that down to the ruin of the Temple, the priests continued to give answers in God's name (though without using means of divination) to those pilgrims who came to offer sacrifice and to pray for favours there: certain psalms and a number of passages in second Isaias can be explained in this way. But this procedure was utterly different from using the ephod with its Urim and Thummim.

5. *The priest as a teacher*

In the Blessing of Levi (Dt 33: 10), a twofold duty is assigned to the Levites; they are to take charge of the Urim and Thummim, and to instruct the people: 'They shall teach thy decisions (*mishpaṭîm*) to Jacob, and thy instructions (*tôrôth*: read the plural) to Israel'. The *tôrah* belongs to the priest, as the virtue of judgment belongs to the king, or wisdom to the wise man, or vision and message to the prophet. Three texts state this clearly: 'Its princes give judgment in return for presents, its priests teach for reward, its prophets speak out in return for money' (Mi 3: 11) 'The priest shall not be found lacking in the *tôrah*, nor the wise man in counsel, nor the prophet in words' (Jr 18: 18). 'They shall ask the prophet for a vision, and the priest will be found wanting in the *tôrah*, and the elders in counsel' (Ez 7: 26).

It has been suggested that *tôrah* comes from the verb *yarah*, meaning 'to throw', and occasionally 'to cast lots' (Jos 18: 6); consequently, this rôle of the priest has been linked with his rôle as a man who gives oracles, and a comparison has been drawn with the Assyrian *tertu*, which means 'an oracle'. But the way in which the word is used and the verbs which are used with it indicate that its root is rather *yrh*, which is frequently employed in the factitive form with the meaning 'to show', to 'teach'. The *tôrah* is, therefore, in the strict sense 'instruction' and the usual translation of this word as 'law' is not quite accurate.

This 'law' came from God, but he entrusted it to the priests (Dt 31: 9, 26). According to Dt 33: 10, the priests are to teach the *tôrôth* of Yahweh to Israel (cf. Os 4: 6) and the priest as a teacher is a 'messenger of Yahweh Sabaoth' (Ml 2: 7). Naturally enough, this instruction was delivered in the sanctuary to which the priest belonged and where men came on pilgrimage, or to offer sacrifice, or simply to consult the man in charge of the sanctuary; as a result, the teaching of the *tôrah* was, in pre-exilic days, confined to the Temple, and texts like Is 2: 3=Mi 4: 2; Dt 31: 10-11 reflect a most ancient custom.

The *tôrah* was originally a short instruction on a particular topic, a rule of practical conduct, more especially about how to perform cultic worship, in which the priest was a specialist; he had to decide what was sacred and what was profane, what was clean or unclean, and to instruct the faithful on the point (Lv 10: 10-11; Ez 22: 26; 44: 23). After the return from the Exile, the prophet Aggaeus asked the priests for a *tôrah* about the effects of touching clean and unclean things (Ag 2: 11-13), and on other occasions the priests were asked whether it would be opportune to hold a fast (Za 7: 3).

But it would be a grave error to restrict the teaching rôle of priests to casuistry of this kind. Whatever may have been true in very early days, texts like Os 4: 6 and Jr 2: 8 shows that the priests' competence extended far beyond strictly cultic precepts. The priestly *tôrah* became the Torah, the Law, a collection of precepts governing the relations of man with God, and the priests were recognized as its interpreters; at the same time, men became ever more anxious to have the right interior dispositions which would make their worship agreeable to God; and as these two changes made themselves more widely and more deeply felt, the priests became teachers of morality and of religion. The prophets played the same part, but in a different way. A prophet was a man of the *dabar*, of the word, a spokesman of God, therefore, who was directly inspired by God to give a particular message in definite circumstances; he was an instrument through whom God actually revealed himself. The priest, on the other hand, was the man of the *tôrah*; knowledge (*da'ath*) was entrusted to him for interpretation, and though this knowledge certainly came from God long ago, it was handed down to men century after century by teaching and practice.

From the time of the Exile onwards, the priests ceased to have the monopoly of teaching the Torah. The Levites, who by then had been taken away from strictly priestly functions, became preachers and catechists. In the end, teaching was given quite apart from worship, in the synagogues, and a new class arose, of scribes and teachers of the Law. This class was open to all, priests and Levites and layfolk alike, and eventually it displaced the priestly caste in the work of teaching.

6. *The priest and sacrifice*

In the Blessing of Levi, those functions which are strictly connected with worship are mentioned last of all: 'They shall put incense in thy nostrils, and the sacrifice upon thy altar' (Dt 33: 10). The low position assigned to sacrifice in this hierarchy of functions may astonish anyone who thinks of later theology in which the offering of sacrifice is seen as the principal function of a priest. Philo (*De Vita Moysi*, II (III), 29) says that at the Passover all are priests because everyone offers the lamb, and the Epistle to the Hebrews says that 'every high priest is appointed to offer gifts and sacrifices' (He 5: 1; 8: 3). But these texts come at the end of a long development, of which Dt 33: 10 is merely one stage. We may pass over in silence the period of the Patriarchs, when there was no official priesthood. In the time of the Judges, God ordered Gideon to construct an altar and to offer a holocaust (Jg 6: 25-26), and the Angel of Yahweh invited Manoah, Samson's father, to offer a holocaust, which was accepted (Jg 13: 16-23). In the old account of Samuel's childhood, his father Elqanah himself ordered a sacrifice at Shiloh (1 S 1: 3, 4, 21; 2, 19), and the priest Eli seems to be the guardian of the sanctuary (1 S 1: 9); the 'priest's right', against which his sons offended, refers only to the right the priests had to a part of the victims (1 S 2: 12-17), and that part of the story which states that only priests might go up to the altar and set fire to the holocaust is an addition to the primitive text (1 S 2: 27-36).

Saul, David and Solomon all offered sacrifice, and we have explained elsewhere[1] that this does not mean that the kings of Israel were priests; but neither does it mean that priests did not offer sacrifice at that time. Achaz himself offered the first sacrifice on the new altar he had built, but the priest Uriyyah was entrusted with the care of it afterwards (2 K 16: 12-16). Shortly before this time, presumably between 800 and 750 B.C., the Blessings of Moses (Dt 33) were given their final form in the Northern kingdom; in this chapter, verses 8-11 are about Levi, and they recognize that the offering

1. Cf. pp. 113-114.

of sacrifice is a privilege of the priests. Before the Exile, in Jerusalem, the men who compiled the Law of Holiness based the special rules of cleanliness for priests on the holiness of their functions: they must be clean because they place on the altar the holocausts and the parts of other sacrifices (Lv 21: 6).

For (and this is important) the priest in the Old Testament is not strictly a 'sacrificer' in the sense of an 'immolator'. He may at times have taken care of the slaughtering of a victim, but this was always an accessory function and was never his exclusive privilege. According to Ex 24: 3-8 (generally regarded as Elohistic tradition) Moses ordered some young men (and there is no indication that they were priests) to immolate holocausts and communion-sacrifices, but it was Moses himself who took the blood and sprinkled it on the altar and on the people. The law on sacrifice expressly stipulated that the victim was to be killed by the man making the offering (Lv 1: 5; 3: 2, 8, 13; 4: 24, 29, 33). If the man making the offering was not ritually clean himself, or if it were one of the great public sacrifices (2 Ch 30: 17; Ez 44: 11), then the animal was killed by someone from the lower ranks of the clergy. The priest's rôle began when they had to use the blood, partly because this was the holiest part of the victim (Lv 17: 11, 14), but mainly because the blood had to be brought into immediate contact with the altar; similarly, it was always a priest who presented and who placed upon the altar that part of the sacrifice which belonged to God. Indeed, this ruling was so absolute that when the victim was a bird and had to be killed on the altar itself, the person bringing it lost his right to put it to death (Lv 1: 14-15; 5: 8). Similarly, when the writer wants to say, in 2 K 23: 9, that the priests of the high places were deposed after the reform of Josias, he simply says that they could not 'go up to the altar'. A text written about the same time says that priests were chosen to 'go up to the altar' (1 S 2: 28). Again, incensing was a privilege of the sons of Levi because the incense had to be burnt upon the altar (according to Dt 33: 10); according to Nb 17: 5; 1 Ch 23: 13 it was a privilege reserved to the descendants of Aaron, and 2 Ch 26: 16-18 says that king Ozias was punished for usurping this right. The priest was, then, in a very real sense, the 'minister of the altar' and this Christian expression can trace its ancestry far back into the Old Testament.

If we understand it in this very precise way, then the rôle of the priest in sacrifice is certainly very ancient, but as time went on, this part of their work came more to the fore, for people ceased to ask them for oracles, and others came to share with them the rôle of teaching. Conversely, the offering of sacrifice was reserved to them more and more as time went on; it became an essential function of the priesthood, and as a result the ruin of the Temple marked the end of their influence. The religion of the Torah replaced the ritual of the Temple, and the priests were replaced by rabbis.

7. *The priest as mediator*

All these various functions have a common basis. When the priest delivered an oracle, he was passing on an answer from God; when he gave an instruction, a *tôrah*, and later when he explained the Law, the Torah, he was passing on and interpreting teaching that came from God; when he took the blood and flesh of victims to the altar, or burned incense upon the altar, he was presenting to God the prayers and petitions of the faithful. In the first two rôles he represented God before men, and in the third he represented men before God; but he is always an intermediary. What the Epistle to the Hebrews says of the high priest is true of every priest: 'Every high priest who is taken from among men is appointed to intervene on behalf of men with God' (He 5: 1). The priest was a mediator, like the king and the prophet. But kings and prophets were mediators by reason of a personal charisma, because they were individually chosen by God; the priest was *ipso facto* a mediator, for the priesthood is an institution for mediation. This essential feature will reappear in the priesthood of the New Law, as a sharing in the priesthood of Christ the Mediator, Man and God, perfect victim and unique Priest.

CHAPTER SIX

THE LEVITES

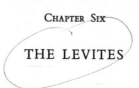

THERE are many texts in the Bible which refer to the clergy as 'Levites' or 'sons of Levi', and which state or imply that only those men who were descended from Levi could undertake sacred functions. These texts raise a number of difficult problems which must be examined, though we shall not be able to give a satisfactory solution to all of them.

1. *Etymology*

The etymology of the word *lewy* is not known for certain. In Hebrew, the root *lwh* has three meanings, each of which has been attributed to the noun, *lewy*:

(1) *lwh* can mean 'to turn around, to whirl around', and one suggestion is that the Levites were men who performed ecstatic dances, rather like the whirling dervishes and prophets;

(2) another meaning of *lwh* is 'to accompany someone, to be attached to someone', and this is the etymology put forward in the Bible itself. Leah called her new-born child Levi because, she said, 'This time my husband will cling to me' (Gn 29: 34); similarly, the members of the tribe of Levi were 'attached' to Aaron (Nb 18: 2 and 4). The corresponding root in Arabic is *wly* (with inversion), from which is derived the noun *wely*, meaning, 'one who is attached to God, a holy person';

(3) *lwh* can also mean 'to lend, to give as pledge or surety'. Although the Bible never uses the verb *lwh* in this sense when it is referring to the Levites, it does contain some very similar expressions: the Levites were 'given' to Yahweh instead of the first-born (Nb 3: 12; 8: 16), and Samuel was 'given over' to Yahweh as a boy (1 S 1: 28). Again, several Minaean inscriptions in Arabia use the word *lw'* of things and persons consecrated or vowed to a divinity.

The first derivation can be rejected as quite arbitrary. The second can claim the support of biblical texts, but we know that the etymologies advanced in the Bible do not always give the true meaning of a word. The third raises the whole problem of how the Levites originated, which we shall examine at the end of the chapter. All three hypotheses try to explain *lewy* as if it denoted a function, but according to the Bible the word originated as the proper name of one of Jacob's sons. This proper name could be a shortened form of Levi-El, which has been discovered in texts from Mari (*La-wi-ili*), and was previously known in an Egyptian form (*Rw'r*). The name seems to mean 'attached to God, a client of God' or something similar.

2. *The hereditary priesthood*

In the ancient East, professions were generally hereditary, and crafts were handed down from father to son.[1] This was particularly true of Egypt, where, at one time, no one was allowed to practise any trade other than that practised by his father. Long genealogies show how highly this system of succession was esteemed, and under Darius I, one architect even pretended that he could trace his ancestry back through twenty-four generations to Imhotep, the builder of the pyramid at Zaqqara.

Such a system was particularly suitable for the priesthood; it ensured that sanctuaries were well looked after and kept in good repair, and that religious rites were left unchanged: the father would initiate his son into the skills required of him. We know that the priesthood was hereditary in Egypt at least from the XIXth Dynasty onwards, and anyone who could prove his priestly ancestry was assured of entry into the priestly caste. In Assyria, at least among certain categories of priests, the succession passed from father to son. There is evidence of priestly houses in Phoenician and Punic inscriptions, too; at Palmyra, the priesthood seems to have been restricted to certain families; among the pre-Islamic Arabs, every sanctuary belonged to a particular family which owned it from generation to generation; and finally, we may recall, as an example from another civilization, the great priestly families attached to the sanctuaries of Greece.

It is not surprising, then, that the priesthood was hereditary in Israel, too. A few examples from the texts which everyone recognizes as ancient will suffice to illustrate this remark. The Levite whose services Mikah had engaged became custodian of the sanctuary at Dan, and his descendants continued to serve there (Jg 18: 30). Eli was the priest at Shiloh, and two of his sons were also priests there (1 S 1-2). When the Ark was at Qiryath-Yearim, the priesthood remained in the line descended from Abinadab (1 S 7: 1; 2 S 6: 3). At Nob, Ahimelek had around him 'all the house of his father, the priests of Nob' (1 S 22: 11), eighty-five of whom were put to death by Saul (1 S 22: 18); another, Ebyathar, escaped and lived to become David's priest (1 S 22: 20-23).

On the other hand, these same ancient texts depict the Levites as strangers to the places where they exercise their functions. The Levite mentioned in Jg 17-18 was first a resident alien, a *ger*, in Bethlehem of Judah; later he tendered his services to Mikah in the hill-country of Ephraim, and in the

1. Cf. pp. 49 and 77.

end he migrated, with the men of Dan, to the North. The Levite in Jg 19 was a resident alien in the hill-country of Ephraim, but he had a woman from Bethlehem in Judah as his concubine; and when he wished to avenge the crime of Gibeah, he appealed not to his kinsfolk, as the law of blood-vengeance required, but to all the tribes of Israel. From the texts listed in this and the preceding paragraph, three conclusions may be drawn: first, that the priesthood was hereditary in certain families; secondly, that these families could stay in one sanctuary for generations; thirdly, that they were not bound to stay in the same place, for they were not tied to a particular region. All this suggests that these families formed a group which was bound together not because it lived in one region, but because all its members performed the same functions; they formed a priestly tribe.

3. *The priestly tribe of Levi*

This, in fact, is how the Israelite priesthood is presented in the Bible as we have it to-day. The descendants of Levi, Jacob's son, were set apart to perform sacred functions by a positive intervention of God (Nb 1: 50; 3: 6f.). They were taken by God, or given to God, instead of the first-born of Israel (Nb 3: 12; 8: 16). According to Nb 3: 6, they were to assist Aaron, but according to Ex 32: 25-29, they were chosen in opposition to Aaron since he had encouraged idolatry among the people; lastly, according to our present text of Dt 10: 6-9, it was only after the death of Aaron that they were chosen by Moses.

They held, in consequence, a special place among the people: they were not counted in the census of the other tribes (Nb 1: 47-49; all chapter 4; 26: 62). They had no share in Israel (Nb 18: 20; Dt 18: 1), and were not allotted any territory in the division of Canaan, for 'Yahweh is their inheritance' (Jos 13: 14, 33; 14: 3-4; 18: 7). Instead, they were provided with revenues or tithes (Nb 18: 21-24), and with real estate in the territories of the other tribes, *i.e.* the Levitical towns (Nb 35: 1-8; Jos 21: 1-42; 1 Ch 6: 39-66). Hence the members of the priestly tribe are commonly referred to as sons of Levi or Levites.

One branch within this tribe received the promise of a perpetual priesthood, as a result of which the other Levites were relegated to a subordinate position and restricted to the less important functions of the cult: this branch was the family of Aaron, Moses' brother (Ex 29: 9, 44; 40: 15). The priesthood was handed on to the sons of Aaron, Eleazar and Ithamar (Nb 3: 4), and the promise was later renewed in favour of Phinehas, the son of Eleazar (Nb 25: 11-13). According to 1 Ch 24: 3, the priesthood of Shiloh, of Nob and of Jerusalem itself, until the dismissal of Ebyathar, was descended from Ithamar. Sadoq, who replaced Ebyathar (1 K 2: 35) traced his ancestry back to Aaron through Eleazar, and his family retained the priesthood until the ruin of the Temple (1 Ch 5: 30-41; 6: 35-38; Esd 7: 1-5).

The Bible contains several examples of Levitical genealogies (Gn 46: 11; Ex 6: 16-25; Nb 26: 57-60 and especially 1 Ch 5: 27 to 6: 38, which goes down to the Exile). One incident which took place after the return from the Exile underlines the importance of these genealogies: those who could not bring evidence of their ancestry were excluded from the priesthood (Esd 2: 62; Ne 7: 64).

4. *Historical development*

Nevertheless, if we compare these various texts with one another, the differences between them become evident. We have already mentioned that it is not certain when, or why, the Levites were chosen for the service of the sanctuary. Even the genealogy in Ex 6: 16-25 is composed of different elements, and that in Nb 26: 57-58 gives two different divisions of the clans of Levi. The genealogies in 1 Ch 5-6 combine and harmonize information of various kinds. In addition, some of the texts were not edited until a fairly late period, and the data they contain are by no means in perfect harmony with what the older texts say. The editors of these later texts knew that the tribe of Levi alone had the right to perform liturgical functions, and saw the pre-eminence of the priesthood of Jerusalem; they must have regarded these two privileges as dating back to the earliest period of the people's history, though in fact they emerged only after a long development.

(a) *Non-Levitical priests.* In the period of the Judges and at the beginning of the monarchy, not all priests were 'Levites'. Mikah, a man of Ephraim, appointed his own son a priest (Jg 17: 5). Samuel, too, was an Ephraimite (1 S 1: 1), but he was attached to the sanctuary at Shiloh, wore the priest's loincloth (1 S 2: 18), and offered sacrifices (1 S 7: 9; 9: 13; 10: 8); it was only centuries later that he and his ancestors were given a place in a Levitical genealogy (1 Ch 6: 18-23). Abinadab was a man of Qiryath-Yearim, but his son Eleazar was appointed to be the priest in charge of the Ark (1 S 7: 1). In the lists of David's chief ministers, the sons of David are mentioned as priests, and they must have belonged to the tribe of Judah (2 S 8: 18). Ira the Yairite, who belonged to a clan of Manasseh (2 S 20: 26) is also called a priest, and in spite of 1 Ch 18: 17, there is no reason to think that the word *kohen* has any other meaning in this context.

The action of Jeroboam I must be given separate consideration: according to 1 K 12: 31; 13: 33 (cf. 2 K 17: 32); 2 Ch 13: 9, he appointed to the royal sanctuary at Bethel priests who were not of Levi's line. It is, of course, possible that Jeroboam appointed non-Levitical priests, like those just mentioned; later we shall consider the same possibility with reference to the priests who served the Temple in Jerusalem.[1] But the texts which record this action of Jeroboam were edited by men in the school of Deuteronomy, whose home lay in Judah, and who were anxious to condemn a hated rival to the Temple; is it not possible that they were trying to blacken Jeroboam, Bethel and its priests? After all, there were Levites in other sanctuaries of the Northern kingdom (cf. Dt 18: 6 and 2 K 23: 9), even in the other royal sanctuary set up by Jeroboam at Dan (Jg 18: 30).

This latter sanctuary traced its origin back to the migration of the men of Dan, and the story of their migration throws light on the history of the priesthood (Jg 17-18). Mikah had installed his son as priest when a Levite passed by. He engaged the Levite immediately and exclaimed: 'Now I know that Yahweh will grant me prosperity, because I have this Levite as priest' (Jg 17: 13). The Levite was Yehonathan, son of Gershom, Moses' son (Jg 18: 30). There is no reason to doubt the truth of this detail in such an ancient story, though it scandalized the Massoretes so much that they added a letter to make the text read 'Manasses' instead of 'Moses'. Nor is there any reason to deny the Levitical ancestry of Moses himself, which is asserted by Ex 2: 1 (Elohistic tradition) and traced in detail both by the Priestly tradition (Ex 6: 20; Nb 26: 59) and by the Chronicler (1 Ch 5: 29; 23: 13).

Therefore we can say that even from the period of the Judges, the Israelites preferred to have a Levite as priest, and the only Levite of the period whose genealogy we can trace is a descendant of Moses, and, through Moses, of Levi. In the first half of the eighth century, at the very latest, the priestly tribe of Levi was quite certainly in existence, and alone exercised the priesthood (Dt 33: 8-11). Like the other tribes of Israel,[2] this tribe must have incorporated into itself other stock, but these newcomers were received into an already existing line.

(b) *Levite-priests*. The Books of Kings are interested only in the priesthood of Jerusalem, which we shall study later.[3] Apart from the accusation against Jeroboam (which, we said, may be without foundation), they never once mention the Levites, and to find any record of them under the monarchy, one must open Deuteronomy. It is still the common opinion that this book equates priests and Levites, and attributes to both the same functions. The entire tribe of Levi was set apart to carry the Ark, to serve God and to bless the people (Dt 10: 8), and members of this tribe are called 'the priests, the Levites' (Dt 17: 9, 18; 18: 1; 21: 5; 24: 8; 31: 9). The text of Dt 18: 1 should be translated: 'the Levite priests, all the tribe of Levi', with the two phrases in apposition, and not 'the Levite priests and all the tribe of Levi'. The text could scarcely bear the latter meaning, for this would make a distinction between Levites who were priests and others who were not. There are, of course, texts which use the word 'priest' alone, or 'Levite'

1. Cf. pp. 372 ff. 2. Cf. p. 6. 3. Cf. p. 372.

alone, but a comparison of these texts proves that the terms are employed as synonyms. Thus, in Dt 31: 9, it is 'the priests, the Levites' who carry the Ark, whereas in Dt 31: 25 it is the Levites; again, Dt 18: 6-7 makes provision for a Levite, when he comes to the central sanctuary, to perform the functions of a priest together with all his brother Levites.

Nevertheless, within the book of Deuteronomy itself, a certain distinction can be perceived. It has recently been argued that the 'Levite-priests' were the servants of the central sanctuary; in general, this is true, but it does not apply to Dt 21: 5, where the Levite-priests are those in any town near which a murder has been committed. Conversely, in Dt 18: 7, we read of 'Levites', not 'Levite-priests', although the text refers to the central sanctuary. The terminology of Deuteronomy then, is not hard and fast, and the book implies that all the Levites could perform priestly functions. In practice, however, the great number of Levites made it impossible for everyone of them to find employment at the central sanctuary in Jerusalem. Those Levites who were not employed in the service of the altar did not, of course, share its emoluments (Dt 18: 1-4), and since their tribe had no territory assigned to it, they had no source of income. Hence the writer of Deuteronomy commends to the charity of the Israelites 'the Levite who dwells in thy gates' along with the stranger, the fatherless and the widow, *i.e.* all those who had no assured means of livelihood (Dt 12: 12, 18, 19; 14: 27, 29; 16: 11, 14; 26: 11-13). But every Levite retained his priestly rights, and when he came to the central sanctuary, he not only officiated there but received a stipend equal to that of his brother Levites who were attached to the sanctuary (Dt 18: 6-7).

These prescriptions are not a codification of the reform of Josias. They date from before it, and could not be applied in their entirety even at the moment of reform, cf. 2 K 23: 9: 'Nevertheless, the priests of the high places could not go up to the altar of Yahweh in Jerusalem, though they ate unleavened bread among their brothers'. These 'priests of the high places' were Levites, and the clergy of Jerusalem, jealous of their own privileges, did not allow them to take part in the liturgy; the mention of unleavened bread is no doubt a reference to the great Passover which closed the reform (2 K 23: 21-23); *i.e.* instead of applying the rules of Dt 18: 6-7, the priests of Jerusalem followed the line of conduct indicated in Dt 12: 11-12.

The position of the Levites, then, as described in Deuteronomy, was not the result of Josias' reform, but it must have been connected with some movement which sought to centralize worship; here we meet once more the problem already discussed when we were speaking about the Deuteronomic law allowing only one sanctuary.[1] The inequality in position between those Levites who were ministers of the sanctuaries and those who were scattered among the tribes was either a result of some attempted reform in

1. Cf. pp. 338-339.

the Northern kingdom, or a reflection of the reform attempted by Ezechias. The question of the priesthood is, however, more complicated, and a third solution is possible. Before there was any reform or any project of reform seeking to restrict legitimate worship to one place, there was both in Israel and in Judah a movement to draw the faithful to the great national sanctuaries of Jerusalem and Bethel. The local sanctuaries continued in existence, but their guardians had suffered from the competition, their revenues had decreased and many of their members had lost their positions; they could still have offered their services as priests, but in the meantime they were reduced to the position of resident aliens, *gerîm*, as Deuteronomy describes them. Thus a distinction already existed, *de facto* though not *de jure*, between the priests of the large sanctuaries (or, during the attempts at reform, of the sole sanctuary) and the priests in the provinces.

(c) *Priests and Levites.* In Deuteronomy, the distinction between priests and Levites lies under the surface; in Ezechiel it is explicit. The main text is Ez 44: 6-31. The Israelites sinned by introducing uncircumcised men into the service of the Temple: this is a reference to the public slaves employed in the Temple, the descendants of those slaves employed by Solomon (cf. Esd 2: 55-58), the '*nᵉthînîm*' ('given')[1] whose origin went back to David, according to Esd 8: 20. These men, says the prophet, will be replaced by the Levites who helped Israel to commit idolatry; but as a punishment, the Levites will be forbidden to perform strictly priestly functions and will be relegated to lower offices: they will slaughter the victims and be at the service of the people (Ez 44: 6-14). Clearly, Ezechiel is not referring to priests who worshipped idols; he could never assign to them a place in the future Temple. He is referring to Levites who had served the small sanctuaries where worship was not always pure; they are the Levites in the provinces mentioned in Deuteronomy, those whom 2 K 23: 9 calls the 'priests of the high places', those whose worship was suppressed in Josias' reform. In Ezechiel, we can perceive a distinct echo of this reform, and of the incidents which it provoked; the violence of Ezechiel's protest shows that these struggles did not happen in the distant past. And yet the prophet is anxious to give these Levites a recognized standing; they are to be accepted among the clergy, but in an inferior rank.

Ezechiel contrasts them with the Levite priests, and this term too reminds us of Deuteronomy. Priestly functions are to be reserved to this class: these alone may approach Yahweh, offer up fat and blood, and go into the sanctuary. This close contact with holy things binds them to observe special rules of purity (Ez 44: 15-31). They are called sons of Sadoq in Ez 44: 15, and also in Ez 40: 46; 43: 19; 48: 11: in short, this class represents the priesthood belonging to the Temple of Jerusalem. Here again, Ezechiel gives his approval to the reform of Josias.

1. Cf. p. 89.

There are still other texts which tell of a distinction within the ranks of the clergy. There was one room for the 'priests who serve the Temple' and another for the 'priests who serve the altar, *i.e.* the sons of Sadoq' (Ez 40: 45-46). Some land was reserved for priests who served the sanctuary, and some other land for the Levites who served the Temple (Ez 45: 4-5). There were kitchens for the 'priests' to cook the sacrifices offered for sin, and other kitchens for 'those who serve the Temple' to cook the sacrifices for the people (Ez 46: 20-24). The territory around the Temple was allotted to the priests, the sons of Sadoq, who had not gone astray, and a different area was allotted to the Levites, who had gone astray (Ez 48: 11-14). All these distinctions repeat, and are in conformity with, the distinction drawn in Ez 44: 6-31, where the Levites are 'those who serve the Temple' (v. 11), and the priests are 'those who serve the sanctuary' (v. 15). But it is interesting to note that in Ez 40: 45-46, both categories are called 'priests'. The passage must have been written soon after Deuteronomy.

Ezechiel, then, is not a radical innovator; he is merely trying to regularize a situation which had long existed and which had deteriorated as a result of Josias' reform. We must now compare this project with the legislation of the priestly writings. The supposed background to this legislation is the sojourn in the desert. According to Nb 3: 6-9, the Levites were placed at the service of Aaron and his sons, were 'given' to them, and served the Dwelling; according to Nb 8: 19, they were 'given' to Aaron and his sons for the service of the Tent; according to Nb 18: 1-7, which is the principal text, they were to serve Aaron and the Tent and they were 'given', but Aaron and his sons performed the strictly priestly functions, such as the service of the altar and the sanctuary, and of 'everything which stands behind the veil'. Here there is an evident parallel with Ezechiel: the Dwelling, the Tent of desert days, is here equated with the Temple of Ezechiel; the Levites are 'given' and, as in Ezechiel, they take the place of those 'given' men who had formerly been attached to the Temple. Thus far there is harmony, and the differences are by comparison of secondary importance: the main one is that Numbers ascribes the priesthood to Aaron, whereas Ezechiel called the priests 'sons of Sadoq'; we shall see later what this difference of names implies.[1] Clearly, the text of Numbers was edited after Ezechiel: it is more precise, more calm, and devoid of any polemical note; the Levites were not identified with the 'given' servants until after the return from the Exile (cf. the lists in Esd 2 and Esd 8: 20), and the Aaronitic ancestry of the priests is stressed only in secondary passages in the books of Esdras and Nehemias (Esd 7: 1-5; Ne 10: 39; 12: 47). On the other hand, it is hard to admit that legislative arrangements like those in Numbers can have been inspired by an idealistic description like that in Ezechiel. It is more probable that both texts, Numbers and Ezechiel, represent two parallel

1. Cf. pp. 394-397.

trends originating from a common source, *i.e.* the situation created in Jerusalem by the reform of Josias. Indeed, it is not impossible that the laws in Numbers are a development of rules issued towards the end of the monarchy by the priests in the Temple.

Whatever solution be preferred, the Levites were distinguished from the priests and relegated to an inferior position, and this explains why they were not over-anxious to return from exile. In the list of Esd 2: 40 = Ne 7: 43, there were only 74 Levites as against 4,289 priests, and in his own caravan, Esdras had difficulty in mustering a mere 38 Levites (Esd 8: 18–19). When we discuss the priesthood of the Second Temple, we shall see how the Levites tried to improve their status.[1]

5. *Levitical towns*

Deuteronomy describes the Levites as scattered throughout the land, living as resident aliens, and deserving of charity from those who possess the land; Ezechiel planned to group them together in a region near Jerusalem; but the book of Josue allots them 48 towns, including the environs, and these towns are divided equally among the twelve tribes; Josue's list is repeated, with some variations, in 1 Ch 6: 39–66. According to Jos 21: 2, God himself had ordered Moses to grant cities of this kind to the Levites, and this is explicitly asserted in Nb 35: 1–8 also. Lastly, the law of Jubilees contains a special clause concerning these towns (Lv 25: 33–34). The essential text is Jos 21, on which the others depend.

The problem raised by these texts is far from simple. At first sight, the institution of Levitical towns seems to be a Utopia thought out in later days. Many of the 48 towns, theoretically four in each tribe, were important centres, and it is impossible to imagine their being left exclusively to the Levites. And, we should add, the Levites were to possess also the land around these cities, to a greater or lesser extent (Nb 35: 5). Next, the list includes the six cities of refuge (Nb 35: 6; Jos 21: 13, 21, 27, etc.), which were, basically, a very ancient institution[2]; but the connection between the cities of refuge and Levitical towns was introduced at a later date, and those texts which give independent witness to cities of refuge do not consider them as Levitical towns. Lastly, the list presumes that there is a clear distinction between priests and Levites, that the Levites are divided into three classes, and that the priests are known as 'the sons of Aaron'; none of these things is ever mentioned in a pre-exilic text.

In its present form, then, Jos 21, like Jos 20 on the cities of refuge, belongs to the latest edition of the book of Josue; for our present purposes, it matters little whether we ascribe this edition to someone of the priestly school or to a later Deuteronomic editor. But the chapter on cities of refuge has a kernel of ancient tradition within it, and the list of Levitical towns might

1. Cf. pp. 393–394. 2. Cf. pp. 160–163.

also be based on a pre-exilic tradition. Two hypotheses have recently been put forward. The first states one important fact: the cities in the list were in existence and ruled by the Israelites only towards the end of David's reign and under that of Solomon; therefore the original list and the institutions of Levitical towns must date from this period, from the first half of Solomon's reign. The second hypothesis brings forward an objection to this view which is rather shrewd: if we plot these towns on a map, there are only two zones not occupied by the Levites, the centre of the kingdom of Judah to the south of Jerusalem and the centre of the kingdom of Israel (Shechem is an insertion). The explanation of this fact may be sought in the reform of Josias: the king brought all the priests in Judah to Jerusalem (2 K 23: 8), and put to death all the priests of the high places in the towns of Samaria (2 K 23: 19-20). The list therefore belongs to the time of Josias, or to some period after him, but was written before the return from the Exile. This interpretation is not convincing. The historicity of 2 K 23: 19-20 is not above suspicion, and 2 K 23: 8 expressly states that the towns of Judah from which the priests came stretched 'from Geba to Beersheba', *i.e.* from the entire kingdom of Judah, in which there were a dozen Levitical towns outside the centre. The only remaining possibility is that the list represents a partial execution of the measures taken by Josias. The first hypothesis does not explain the lacunae, but the second explains only the lacunae and gives no reason for the rest.

In the end, we must confess that this list is a riddle. Its systematization is certainly Utopian, but otherwise it must be based upon an ancient document, and must at some time have reflected a real situation. Several of the towns mentioned are referred to elsewhere in the Bible as the home-towns of priestly families. On the other hand, it does not represent a list of sanctuaries served by Levites; in fact, it seems rather to represent the home-towns of Levites who were not employed at the big sanctuaries, *i.e.* Levites who had no assured source of income and who were therefore in the position of the Levites described in Deuteronomy. Let us propose a slight modification of the first of the hypotheses just mentioned, and take the risk of stating our own view: the list originally represented the dispersal of the Levite population after the foundation of the Temple and after the organization of the official cult at Bethel. The foundation of the Temple would explain why no other Levites are mentioned in the immediate environs of Jerusalem, and the foundation at Bethel would explain why there were no Levitical cities in the centre of Israel either.

6. *Was there ever a non-priestly tribe called Levi?*

According to the Bible, this priestly tribe originated from Levi, one of twelve sons of Jacob. We have already stated that in the blessings of Moses

(Dt 33: 8-11) this same Levi, considered as representing his descendants, received as his inheritance the functions of the priesthood. But two other texts present the man in a very different light. In the blessings of Jacob (Gn 49: 5-7), Levi and Simeon are condemned together for their violence; they have killed men and mutilated bulls and will therefore be scattered throughout Israel. This text is evidently connected with the same tradition as Gn 34: in order to avenge the honour of their sister Dinah, Simeon and Levi made a treacherous attack on the inhabitants of Shechem, killed the men and made off with the cattle, and for this crime they were condemned by Jacob. Other texts show that Simeon was a non-priestly group which very soon lost its autonomy and whose members were scattered throughout the territory of Judah. It is reasonable to conclude that there was also a non-priestly tribe called Levi which suffered the same fate.

Some critics, however, reject this conclusion. They hold that the story in Gn 34 is mere legend, and that the oracle in Gn 49 is an artificial explanation of the unusual situation in which the priestly tribe of Levi found itself: they hold, then, that the tribe of Levi had always been priests, that it had never had any part in politics, and that its members lived scattered among the other tribes. Against this, we know that Levi formed part of the old system of the Twelve Tribes; it is improbable that at some later date, when tribal divisions corresponded to territorial divisions, a tribe which had no territory was introduced into the Twelve Tribes. The blessings of Jacob, in their present form, go back to the reign of David, and some oracles among them are even older. And Gn 34 has none of the characteristics of an aetiological narrative; nor does it contain any allusion to the dispersal of Simeon and Levi; yet, according to the thesis we are opposing, it was written to explain this dispersal! Gn 34 relates a fact, and Gn 49: 5-7 gives the consequences of that fact. The fact itself is an episode from the pre-history of Israel. The groups which belonged to Simeon and Levi had a serious quarrel with the indigenous population near Shechem; the quarrel may have occurred when they were passing through the area with their flocks, or perhaps when they had settled in the region before Ephraim and Manasseh arrived and drove the remaining members of these tribes further south. We can only make up hypotheses, but we should not reject this very ancient tradition which takes us back before the time of Moses; there was a non-priestly tribe of Levi, and its ancestor's name is found, in its unabbreviated form, both in cuneiform and in Egyptian inscriptions.

And yet the problem with which we are concerned is not thereby resolved. One could suppose (and some have done so) that the connection of this profane tribe of Levi with the priestly tribe of Levites was purely accidental: the latter would have been called Levites because the word expressed their function. Eventually the function became hereditary, and the similarity between the name given to the priests and the name of Jacob's son would then have led people to connect these men, now a priestly tribe, with the old, profane tribe which had disappeared. This leads us to our last question: what was the origin of the Levites?

7. *The origin of the Levites*

In Hebrew, the same word is used for 'Levi' and 'Levite': *lewy*. Even those texts which refer to the tribe of Levi use the same word, but with the article, to make it a common noun: *hallewy* (Ex 6: 19; Nb 3: 20; Dt 10: 8, etc.). All the many texts which speak of the Levites employ the plural of this word, *lᵉwiyyim*, as if it were the name of men performing a function.

On the other hand, among the inscriptions discovered in the Minaean script and dialect at El-Ela, the ancient Dedan, in Northern Arabia, there are several which contain the word *lw'* or, in the feminine, *lw't*. This word has sometimes been translated 'priest' or even 'Levite', by reason of its resemblance with the Hebrew *lewy*; and some writers have concluded that the Israelites adopted the institution of Levites from those early Arabs with whom they had been in contact at Sinai. Consequently, the connection of the Levites with a profane tribe of Levi (whether the latter existed or not) is quite artificial.

Close study of these inscriptions, combined with more accurate research into the epigraphy and history of ancient Arabia, has led to a very different solution. The words *lw'* and *lw't* do not mean 'priest' or 'priestess', but denote an object given to a god, a pledge. This object may be a person, man or woman, or a thing; but it is never a person engaged in performing the cult. Since this meaning is quite different from that of the Hebrew *lewy*, it is quite possible that there is no connection between the terms. Even if we admit that the primary meaning is 'consecrated, given', and that the word evolved differently in the two languages, this does not mean that the Hebrew borrowed from the Minaean. In fact, the Minaeans were a people from the South of Arabia, and their kings did not rule the region around Dedan in Northern Arabia until the 4th century B.C., at the earliest. Now the words *lw'* and *lw't* are found only in Minaean inscriptions from Northern Arabia, at Dedan, and never in those from the South, nor in any other South Arabian dialect. It is quite possible then, that they were borrowed from a population of Dedan which was neither Minaean nor even proto-Arab in the widest sense. Again, we should not forget that, according to Arabic authors writing in the early days of Islam, the oasis of Dedan was then occupied by Jews, who seemed to have been there a very long time. A recently discovered inscription of Nabonidus states that this king installed a colony of soldiers in Northern Arabia, at Dedan itself, and that these soldiers were recruited, for the most part, from the West of his empire. There probably were Jews among them, and if so, then Jews, including Levites, would have been living at Dedan two centuries before it came under the control of the Minaeans. If anyone borrowed the word *lewy*, it was the Minaeans, who modified the sense of the term and gave it a feminine which did not exist in Hebrew.

Furthermore, it is not so evident as is sometimes claimed that 'Levite' in Hebrew is primarily the name of a function. It is significant that in the Bible this word occurs only once in the construct state, as a common noun (Ne 10: 1), whereas *kohen* is often used in this way ('the priests of Yahweh, of the high places', etc., 'my priests, your priests, their priests', etc.). In its form and usage, 'Levite' is first and foremost a *nomen gentilitium*: it means 'a descendant of Levi' and there is no reason to reject the biblical tradition which constantly connects the Levites with their ancestor Levi.

After the very ancient episode recorded in Gn 34, we find the remainder of the tribe of Simeon associated with Judah in the South. The survivors of the tribe of Levi probably accompanied them. But, whereas the Simeonites integrated themselves into the surrounding population, the descendants of Levi specialized in cultic functions. Ethnology and history provide other examples of the way in which an ethnic minority has specialized in a particular profession or trade, not excluding professions associated with worship. The ancient accounts of relations between the Levites and Judah and the South are clear enough. According to the patriarchal traditions, Levi was a son of Leah, like Simeon and Judah; and according to the traditions about the wanderings in the desert, the Levites were set apart for the cult during this period; they are closely associated with Moses, and he is one of them. Moses had certainly been in Egypt, and the Levites with him; this would explain the surprisingly high proportion of Egyptian names found among them. The text of Nb 26 : 58 has preserved a division of Levites into clans which does not harmonize with the canonical division into three classes, representing three families, the Gershonites, Qehathites and Merarites. The text in Nb 26 however, lists five clans: Libnite, Hebronite, Mehlite, Mushite, Qorahite. The Greek version omits the Mahlite clan: of the other four names, Mushite is generally interpreted as a *nomen gentilitium* derived from Moses, and Qorahite is connected with the Qorah of 1 Ch 2: 43 (a list of the 'sons' of Caleb, most of which are place-names: Qorah is listed between Hebron and Tappuah). The Libnites and Hebronites were obviously the inhabitants of Libnah and Hebron. This list is very ancient, certainly pre-monarchic; it tells us where the Levites lived, and seems to place them all in the territory of Judah. From the time of the Judges they began to spread further afield. The Levite who figures in the story of the crime of Gibeah lived in the hill-country of Ephraim, but he still had contacts with Judah, where he had taken a concubine (Jg 19: 1). The Levite engaged by Mikah was connected with a clan of Judah (Jg 17: 7) and was recognized by the men of Dan (and therefore must have lived among them, Jg 18: 3); he was engaged by Mikah in the hill-country of Ephraim (Jg 17: 1), and later followed the men of Dan north to the sources of the Jordan (Jg 18: 30); yet there is nothing whatever to make his Levitical ancestry suspect; indeed, it is expressly affirmed by the last text, and he would evidently belong to the Mushite clan. This is just one example of the way in which men of this tribe spread over the country away from Judah, and when the document which forms the basis of the list of Levitical towns in Jos 21 was first edited, the Levites were already scattered through all the tribes of Israel.

This geographical expansion was accompanied by a corresponding expansion in the original nucleus of the tribe. Levi, like the other tribes, presumably adopted into its ranks individuals and even groups; entire families which had officiated as priests in the various sanctuaries would thus be integrated into the tribe of Levi, whatever their ancestry.

We are very ready to admit that this reconstruction of the early history of the Levites is still a hypothesis, but it seems to take into account those rare ancient texts which are certainly trustworthy; it also explains how the profane tribe of Levi (which certainly existed) was transformed into the priestly tribe of Levites, and how this latter became one of the great institutions of Israel. But there is certainly no need to look for the origin of this institution outside Israel.

CHAPTER SEVEN

THE PRIESTHOOD IN JERUSALEM UNDER THE MONARCHY

THOUGH there were many sanctuaries in Palestine from the early days of the monarchy down to the reform of Josias, we have no detailed information about the priests who served in these sanctuaries. Jerusalem is the only exception, and this is not surprising. The Temple at Jerusalem was the richest and the most frequented centre of worship; it was the official sanctuary of the kingdom of Judah, and its priests were the only priests who played any part at all in the political life of the nation. Furthermore, the only sources we can use are the Books of Samuel and Kings, all four of which were written in Judah under the influence of Deuteronomy, and edited, therefore, by men who refused to acknowledge the legitimacy of any sanctuary other than the Temple. Yet even the information which these books provide is scanty, and often difficult to interpret. We should be able to present a more complete picture if we could feel safe in using everything which the Books of Chronicles relate about the organization of the clergy by David (1 Ch 23-26); unfortunately, the clergy (whose divisions and tasks are described in minute detail) are there spoken of as serving in the Temple, and the Temple, in David's time, had not yet been built. The only possible conclusion is that this picture reflects the ideal of the Chronicler, and that it was inspired by the situation in his own day; we shall use these chapters, therefore, for the history of the priesthood after the Exile.

1. *Ebyathar and Sadoq*

1 S 22: 20-23 says that the sole survivor after Saul's massacre of the priests in Nob was called Ebyathar, the son of Ahimelek and grandson of Ahitub, through whom he could trace his ancestry to Eli, the priest of Shiloh (1 S 14: 3, cf. 1 K 2: 27). It is impossible to trace his ancestry any further in pre-exilic texts, but the names of Eli's two sons, Ophni and Phinehas, show that the family was of Levitical origin (cf. also 1 S 2: 27, which is the work of a later editor). Ebyathar took refuge with David and followed him in his wanderings, acting as his priest (1 S 23: 6, 9; 30: 7).

The next time Ebyathar is mentioned is after the conquest of Jerusalem, and he is then in the service of the Ark, along with another priest, Sadoq

(2 S 15: 24-29). These two priests are always mentioned together right to the end of David's reign (2 S 17: 15; 19: 12), and are named next to each other in both lists of David's chief officials (2 S 8: 17 and 20: 25). In every text Sadoq is mentioned before Ebyathar; Ebyathar seems, therefore, to have been relegated to a secondary position after the king had moved his capital to Jerusalem. In the intrigues over the succession to David, Sadoq supported Solomon; but Ebyathar (who had always remained faithful to David himself, cf. 1 K 2: 26) supported Adonias against Solomon (1 K 1: 7, 19, 25; 2: 22), and consequently, when David died, he soon found himself banished by Solomon to his family estate at Anathoth (1 K 2: 26-27). This was a Levitical town (Jos 21: 18) and the nearest one to the disused sanctuary at Nob where Ebyathar had begun his career.

Sadoq became the sole holder of the priestly office (1 K 2: 35). He must have died shortly afterwards, for he is never again mentioned in the history of Solomon's reign; and in the list of the main officials which was compiled in the middle of the reign, it is his son Azaryahu who holds the title of priest (1 K 4: 2). (The mention of Sadoq and Ebyathar in verse 4 of this list is obviously an interpolation.)

Sadoq, then, appears in history only after the conquest of Jerusalem; at first he shares the priesthood with Ebyathar and in the end ousts his partner. What was his origin? The question is extremely obscure, because the Bible has provided him with two genealogies. The first makes him a descendant of Eleazar (1 Ch 24: 3), and 1 Ch 5: 29-34 and 6: 35-38 give his complete genealogy from Aaron through Eleazar. The second (cf. the Hebrew text of 2 S 8: 17) calls Sadoq the son of Ahitub, and seems to connect him with the family of Eli. The genealogies on Chronicles, however, are artificial, and Sadoq cannot possibly have been a descendant of Eli since his appointment is presented as the fulfilment of the curse pronounced against the house of Eli (1 K 2: 27; cf. 1 S 2: 27-36; 3: 11-14). Furthermore, there is, in 2 S 8: 17, an indication that the verse is in disorder: it reads 'Sadoq, son of Ahitub, and Ahimelek, son of Ebyathar, were priests'; now Ebyathar was the son of Ahimelek, not his father (1 S 22: 20). The Syriac version has made this correction, but we must go further: in 1 S 22: 20, Ebyathar is called 'son of Ahimelek, the son of Ahitub', and it may be that in 1 S 8: 17 Ahitub has been transferred to make him father of Sadoq, perhaps by accident, or perhaps on purpose. The original reading would then be: 'Sadoq and Ebyathar, son of Ahimelek, son of Ahitub'. Thus Sadoq is left without any genealogy.

Several hypotheses have been advanced about his origin. Some suggest that he may have been the high priest of Gibeon. It is an idea of the Chronicler (1 Ch 16: 39) which has been adopted by some modern scholars: under David, Ebyathar would then have been in the service of the Ark, and Sadoq in the service of the Tent, which, at the time, was kept at Gibeon (cf. 2 Ch 1: 3). In the early texts, however, Sadoq is never mentioned except, like Ebyathar, in connection with the Ark. A second suggestion is that Sadoq was one of the priests at Qiryath-Yearim (1 S 7: 1), and that he took part in the transfer of the Ark to Jerusalem; according to 2 S 6: 3-4, the cart was driven by Uzzah and 'Ahyo'; it is suggested that instead of 'Ahyo', we should read ''*ahiw*', meaning 'his brother'. This brother would in fact be Sadoq, who afterwards remained at Jerusalem as one of the two men who carried the Ark: and Uzzah would have been replaced by Ebyathar (2 S 15: 29). There is no text which formally contradicts this theory, but neither is there one which gives it positive support; it is certainly possible, but it is not proven.

A third, and last, hypothesis enjoys great favour at the moment. Since Sadoq does not appear until after the capture of Jerusalem and since his genealogy is not given, may he not have belonged to the city of Jerusalem itself? His name reminds us of the ancient names connected with Jerusalem, such as Melchisedech in the time of Abraham, and Adoni-Sedeq at the time of the conquest. The suggestion is that he was the priest of the Jebusite sanctuary, and therefore the heir of Melchisedech (Gn 14: 18-20; Ps 110: 4).[1] David would have placed the Ark in the old sanctuary, and retained the services of its priest in order to win over those Jebusites who remained in the town. Certainly, there is nothing impossible in this idea of utilizing an old sanctuary, and of employing the priests who served that sanctuary; we have seen several examples of the way in which the early Israelites took over the sanctuaries of Canaan. Indeed, the character of the god who was worshipped in Jerusalem could have facilitated the change; it was not Baal, but El-'Elyon, one of the forms of El under which the Patriarchs had worshipped the true God,[2] and one of the titles Yahweh had appropriated.[3] The meeting between Abraham and Melchisedech (Gn 14: 18-20) could have been cited to justify the rights of Jerusalem's priesthood and to prove its ancient origin. If we hesitate to adopt this solution, it is for lack of positive evidence. First, it implies that a sanctuary of El-'Elyon was later used for the cult of Yahweh, and the texts never once mention any such sanctuary; the Ark was kept in a Tent until the end of David's reign. Secondly, Sadoq is never mentioned in the Bible except in connection with the Ark and the Tent of Yahweh.[4]

It is safer to admit that we do not know where Sadoq came from. Possibly he really was of Levitical origin, though not from the same branch as the house of Eli, and the later tradition in Chronicles may rest on a firm basis. We do know, however, that his descendants kept their position in Jerusalem until the Exile, and that the legitimacy of their priesthood was never called in question, though a feud continued between the house of Sadoq and the family of Ebyathar, which they had ousted.

1. Cf. p. 114.
2. Cf. p. 294.
3. Cf. p. 310.
4. Cf. p. 311.

2. *The descendants of Sadoq*

1 Ch 5: 34-41 gives a list of the men who succeeded Sadoq as head of the clergy in Jerusalem. It contains eleven names from Ahimaas (Sadoq's son) to Yehosadaq (the father of Josue, who was the first high priest after the Restoration, Ag 1: 1). This gives exactly twelve generations of priests from the building of the Temple under Solomon to its reconstruction after the Exile. Now the list of Sadoq's ancestors is given immediately before (1 Ch 5: 29-34), and this too has exactly twelve generations from the making of the Tent in the desert to the building of the Temple; and 12 generations of 40 years make exactly 480 years, as given in 1 K 6: 1. Thus the foundation of Solomon's Temple would mark the middle year in the history of Israel's sanctuary. This symmetry is deliberate, and other facts underline the artificial character of these lists. Ahimaas was undoubtedly Sadoq's son (2 S 15: 36), but Azaryahu, who was priest under Solomon, was another son of Sadoq, not his grandson (as 1 Ch 5: 35 has). Moreover, the list is incomplete; though it contains some names which are found elsewhere in the Bible (Azaryahu, 1 K 4: 2; Hilqiyyahu, 2 K 22: 4; Serayah, 2 K 25: 18; Yehosadaq, Ag 1: 1), it omits Yehoyada, the priest under Joas (2 K 12: 8), Uriyyah, the priest under Achaz (2 K 16: 10), and at least two others who are mentioned in the narrative part of Chronicles itself (an Azaryahu under Ozias, 2 Ch 26: 20, and an Azarya under Ezechias, 2 Ch 31: 10). Another difficulty is that the series Amarya-Ahitub-Sadoq recurs in identical form among the immediate ancestors of Sadoq (vv. 33-34) and among his descendants (vv. 37-38). The list, then, expresses a real fact, namely, the continuity of Sadoq's line, but it cannot be used to write a detailed history of his house.

The Books of Kings tell us very little about this history, apart from what they say about the relations between the priests and the kings, which will be studied later. It seems that the descendants of Sadoq were a conservative-minded family, with little liking for innovations which might change their way of life. We know, for example, that the religious reforms were initiated by the kings, not by the priests: cf. the reforms of Asa (1 K 15: 12-13; cf. 2 Ch 14: 2-4; 15: 1-15), of Ezechias (2 K 18: 3-4) and of Josias (2 K 23). The only exception to this is the revolution against Athaliah, directed by the priest Yehoyada, which culminated in the destruction of the temple of Baal (2 K 11: 18); but this revolt was primarily a reaction against the foreign queen and her entourage. The same Yehoyada is blamed for having neglected the upkeep of the Temple, and the integrity of the lay craftsmen is contrasted with the mean behaviour of the priests (2 K 12: 8 and 16). Here, as on other occasions, the kings and the priests were in opposition to each other; yet Sadoq's descendants never lost their standing and they even won a victory against Josias' reform when the Temple clergy succeeded in preventing the application of the law of Deuteronomy to the provincial priests who came to Jerusalem (2 K 23: 9).

The principal opponents of this Sadoqite monopoly were the descendants of Ebyathar. A trace of this struggle can be seen in the verses added to the history of Eli by someone from the Sadoqite camp; in 1 S 2: 27-36, Yahweh is made to say to Eli: 'I shall keep one of thy line near my altar to wear out his eyes with weeping and to break his spirit . . . I shall raise unto myself a faithful priest (*i.e.* Sadoq) . . . I shall ensure that his house endures . . . Every survivor of thy family will come and bow before him to have a little bit of money and a piece of bread'. The Sadoqites certainly rejoiced at the humiliation of their rivals, but the party of Ebyathar had one voice to speak in reply—that of Jeremias. This prophet came from a priestly family at Anathoth, the village to which Ebyathar had been banished, and he aroused the fury of the priests when he began to preach, in the Temple itself, against the Temple and its cult (Jr 7 and 26). In two texts, Jr 7: 14 and 26: 6, he predicts that the Temple at Jerusalem will meet the same fate as the sanctuary at Shiloh; we have just seen how the Sadoqites used to taunt their luckless rivals with the curse pronounced at Shiloh against the house of Eli, and it is hard not to see in these words of Jeremias a retort that their own Temple and priesthood will suffer the same fate.

It is unlikely that the Sadoqites, in their resistance to religious reform, confined themselves to polemic of the kind just mentioned, and it is probable that they tried to put forward a code of law which would be a rival to that of Deuteronomy. The basic laws which underlie the Law of Holiness in Lv 17-27 seems to stem from the priests of Jerusalem in the last years of the monarchy. In the next chapter we shall see how a compromise between these two conflicting parties and their tendencies was worked out in the post-exilic period.

3. *The priests and the kings*

The Temple in Jerusalem was a state sanctuary, and its priests were civil servants appointed by the king. The head of the clergy is mentioned among the king's officials (1 K 4: 2) and he was appointed and dismissed by the king (1 K 2: 27 and 35). The king issued all orders concerning the upkeep of the sanctuary and the furnishings to be used in worship. Even Yehoyada, who had placed Joas on the throne, had to bow to two orders of this same king, the second of which revoked one of the priests' privileges and placed them under the control of a lay official (2 K 12: 5-17); even the successors of Yehoyada could not emancipate themselves from this control (2 K 22: 3-7). Or, to take another example, when Achaz ordered Uriyyah to build a new altar, the priest obeyed without a word of protest (2 K 16: 10-16).

This last text is a reminder that the power of the king included more than the administration of the Temple; Achaz 'went up' to the altar he had ordered the priest to make, and there offered sacrifice. We discussed the intervention of the kings in public worship when we were treating royal institutions,[1] and we concluded that it was based on the sacral character of the king. He was not a priest in the strict sense, nor even the head of the clergy; but he was the patron of the priesthood.

Conflicts between the priests and kings were not unknown. The priest Yehoyada led the revolt which overthrew the regime of Athaliah (2 K 11). According to 2 Ch 24: 17-26, king Joas fell into evil ways after the death of Yehoyada, and ordered Zacharias, the son of Yehoyada, to be stoned to death; 2 K 12: 21-22 records without comment the subsequent assassination of the king, but the Chronicler presents it as the revenge of the priest's party. This story was not made up by the Chronicler; he must have taken it from the midrash on the Book of Kings to which he refers in 2 Ch 24: 27. Again, the conspiracy against Amasias was hatched in Jerusalem (2 K 14: 19; 2 Ch 25: 27), and it is often said that it was inspired by the priests. The Bible does not say so explicitly, but the revolts against Joas and against Amasias both followed a plundering of the Temple treasury, necessitated by the bad policies of these two kings (2 K 12: 19; 14: 14). Understandably, the priests would have been annoyed, but their annoyance was only one element amid the general dissatisfaction of the population. On the whole, the priests probably did try to prevent the king from intervening in the Temple and in affairs concerning the cult, and this opposition is described in a late narrative in Chronicles (2 Ch 26: 16-20): it tells how the priests dragged Ozias from the altar of incense when he was on the point of offering incense there. There certainly was friction, though the texts which record it are mainly post-exilic: the 'perfect peace' which Za 6: 13; cf. 4: 14 and the late passage in Jr 33: 17-26 foretold for the Messianic age did not always reign. Yet at least the alliance between the descendants of David and the line of Sadoq was never broken up; as a text of Sadoqite inspiration puts it, a 'faithful priest' always walked before Yahweh's Anointed (1 S 2: 35).

4. *The hierarchy*

There was in Jerusalem, as in all the great ancient sanctuaries, a large number of priests. Lucian (*De Dea Syra,* 42-43) says that there were at least three hundred priests at Hierapolis, not counting the singers and the Galli. Strabo (XII, ii, 3) says that the temple of Comana in Cappadocia had a staff of six thousand priests. The accounts from Citium show that there must have been many there also, and examples of this kind could be multiplied. Under Saul, the sanctuary at Nob was looked after by Ahimelek and eighty-five priests descended from Eli (1 S 22: 16, 18). Certainly, there

1. Cf. pp. 113-114.

must have been still more in the Temple at Jerusalem, but it is impossible to give any precise number.

These priests must have been organized in some way; who, then, was their head? The term 'high priest' (*hakkohen haggadôl*) is found only four times in pre-exilic texts (2 K 12: 11; 22: 4, 8; 23: 4); but in the parallels to these texts, 2 Ch 24: 11 (=2 K 12: 11) has *kohen harôsh* ('the head priest'), 2 Ch 34: 14, 18 (=2 K 22: 4, 8) has merely *kohen* and the Greek version of 2 K 23: 4 also presumes the reading *kohen*. Thus all four references to the 'high priest' before the Exile seem to be later modifications. Since the title 'high priest' did not exist before the Exile, some writers have argued that the king performed the functions attached to the office, just as the high priest after the Exile took the place of the king. In fact, the question is more complicated. We shall see in the next chapter how Josue, the first priest of the new Temple, was also the first to be called 'the high priest'; but beside Josue stood Zorobabel, the supreme civil authority, and the 'royal' character of the high priest was asserted only little by little. Nevertheless, it is quite true that before the Exile the king had supreme control over the Temple and its clergy; and that in certain circumstances, he officiated himself; yet the king was never a member of the hierarchy of priests.

The head of the clergy is usually referred to in the Bible as 'the priest', without any qualification; he was *the* priest (cf. the list of Solomon's ministers, 1 K 4: 2; Yehoyada 2 K 11: 9f.; 12: 8f.; Uriyyah, 2 K 16: 10f.; Is 8: 2; Hilqiyyahu, 2 K 22: 12, 14: all these were quite evidently heads of the clergy). The title 'head priest' (*kohen harôsh*) is found once in Kings (2 K 25: 18 and its parallel in Jr 52: 24) and several times in Chronicles (2 Ch 19: 11; 24:6 (?) and 11; 26:20); the formula is expanded in 2 Ch 31: 10 to 'the priest, the head of the house of Sadoq'.

But even if we leave aside the question of his title, it is quite evident that the clergy had someone at their head. (Similarly, we read of a 'head of the priests' in the texts from Ras Shamra and in several Phoenician inscriptions.) But one should not imagine that this head of the priesthood had the importance or the rank which the high priests had after the Exile. Before 587, the principal priest had control over the clergy of Jerusalem only, and he was himself responsible to the king (cf. 2 K 12: 8; 16: 10), whereas the high priest after the Exile was the religious and civil head of the community. Indeed, during that brief period when the Jews gained their independence under the Hasmoneans, the high priest acted as their king, and he even took the title of king from 104 onwards (Aristobulus I).

Immediately under the head priest was the 'second priest' (*kohen mishnê*, 2 K 23: 4 and 25: 18=Jr 52: 24, where the name is given, Sephanyahu). Sephanyahu is mentioned several times in the Book of Jeremias (Jr 21: 1; 37: 3); in Jr 29: 24-29 he is called 'the superintendent of the Temple' and he seems to have been responsible for policing the sanctuary; his predecessor in this office was called Yehoyada (Jr 29: 26), who had succeeded a man called Pashehur (Jr 20: 1-2).

After the head priest and the second priest, 2 K 23: 4 and 25: 18=Jr 52: 24 mention the 'keepers of the threshold'. These men are therefore the senior officials of the Temple, not mere door-keepers (2 Ch 34: 9 [cf. also 1 Ch 9: 22] seems to have confused them with the Levites who looked after the entrances). These officials were only three in number, according to 2 K 25: 18, and Joas placed them in charge of the collections from the people (2 K 12: 10; 22: 4).

As well as the five principal officers of the Temple, the 'elders of the priests' held an important position among the clergy. Ezechias sent them, along with the master of the palace and the royal secretary, to consult Isaias (2 K 19: 2; Is 37: 2). Jeremias took as witnesses some elders of the people and some elders of the priests (Jr 19: 1, in the Hebrew: the Greek text reads 'some priests'). If the analogy with the 'elders of the people' holds good,[1] the 'elders of the priests' must have been the heads of the priestly families; thus they would be forerunners of those men who headed the various divisions of the clergy after the Exile, the origins of which are attributed to the time of David by 1 Ch 24: 1-18.

5. *The revenues of the clergy*

Unlike the temples of Mesopotamia and of Egypt, the Temple in Jerusalem did not possess vast tracts of real estate; it was, however, a state sanctuary, and one must conclude that the king paid the normal expenses of public worship and the cost of repairs to the building. At least, he must have done so until the time of Joas, who, as we shall see, gave particular instructions about the cost of repairs. Yet there is no indication that the king contributed to the upkeep of the clergy. There is little information available for the period of the monarchy, and it is sometimes difficult to interpret what there is.

There was a universal ruling that the priest should gain a livelihood from the altar; he was entitled to a part of the sacrifices offered there, except for the holocaust, which was completely burnt. The story of Eli's sons (1 S 2: 12-17) records how this right of the priests was interpreted at Shiloh: after every sacrifice, one of the priest's servants took some of the meat out of the pot in which it was cooking. The fault of Eli's sons lay, not in taking their portion of meat, but in demanding the meat raw, *i.e.* before the fat had been offered upon the altar; they were thus serving themselves before they had served Yahweh. Osee accuses the priests of feeding on the 'sin' of the people (Os 4: 8). Now in sacrifices for sin, the priest kept

1. Cf. p. 69.

everything which was not offered on the altar (according to Lv 6: 19); it is possible, however, that Osee is referring not to this custom, but to sacrifices in general which are offered with bad dispositions and are therefore considered by him as a 'sin' (cf. Os 8: 11); in either case, the priest was taking his food from sacrifices. The same principle was certainly applied in the Temple at Jerusalem, with some modifications of the ritual.

The priest was also entitled to a part of the collections given to the Temple, as we learn from the two edicts of Joas (2 K 12: 5–17; cf. 22: 3–7). The first edict left the priests all the money the faithful gave, compulsory taxes and voluntary offerings alike, with the condition that the priests should undertake the repairs which were then needed in the Temple. But, as the following verses show, the novelty of this lay not in giving the priests a right to the revenue, but in imposing on them a charge which diminished their revenue. When the priests failed to carry out the repairs, the king issued a second order taking away from them the greater part of this revenue, and leaving them only the money given as satisfaction for a crime or a sin; it does not matter, for our present purposes, whether this refers to a fine for faults similar to those which were expiated by sin-offerings, or to a contribution which was made along with sin-offerings, or to a contribution made instead of them.[1]

The rights of the priests are contained in Dt 18: 1–5: Levite priests shall live on the meat offered to Yahweh because they have been chosen for the service of God; they are to be given the shoulder, the jaw and the stomach of all victims sacrificed, and also the best (*rêshîth*) of the wheat, of the wine or oil, and of the wool from shearing. This text is most precise, but it seems difficult to reconcile with other prescriptions in the same book of Deuteronomy. The Israelites are commanded to bring to the central sanctuary their sacrifices and all their offerings, tithes (*ma'aser*), first-born (*b'kôr*), etc., and to eat them in the presence of Yahweh along with their family, their servants and the Levite who dwells with them (Dt 12: 6–7, 11–12, 17–19). The same command is repeated in the law about the first-born (*bikkûrîm*, Dt 26: 1–11), but elsewhere a further directive is given about tithes and the first-born: if the central sanctuary is too far away, then they may sell their offerings and bring the money to the sanctuary to buy on the spot what they need to make a feast before Yahweh; and they are not to forget 'the Levite who is in thy towns' (Dt 14: 22–27). Lastly, Dt 14: 28–29 and 26: 12–15 prescribe that every three years the tithes are to be kept at home and there distributed to the Levites, the stranger, the fatherless and the widow; instead of presenting this tithe at the sanctuary, the pilgrim shall make a declaration that he has used it according to the law (Dt 26: 13). The Levites to whom these texts refer lived scattered throughout the land of Israel; they could accompany pilgrims to the sanctuary, and they were

1. Cf. p. 430.

commended to the charity of the Israelites; there is no reference here to the Levite priests who officiated in the sanctuary. From this some scholars have argued that Dt 18: 1-5, which describes the rights of Levite priests, is a later text, and that Deuteronomy originally made no provision for the priests who served the sanctuary.

Such a conclusion fails to take into account the character of Deuteronomy, which is a code of reform (cf. Dt 12: 8 for the subject under discussion). Sacrifices, dues and tithes existed before Deuteronomy, and so did the rights of those priests who served the various sanctuaries. Deuteronomy is promulgating a new law insisting on one sole sanctuary; this law naturally entailed new measures, and all the texts about the Levites can be explained against this background. The suppression of the local sanctuaries would deprive their guardians of their revenues, and the Israelites are therefore ordered to maintain them out of the things owed to Yahweh, exactly as they had done before: those Levites who might take part in pilgrimages were to be invited to the religious meals, and all Levites were to share in the tithe every third year. Yet no one can possibly imagine that the Israelites and their guests ate everything they brought to the sanctuary, for the offering would then be almost meaningless; they must, therefore, have given part of that offering to the servants of the sanctuary, even though no text mentions it. Thus we can harmonize all the other references with Dt 18: 1-5; this text refers to the priests of the sole, central sanctuary, not to the priests and Levites from the provinces. The latter, however, are affected by the statute which follows immediately afterwards: if Levites from the provinces come to live at the central sanctuary, they may exercise their priestly office and share the revenues attached to it (Dt 18: 6-8).

It is impossible to say how far these prescriptions were followed, and we know that the last one, at least, could not be enforced by Josias (2 K 23: 9). But, far from showing that the priests had no means of livelihood, these texts all presuppose that they lived on the revenues from public worship.

Nor is this conclusion weakened by the silence of the oldest laws: the Elohistic code of the Covenant (Ex 23: 19) and the Yahwistic Code (Ex 34: 26) both command that the best of the first-fruits of the earth should be brought to the house of Yahweh. There is no mention of any part of these first-fruits being allotted to the priests, but then these two codes of law never mention priests at all; we know that the priests shared in the sacrifices, from the very beginning, and it would seem normal enough for them to have shared in the first-fruits, too. The same principle would seem to apply to tithes, which are not mentioned in either of these two codes; but the tithe was certainly a very ancient institution, attested, for the sanctuary at Bethel, by Am 4: 4 and by the foundation-story contained in Gn 28: 22. In a word, the situation which Ezechiel describes in his plan of the future Jerusalem (Ez 44: 29-30) is the situation which obtained under the monarchy; there is no need to eliminate part, or all, of these verses, as some recent authors have done. On this matter of the revenues accruing to the clergy, there is not such a pronounced contrast between the first and the second Temple as most writers claim. But there certainly was a development, and more precise rulings, about which we shall speak in the next chapter.[1]

6. *The lower-ranking personnel*

The Chronicler attributes to David not only the division of priests into classes, but also the institution of twenty-four classes of singers (1 Ch 25), and of several classes of door-keepers who were to keep watch for twenty-four hours a day (1 Ch 26: 1-19). In these chapters he is describing a later situation in which door-keepers and singers had been incorporated into the Levites; but he is not inventing everything. Though the pre-exilic texts never mention the singers or the door-keepers, every large sanctuary in ancient times had them, and the liturgical services of the Temple always needed such men. Our present Psalter contains psalms which were sung in the Temple by professionals, sometimes accompanied by musical instruments. Amos refers to the religious music in the sanctuary at Bethel (Am 5: 23), and Yahweh had to have his singers, exactly as the king had his.[2] The names of the three heads of the families of singers in Ch 6: 18-32; 25: 1 (Asaph, Heman and Ethan or Yeduthun) are also a proof of the antiquity of the institution. We cannot, of course, set much store by the Psalm titles which ascribe twelve psalms to Asaph, one to Heman, one to Ethan and three to Yeduthun. But 1 K 5: 11 mentions Heman and Ethan along with Kalkol and Darda as famous wise men in order to stress how much wiser Solomon was, and we know that in ancient times singers also gave lessons in wisdom; moreover, in this same text, Heman, Kalkol and Darda are called 'sons of *maḥôl*', which is not a proper name, but a common noun; they were 'sons of the choir', *i.e.* choristers. The names are not Israelites, and Kalkol is found, in an Egyptian inscription from Megiddo, as the name of a woman singer from Ascalon. Ethan, on the other hand, is called the Ezrahite, literally, an indigenous person, and therefore, in this context, a Canaanite. It is not too bold to think that the first choir of singers for the Temple at Jerusalem was recruited from among non-Israelites. Lastly, since singers and door-keepers returned from the Exile (Esd 2: 41-42=Ne 7: 44-45), their offices must have existed before the Exile, though in those days they would not have been Levites. The 'keeper of the vestments' who is mentioned in 2 K 22: 14 was also, very probably, an employee of the Temple; there is a similar reference in 2 K 10: 22 to a keeper of the vestments in the temple of Baal at Samaria.

The door-keepers and the singers were presumably free men, but slaves

1. Cf. pp. 403-405.

2. Cf. pp. 121-122.

also were attached to the Temple. The list of the caravans returning from exile mentions, after the singers and the door-keepers, the '*n*^{e}*thînîm*' or 'given' persons, and 'the descendants of the slaves of Solomon', and the two groups are counted together (Esd 2: 43-58=Ne 7: 46-60). There were 'given' men in the group led by Esdras also (Esd 8: 20). Some of their names are of foreign origin: these would be the descendants of the public slaves in the time of the monarchy,[1] when a number of such slaves were directed to work in the Temple. Esd 8: 20 says that David put them under the control of the Levites; Jos 9: 23 says they originated in the days of Josue, and the editor of the book knew that in his own day Gibeonites were still employed in the Temple as wood-cutters and water-carriers (Jos 9: 27; cf. Dt 29: 10). Ezechiel condemned this custom of using uncircumcised foreigners for the service of the Temple (Ez 44: 7-9).

Were there any women employed in the Temple? Ex 38: 8 speaks of the 'women who served at the entrance of the Tent of Reunion' and who gave their mirrors to make the bronze basin; the text is repeated in a gloss of 1 S 2: 22, which is not found in the Greek version. No one really knows how to interpret this information. The women who served at the Tent remind us of the young girls who used to guard the sacred pavilion among the pre-Islamic Arabs,[2] but there is no indication that they had any office to perform in public worship. Perhaps the late text in Ex is based on 2 K 23: 7, stripped of its syncretism: the verse in Kings tells how, as part of his reform, Josias dismantled the house of the sacred prostitutes which stood inside the Temple enclosure, and in which women used to weave veils for Ashera. This house, however, was one of those Canaanite intrusions into Yahwism of which we shall speak later. Another text cited as referring to women is the title of Ps 46: '*al 'ălâmôth*, which is sometimes translated 'for the young girls'; the theory is that there were women in the Temple choir, and in support of this, our attention is called to Esd 2: 65, which lists male and female singers in the caravan returning from Babylonia. In Esdras, however, the musicians are not listed with the staff of the Temple; they were layfolk, the servants of rich families in exile. And though the meaning of the title of the psalm is not certain, it is definitely not 'for young girls'; the same phrase is found in 1 Ch 15: 20, in connection with male singers, and must mean either a musical instrument or a key. It is even more daring to make the '*almah* of Is 7: 14 and the '*ălâmôth* of Ct 1: 3; 6: 8 persons connected with the liturgy. Though it is quite true that women are represented as singing and dancing at religious festivals (Ex 15: 20; Jg 21: 21; Ps 68: 26), this does not mean that they formed part of the staff regularly appointed for the cult. And the suggestion that there were women among the clergy of the Temple clashes with an important linguistic fact: there were priestesses in Assyria, priestesses and high priestesses in Phoenicia, where

1. Cf. p. 89.   2. Cf. p. 296.

they are known by the feminine of *kohen*; in the Minaean inscriptions, there was a feminine form of *lw'* which some scholars would link with the Hebrew *lewy*[1]; but Hebrew has no feminine noun corresponding to *kohen* or *lewy*[1]; no women ever held a place among the Israelite clergy.

There were, nevertheless, periods in which religious syncretism defiled the cult in the Temple, when men and women were brought there to practise something which Yahwism rejected with horror. The women who wove veils for Ashera lived in the 'house of the sacred prostitutes' (2 K 23: 7). Prostitutes of both sexes (*q'deshîm* and *q'deshôth*) were attached to Canaanite sanctuaries, and Israel had followed this practice (Os 4: 14; 1 K 14: 24; 15: 12; 22: 47). And in spite of the condemnation in Dt 23: 18-19, they had made their way even into the Temple at Jerusalem (2 K 23: 7; perhaps also Ez 8: 14).

7. *Were there prophets attached to the Temple?*

There is an inaccurate but widespread theory which asserts, without nuances, that the priests were the ministers of public worship, and the prophets its enemies. Some recent studies, reversing this judgment, have tried to show that there were some prophets attached to the Temple in an official capacity, 'cultic prophets'. In fact, the Bible often does mention the priests and the prophets together (2 K 23: 2; Jr 23: 11; Lm 2: 20; Os 4: 4-5 and especially Jr 26, where Jeremias is preaching against the Temple, in the Temple itself, in the presence of the priests, of the prophets and of all the people; he arouses opposition among the priests and the prophets, but he is defended by the people and by the magistrates). On the other hand, the Psalter contains certain prophetical compositions which were written to be recited or sung in the Temple, and these have been attributed to the cultic prophets. Furthermore, 1 Ch 25: 1 describes Asaph, Heman and Yeduthun, the ancestors of the singers, as 'prophets' (*n'bi'îm*); the passage goes on to say that they 'used to prophesy' and that Heman was the 'seer' of the king (1 Ch 25: 2, 3, 5). From this, some modern scholars have concluded that the singers in the post-exilic Temple were the successors of the prophetical guilds in the first Temple, and that the latter were themselves a continuation of those brotherhoods of prophets (*n'bi'îm*) which are mentioned so often in the stories of Samuel, of Saul and of Eliseus, sometimes in connection with a particular sanctuary. The supporters of this theory also appeal to analogies in neighbouring countries: Mesopotamian temples had their seers and ecstatics, and Canaan had its prophets. Since Jehu assembled the prophets and the priests of Baal in the temple of this god (2 K 10: 19), it is probable, they argue, that the Temple of Yahweh had its prophets too.

The more moderate among these writers admit that, apart from the anonymous compositions in the Psalter, these cultic prophets have left no

1. Cf. p. 369.

trace of their existence; some will even admit that they should be identified with the false prophets, the 'professionals' who are condemned by the Bible. Others, however, go much further. They hold that our prophetical books are to a large extent the works of cultic prophets: Isaias had his inaugural vision in the Temple, Jeremias and Ezechiel were both priests, and the Books of Joel, Habaquq, Nahum and Sophonias are, they claim, liturgical compositions.

This extreme position is quite untenable. We may grant that the Books of Nahum and of Habaquq are imitations of liturgical works, that the prophecy of Joel may have been delivered in some rather extraordinary cultic ceremony, and that the Lamentations attributed to Jeremias may have been used for religious services on the site of the ruined Temple during the Exile; but this does not make the prophets officials of the Temple. As far as the great Prophets are concerned, the question ought never to have been raised: Ezechiel is a priest, but all his prophetical activity took place after the ruin of the Temple; Jeremias was a priest, but since he belonged to the line of Ebyathar, he was debarred from any official service by the Sadoqites, and his behaviour in the Temple proves that he did not belong to the regular staff there; and the fact that Isaias received his vocation in the Temple does not imply that he held an office there.

The more moderate position, which does not count the literary prophets among the Temple staff, is itself far from certain. It is unscientific to apply indiscriminately to Israel everything which happened in neighbouring religions, especially where biblical evidence is lacking. As for 1 Ch 25: 1f., we have endeavoured to show above that the post-exilic singers traced their ancestry from the singers of the first Temple. The Chronicler is the only one who calls them *n^{e}bi'îm*, and this term, it must be remembered, has various meanings: the Chronicler considers them as 'inspired' and he may have done so merely because the writing and singing of psalms required a kind of inspiration; in the very same passage, 'to prophesy' alternates with 'to sing' (1 Ch 25: 6). When the Chronicler wants to speak of true prophetical inspiration, he uses other words: Josaphat panicked during an invasion, and assembled the people in the Temple: then 'the Spirit of Yahweh came upon Yahaziel' and he spoke out like a great prophet. Yahaziel was one of the sons of Asaph, and the text is used by the champions of cultic prophets to prove that the singers were in fact cultic prophets. There is, however, a close parallel in 2 Ch 24: 20 where, in the Temple, 'the Spirit of God enveloped Zacharias', who then spoke like a second Jeremias; but Zacharias was the son of the priest Yehoyada, not one of the singers. In spite of the terms used in 1 Ch 25: 1f., there never was a class of prophets in the second Temple, and apparently the Chronicler himself did not think there had been such a class of men in the Temple before the Exile. Finally, the old brotherhoods of *n^{e}bi'îm* are never mentioned in connection with the Temple in Jerusalem, and though they had connections with other sanctuaries, they did not, apparently, form part of the regular staff of those holy places.

The only point to be retained is that we should not pretend that the priests and the prophets were in complete opposition to each other. Prophets, whether true or false, had connections with the cult and with the Temple where it was celebrated. Conversely, the priests had something in common with the prophets, not so much because they gave oracles, for that function had died out,[1] but rather because they taught the people religion.[2] But it is impossible to prove that prophets were once attached to the Temple at Jerusalem, or that they formed a particular section of its clergy.

1. Cf. pp. 352-353.

2. Cf. pp. 353-355.

Chapter Eight

THE PRIESTHOOD AFTER THE EXILE

THE fall of Jerusalem brought disaster to the clergy of the Temple. The head priest, the second priest and the three keepers of the threshold, *i.e.* all the leading Temple officials, were taken prisoner and executed by Nabuchodonosor at Riblah (2 K 25: 18–21=Jr 52: 24–27; 39: 6). The two deportations affected first and foremost the population of Jerusalem (2 K 24: 14; 25: 11=Jr 52: 15; 39: 9). Most of the Sadoqite clergy and of the other persons in the service of the Temple were taken away into exile. Those members of the tribe of Levi who were not employed at the Temple (*e.g.* the family of Ebyathar) were deported with the rank and file of the population. We have shown above[1] how the *de facto* distinction between priests and Levites which resulted from Josias' reform became more clear-cut in Babylonia. On the other hand, the superiority of priests over Levites had no practical consequences during the Exile, because there was no sanctuary where priests could exercise their office.

The deportations did not, however, empty Palestine of all its inhabitants. Part of the tribe of Levi stayed on in Judah: the members of the line of Ebyathar or the Levites who lived up and down the country were counted among the common people whom the Chaldeans left to work the land (2 K 24: 14; 25: 12=Jr 52: 16; 39: 10). Moreover, the community in Judah still kept up its religious and liturgical life in some way; the people continued to frequent the provincial sanctuaries which had been reopened after the failure of Josias' reform, and the same syncretist cult was practised there as in the days before the reform. Some of the people, however, remained faithful to the legitimate forms of Yahwism: at least some of the Lamentations ascribed to Jeremias were probably used for liturgical assemblies in Judah: men fasted on the anniversary of the destruction of the Temple (Za 7: 1–3) and some even came to offer sacrifices amid its ruins (Jr 41: 4–5). Thus the Levite priests who stayed in Palestine found work once again, now that the monopoly of the Sadoqites no longer existed.

Such was the situation, in Babylonia and in Judah, and it must be kept in mind in order to understand how the priesthood was reconstituted in Jerusalem after the Return.

1. Cf. pp. 364–366.

1. *Priests and Levites down to the period of Esdras and Nehemias*

In the first caravans to return to Jerusalem after the Exile (according to the statistics in Esd 2: 36–39 and Ne 7: 39–42), there were 4,289 priests divided into four families, called after Yedayah, Immer, Pashehur and Harim. The family of Yedayah was the smallest in number, but it is named first because Josue, the first high priest after the Exile, belonged to it; the second family is named after the Immer mentioned in Jr 20: 1. The heads of the other two families are not referred to elsewhere in the Bible. By contrast, these first caravans brought with them only 74 Levites (Esd 2: 40; Ne 7: 43).

The same disproportion between priests and Levites is found in the caravan led by Esdras. He assembled a group containing two families of priests (no number is given, Esd 8: 2), but not a single Levite, and it was only after an urgent appeal that he mustered 38 (Esd 8: 15–19). Two reasons explain the small numbers of Levites in these caravans: first, far more priests than Levites had been deported to Babylonia, and secondly, those Levites who had gone into exile had little inclination to return to Judaea, where discrimination would be practised in favour of the priests, and where they would become mere 'servants of the Temple' (Esd 8: 17).

Though the biblical texts give no precise information about the origin of the four priestly families which returned, all four of them very probably claimed Sadoqite ancestry. Jr 20: 1 proves that this was true of the family of Immer; again, Josue, who belonged to the family of Yedayah, was the son of Yehosadaq (Ag 1: 1), and therefore, according to 1 Ch 5: 40, the grandson of Serayah, the last Sadoqite high priest before the Exile (2 K 25: 18); and there is no reason to doubt the value of this text in Chronicles. Besides, it was principally the Sadoqite priests who had been deported. When Esdras arrived in Jerusalem, the entire priesthood there was drawn from these four great families still (Esd 10: 18–22), and it is presumably by a mere accident of textual tradition that only three of them (Yedayah, Immer and Pashehur) are mentioned in the list of Jerusalem's population compiled under Nehemias (Ne 11: 10–14; note that the family of Yedayah is here expressly related to Sadoq).

By contrast, the priests in Esdras' caravan were of mixed origin: one group was descended from Phinehas and another one from Ithamar (Esd 8: 2). Phinehas was the son of Eleazar, the ancestor of Sadoq, according to the genealogies in 1 Ch 5: 30–34; 6: 35–38. The descendants of Ebyathar had claimed Ithamar as ancestor (1 Ch 24: 3; cf. 1 S 22: 20). Thus, when this caravan reached Jerusalem, that branch which was rival to the Sadoqites at last recovered its right to exercise the priesthood. Eleazar and Ithamar were both sons of Aaron, and we shall see[1] shortly how, after the time of Esdras

1. Cf. pp. 394–397.

the expression 'sons of Aaron' replaced the terms 'sons of Sadoq': both phrases mean simply 'priests'.

In the early caravans, there were only three families of Levites (Esd 2: 40; Ne 7: 43). Two other families returned with Esdras. In the meantime, the number of Levites increased by the integration into these families of others who had not gone into exile; other names appear in the account of the rebuilding of the city walls under Nehemias, and the entire district of Qeilah seems to have been occupied by Levites (Ne 3: 17–18); the famous pledge taken by the whole community (Ne 10: 10–14) was signed by the heads of the three families mentioned in Esd 2: 40, but it bore the signature of fourteen other Levites as well. The list of the population of Jerusalem compiled under Nehemias gives 284 Levites resident in the city (Ne 11: 18), apart from others who lived in the province (Ne 11: 20). One writer has recently suggested that the list in Ne 11: 25*b*–35, cf. 36, represents the places where these Levites lived, but all one can say for certain is that the list mentions three towns (Hebron, Geba and Anathoth) which also occur in the list of Levitical towns in Jos 21.

In the caravans, the singers are all called sons of Asaph; they are listed separately from the Levites, and are more numerous than them (Esd 2: 41; Ne 7: 44). The priests and the Levites settled in Jerusalem, but the singers and the door-keepers and the 'given' men went to live in their own home towns (Esd 2: 70; Ne 7: 72). This distinction between singers and Levites is maintained in the authentic parts of Esdras' account (Esd 7: 7, 24; 10: 23–24), and also, it would seem, in Nehemias' memoir about his second mission (Ne 13: 5). The other passages in the Books of Esdras and Nehemias, in which the singers are included among the Levites, were either edited by the Chronicler, or inserted by a later glossator. There is only one text which causes any difficulty: in the list of the population of Jerusalem, the singers are mentioned among the Levites (Ne 11: 17), and though this list is not part of Nehemias' memoir, it is a trustworthy document from some archives, contemporaneous with the events it describes. Perhaps it was retouched on this point, or perhaps singers and Levites were then beginning to amalgamate. This solution would also explain why, in Ne 13: 10, the word 'Levites' is explained as 'the Levites and the singers who did the work'.

The integration of the door-keepers into the body of Levites took place even more slowly. The door-keepers who returned with the first caravans (Esd 2: 42; Ne 7: 45) are listed separately from the Levites and from the singers; there were six families of door-keepers, all small in number, and this denotes that they did not have the social standing of the singers, who together formed one large family. These door-keepers have nothing in common with the three 'keepers of the threshold' in the monarchic period; in fact, we never hear of these three officials after the Exile. No door-keepers are mentioned in the caravan of Esdras, but they are mentioned, along with the Levites and the singers, in the memoirs of Esdras and of Nehemias, in the passages cited in the last paragraph; but even in those texts where the singers are included among the Levites (*e.g.* Ne 11: 19), the door-keepers are listed apart. They are, however, named along with the Levite-singers in the editorial passage in Ne 12: 25; this is the Chronicler's point of view, for in his day the door-keepers definitely belonged to the Levitical class.

We have already spoken of the 'given' men and of 'the descendants of the slaves of Solomon' in reference to the staff of the Temple in the monarchic period.[1] The number of these who joined the caravans returning from exile was relatively large (392 in the first caravans, Esd 2: 58; Ne 7: 60, and 220 in the caravan led by Esdras, Esd 8: 20); yet the number of persons in each family was relatively small; these two facts would indicate that they were not well-off in Babylonia and that they hoped to better their fortunes by returning to Palestine. They must certainly have been integrated into the people of Israel, or Esdras would never have accepted them for the service of the Temple (cf. Ez 44: 7-9). They were housed on the hill of Ophel (Ne 11: 21), and near the Temple there stood a house which the 'given' men shared with the Temple merchants (Ne 3: 31). They are never again mentioned but it is doubtful whether more than a few individuals were ever absorbed into the Levites.

More probably, the institution itself went out of existence, and the work was done by the Levites: hence later ages considered the Levites as having been 'given' to the priests for the service of the sanctuary (Nb 3: 9; 8: 19).

2. *The Levites in the work of the Chronicler*

After Esdras and Nehemias, more than a century passes before we have any further information about the status of the clergy in Jerusalem. Our next source is the work of the Chronicler, the author of 1 and 2 Ch, Esd and Ne; he probably composed his work about the year 300 B.C., but it was retouched at a later date. The longest additions to his work are 1 Ch 1-9 and 23-27, all of which chapters are particularly important for a study of the priesthood. All the information we can gather must be picked out of this great work which traces the history of Israel down to the restoration after the Exile; what makes it difficult is that the author ascribes to ancient times situations and ideas which were unheard of until much later. Indeed, he includes ideas from his own day, and ascribes them to ancient times; to make it worse, the annotators of his work have added ideas and customs from their day, too, and backdated them as well. In the period which separates the memoirs of Esdras and Nehemias from the work of the Chronicler, several changes took place which are of interest to us here. The Priestly laws of the Pentateuch were put into practice, with modifica-

1. Cf. p. 383.

tions as the occasion demanded, and certain changes were made in the rules governing the clergy; the changes took place gradually, but the different stages of development have not been recorded. All these factors explain why it is so difficult to reconstruct a coherent picture out of the work of the Chronicler, and we shall restrict ourselves to the broad outlines. Since the distinction between Levites and priests at this period is an undisputed fact, we shall treat of the priests in the next section, and begin with the Levites.

Anyone who reads Chronicles alongside the Books of Samuel and Kings (which cover the same period) will be struck at once by the importance which the Chronicler gives to the Levites. They have the principal rôle in looking after the Ark of the Covenant (1 Ch 15-16); their duties in the Temple are laid down even before it is built, and there too they play the principal part (1 Ch 23-26). They are the predominant figures in the religious reforms of Ezechias (2 Ch 29-31) and of Josias (2 Ch 34-35). But even apart from these long texts, they are found intervening everywhere, whether their action is relevant or not. The attention paid to genealogies, which was already showing itself in the days of Esdras, develops even further. The ancestry of all the Levites is traced to the three sons of Levi, Gershom, Qehath and Merari (1 Ch 6: 1-32; 23: 6-24), in perfect harmony with the Priestly tradition recorded in Nb 3-4; even people like Samuel, who, in the pre-exilic books, had no Levitical ancestry, are given a place in these genealogies.

(a) *The Levites and the Ark.* The theory of the original Chronicler was that the Levites were primarily meant for the service of the Ark: 'the Ark of God may be carried by Levites only' (1 Ch 15: 2). They looked after it at Jerusalem until the Temple was built (1 Ch 16: 4f.) while the priests remained at Gibeon with the Tent (1 Ch 16: 39). The Levites (not the priests, as in 1 K 8: 3) carried the Ark into Solomon's Temple (2 Ch 5: 4; and cf. also 2 Ch 35: 3). This idea does not originate from the Priestly tradition, for in this the Levites are connected with the Tent (Nb 1: 50; 3: 8); its source is Deuteronomy (Dt 10: 8), to which 1 Ch 15: 2 certainly refers. It is a way of giving the support of tradition to Levitical claims: since the Levites carried the Ark into the Temple, their presence in the Temple is in accordance with the Law, and therefore they have rights there. In the additions made to the Chronicler's work, this claim has been obscured by the Priestly tradition; the Priestly editors say that the Levites carried the Tent and that they were under the authority of the sons of Aaron (1 Ch 23: 26-28).

(b) *The singers.* Once the Ark had been laid to rest in the Tent which David made for it, and later in the Temple which Solomon built, the Levites had no more work to do as porters (1 Ch 23: 25-26; cf. 2 Ch 35: 3). David set some of them apart for choral service (1 Ch 16: 4). Thus the singers in the second Temple, who were definitely counted among the Levites, traced their foundation back to David, the first singer of Israel. Indeed, one of the dominant features of the Chronicler is this interest in sacred music. Singing had come to occupy an important place in the liturgy, and the status of the singers had risen as a result. The body of singers had grown larger, too. Only one group, that of Asaph, had returned from exile (Esd 2: 41; Ne 7: 44), but the Chronicler mentions three families of singers in the time of David: Asaph's family was connected with the Ark, and the two families of Heman and Yeduthun (or Ethan) were employed at the sanctuary of Gibeon (1 Ch 16: 37, 41). This would seem to imply that the guilds of Heman and Yeduthun were descended from Temple singers of monarchic times[1] who had not gone into exile; in the Chronicler's day, all three families were counted as Levites.

The later additions to the book are meant to show the legitimacy of the institution of singers, and to give a more exact definition of their rights. The three head singers under David have their ancestry traced to the three sons of Levi: Heman is the descendant of Qehath, Asaph of Gershom, Ethan (Yeduthun) of Merari (1 Ch 6: 18-32). In 1 Ch 25, the sons of Asaph, Heman and Yeduthun (v. 1) or, as verse 6 has it, the sons of Asaph, Yeduthun and Heman, are divided into twenty-four classes, each composed of twelve members. The artificial character of this list, referring to the time of David, is too obvious for words, and the most curious feature in it is that the names of Heman's nine last sons (v. 4) when put together, form a little poem, a fragment of a psalm. Note, too, that the names of the ancestors are not always in the same order; this variation reflects rivalry between the different groups. The sons of Asaph, who had been in exile, were given seniority, but the sons of Heman also claimed it (cf. 1 Ch 6: 18; 15: 17, 19) on the grounds that they were descended from Qehath, from whom Aaron and the priests were also descended, and that they formed the largest group.

(c) *The door-keepers.* Eventually, the door-keepers too were shown to be Levites. The six families which returned from the Exile were not Levites (Esd 2: 42; Ne 7: 45; cf. Ne 11: 19), but when Chronicles is repeating the list given in Ne 11, it gives the door-keepers a Levitical ancestor, Qorah (cf. 1 Ch 6: 7): from the days in the desert, says 1 Ch 9: 19, the door-keepers kept watch over the Tent and the camp. Apart from the Qorahites (1 Ch 26: 1f.), there was another class of door-keepers, also Levites, called the Merarites (1 Ch 26: 10 f., 19). Between these two classes, 1 Ch 26: 4-8 lists the sons of Obed-Edom. Though this man was not an Israelite, the Ark had been left in his house (2 S 6: 11), and 1 Ch 15: 24 says that David appointed him a door-keeper in the service of the Ark; 1 Ch 16: 38 adds that he was a son of Yeduthun, and therefore a Levite. A group of door-keepers in the second temple claimed to be descended from him.

But the claims of these door-keepers did not stop there; they aspired to

1. Cf. p. 382.

the position of singers. Now, since Yeduthun had been a singer, it was natural that his son too, should have been a singer; at least, this is what 1 Ch 15: 21 and 16: 5 suppose. The Qorahites disregarded the ill-defined border between the two classes, and promoted themselves: they are listed as singers in 2 Ch 20: 19, and in the titles of the Psalms, no less than twelve are attributed to the sons of Qorah.

(d) *Other Levitical functions.* The reader will have noticed that much of our information about the singers, and almost all our information about the door-keepers, comes from passages inserted into the Books of Chronicles after the original work was completed. These passages describe the very end of a long development, and the number of references cited may mislead a person into thinking that the Levites were merely singers or door-keepers.

According to 1 Ch 23: 3-5, the Levites mentioned in David's census were employed as follows: 24,000 looked after the Temple's affairs, 4,000 were employed as clerks and judges, 4,000 were door-keepers, and 4,000 'praised Yahweh on musical instruments'. What interests us here is not the figures (which are fantastic), but the proportion between the figures: the great majority of Levites were engaged in the service of the Temple, and only a relatively small proportion of them were musicians; it would be quite arbitrary to say that the first class were singers and the second the accompanists. This conclusion is confirmed by 1 Ch 23: 25-32 (though the text belongs to another tradition, since the age at which Levites begin service is here fixed at twenty years, not thirty, as in verse 3): the Levites will no longer have to carry the Ark, since Yahweh will henceforth dwell in Jerusalem, but they are to do all the work in the Temple, and their choral duties are mentioned only at the end.

The Levites, therefore, were placed at the service of the sons of Aaron (1 Ch 23: 28), or at the service of the faithful, according to 2 Ch 35: 3-6 (a parallel text, but it refers to the unusual circumstances at the celebration of the great Passover under Josias). They are responsible for the administration of the Temple (1 Ch 9: 26; 26: 20f.; 2 Ch 24: 6, 11; 31: 11-15), but they have duties in connection with worship also: they are to purify the holy things, to prepare the shew-bread and vegetable offerings (1 Ch 23: 28-29); they are to take charge of the slaughtering and of the carving up of victims (2 Ch 29: 34; 35: 11). Thus their work touches on the domain reserved to the priests, and there must have been conflicts, though they are not mentioned explicitly in Chronicles. The story of Qorah and his followers in Nb 16 clearly reflects this tension (cf. especially Nb 16: 8-11): Qorahites were always the same, full of intrigue, battling their way forward, first as door-keepers, then as singers,[1] and finally even usurping Priestly functions!

David's census of the Levites included clerks and judges also, according to 1 Ch 23: 4. These clerks could have been secretaries, for the Temple

1. *V. supra.*

would certainly have needed secretaries for its administration (cf. 2 Ch 34: 13), and a letter of Antiochus III cited by Josephus (*Ant.* XII, iii, 3) lists the categories of the clergy in Jerusalem as 'the priests, the Temple scribes and the sacred singers'. But the *shôṭrîm* whom Chronicles lists alongside the judges were clerks of the courts, assistant officials,[1] and they were appointed for 'outside' duties in Israel (1 Ch 26: 29). This last phrase does not mean Temple affairs unconnected with worship (as it does in Ne 11: 16), but affairs which have nothing to do with the Temple. We may compare them with the Levites whom Josaphat appointed to judge cases along with the priests and the elders (2 Ch 19: 8); indeed, Josephus presumes, in *Ant.* IV, viii, 14, that every town had a tribunal consisting of seven judges and fourteen Levite assistants.

Lastly, the Levites were also teachers. The Chronicler first refers to this privilege in the report of Esdras (Ne 8: 7, 9). He attributes the same rôle to them under Josaphat, saying that the king sent them out 'armed with the Law of Yahweh, to teach Judah'; the group he sent comprised eight Levites and only two priests (2 Ch 17: 8-9). In 2 Ch 35: 3, the Levites are called 'men who have understanding', *i.e.* knowledge of the things of God.

The Chronicler's work, then, gives wide testimony to the ever-increasing influence of the Levites in the second Temple. It seems, too, that their struggle for emancipation continued in the last centuries before the Christian era. In the Apocrypha, *e.g.* in the Book of Jubilees or in the Testament of Levi, the figure of their great ancestor is exalted: in these books, it is no longer Aaron but Levi himself who was appointed priest by God, and all his sons after him hold this rank. From the historical point of view, this new attitude may have been connected in some way with the eviction of the Sadoqites by John Hyrcanus, who himself came from a Priestly family of secondary importance; there is no way of knowing, however, whether the general body of Levites ever really profited from his action. Nevertheless, they continued their intrigues to the end: some years before the ruin of the Temple, the singers persuaded Agrippa II to let them wear linen vestments, as the priests did, and the other Levites who served in the Temple were all promoted to the rank of singers (*Ant.* XX, ix, 6).

3. '*Sons of Sadoq*' *and* '*Sons of Aaron*'

From Solomon to the Exile, the descendants of Sadoq provided the priesthood of the first Temple, and in Ezechiel, the priests are always called 'sons of Sadoq'. Yet in the priestly documents of the Pentateuch, in Chronicles and in some post-exilic Psalms, they are called 'sons of Aaron'. In the present section we shall try to explain what this change of name signified, and how it came about.

In the oldest traditions of the Pentateuch, Aaron is a rather hazy figure at

1. Cf. p. 155.

first, but little by little his character becomes more defined; unfortunately, it is impossible to make a clear distinction between the earlier and later sources, and to assign the precise order in which the texts should follow one another. Aaron was Moses' brother, and he was called 'the Levite'; he was Moses' spokesman before the people (Ex 4: 14-16) and before Pharaoh (Ex 7: 1f.); he even worked miracles (Ex 7: 9, 19; 8: 1, etc.). He stands at Moses' side during the battle against the Amelekites (Ex 17: 8, 10), at the meeting with Jethro (Ex 18: 12) and at Sinai (Ex 19: 24; 24: 1, 9). In these traditions, however, he is never once mentioned as a priest or as an ancestor of priests. On the contrary, he opposes Moses on religious questions, by making a golden calf (Ex 32; cf. Dt 9: 20), and by leading a revolt in company with his sister Miriam (Nb 12).

In the Priestly tradition of the Pentateuch, Aaron is quite a different character: here he is the first high priest of Israel, his sons are the only lawful priests, and the other members of the tribe of Levi are given to them as servants (Ex 28-29; 39; Lv 8-10; Nb 16-18). This new picture of Aaron was built around the old tradition of Aaron 'the Levite', and it marks the triumph of a trend which had to overcome considerable opposition: the stories in Ex 32 and Nb 12, with their unfavourable account of his actions, are an echo of this opposition.

The differing accounts of Aaron's rôle during the Exodus reflect a struggle between different groups of priests; unfortunately, we cannot trace this development in detail, so we must fall back on hypotheses. One suggestion, which has recently been put forward in an extreme form, is that 'sons of Aaron', is a name for the priests who served the sanctuary at Bethel, where men worshipped a golden calf, as the Israelites had done at Sinai. The sanctuary at Bethel, it continues, was spared destruction after the fall of Jerusalem, and its priests stayed on there; they continued to exercise their ministry, and so became the dominant religious force in Palestine during the Exile. Those priests who returned from Babylonia had to reckon with the group at Bethel, and the latter would have instigated all kinds of obstacles to the rebuilding of the Temple; finally, Za 7: 1-3 means that men were sent from Jerusalem to consult the priests of Bethel, who were in the end recognized by the Sadoqites, on condition that the Sadoqites should retain their precedence. The foundations on which this theory rests are far from solid: the text of Za 7: 1-3 is undoubtedly obscure, but it certainly does not bear the meaning given to it here; there is not a single fact to prove that the sanctuary of Bethel took on a new lease of life after the reform of Josias, or that it was active during the Exile; and the connection between the cult practised at Bethel and the episode of Aaron's golden calf can be interpreted in a number of ways.[1]

A more moderate and more widespread theory is that the priests who

1. Cf. p. 334.

returned from Babylonia had to amalgamate with a non-Sadoqite group which had maintained continuity of worship in Jerusalem during the Exile; this latter group claimed descent from Aaron. Against this, the only evidence in our texts would seem to indicate that the Aaronite group was formed in Babylonia, not in Jerusalem. We have seen[1] that the first caravans to return included priests who were probably Sadoqites, and the evidence given in the Books of Esdras, Aggaeus and Zacharias about the restoration of worship in Jerusalem contains no trace of any opposition from a non-Sadoqite group which was already in possession of the Temple. The first time two different groups of priests returned from Babylonia was when Esdras brought with him the families of Phinehas and of Ithamar (Esd 8: 2). This was the period when everyone was preoccupied with genealogies: the Sadoqites priests traced their ancestry back to Phinehas (cf. 1 Ch 5: 30–34), to whom God had promised an everlasting priesthood among his descendants (Nb 25: 10–13), and Phinehas was the son of Eleazar, to whom Aaron's priesthood had been transferred by God himself (Nb 20: 24-26). The only explanation for the references to Phinehas in Esd 8: 2 is that at some date between Zorobabel and Esdras, the Sadoqites had begun to claim Aaron as their ancestor. They probably did so in order to counteract the claims of another group of priests who were tracing their ancestry back to a far more ancient and far more noble figure than David's priest, Sadoq, *i.e.* to a near relative of Aaron 'the Levite', Moses' brother. This group of rivals can be identified as the family of Ebyathar, who represented the house of Eli and who boasted (rightly, it seems) of their Levitical origin. The verses inserted in 1 S 2: 27–36 were certainly written before Esdras, and may date from shortly after the reform of Josias; and this text states that the house of Eli had been chosen as priests when the Israelites were still in Egypt. Only the name of their ancestor was lacking, and once Aaron had been acknowledged as the first high priest of Israel, they claimed descent from him. Eventually an agreement was reached between the descendants of Sadoq and those of Ebyathar; the former traced their ancestry to Eleazar (or to his son Phinehas), and the latter to Ithamar.

They reached this agreement in Babylonia, and Esdras gave it his blessing by taking with him representatives of both the great Priestly families. But this does not mean that there was no parallel movement in Palestine, where descendants of Ebyathar had stayed on through the Exile, and to which descendants of Sadoq had returned after the Exile; similarly, there may have been a combined movement both in Palestine and in the land of Exile; but the agreement was actually concluded in Babylonia. When Esdras reached Jerusalem, he found the Priestly offices held by the same families as had held them in the first days after the return (Esd 10: 18-22 and Esd 2: 36–39). The sons of Aaron did not occupy any positions at that time.

1. Cf. p. 388.

After Esdras' reform, the situation was straightened out, and from that time onwards the two families shared the priesthood, which thus became the privilege of all the sons of Aaron. Their titles to this office are given in the work of the Chronicler in his genealogies of Levi and of Aaron (1 Ch 5: 27–29; 6: 34–38, and above all in the organization he ascribes to David, 1 Ch 24: 1–6): this last text states that all Aaron's sons were priests, though the two eldest, Nadab and Abihu, died childless in punishment for a crime against the cult: hence the two youngest, Eleazar and Ithamar, inherited the priesthood (cf. Lv 10: 1–3; Nb 3: 1–4). Sadoq was a descendant of Eleazar, and Ebyathar a descendant of Ithamar. David divided the work between the two families by instituting twenty-four classes of priests; sixteen belonged to the family of Eleazar, which was the more numerous, and eight to the family of Ithamar. The following passage (1 Ch 24: 7–18) gives a list of these twenty-four classes, but the text was retouched in the Maccabean period, for the first class is that of Yehoyarib, the ancestor of the Maccabees (1 M 2: 1), who is never previously mentioned in an authentic text.

Thenceforward all the priests could be called 'sons of Aaron', but the Sadoqites still retained a certain distinction: their ancestor Eleazar is presented as more noble than Ithamar, since he is the only priest mentioned in the stories about the end of the desert wanderings (Nb 25: 11; 26: 1; 31 *passim*). According to the Chronicler (Esd 7: 1–5), Esdras himself was a Sadoqite, and the family filled twice as many classes as the sons of Ithamar. Finally, they continued to provide the high priest down to the time of Antiochus Epiphanes.

4. *The high priest*

(a) *His titles.* We said above that the title 'high priest' (*hakkohen haggadôl*) was not used to indicate the head of the priesthood before the Exile. We must now emphasize that even after the Exile it was used only rarely, and that it did not become the regular title until very long afterwards.

In the Law of Holiness, which is the oldest part of Leviticus, the head of the priesthood is called *hakkohen haggadôl me'eḥaw*, *i.e.* 'the greatest priest among his brothers' (Lv 21: 10); the rest of the phrase is an addition (see below), but this formula is a description, not a title. The formula is never once found in Ezechiel, and only three times in the entire Pentateuch, in a passage belonging to its last redaction (the ruling on cities of refuge: Nb 35: 25, 28 and 32? cf. the Greek). The 'high priests' in the desert, Aaron, Eleazar and Phinehas, are never called by any name other than 'the priest'. In the Chronicler, the title is found only four times: 2 Ch 34: 9 uses it of Hilqiyyah before the Exile, Ne 3: 1, 20 and 13: 28 use it of Elyashib. In contrast to this, 'high priest' is found eight times in Aggaeus and in Zacharias, and it refers on every occasion to Josue, the son of Yehosadaq, and the contemporary of Zorobabel (Ag 1: 1, 12, 14; 2: 2, 4; Za 3: 1, 8;

6: 11). Lastly, the Hebrew text of Si 50: 1 eulogizes Simon 'the high priest', who lived about 200 B.C. That is the complete list of references in the Hebrew Bible. The title, therefore, certainly existed from the moment of the return from exile. A papyrus from Elephantine, dated 408 B.C., refers to the high priest of Jerusalem, Yehohanan, as *kahna rabba*, which is the Aramaic equivalent of *kohen gadôl*. On the other hand, the term was rarely used, and people usually said simply 'the priest', as they had done before the Exile, and as the Priestly texts of the Pentateuch have it. It is only in the Mishnah and in the Talmudic treatise that the title is commonly used, either in Hebrew (*kohen gadôl*) or in Aramaic (*kahna rabba*).

It is interesting to compare with this the usage of the Greek Bible: the older books of the Septuagint always translate *hakkohen haggadol* by ὁ ἱερεὺς ὁ μέγας. But in the Books of Maccabees, this literal rendering is replaced by a technical term, ἀρχιερεύς, which is regularly applied to all the high priests; the New Testament and Philo follow the same practice. Now, the word ἀρχιερεύς is a term from the Seleucid chancery, and denotes a man whom the king appointed as head of the state religion in a particular district or town. The Hellenistic Jews used the word in this official sense: the first instance of it, in 1 M 10: 20, occurs in a letter of Alexander Balas to Jonathan: 'This day we appoint thee high priest (ἀρχιερεύς) of thy nation'. Greek-speaking Jews continued to use this pagan title when referring to the high priest, and this practice brought the terms *kohen gadôl* and *kahna rabba* into common usage, as the Hebrew and Aramaic equivalents of the Greek word.

The post-exilic books contain a few rare examples of other terms denoting the high priest. In 1 Ch 9: 11; 2 Ch 31: 13; Ne 11: 11, he is the *nagîd* of the Temple. In the language of the period, this word is used of officials and of men of high rank, but in these three texts it may preserve its loftier meaning of a prince or a leader appointed by God.[1] It certainly does have this latter meaning in Dn 9: 25; 11: 22, where the expressions 'Anointed Prince' and 'Prince of the Covenant' refer to the high priest.

The phrase 'Anointed Prince' corresponds with another title of the high priest: in Lv 4: 3, 5, 16 he is called *hakkohen hammashiaḥ*, 'the anointed priest' (cf. Lv 6: 13, 15; 16: 32); an addition to the primitive text of Lv 21: 10 speaks of the priest 'upon whose head anointing oil is poured'. This title brings us to the ritual of investiture.

(b) *The investiture of the high priest.* In the priestly documents of the Pentateuch (Ex 29: 4–7 and Lv 8: 6–12), the consecration of Aaron is described in three stages: purification, clothing and anointing. First he washes himself, then they clothe him with the tunic, with the cloak, with the ephod and with the breast-plate or pectoral: next they place upon his head a turban (*miṣnepheth*), on the front of which the holy *nezer* is fixed. (We shall discuss

1. Cf. p. 70.

the meaning of *nezer* in a moment.) Finally, anointing oil is poured over his head.

Ex 28 and 39 give a detailed description of the high priest's vestments. We shall confine ourselves to what they say about the turban. In Ex 28: 36, the decoration on the turban is called *ṣiṣ*, not *nezer*, whereas in Ex 39: 30, *ṣiṣ* and *nezer* are used together, as in Lv 8: 9. The basic meaning of *nezer* is 'consecration', and here 'a sign of consecration'. The usual translation 'diadem' is inaccurate, for the shape of this 'sign of consecration' is indicated by the other noun *ṣiṣ*, which means 'a flower'. Thus the high priest wore above his forehead, on his turban, a golden flower, as a symbol of life and of salvation. This flower had on it the inscription 'consecrated to Yahweh' (Ex 28: 36; 39: 30); it was, as it were, the seal of his consecration.

It is most interesting to compare these texts with Za 3: 1–9, which describes the consecration of Josue, the first high priest after the Exile. Here, too, a ceremony of purification precedes the ceremony of clothing: when Josue is stripped of his dirty clothes, his 'impiety' is taken away; thereupon he is clothed in rich vestments, and they place a turban (*ṣaniph*) upon his head; finally, a stone is placed in front of him, upon which Yahweh himself is going to engrave an inscription. Though the interpretation of this last detail is debated, the most probable meaning is that the stone was a precious stone which had to be engraved before the high priest began to wear it. The parallelism with the priestly documents is striking: *miṣnepheth* and *ṣaniph* mean respectively a flower engraved like a seal, and a precious stone inscribed in some way.

Josue's consecration, however, stops at his clothing: similarly, in Nb 20: 26–28, Eleazar is installed as Aaron's successor once he has been clothed in the vestments which the first high priest had worn. In both instances, there is no anointing. Some authors would see a reference to anointing in the subsequent vision of Zacharias (Za 4: 1–14), where Zorobabel and Josue are represented by two olive trees; the angel explains that they are 'the two sons of oil'. This is sometimes translated as 'the two anointed ones', on the grounds that Josue had been anointed priest, and that the writer hoped Zorobabel would be anointed king; but such a translation presupposes that a rather difficult problem of exegesis has been solved in a particular way. In fact, it is unlikely that the text refers to anointing at all; the expression 'sons of oil' is never used anywhere else for 'anointed one', and the word used for oil is not the one used for anointing-oil. Moreover, Zorobabel was an official appointed by the king of Persia, and he was never anointed as king; nor is there any other text to indicate that Josue was anointed as high priest. Indeed, the vision in Za 3 would seem to indicate, by its silence, that he was not.

It is hard to say when the rite of anointing was introduced. Ex 29: 7 and the passages of Leviticus cited above presuppose it, but we cannot say for certain when these passages were edited: they do not belong to the very last redaction of the Pentateuch, in which all priests are said to be anointed[1] (though this prescription, it would seem, was never put into practice). In all probability, the custom of anointing the high priest was already practised from the end of the Persian period, though the first written evidence we can date with certainty comes much later. The texts are Si 45: 15, in its eulogy of Aaron, Dn 9: 25-26, which calls Onias III the 'Anointed Prince' and 'The Anointed', and 2 M 1: 10, where the dynasty of high priests is called the race of anointed priests. Nor do we know when the practice died out; it may have lasted until the end of the dynasty of the Hasmonean king-priests. Certainly it was not practised any more in the Herodian and Roman period, for in those days the sole rite used at the installation was the clothing. The rabbis no longer remembered the time when the high priests were anointed; according to some of them, the practice was suppressed under Josias.

(c) *The high priest and the idea of kingship.* These rites of investiture (accompanied by anointing) made the high priests of post-exilic times rather like the kings before the Exile. Anointing was the principal ceremony in the coronation, for it made the king the Anointed of Yahweh.[2] The clothing worn by the high priest is equally significant: the turban (*ṣaniph*) which Josue receives is a royal head-dress in Is 62: 3; Si (Hebrew text) 11: 5; 40: 4; 46: 16, and the *miṣnepheth* mentioned in the Priestly texts is worn by the prince in Ez 21: 31. In addition, Si 40: 4 says that the king's *ṣaniph* had on it a *ṣiṣ*, *i.e.* a flower as worn in front of the turban by the high priest. *Nezer*, the equivalent of *ṣiṣ*, is a sign of royal rank in 2 S 1: 10; 2 K 11: 12; Ps 89: 40, and the meaning we ascribed to *nezer* is confirmed by a royal psalm (Ps 132: 18): 'his *nezer* shall blossom'. Last of all, the breast-plate covered in precious stones (Ex 28: 15f.) recalls the rich breast-plate worn by the Pharaohs, and by the kings of Syria in imitation of them, as the finds at Byblos show; it is quite likely that the kings of Israel also wore a similar breast-plate.

Once the monarchy had disappeared, all this royal paraphernalia was appropriated to the high priest. This does not mean merely, or mainly, that the high priest inherited the cultic privileges of the king, for we have proved that the king's rights in the exercise of worship were far from unrestricted. What it does mean is that the high priest became the head of the nation, and its representative before God, as the king had been in days gone by. But it was only gradually that this idea of the high priest as head of the nation took shape. We have seen that at first he was not anointed, and in the original text of Za 6: 9-14, the crown (*'aṭarah*)—a royal ornament, cf. 2 S 12: 30; Jr 13: 18; Ez 21: 31—was destined for Zorobabel; he was to be clothed with royal majesty and he was to be enthroned with the priest

1. The texts are cited on p. 105. 2. Cf. pp. 103-106.

standing at his right hand. Later on, these royal prerogatives were transferred to Josue, and his name was substituted in the text for that of Zorobabel.

Under the Hasmoneans, this ideal became a reality: the eight heads of this dynasty, from Jonathan to Antigonus, were both high priests and heads of the Jewish nation. They also took the title of king, probably from the time of Aristobulus I (104-103 B.C.).

(d) *The succession of high priests.* The advent of the Hasmoneans marked a turning-point in the history of the priesthood from other points of view also. The Chronicler has inserted into the Book of Nehemias (Ne 12: 10-11) a list of the high priests from Josue to Yaddua, *i.e.* down to the time of Darius II (cf. Ne 12: 22), *viz.* until about 400 B.C. (Darius died in 405 B.C.). This list may be incomplete, and it presumes, too, that the succession always passed from father to son; yet it does collect together the information given in Nehemias' memoir, and the last name but one (Yohanan) is given in the papyrus of Elephantine as the name of the high priest in 411 and again in 408.

There is no information extant about the following century and a half. After this, Josephus and the Book of Maccabees allow us to trace the line of Onias' descendants, from Onias I in the middle of the 3rd century B.C. to Simon the Just, eulogized in Si 50: 1f., and to Onias III, who held the office of high priest when Antiochus Epiphanes succeeded to the throne in 175 B.C. He was deposed by the new king and replaced by his brother Jason, and three years later, treacherously assassinated (2 M 3-4).

There is no reason to doubt that the high priesthood remained in the Sadoqite family until the death of Onias III, its last legitimate representative. His brother Jason obtained the post by bribing Antiochus and by introducing Greek customs into Jerusalem (2 M 4: 7-20). Thereafter, the office became a prize in the troubled politics of the period. Jason was dismissed when Menelaus made a higher bid (2 M 4: 23-26): this Menelaus was of the tribe of Benjamin, according to the Greek text of 2 M 3: 4; cf. 4: 23, and therefore not a priest at all; more probably, he belonged to the class of Bilga, as the Vetus Latina reads, *i.e.* he was a priest belonging to a family of secondary importance (Ne 12: 5, 18). It was the intruder Menelaus who arranged the murder of Onias III (2 M 4: 30-38); once he had sold his services to Antiochus, he upheld the king's policy of Hellenization and retained his position even after the first victories of the Maccabees, though his rank was, from this time onwards, merely nominal. He spent most of his time in Antioch, where he continued to intrigue and to pose as the spokesman of the Jews (2 M 11: 27-33) until he was put to death on the orders of Antiochus V, according to 2 M 13: 3-8. His successor was called Alkimus, one of the sons of Aaron (1 M 7: 14), but not of the Sadoqite branch. After the fall of Antiochus V, Alkimus secured confirmation of his position from Demetrius I (1 M 7: 9; 2 M 14: 3, 13). In Jerusalem itself, he began to knock down the wall separating the two courts of the

Temple,[1] but he died of a thrombosis in 159 B.C. (1 M 9: 54-56); the office of high priest then remained vacant for seven years.

In the end, Jonathan, the brother of Judas Maccabaeus and his successor in the struggle for independence, was named high priest (ἀρχιερεύς) by Alexander Balas, the pretender to the throne, who shortly afterwards defeated Demetrius I (1 M 10: 17-20). Jonathan was clothed in the sacred vestments at the Feast of the Tents in the year 152 B.C. He was both the high priest and the leader of the nation, for Alexander quickly promoted him *strategos* and *meridarches*, *i.e.* military and civil governor of Judaea (1 M 10: 65). Jonathan was certainly of priestly descent, for his father Mattathias, who had started the Jewish revolt against Antiochus Epiphanes, was a priest of the line of Yehoyarib (1 M 2: 1). This was, however, an obscure family which was placed at the head of the Priestly classes in 1 Ch 24: 7 only after the triumph of the Hasmoneans; it was a late date for such a correction, and since the family was not Sadoqite, those who were partisans of traditionalism could consider the Hasmonean high priests as illegitimate usurpers. On the other hand, the office became less and less a purely religious one: the high priest held an official rank in the Seleucid Empire and he was appointed by the sovereign; his rôle as civil and military governor also involved him in purely political affairs. The century following Jonathan's appointment saw a development of this political rôle: Simon, his brother, became high priest, *strategos* and *hegoumenos* of the Jews (1 M 13: 42); when the people decreed that he should be styled *ethnarches* (1 M 14: 47), a title higher than *strategos* but lower than that of king, Antiochus VII acquiesced (1 M 15: 2). John Hyrcanus, Simon's son, broke away from his Seleucid protectors and secured national independence; he even began to strike coins, which bore the inscription: 'Yehohanan the high priest, head of the Jewish community'. He decided that the time was not yet come to take the title of king; it was Aristobulus I who took this step, according to Josephus, and the title of king was quite certainly used by Alexander Jannaeus, according to Strabo and the inscriptions on coins. The new title certainly underlined the kingly rôle of the high priest, but it was a blow to religion, and the traditionalists among the Jews no longer recognized in these political high priests the spirit which had made the Maccabees national heroes. Opposition movements began to form: the Pharisees were hostile, and the group which founded the community at Qumran seceded from the regular worship of Judaism.

The final turning point came with the end of the Hasmonean dynasty: Antigonus Mattathias, the last king and high priest of this line (40-37 B.C.) was displaced by Herod the Great. From then onwards the office of high priest was at the disposal of the sovereign, who could appoint and dismiss nominees at his own caprice. There were no less than twenty-eight high

1. Cf. p. 325.

priests, chosen from several different priestly families, between 37 B.C. and A.D. 70. The members of these families thus formed a Priestly aristocracy, that group of 'high priests' (in the plural) which is referred to so often in the New Testament. Their history, however, is outside the scope of this book.

5. *The revenues of the Temple and of the clergy*

(a) *The Temple.* Before the Exile, the Temple was a state sanctuary, and the king provided for the expense of public worship.[1] Ideally, according to Ezechiel, the prince would receive the contributions of the people, but he would be responsible for the offerings and for all the sacrifices offered on behalf of the house of Israel (Ez 45: 13-17). After the return from exile, however, there was neither king nor prince. Darius, of course, issued an edict that in addition to the cost of reconstructing the Temple, which Cyrus had already authorized (Esd 6: 4), everything necessary for sacrifice and for offerings should be furnished to the priests out of the provincial treasury (Esd 6: 9-10); but these orders were not obeyed for long. The letter of credentials which Artaxerxes gave to Esdras contained important provisos about finance: Esdras was to take with him contributions from the king and from his counsellors, from the rich men of Babylon and from the Jews, and he was to spend this money on victims, offerings and libations to be used for sacrifice in the Temple (Esd 7: 15-18). This letter implies that the edict of Darius had not been applied, and that the Temple was desperately poor. Help such as this, however, was exceptional, and the Temple needed a regular income.

Ne 10: 33-35 tells how a regular source of income was arranged. Each man was to give one-third of a shekel per annum for the purposes of public worship and for all the service of the Temple (*i.e.* for its general maintenance), and there was to be an annual delivery of wood (cf. also Ne 13: 31). There is an allusion to this measure in the Priestly redaction of the Pentateuch (Ex 30: 11-16): everyone of twenty years and over is to contribute half a shekel for the service of the Tent of Reunion. This Temple tax was still collected in New Testament times (Mt 17: 24).

However, the generosity of the Persian kings was copied on several occasions by the Seleucids, according to documents cited by Josephus and by the Books of Maccabees; the authenticity of these documents has recently been questioned, but it seems well-founded. There is a vague allusion in 2 M 3: 3 which says that the founder of the Seleucid dynasty paid for all the sacrifices out of his personal income; but, more important, a letter of Antiochus III is quoted by Josephus in *Ant.* XII, iii, 3; the king has decided to contribute twenty thousand drachmas for victims to be offered in sacrifice, and also a large quantity of flour, of corn and of salt. Demetrius I,

1. Cf. pp. 320 and 379.

in his struggle for power, offered Jonathan all the revenues from Ptolemais and from its environs, and an annual subsidy from the royal list to cover the expenses of worship; he even promised to pay for all the work necessary in repairing the Temple (1 M 10: 39-45). And yet verse 47 tells us that the Jews decided in favour of Demetrius' rival, Alexander Balas, 'because, in their opinion, he offered them more help'.

Such were the sources of income, some of them permanent, others ephemeral; in addition, the Temple received voluntary donations and probably part of the votive offerings, the other part being reserved for the priests. In the course of time, the wealth of the Temple continued to increase, and many covetous eyes were turned on it: cf. the history of Heliodorus (2 M 3), the plundering by Antiochus Epiphanes (1 M 1: 21-24), the tribute of 10,000 talents demanded by Pompey (Josephus, *Ant.* XIV, iv, 5), the confiscation by Crassus of 2,000 silver talents left by Pompey and of 8,000 gold talents as well (Josephus, *Ant.* XIV, vii, 1), and the final sacking of the burnt-out Temple by the soldiers of Titus (Josephus, *Bell.* VI, v, 2, vi, 1).

(b) *The clergy*. Ezechiel drew his inspiration, presumably, from the situation which obtained in the last years of the monarchy, when he assigned to the priests part of the sacrifices, everything which was vowed to the Temple, the best of the first-fruits and of the dues, and the best of the flour which was offered to the sanctuary (Ez 44: 29-30).

The dispositions made in Nb 18: 8-32 are far more detailed and even more favourable to the clergy. Different arrangements are there made for the priests and for the Levites. The priests are to take their food from the sacrifices and from the offerings brought by the people. Lv 6-7 expressly states the part which falls to the priests in every instance, and he is better off than in the parallel ruling given in Dt 18: 3: instead of the shoulder, the jaw and the stomach, the priest is now to receive the breast and the right leg. the finest pieces (Lv 7: 30-34); Dt 18 does not mention the sacrifices for sin and the sacrifices of reparation, but Lv 7: 7-10 entitles the priest to everything from these sacrifices which is not burnt upon the altar—in short, almost everything; he is to keep also the skin of the victims offered as holocausts, and all vegetable offerings. The priests are also to have (as in Ezechiel) the best (*rêshîth*) of the produce of the land, the first-fruits (*bikkûrîm*) and everything which is vowed by an anathema (*ḥerem*), according to Nb 18: 12-14; Nb 18: 15-18 adds to this the first-born (*b'kôr*), which must be offered in the sanctuary or else, if it is a man or an unclean animal, redeemed.

The Levites were to be supported by the tithes (*ma'aser*) on corn and new wine. Yet one-tenth of this tithe was to be considered as a levy for Yahweh, and the Levites had to pay this to the priests, who thus had a further increase in their income (Nb 18: 20-32). The obligation of paying a tithe was extended to cattle by Lv 27: 30-33, though the cattle, like the farm-produce, could be redeemed; there is an allusion to this tithe on cattle in 2 Ch 31: 6, but it is impossible to say whether it was ever paid.

Certainly, the tithe on cattle is not mentioned in the parallel texts in the Book of Nehemias. When Nehemias arrived on his second mission, he was informed that the Levites had left the Temple because the tithes, their only source of income, were not being paid. Nehemias placed the blame on the upper classes, brought back the Levites, and set up a committee to administer the stores (cf. Ne 13: 5) and to distribute them (Ne 13: 10-14). To prevent the recurrence of the abuses he had found, Nehemias then made the community undertake a number of solemn promises, in which the income due to the clergy was not forgotten: the first-fruits of the land and of fruit-trees, the first-born, the best of the wheat flour, of the fruits, of new wine and of oil were to be given to the priests, and the tithes were to be given to the Levites (Ne 10: 36-38*a*). He was putting into practice the laws of Nb 18. Yet it appears that the obligation was not always well honoured: Malachi probably preached about this time, and he accuses the people of not paying tithes and of not making offerings to the Temple treasury (Ml 3: 7-10). An insertion in Nehemias (Ne 10: 38*b*-39) probably belongs to these same years; it allows the Levites to go themselves to collect the tithes in the towns, under the direction of a priest.

The system was functioning smoothly at the time when the Chronicler was writing, and he, forgetting the difficulties of bygone days, paints the period of the Return as a golden age for the clergy: 'Judah rejoiced in the priests and in the Levites who served there. . . . In the time of Zorobabel and in the time of Nehemias, all Israel paid the singers and the door-keepers their dues, in accordance with their daily needs. They gave the Levites the sacred dues, and the Levites gave part of them to the sons of Aaron' (Ne 12: 44-47).

This prescription remained in force (cf. Si 7: 31; Jdt 11: 13), and the cost to the faithful grew heavier when old obligations, which these new measures had replaced, were also re-enforced; the tithe of Dt 14: 22-26 was understood as a 'second tithe' which was changed into money and spent at the sanctuary, and the three-yearly tithe of Dt 14: 28-29 became 'a third tithe'. Yet all these tithes were paid by the pious Tobias, as a man who faithfully observed the Law (Tb 1: 6-8).

Chapter Nine

ALTARS

THE altar is an essential element in a sanctuary; and in the stories about the Patriarchs, the phrase 'setting up an altar' means, in effect, founding a sanctuary (Gn 12: 7, 8; 13: 18; 26: 25; 33: 20). From the beginning, the priest's office consisted in the ministry of the altar, and as time went on, his work became more and more restricted to this ministry; sacrifice, the principal rite in public worship, means the offering of a gift upon an altar. Before passing, then, from the study of the priesthood to the study of sacrifice and ritual, we must say something about altars.

The Hebrew word for an altar is *mizbeaḥ*, from a verbal root meaning 'to slaughter', and therefore 'to slaughter with a view to sacrifice'. The word took on a broader meaning when the ritual became more developed: in the Temple, victims other than birds were killed at some distance from the altar and then placed upon it; vegetable offerings were also placed on the altar; and the same word was used for the altar of incense. An altar, then, was a place where men offered sacrifices, whatever their nature.

1. *Pre-Israelite altars in Palestine*

In Palestine, sacrifice was offered on various types of altars: the altar might be just the natural surface of the rock, or a rock which had been hewn into a certain shape, or a piece of rock jutting up on its own; and there were, of course, man-made altars.

Excavations in Palestine have revealed many rocky surfaces which have been artificially hollowed out. It would be an exaggeration to say that everyone had some connection with worship. The majority of them could have served a profane purpose: for example, those which stand near a well or a cistern or a spring may have been used as watering-troughs for animals, and the largest of them may have been used to do the laundry; those which are near a press are obviously connected with the making of wine or of oil. And when they are found near tombs, they are to be explained by funeral rites, but not necessarily by sacrifices: the dead could be hungry and thirsty.[1]

There are, however, examples in which other evidence proves that some of these hollowed rocks were used in connection with sacrifice. We shall

1. Cf. p. 60.

speak in a moment of the rock altar at Sar'a; at Gezer, the hollows in the surface of the rock lead down to a cave where the bones of pigs offered in sacrifice were found. But where evidence of this kind is wanting, it is impossible to decide whether a surface of rock, with or without such hollows, was used as an altar. At least two passages in the Bible, Jg 6: 19–23 and 13: 19–20, indicate that the custom of using such rocks existed.

Everyone quotes, as examples of altars hewn out of the natural rock, those found at Petra and in the district around; the altars there are cut out of the surrounding rock, and steps are even hewn in front of them. Petra became an important Nabatean centre in Hellenistic times, but there is no reason why these installations should not be even older; on the other hand, it must not be forgotten that tombs and houses carved out of the rock are also a characteristic feature of Petra; it would be imprudent, then, to make generalizations about altars from observations which may not be valid outside this region.

A large stone or a detached piece of rock could serve as an altar. We shall cite only two examples: near Sar'a, a large, cubic piece of stone stands in a field; it is rough-shapen, about four feet three inches high, with steps near the top, and hollowed out on top in several places. It is called, without any proof, the altar of Manoah (Jg 13: 19–20). Recent excavations at Hazor have unearthed an enormous rectangular block weighing about five tons, with a basin hollowed out on one of its surfaces; the site in which it was found was a Canaanite temple of the 13th century B.C.

Lastly, we have man-made altars. Here we must recall what was said about the 'high places'.[1] The *bamah* was a knoll or a mound upon which sacrifice was offered, but not every *bamah* had an altar erected upon it; the knoll itself could take the place of an altar. Platforms of large stones have been uncovered in the excavations at Megiddo, at Nahariyah near Haifa and at Hazor in Galilee.

In other pre-Israelite sanctuaries, altars have been discovered standing against the back wall, built of large stones and earthen mortar, or built in plain brick. Recent excavations have provided examples for all periods: at Megiddo, for the periods around 3000 B.C. and around 2000 B.C., at Et-Tell (Ai) for a period between 3000 and 2000 B.C., and at Tell ed-Duweir (Lakish) for the 14th-13th centuries B.C.

2. *Israelite altars outside the main sanctuary*

Examples of the different types of altars are found in the most ancient biblical texts. In Jg 6: 19-23, Gideon wanted to offer a goat and some unleavened bread to the Angel of Yahweh; the Angel ordered him to put the meat and the bread on a rock, where they were burnt up by a fire which shot

1. Cf. pp. 284-285.

out of the rock: it was a sacrifice. In Jg 13: 19-20, Manoah, the father of Samson, offered up a goat as a whole-burnt offering to Yahweh; he offered it upon a rock, and in the following verse the rock is called an 'altar'.

Other examples show that large stones were used as altars. When the Ark was being brought back from Beth-Shemesh, the wooden chariot and the cows which had drawn it were used for a whole-burnt offering on a 'large stone' which stood nearby (1 S 6: 14). In Saul's war against the Philistines, the people began to slaughter the captured sheep on the ground itself; thereupon Saul intervened with the command 'Roll a big stone over here towards me!' and he insisted that the beasts should be slaughtered on the stone: the implication is that this was an altar, for all slaughtering of animals had a sacrificial character until the time of Deuteronomy (Dt 12: 20-25).

As a general rule, however, all the altars mentioned in the Bible (with the exception of those in the Temple) were altars built out of stone: *e.g.* those which the Patriarchs set up, those in the period of Josue (Jos 22: 10) and of the Judges (Jg 6: 24: the altar built on the rock where the meal prepared for the guests had been burnt up by fire from Yahweh, and 6: 26: a parallel tradition); this is true of all the altars down to the time when David built an altar on the site of the future Temple (2 S 24: 25). Elias restored the altar of Yahweh which had stood on Carmel and which had been demolished; then he laid on it the wood and the quarters of the victims which were to be sacrificed (1 K 18: 30 and 33). A gloss inspired by Ex 24: 4; Jos 4: 1-9 states (vv. 31-32*a*) that this altar was made of twelve stones to symbolize the twelve tribes of Israel.

Apart from this gloss, we are never told whether the altars were made of (plain) bricks or of stones. As we have seen, both kinds of material were used for pre-Israelite altars in Canaan, and both kinds are authorized by the law of Ex 20: 24-26: the altar must be of earth (*i.e.* plain bricks); if it is made of stone, the stone must not be trimmed with a chisel. Dt. 27: 5 repeats this command: an altar of stones untouched by any iron is to be erected on Ebal; the order was carried out by Josue, according to the Deuteronomic passage in Jos 8: 30-31. The rabbis found some very subtle explanations of this precept forbidding trimmed stones to be used for an altar: 'The altar is for forgiving, and iron is for punishing', or 'The altar prolongs life, but iron cuts it short'. Ex 20 merely says that iron 'desecrates' stone; the meaning is that things should be used for the service of God only in their natural condition, before they have been interfered with in any way by man (cf. Nb 19: 2; Dt 21: 3-4; 1 S 6: 7, etc.); the principle reminds us of altars erected on rocks or upon a large unhewn stone. The law of Ex 20: 26 also forbids steps leading up to the altar. Some Canaanite altars had them, and later Israelite altars were approached by a series of steps or by a ramp. Ex 20: 26 gives modesty as the reason for this prohibition: a priest wearing only a loincloth might expose himself as he was stepping up to the altar; consequently, when, in later ages, the high altar was approached by a series of steps, another law was introduced by which the priests were obliged to wear a pair of drawers (Ex 28: 42-43). The explanation advanced in Ex 20: 26 does not seem to be the original one; the prohibition was originally based, it would appear, rather on the sacred character of the altar, which was to be as far removed as possible from anything profane: steps which touched the altar and upon which the priest trod would bring the altar into contact with the profane.

We shall discuss later the little movable altars which were used for offerings of incense.[1]

3. *The altars used in the desert*

According to the description of the desert sanctuary, the Tent or the Dwelling had two altars: one was the altar of holocausts which stood immediately in front of the entrance to the Dwelling (Ex 40: 6, 29; cf. Lv 4: 18), and the other was the altar of incense which stood inside the Dwelling, in front of the veil which cut off the rear part where the Ark was kept (Ex 30: 6; 40: 5, 26).

The altar of holocausts is described in Ex 27: 1-8 and 38: 1-7. It was constructed of planks of acacia-wood, five cubits long, five cubits wide and three cubits high. Bronze plates were fitted over these planks, and the altar is sometimes called 'the bronze altar'. It had a bronze grating (*i.e.* some kind of trellis work), a cornice or rim, and four rings for the bars by which it was carried. Also, it was hollow. This description is obscure; in particular, it is hard to see how the trellis work fits in with the rest, and very difficult indeed to see how victims could have been burnt on this wooden chest, even if it was covered in bronze. Some exegetes have suggested that the structure was filled with earth and with stones each time the people pitched camp, but this is not stated in the text and the grating would make it impossible. Finally, its height is given as four and a half feet; this means a step would have been needed, but the text does not mention one.

The altar of perfumes is described in Ex 30: 1-5 and 37: 25-28: its surface was one cubit square, its height two cubits. It was made of acacia wood, and the upper part was plated with gold; it had golden horns, and four golden rings by which it could be carried (hence it is sometimes called simply 'the golden altar'). The description is clear, but it seems that the mention of this altar as among the appurtenances of the desert sanctuary is a later insertion into the text. The altar is not mentioned among the furnishings of the Dwelling in Ex 25; nor is its siting indicated where one would expect it, in Ex 26: 33-37; instead, the altar itself, its site and its use are described in Ex 30: 1-10, which looks very like a passage out of context. Lastly, this altar is never mentioned in the stories about the desert: in the desert, offerings of perfume were made with a little incense-shovel (Nb 16: 6-7, 17-18; 17: 11-12).

1. Cf. p. 411.

Israelite tradition, then, was not certain that there had been an altar of perfumes in the desert sanctuary, and only included it among the furnishings of the Tent in order to make the Tent a copy of the Temple of Jerusalem. Indeed, the altar of holocausts itself is a movable replica of the altar in the Temple. Thus we reach the same conclusion from studying the furnishing of the Tent as we reached from examining the priestly description of it.[1]

4. *The altars in Solomon's Temple*

Like the Tent, Solomon's Temple had two altars, standing in the same position to each other as the two altars in the Tent: the altar of holocausts stood in front of the Temple (2 K 16: 14), and the altar of perfumes stood in the Hekal, in front of the Debir (1 K 6: 20–21). (The exact position of the altar of holocausts on the modern Haram esh-Sherif depends on the view one takes about the general site of the Temple.[2])

(a) *The altar of holocausts.* One curious fact to be noticed is that the altar of holocausts is never once mentioned in the long description of the Temple and its furniture (1 K: 6–7). There are allusions to it in 1 K 8: 22 and 54 (which are part of the Deuteronomic redaction) and also in 1 K 8: 64 and 9: 25 (which are older texts). Several explanations have been given for this strange silence. It is not likely that Solomon simply transferred into his Temple the altar which David had built (2 S 24: 25), for he had a habit of ordering new and costly things. It is more likely that he installed a new altar, which (according to 1 K 8: 64 and 2 K 16: 15) was called a bronze altar and which (according to 2 K 16: 14) was movable: it would then be a large grille upon which sacrifices could be burnt. Possibly the editor of 1 K 6–7 suppressed the description of this altar because it was not the kind of altar demanded by the customs and laws of Israel (Ex 20: 24–26); it was, in fact, a type used by the Phoenicians, as two inscriptions tell us. The Chronicler has made good this omission by attributing to Solomon the construction of a bronze altar ten cubits square and five cubits high (2 Ch 4: 1): the measurements he gives, however, seem to be more in accord with the altar built by Achaz, or with the one which must have existed in the Chronicler's own day.

In the time of Achaz, Solomon's altar was replaced by a new one modelled on an altar the king had seen at Damascus when he went there to take an oath of fealty to Tiglath-Pileser (2 K 16: 10–16). In all probability, the model Achaz copied was Syrian, not Assyrian (though many writers defend the latter view): the new altar was of imposing dimensions (v. 15) and it was approached either by steps or by a ramp (v. 12); it was a copy of the large altar in the temple of Hadad-Rimmon at Damascus (cf. 2 K 5: 18). The old bronze altar was moved a little to the north, and Achaz kept it so that he could use it in examining victims for omens: this interpretation of the final

1. Cf. p. 296. 2. Cf. pp. 318–319.

phrase in v. 15 is quite possible, for the verb *biqqer* could have this meaning. In spite of its origin, which was not above suspicion, the new altar remained in use until the Exile, and the altar in the second Temple was apparently of the same shape, though perhaps larger.

(b) *The altar of perfumes.* Some authors have denied, though without convincing arguments, that there ever was an altar of perfumes in Solomon's Temple. There is a reference to it in the overloaded and confused text of 1 K 6: 20-21, which may be reconstructed thus with the help of Greek texts: 'He made an altar of cedar ⟨ ⟩ in front of the Debir, and covered it with gold'. It is referred to as the 'golden altar' in 1 K 7: 48. Moreover, in the inaugural vision of Isaias (where the Temple either is, or is imagined to be, the place where Yahweh speaks to him) one of the Seraphim takes a piece of burning coal from an altar: and since the altar is inside the Temple, it can only be the altar of perfumes. The last reference occurs in 2 Ch 26: 16: Ozias tried to offer incense on the altar of perfumes, inside the Hekal.

In 1 K 7: 48, this altar is called simply 'the golden' one (*zahab*), and the same term is sometimes used for the corresponding altar in the desert Tent. A new explanation of this name has recently been put forward: in Southern Arabia *dhb* was used both for 'gold' and for 'perfume', and the word has been discovered in an engraving on a small perfume-brazier, along with the names of other aromatic perfumes. It is suggested, therefore, that the 'golden altar' (*mizbeaḥ hazzahab*) of 1 K 7: 48 should be translated 'altar of perfumes'. The rendering is certainly possible, but if it is accepted, one must admit that the original meaning was very soon lost: both 1 K 6: 20-21 (describing the altar in Solomon's Temple) and Ex 30: 1-5 (describing the altar in the Tent) lay great stress on its covering of precious metal in order to justify its name (*mizbeaḥ hazzahab*); and all the Greek texts, biblical or non-biblical, in referring to it speak of it as 'golden' altar.

Palestinian archaeology enables us to trace the development of this kind of altar. The Canaanites used cylindrical or rectangular objects made out of baked earth in order to burn perfumes. From the beginning of the Israelite monarchy, limestone altars are found, shaped like square pillars; usually, they have four horns on the top corners. (Examples of this type have been unearthed at Shechem and at Megiddo.) This is the shape of the altar of perfumes described in Ex 30: 1-5, but the specimens found in excavations are not as big as that described in this text. One specimen of a very tiny altar of the same type, dating from the eleventh century, was found at Tell Beit Mirsim, and a large group of similar small ones, dating from the Persian period, was found at Lakish. The use of these altars outside the central sanctuary was eventually condemned,[1] but an altar of the same type, only more imposing, must have stood in the Temple from the time of Solomon.

1. Cf. pp. 286-287.

5. *The altar of Ezechiel*

Yet we should note that when Ezechiel is describing the future temple, he makes no mention of the altar of perfumes. Ez 41: 21–22, which is often cited in this connection, refers to the table of shewbread. By contrast, the altar of holocausts is described in minute detail (Ez 43: 13–17), but this description (with the later insertion about the consecration of the altar, Ez 43: 18–27) seems to have been added at a later date; it certainly does not stand in its original context. The altar described by Ezechiel had three tiers, and seems to be a small-scale model of the many-storied tower (the ziggurat)[1]; the terms used for its different parts are evidently taken from a Babylonian background. The base is called *ḥeq ha'areṣ*, *i.e.* 'bosom of the earth', which is a translation of the Akkadian *irat erṣiti*, the name given to foundations of a temple or ziggurat. The upper part is called *'ari'el*; or *har'el*; the word *har'el* means 'mountain of God', and is a Hebrew interpretation of the Akkadian term *arallu*, which stands both for the world underneath the earth and for the mountain of the gods. The top platform had horns at the four corners, and was approached by a flight of steps on its eastern side.

Ezechiel planned that this new altar should be ten cubits high, and from eighteen to twenty cubits square at the base: this is more or less the size of the altar in Solomon's Temple, according to 2 Ch 4: 1. Ezechiel may have been thinking of the altar in the first Temple, for he had himself seen it, but the shape of the new altar and the names given to its parts are of Babylonian inspiration, as is the symbolism which results. There is no evidence whatever that the altar built after the Return was modelled on the description given by the prophet.

6. *The altars in the second Temple*

We have already stated that Chronicles refers to Solomon's altar (2 Ch 4: 1) and to the altar of perfumes (2 Ch 26: 16): these two references may preserve information about the first Temple, or they may have been inspired by what the Chronicler saw in the second Temple, but otherwise we have no information in the Hebrew Bible about the altars in the post-exilic Temple. Two non-biblical texts are extant, both dating from the Hellenistic period. According to the Pseudo-Hecataeus (cited by Josephus, *C. Apionem* I 198), there stood in the Temple enclosure a square altar, twenty cubits wide and ten cubits high, built of untrimmed stones. Beside it there was a building containing a golden altar and a golden chandelier. This text confirms the existence of two altars, one for whole-burnt offerings and one for perfumes; the dimensions of the altar of holocausts are those given by 2 Ch 4: 1, and it is presented as if it had been built in accordance with the law of Ex 20: 25. This perfect harmony with the biblical texts is, however, disconcerting

1. Cf. pp. 281–282.

rather than probative, for the Pseudo-Hecataeus is a work of Jewish propaganda written at Alexandria shortly after 200 B.C. The second text, in the Letter of Aristeas, comes from the same place, and from almost the same period: it says, quite simply, that 'the size of the altar's structure was in proportion to the place where it stood, and to the victims burnt upon it: it was approached by a ramp of similar proportions. The place had a slope, for the sake of propriety'. All these facts, too, are an echo of biblical texts.

Shortly after these propaganda works were written, Antiochus Epiphanes launched his persecution, and the altars in the Temple did not escape. In 169 B.C., Antiochus plundered the Temple and took away the golden altar, *i.e.* the altar of perfumes (1 M 1: 21); in December, 167, he erected an altar to Zeus Olympios over the altar of holocausts, and had sacrifices to Zeus offered there (1 M 1: 54, 59; 2 M 6: 2, 5). The pagan altar is 'the abomination of desolation' referred to in 1 M 1: 54 and Dn 9: 27.

As soon as the Maccabees had regained freedom for the Jews to practise their religion, they made away with this scandal: a new altar was built, and the stones of the old one, which had been desecrated by the pagan worship performed over it, were put away in a side-building of the Temple (1 M 4: 44-47; 2 M 10: 3). A new altar of perfumes was also put in the Temple (1 M 4: 49).

7. *The religious significance of altars*

In Israel, the altar had the same significance as in other ancient religions, but with appreciable nuances. The altar is only rarely referred to as the table of Yahweh (Ez 44: 16; Ml 1: 7, 12), and never in ancient texts: conversely, the table of shewbread is said to be 'like an altar' in Ez 41: 21-22. This distrust of the word 'table' is based on a reaction against the idea that a sacrifice provided the god with a banquet (cf. Is 65: 11 and the satire in Dn 14: 1-22).

Since the Temple was the house of God, it had to have a hearth, and the altar was this hearth. The idea is not expressed in explicit terms, for the *'ari'el* of Ez 43: 13-17 does not mean (as we have seen above) a 'hearth', though many writers have thought so. The idea is expressed in another way: a fire must always be burning upon the altar (Lv 6: 5-6; cf. 2 M 1: 18-36), just as the lamp must always be kept alight in the Temple (Ex 27: 20-21; Lv 24: 2-4).

The altar was the sign of God's presence. In the earliest period of Israel's history, it commemorated a theophany (Gn 12: 7; 26: 24-25) or was called by some name which reminded men of God: Jacob called the altar he erected at Shechem 'El, God of Israel', and Moses called the altar he erected after the defeat of the Amalekites 'Yahweh-Nissi', 'Yahweh is my rallying-standard'. Later on, the altar was specially consecrated, and purified each year on the Day of Atonement: it thus acquired an altogether exceptional holiness (Ex 29: 36–37; 30: 10; Lv 8: 15; 16: 18–19).

This holiness was connected in a particular way with the 'horns' of the altar, those four parts which stuck out at the top corners of the altar of holocausts and of the altar of perfumes. The blood of victims was rubbed on them to consecrate the altar, or in rites of expiation to make atonement (Ex 29: 12; 30: 10; Lv 4 *passim*; 8: 15; 9: 9; 16: 18; Ez 43: 20). A fugitive claiming asylum would grasp the horns of the altar (1 K 2: 28). It is not quite clear what these horns stand for: in the Bible, a horn is a symbol for power, but this interpretation is inadequate in the present context; nor is it likely that these horns represent the horns of the victims slaughtered, like the bucrane often found on Roman altars. Possibly they took the place of little steles, *i.e.* of small *maṣṣebôth*, which had once been placed on the altar as emblems of the divinity; possibly they are just visible symbols emphasizing the special importance and holiness of the extremities of the altar. The extremities of a priest's body (the lobe of his ear, his thumb and his big toe) were rubbed with blood in the late ritual for investing a priest in his office (Ex 29: 20), and the same parts were rubbed with blood and anointed with oil in the rite for the purification of a leper (Lv 14: 14–17).

Lastly, the altar was used as an instrument of mediation. The offerings of men were placed upon it and there burnt: by this ceremony, the offerings were taken out of man's domain and given to God, and God replied by bestowing blessings (Ex 20: 24). Thus the Covenant itself between God and his people was maintained in force, or re-established, upon the altar of sacrifice.

CHAPTER TEN

THE RITUAL OF SACRIFICE

THE altar was the place of sacrifice, and sacrifice was the principal act in Israel's cult. We shall endeavour to define the meaning of sacrifice in the religion of Israel, but before we can do so, we must first make a study of the rites connected with sacrifice, and trace their development. For the moment, we may give the following provisory definition: sacrifice is any offering, animal or vegetable, which is wholly or partially destroyed upon an altar as a token of homage to God. The study of the ritual is complicated by the fact that several terms are used for sacrifice, and they are not always clearly distinguished: one and the same word can denote several kinds of sacrifice, and one kind of sacrifice can be described by a variety of terms. The vocabulary reflects an historical development and the fusion of various practices, similar to one another, but originating from different backgrounds.

We shall start with the latest and most complete ritual, and we shall then endeavour to retrace the history of sacrifice to its origin. The code of sacrifices followed in the second Temple is contained in Lv 1-7. These chapters belong to the last redaction of the Pentateuch: they are legislative in character, and break the story of the institution of worship in the desert which ought to continue straight on from the erection of the sanctuary (Ex 40) to the installation of the priests (Lv 8-10).

1. *Holocausts*

The English word 'holocaust' comes, through the Vulgate, from the Septuagint, and in the Septuagint it is a translation of the Hebrew *'olah*, from a root meaning 'to go up': a holocaust, then, is a sacrifice which is 'taken up' on to the altar, or, more probably, whose smoke 'goes up' to God when it is burnt. The characteristic feature of this sacrifice is that the entire victim is burnt and that nothing is given back to the man who offers it or to the priest (except the skin). This is why the Greek translates it 'holocaust' (meaning, 'wholly burnt'), and why the term *'olah* has sometimes been replaced by the word *kalil*, meaning a 'total' sacrifice (1 S 7: 9; Dt 33: 10; cf. Ps 51: 21, where *'olah* is used alongside *kalil*).

In the ritual of Lv 1, the victim must be a male animal without any blemish (cf. the older Law of Holiness, Lv 22: 17-25); it may be a small or a large beast, or a bird (though only a turtle-dove or a pigeon). The victim is presented by the man making the offering and he must be in a state of ritual purity. He lays his hand upon the head of the victim. This action is not a magic gesture to establish contact between God and man, nor is it a symbolic action implying that the victim is a substitute for the man, whose sins are thereby transferred to the victim for expiation. (It is true that in the ceremony of the scapegoat, Lv 16: 21,[1] the sins of the people are transferred to the goat by the same gesture, but precisely because the scapegoat is thereby loaded with the sins of the people, it is regarded as defiled, and unworthy to be sacrificed.) Nor is this laying of hands on the victim a simple *manumissio* or abandoning of the victim to God: rather, it is a solemn attestation that this victim comes from this particular individual who is laying his hands on it, that the sacrifice which is going to be presented to God by the priest is offered in his name, and that the fruits of this sacrifice shall be his.

The man making the sacrifice would himself cut the throat of the victim at some distance from the altar. The priests and the Levites slaughtered only the animals offered in public sacrifices (2 Ch 29: 22, 24, 34; Ez 44: 11). The priest's rôle, properly speaking, did not begin until the victim was brought into contact with the altar, and it consisted in pouring the blood around the altar. The blood contained the life; indeed, in the Hebrew mind, the blood was life: 'the life of all flesh is its blood' (Lv 17: 14; cf. Gn 9: 4; Dt 12: 23; Lv 7: 26-27), and therefore the blood belonged to God alone.

Afterwards, the victim was skinned and cut up, and its four quarters were put on the altar by the priests, there to be burnt by the fire which was always kept alight (Lv 6: 5-6). (The reference to the lighting of the fire in Lv 1: 7 applies only to the first sacrifice ever offered, which is represented as taking place after the promulgation of the Law.) Everything, including the head, the intestines and the hooves or feet, was first washed, then placed on the altar, and then burnt.

When the victim was a bird, the ritual was modified: the man bringing the offering did not lay hands on it, nor did he cut its throat; instead, everything was done on the altar, and therefore done by the priest. Lv 5: 7 and 12: 8 show that these sacrifices of birds were offered by the poor as a substitute for sacrifices of beasts, which only the rich could afford. For the same reason, sheep and goats were more common offerings than cattle.

The latest rituals in Israel's history lay down that, along with the holocaust, there must be an offering (*minḥah*) of flour kneaded with oil, and a libation of wine; this ruling applied to the feast of Weeks (according to Lv 23: 18), to the daily holocausts (according to Ex 29: 38-42) and to all sacrifices of '*olah* and *zebaḥ* (according to Nb 15: 1-16). The flour was burnt, and the wine was poured out at the foot of the altar, like the blood of the victim (cf. Si 50: 15).

1. Cf. pp. 508-509.

This first chapter of Leviticus presents us with the whole problem of the fluidity of the terms used in sacrificial language. The holocaust is called a *qorban* in Lv 1: 2, 10, 14, *i.e.* that which a man 'brings near' God or the altar: the same term is used by Leviticus, Numbers and Ezechiel for all sacrifices, and even for non-sacrificial offerings, such as the material destined for use in the sanctuary (Nb 7 *passim*); and in later Judaism, it acquired the meaning of 'consecration'. In the same chapter, the holocaust is also called an *'ishsheh* (Lv 1: 9, 13, 17). The etymology of this word is still a subject of debate, but whatever it is, there is no doubt that the editors of the Bible thought the word applied to any offering which was wholly or partially destroyed by fire (*'esh*). The word, which is frequently found in the Priestly writings and which occurs also in the Hebrew version of Si (45: 20; 50: 13), is used only three times elsewhere, *viz.* in Dt 18: 1; Jos 13: 14 (Hebrew) and in 1 S 2: 28: all three texts are the work of the Deuteronomists, and all of them refer to the rights a priest has over sacrifices. In the Pentateuch, the word is often accompanied by the expression 'a fragrance pleasing to Yahweh'. This anthropomorphism means that God accepts the sacrifice (cf. Gn 8: 21, where it corresponds to a similar, but cruder, expression in the Babylonian account of the Flood).[1] The formula, without any materialistic overtones, remained in use in liturgical language.

2. *Communion sacrifices*

We are adopting the translation 'communion sacrifice' for want of a better rendering of what is called in Hebrew *zebaḥ sh^{e}lamîm*, or *zebaḥ* (without qualification) or simply *sh^{e}lamîm* (always in the plural except once, *shelem*, in Am 5: 22). All these terms are equivalent to one another, as is proved by the way in which they are interchanged inside certain passages or in parallel passages, and by the fact that the motives and the rites of this sacrifice are always the same: *zebaḥ sh^{e}lamîm* is the official name in the Priestly rituals which we are studying here, and it is rarely found elsewhere. The renderings 'peace-offering' and 'welcome offering' are inspired by the Greek version, but the ritual and the practice of Israel present it rather as a sacrifice of thanksgiving to God which brings about union with him.

The ritual divides communion-sacrifices into three types: the sacrifice of praise (*tôdah*), Lv 7: 12–15; 22: 29–30, the voluntary sacrifice (*n^{e}dabah*), *i.e.* one offered out of devotion, not because of any precept or promise, Lv 7: 16–17; 22: 18–23, and the votive sacrifice (*neder*), *i.e.* one to which a person has bound himself by a vow, Lv 7: 16–17; 22: 18–23. The distinction between the three types is, however, not very precise.

The principal ritual is described in Lv 3, and its characteristic feature lies in the fact that the victim is shared between God, the priest and the person

1. Cf. p. 433.

offering the sacrifice, who eats it as a holy thing. The victims prescribed are the same as those for a holocaust (though birds are not allowed), but they may be male or female, and minor blemishes are tolerated in a victim offered as a voluntary sacrifice (*n'dabah*), according to Lv 22: 23. The laying on of hands, the cutting of the throat and the sprinkling of blood are carried out exactly as for a holocaust.

The part which is given to Yahweh is burnt upon the altar: this comprised all the fat around the intestines, the kidneys, the liver, and the fat of a sheep's tail, and only the fat. The reason is that fat, like blood, was considered a life-giving part: 'All fat belongs to Yahweh . . . You shall eat neither fat nor blood' (Lv 3: 16–17; cf. 7: 22–24).

Two parts are assigned to the priest: the breast, which was 'weighed' before Yahweh (according to the common explanation of the word *t'nûphah*) but not burnt upon the altar, and the right leg, which was a 'sample' (*t'rûmah*) due to the priest by right (Lv 7: 28-34; 10: 14-15). The two words, however, are often used without distinction, and perhaps they both mean a 'contribution'; both of them may have been borrowed from the terminology of Babylonian contracts.

The remainder of the animal belongs to the person who offers the sacrifice: he eats it with his family and with any guests he may invite, but they must be in a state of ritual purity. The victim of a sacrifice of praise (*tôdah*) must be eaten on the day it is offered (Lv 7: 15), but a victim of a voluntary or votive sacrifice (*n'dabah* or *neder*) can be eaten on the following day, though anything left over must be burned on the third day (Lv 7: 16-17). The *tôdah* sacrifice is to be accompanied by an offering (*minḥah*) of unleavened cakes and of leavened bread. One of the cakes is a 'sample' for Yahweh, and reverts to the priest.

3. *Expiatory sacrifices*

Almost half of the sacrificial code of the second Temple concerns those sacrifices which we call expiatory sacrifices, though the ritual itself does not have one name which is applicable to them all; it treats, sometimes consecutively and sometimes simultaneously, of two kinds of sacrifice whose purpose is to re-establish the covenant with God when it has been broken by the sin of man. They are called respectively, the sacrifice for sin (*ḥaṭṭa'th*) and the sacrifice of reparation (*'asham*). In spite of the length of the passages devoted to them, it is difficult to determine the exact significance of each sacrifice or to say why they are distinguished from each other.

(a) *Sacrifice for sin*. In Hebrew, the word *ḥaṭṭa'th* means both sin and the rite which does away with sin (Lv 4: 1—5: 13; 6: 17-23). The type of victim depended on the rank of the person who had sinned. A bull was to be offered for a sin of the high priest, the 'anointed priest',[1] for his guilt defiled

1. Cf. p. 398.

the entire people; a bull was also prescribed when the people itself had sinned; a he-goat was to be offered for the sin of the 'prince' (*nasi'*), *i.e.* the lay head of the community, in Ezechiel's mind; a she-goat or a sheep was the offering for the sin of a private individual. The poor could offer two turtle-doves or two pigeons instead of these expensive victims: one of the birds was used as a sacrifice for sin (*ḥaṭṭa'th*), and the other was offered a holocaust. The poor could make an offering of flour instead of any of these animals.

The ritual for these sacrifices is distinguished from that used in other sacrifices by two things, the use to which the blood is put, and the way in which the victim's flesh is disposed of. The blood played a more important part in this sacrifice than in any other. When the sacrifice was offered for the high priest or for the entire people, there were three successive rites: the priest who is performing the sacrifice first collected the blood, entered into the Holy Place and there sprinkled the blood seven times against the veil which curtains off the Holy of Holies; next, he rubbed blood upon the corners of the altar of incense, which stood before the veil; thirdly, he poured out the rest of the blood at the foot of the altar of holocausts. These were the only animal sacrifices in which part of the victim was carried inside the Temple building. When sacrifice was offered for the sin of the lay head of the community, or for the sin of a private individual, the blood was put on the horns of the altar of holocausts, and the rest poured out at its base; in these two sacrifices, nothing was taken within the Holy Place.

These rites underline the value which blood has in expiating sin; it can be used to expiate sin because it is the means of life: 'the life of flesh is in its blood. This blood I have given to you, in order that you may perform the rite of expiation upon the altar, for your lives; for blood makes expiation for a life' (or: 'for blood makes expiation, by reason of the life that is in it,' Lv 17: 11). We may compare the parallel text in He 9: 22: 'Without the shedding of blood, there is no forgiveness at all'.

All the fat was burnt upon the altar, as in communion-sacrifices, but the meat was put to a different use: since the person offering the sacrifice admitted his guilt, he received no part of the victim, and everything reverted to the priests. And when the sacrifice of *ḥaṭṭa'th* was offered for the sin of the community, or for the sin of the high priest as head of the community, the priests themselves were not allowed to eat any part of the victim: all the remains were carried outside the sanctuary and placed on the ash-heap. The fact that the fat was burnt on the altar, and that the meat of sacrifices offered for the sins of private individuals was eaten by the priests 'as a most holy thing' (Lv 6: 22) contradicts the theory according to which the victim was loaded with the sin of the person offering the sacrifice and thus itself became 'sin'. On the contrary, it was a victim pleasing to God, and he, in consideration of this offering, took away the sin. It is evidently in this ritual sense that

St. Paul uses the word: 'Christ, who had not known sin, God made "sin" (*ḥaṭṭa'th*: a victim for sin), in order that we might become, in him, God's justice' (2 Co 5: 21).

The rites which are prescribed in Lv 1-7 for the sacrifice of *ḥaṭṭa'th* are not the same as those prescribed in Nb 15: 22-29. In the text of Numbers, there is no mention of a sin committed by the high priest or by the prince, but only of sins committed by the community or by a private individual. Faults which the community has committed inadvertently are effaced by offering a bull as holocaust and a he-goat as a sacrifice of *ḥaṭṭa'th*; faults which a private individual has committed inadvertently are effaced by offering a kid as a sacrifice of *ḥaṭṭa'th*. No details are given about the rites to be followed. If the sin is deliberate, sacrifice cannot atone for the guilt and no forgiveness is possible (Nb 15: 30-31). Perhaps this law is even later than the law in Leviticus.

These sacrifices for sin took on a particular solemnity on the Day of Atonement, which we shall discuss in the chapter about the later religious feasts.[1]

(b) *The sacrifice of reparation*. The other kind of expiatory sacrifice is called an *'asham*. The word means an offence, and then the means by which the offence is righted, and, finally, a sacrifice of reparation. The sacrificial code deals with this kind of offering more briefly (Lv 5: 14-26; 7: 1-6), and states that the rites to be followed are the same as in the sacrifice for sin (Lv 7: 7). This sacrifice, however, was offered only on behalf of private individuals, and as a result, the blood was never taken into Holy Place, and the victim was never burned away from the sanctuary; secondly, the only victim referred to is a ram; thirdly, in certain cases the sacrifice was to be accompanied by the payment of a fine (cf. Lv 5: 14-16, 21-26; Nb 5: 5-8): if the rights of God or of a man had been infringed in a way which could be estimated in terms of money, then the guilty person had to offer a ram for reparation, and to restore to the priests (as representatives of Yahweh) or to the person whom he had wronged the monetary equivalent of the damage, plus one-fifth. It should be stressed, however, that this restitution did not form part of the sacrifice.

(c) *The distinction between sacrifice for sin and the sacrifice of reparation*. It is very difficult to say exactly what distinguishes these two kinds of sacrifice from each other. The ancient writers themselves are not in agreement. Philo (*De Victimis*, 11) thought the *ḥaṭṭa'th* was offered for involuntary faults against another man, and the *'asham* for involuntary faults against God and for all deliberate faults. Josephus (*Ant.* II ix 3) thought the distinction was between sins committed without witnesses, and sins committed in front of witnesses; and the rabbis too had theories of their own. The opinions of modern scholars are generally better founded, but they are just as varied.

1. Cf. pp. 507-510.

The examples cited in Lv 4-5 give the impression that the *ḥaṭṭa'th* covers a wider field, and that the *'asham* relates to faults by which God (or his priests) or a fellow-man has been cheated of his rights; this would explain why the *'asham* is essentially a sacrifice of reparation. And yet, even within the sacrificial code, there are inconsistencies: the *ḥaṭṭa'th* is also called *'asham* in Lv 5: 6, 7; the *ḥaṭṭa'th* is offered when a man sins inadvertently against any commandment of Yahweh (Lv 4: 2), but the *'asham* is offered if a man has unwittingly done something forbidden by the commandments of Yahweh (Lv 5: 17); in general, then, the two sacrifices cover the same offences. The two sacrifices are prescribed for very similar cases: anyone who does not come forward as a witness in court when he ought to, or anyone who makes a declaration in court without consideration, must offer a *ḥaṭṭa'th* (Lv 5: 1, 4), and anyone who commits perjury must offer an *'asham* (Lv 5: 22, 24). The confusion grows worse when we compare certain particular laws with the sacrificial code: for the purification of a leper, three sacrifices must be offered, an *'asham*, a *ḥaṭṭa'th* and a holocaust (Lv 14: 10–32). Similarly, a Nazirite who has been defiled by touching a dead body must offer two turtle-doves or pigeons, one as a *ḥaṭṭa'th*, the other as a holocaust, and, in addition, a lamb as an *'asham* (Nb 6: 9–12). Nor is it possible to state clearly the moral aspect of the sin which is expiated by these sacrifices: the *ḥaṭṭa'th* and the *'asham* are offered when a person has sinned inadvertently (Lv 4: 13, 22, 27; 5: 15, 17 and cf. Nb 15: 22-31). On the other hand, examples are given where there can be no question of mere inadvertence: *e.g.* for the *ḥaṭṭa'th*, the refusal to appear in court as a witness (Lv 5: 1), and for the *'asham*, fraud connected with sureties or with an object which has been found (Lv 5: 21-22).

This confusion and uncertainty can, of course, be partially clarified by literary criticism which can show how the texts have been adapted and recast. But the fact remains that the last redactors who drew up these confused rulings had no clear idea of what exactly was meant by a *ḥaṭṭa'th* and an *'asham*: either they were trying to draw a distinction between two terms which had originally been synonymous or they confused terms whose precise meaning they did not understand. We shall return to the point when we are discussing the history of sacrifice,[1] but enough has already been said to show that the ritual of the second Temple was not written without any reference to older documents or traditions: if it had been, the exposition would have been clearer.

4. *Vegetable offerings*

Vegetable offerings are called a *minḥah* (a word which most probably means 'a gift'). The ritual in Lv 2 distinguishes various kinds of offerings. One was of pure wheaten flour, unbaked, mixed with oil, which was accompanied by an offering of incense: a handful of the flour and all the

1. Cf. p. 429.

incense were burnt upon the altar, and the rest of the flour was given to the priests (Lv 2: 1-2; 6: 7-11; 7: 10). A second kind of offering was of the same mixture of flour, but baked on a tray or in a mould; part of it was burned, and the rest was given to the priests (Lv 2: 4-10; 7: 9). These offerings had to be unleavened and seasoned with salt (Lv 2: 11-13). A third and similar kind of offering is prescribed in Lv 2: 14-16: the offering of first-fruits, parched corn or baked bread, together with an offering of oil and of incense, was treated like the *minḥah*; part of this offering, too, was burnt upon the altar.

In all these offerings, that part which is burnt upon the altar is called *'azkarah*. The precise meaning of this term is not known: it may mean a 'memorial', because the sacrifice reminded God of the person who offered it, or a 'pledge', because the little part which was given to God reminded him of the whole offering and represented the whole.

In special instances, the *minḥah* was offered alone; *e.g.* in the daily offering of the high priest (all of which was burnt, because the priest could not give and receive one and the same offering, Lv 6: 13-16). Similarly, only the *minḥah* was offered on behalf of a poor man, and it then took the place of the sacrifice for sin (Lv 5: 11-13); and only the *minḥah* was offered as the 'sacrifice for jealousy' (Nb 5: 15); in all these instances, no oil or incense was used. More frequently, however, the *minḥah* was offered along with a sacrifice in which blood was shed, *i.e.* along with a holocaust or with a communion-sacrifice, and the *minḥah* was then accompanied by a libation of wine (cf. Ex 29: 40; Lv 23: 13, and especially Nb 15: 1-12).

5. *The shewbread*

Rather similar to the offerings just described is the shewbread, called in Hebrew *leḥem happanîm* ('the bread of the face' (of God), or 'the bread of the Presence') or *leḥem hamma'areketh* ('the shewbread'). According to Lv 24: 5-9, twelve cakes of pure wheaten flour were laid out in two lines on a table which stood in front of the Holy of Holies; they were renewed every sabbath day. They were a pledge of the Covenant between the twelve tribes and Yahweh. These cakes, or loaves, were eaten at the end of the week by the priests, but they were not placed on the altar; incense, however, was placed alongside each line of loaves as an *'azkarah*, and was burnt (on the altar of perfumes) when the loaves were changed. The fact that incense was placed there justifies us in regarding the loaves as something like a sacrificial offering, and Ezechiel himself likens the table on which they were put to an altar (Ez 41: 21-22). This table is described as part of the furniture of the desert Tent (Ex 25: 23-30).

6. *Offerings of incense*

In the last chapter we spoke of the altar of perfumes[1]; and in the present chapter we have frequently referred to the offering of incense along with vegetable offerings. The Hebrew word *qᵉtoreth* means 'that which goes up in smoke', and may be used of any sacrifice which is burnt upon an altar (thus, probably, in 1 S 2: 28; Is 1: 13); in liturgical language, it is applied to offerings of perfumes, the full expression being *qᵉṭoreth sammîm*, which occurs frequently in the Priestly texts. Incense (*lᵉbonah*) is only one constituent of the offering, and Ex 30: 34-38 gives the recipe for the perfume to be used in worship: it contained equal parts of storax, onyx (obtained from certain shell-fish), galbanum and incense. Rabbinical writings contain a recipe for a much more elaborate mixture in which no less than sixteen ingredients were used; perhaps this formula was used in the last centuries of the second Temple. It is not surprising to find such mixtures of perfumes, for they are often mentioned in inscriptions from Southern Arabia. They were imported into Palestine from abroad, and were used in cultic worship as an added refinement. Indeed, they were used in all Oriental religions, as we shall see later on.

In incense-offerings, pieces of coal were taken from the altar of holocausts on a shovel or a scoop, the powder was sprinkled on the glowing embers and the shovelful was placed on the altar of perfumes, in front of the Holy of Holies. This offering was to be made each morning and each evening (Ex 30: 7-8), and could be made only by a priest (2 Ch 26: 16-18; Lk 1: 9). The rite was also performed on the Day of Atonement, and on this day the censer itself was taken inside the Holy of Holies (Lv 16: 12–13). Apart from these instances, in which the offering of perfumes was a special rite in the cult, incense was used in the second Temple only along with a *minḥah*, and in connection with the shewbread; and in these two instances, it was used on its own, not mixed with other substances.

1. Cf. p. 411.

CHAPTER ELEVEN

THE HISTORY OF SACRIFICE IN ISRAEL

THE sacrificial rites described in the preceding chapter were those followed in the second Temple, after the Exile. The final redaction of the Pentateuch assumes that the liturgy had always been practised in this way, from the time when Moses instituted the liturgy of Israel in the desert. Literary critics, however, divided the Pentateuch into several different documents, and by dating these documents, they have reconstructed a history of sacrifice which is very different from that which the last editors of the Pentateuch took for granted. We shall now examine this reconstruction.

1. *The critical theory*

Wellhausen's powerful synthesis, which has had, and still has, so much influence on exegesis, divided the history of sacrifice in Israel into three periods:

In the first period, down to the reform of Josias in 621 B.C., men were not much concerned about rites: their main anxiety was to know to whom they were offering sacrifice, not how to offer it. The rites used in sacrifice did not matter, if the offering was made to Yahweh and was accepted by him. In this period, there were only two types of sacrifice, the holocaust and the communion-sacrifice, and the latter was the more common. This is the situation we find in the ancient parts of the historical books, in the prophets of the eighth and seventh centuries, and in the Yahwistic and Elohistic passages of the Pentateuch.

With the reform of Josias a new period opened. The ritual for sacrifices was not altered, except on one essential point: all sacrifices had to be offered in the Temple at Jerusalem. This new law evidently entailed a unification of the ritual. It was a decisive step towards the systematization of the different usages which had previously obtained in the high places and in the various sanctuaries throughout the provinces. This is the state of affairs which is reflected in Deuteronomy.

From the beginning of the Exile, new trends appeared, and among them was a passionate concern for ritual. It can already be seen in Ezechiel's description of the rites to be followed when the cult was restored, and in his insistence on the idea of expiation. Ezechiel introduced two sacrifices which are not mentioned in earlier texts, namely, the sacrifice for sin and the sacrifice of reparation. These trends underwent several developments and eventually led to the final redaction of the Priestly Code, which contains all the texts referring to sacrificial worship. The ritual was given its definitive form in the days of Esdras, and this code of rites was then followed until the ruin of the Temple.

2. *General considerations*

We have presented the theory in its broad outlines, and without qualifications, but Wellhausen himself made certain reservations, and his followers have stressed them still more. In the years since the theory was put forward, critics have become more and more ready to admit that the late ritual code contains some ancient elements, but these elements, they say, have been integrated into a new system. This change, they hold, took place during the Exile, and it consisted in a fusion of the ideas contained in Deuteronomy with those contained in Ezechiel and the Priestly Code. And it is here that the fundamental weakness of the evolutionary scheme lies. The centralization of worship certainly did precipitate the unification of the ritual, but Deuteronomy cannot be used to reconstitute the ritual followed in the Temple during the years after Josias' reform, because Deuteronomy contains no code of law about sacrifices. It mentions sacrifices only incidentally, and only in connection with two related subjects which it has at heart: the law insisting upon one sanctuary (Dt 12), and the law about rights of priests (Dt 18). Of the cultic terms discussed in the preceding chapter, Deuteronomy mentions only *zebaḥ*, *'olah*, *n'dabah* and *neder*, and makes no reference to *ḥaṭṭa'th* or *'asham* (this is the principal argument for calling these two sacrifices an invention of Ezechiel); but Deuteronomy never mentions offerings, perfumes, incense or the shewbread either, and these things were certainly used in the pre-exilic liturgy. The picture given in Deuteronomy, therefore, is not complete. Moreover, in the story of the reform, everything indicates that when the Temple became the sole legitimate sanctuary, the ritual which had previously been practised there continued in force, for the same priests, and they alone (cf. 2 K 23: 9), held office there. The code of ritual used in the pre-exilic Temple should be sought, not in Deuteronomy, but in the Law of Holiness (Lv 17-26), the basic prescriptions of which probably date from the last years of the monarchy. Now this ritual in Leviticus is quite evidently connected with the thought of Ezechiel, and it bridges the gap between this prophet and the pre-exilic period, *i.e.* it comes from those years in which, according to Wellhausen's school, the great break occurred in the history of sacrifice. And yet the Law of Holiness does not contain a true code of sacrificial law, no more than Deuteronomy does; but it does contain prescriptions about holocausts and about the different kinds of communion-sacrifices (Lv 17: 1-12; 19: 5-8; 22: 18-25, 29-30) which fit in well enough with the sacrificial code of the second Temple. On the disputed issue of expiatory sacrifices, it is the Law of Holiness which contains the most explicit text (Lv 17: 11), and the sacrifice of *'asham* is mentioned in Lv 19: 20–22. We are quite ready to admit that a new edition of the Law of Holiness was written during the Exile, and that additions were made to it even later, but surely it is unsound scholarship to dismiss the passages just cited as the work of a redactor merely because they have no parallels in Deuteronomy and because they are in agreement with Ezechiel? One can only do so if one already accepts a particular theory about the history of sacrifice, and this theory must first be proved.

The fact remains, however, that the evidence contained in the Law of Holiness is not accepted by everyone, and we must therefore try to see how much truth there is in the theory of Wellhausen's school. We shall therefore examine two questions: first, we shall ask to what extent the forms of sacrifice used in the second Temple are mentioned in the historical books, in the pre-exilic prophets and in those traditions of the Pentateuch which are admitted to be ancient: this question will form the subject-matter of the present chapter. We shall then ask whether the neighbours of Israel practised these same kinds of sacrifice in ancient times; and if we find that this is so, we shall then inquire whether the Israelites borrowed their ritual from these neighbouring peoples, and if so, at what period, or whether the similarities can be sufficiently explained by the common racial origin and the common history of Israel and its neighbours: this second question will be studied in the next chapter.

3. *Holocausts and communion-sacrifices*

From the first historical texts to the book of Deuteronomy, there is a continuous line of evidence to show that these two kinds of sacrifice were practised in Israel. We shall mention only the most ancient witnesses.

In the days of the Judges, Gideon offered a holocaust (*'olah* Jg 6: 26, 28). The second tradition about Gideon's sacrifice (Jg 6: 18–22) is not so clear, but the obvious explanation is that at first Gideon does not recognize the Angel of Yahweh, and that he therefore prepares a meal for him as a guest: this meal is then transformed into a holocaust by the fire which shoots out of the rock. There is a similar, but more explicit, story about the holocaust offered by Manoah, the father of Samson (Jg 13: 15–20). Afterwards the Bible mentions the holocaust offered when the Ark is brought back from the land of the Philistines (1 S 6: 14), the holocausts of Samuel (1 S 7: 9; 10: 8), of Saul (1 S 13: 9f.), of David (2 S 6: 17f.) of Solomon, both before and after the building of the Temple (1 K 3: 4; 9: 25), and later, away from Jerusalem, the sacrifice of Elias on Carmel (1 K 18: 38). The victims offered on these occasions are, as in Leviticus, cattle and small livestock. And the characteristic feature of the holocaust, as described in Leviticus, is found in every instance: everything is burnt upon the altar. The sacrifices of Gideon and of Manoah are rather exceptional, but apart from these two, the Bible gives no details about the ritual which was followed, for the rubrics of sacrifice were of no interest to the authors of the historical books. It seems, however, that there was one point on which ancient custom and Leviticus differed: in ancient times, it would appear that the victim was slaughtered upon the altar (cf. the sacrifice of Abraham, Gn 22: 9–10, and the story of the war against the Philistines, 1 S 14: 33–34). In the sacrifice on Carmel, however, the bull was cut into pieces before being placed upon the wood which had been set upon the altar (1 K 18: 23, 33).

The communion-sacrifice is mentioned in ancient texts even more frequently than the holocaust. It is called simply *zebaḥ* in several passages of the historical books (Jos 22: 26f.; 1 S 1: 21; 2: 13, 19; 3: 14; 6: 15, etc.; 2 S 15: 12; 1 K 8: 62; 12: 27; 2 K 5: 17; 10: 24, etc.), in the prophets (Is 1: 11; 19: 21; Jr 7: 22; Os 3: 4; 4: 19; Am 4: 4; So 1: 7, 8, etc.) and in the ancient collections of laws in the Pentateuch (Ex 23: 18; 34: 15, 25). It is also referred to, very frequently, simply as *sh*ᵉ*lamîm* in the historical books (Jg 20: 26; 21: 4; 1 S 13: 9; 2 S 6: 17, 18; 24: 25; 1 K 3: 15; 9: 25; 2 K 16: 13, etc.), in the ancient parts of the Pentateuch (Ex 20: 24; 32: 6, etc.) and in Ezechiel (Ez 43: 27; 45: 15, 17; 46: 12). The singular (*shelem*) occurs once only, in Am 5: 22. By contrast, the expression *zebaḥ sh*ᵉ*lamîm*, which is constantly found in the Priestly writings, is rarely found outside them, and in Ex 24: 5; 1 S 11: 15, cf. Jos 22: 27 we have the phrase *z*ᵉ*baḥîm sh*ᵉ*lamîm*, with the two words in apposition or, perhaps, with one as a gloss to explain the other.

These two names, then, are both very ancient, and they do not seem to denote two different ways of offering sacrifice. One of the words describes the sacrifice by reference to its outward ritual: it is a 'slaughtering' or 'immolation' (*zebaḥ*). The other describes it by a reference to the intention with which it is offered: opinions here vary, but the most probable is that *sh*ᵉ*lamîm* implies the idea of a tribute offered to God to maintain or to re-establish good relations between him and his worshipper (cf. the words *shillem* and *shillum*, meaning 'retribution', and the Ugaritic word *shlmm*, which is used of gifts sent as pledges of peace).[1]

Like the sacrifice described in Leviticus, the communion-sacrifice of ancient times was a joyous sacrifice, in which the priest and the man (or the people) who offered it ate a part afterwards: but the blood was poured out and the fat was burnt upon the altar (1 S 2: 15–16). There is very little information about the ritual which was followed, but we do know that the details of the ritual varied somewhat until after the Exile. If the generally accepted correction of 1 S 9: 24 is the true original reading (and this is not certain), then the fat of a sheep's tail was eaten by the faithful, whereas this part is offered to God in the ritual of Lv 3: 9; 7: 3. The rights of priests

1. Compare the meaning of *shalôm*, p. 254.

developed, too: in ancient times, at least at Shiloh, the priest stuck a fork into the meat as it was boiling in the pot and so took a part at random (1 S 2: 13-14); according to Deuteronomy, he was given the shoulder, the jaws and the stomach (Dt 18: 3); according to Leviticus, he had a right to the breast and the right leg before they were cooked (Lv 7: 34).

The stories and the laws in the Pentateuch presuppose that the Israelites used to offer holocausts and communion-sacrifices before ever they settled in Canaan, while they were still in the desert. Am 5: 25 seems to contradict this: 'O house of Israel, did you make sacrifices and offerings to me during the forty years in the desert?' Jeremias, too, seems to agree with Amos: 'I said nothing, and I gave no commands to your fathers about holocausts or sacrifices when I brought them out of the land of Egypt' (7: 22). These two texts are quite explicit, but precisely because they are so unconditional, they should not be taken literally. The Pentateuch contains ancient traditions about sacrifices in the desert (*e.g.* Ex 3: 18; 5: 3, 8, 17; 10: 25; 18: 12; 32: 6, 8); both Amos and Jeremias must have known of these traditions, Yahwistic or Elohistic, and they did not formally repudiate them. They were familiar, too, with the Yahwistic and the Elohistic codes of the Covenant, both of which speak of sacrifices (Ex 20: 24; 23: 18; 34: 25), and they, like their contemporaries, must have regarded these laws as commandments handed down from the days of Moses; lastly, Jeremias knew of Dt 12: 6-14, and regarded it as a law of Moses. And both these prophets thought of the Passover as an institution dating from the Exodus. There must, then, be some explanation for the two texts cited at the beginning of this paragraph. The words of Amos and of Jeremias quoted there must not be torn out of their immediate context: they form part of oracles directed, not against the cult itself, but against the external and material cult which was practised by their contemporaries. God demands first and foremost an interior religion: he demands that men should 'listen to his voice' (Jr 7: 23), and that they should practise 'right and justice' (Am 5: 24). This ideal had been realized in the desert, according to these same prophets (Jr 2: 2; Am 2: 10), and they are harking back to this ideal here: in the desert, they claim, men did not act as they do nowadays, and to make their argument more striking, they express it without any qualification: in the desert, Israel did not offer sacrifices, and God did not ask them to do so. They ought to have added 'sacrifices like the ones you offer', but they were preachers, not twentieth-century scholars writing a history of Israelite sacrifice. (It is the same principle as that which everyone accepts when speaking of the Priestly authors: they saw the liturgical organization of the Temple in their own day, and ascribed it all to the desert days: yet no one pretends that they were trying to write a critical history of Israelite sacrifice.)

So much, then, for the position adopted by Amos and Jeremias. If we now look at the evidence from the standpoint of modern literary criticism and set aside as late texts all the passages in the Priestly documents, and date the Yahwistic and Elohistic codes of the Covenant to the period when Israel was settling in Canaan, and Deuteronomy to the end of the monarchic period, then one must admit that there is scarcely any information left about sacrificial worship in the desert. Of the very ancient texts quoted above, Ex 1-10 speaks of sacrifices which are to be offered, not of those which actually were offered, and it is a pretext to persuade the Pharaoh to let the Israelites leave Egypt; in Ex 18: 12, it is Jethro who offers the sacrifice, and he is not an Israelite; and in Nb 22: 40; 23: 1f. 14f. 29f. it is Balaq, another foreigner, who offers sacrifice. The sacrifices referred to in Ex 32: 6, 8 were offered to the golden calf, and they are condemned in the present edition of the text. This leaves the Passover, but this is an altogether exceptional kind of sacrifice in which everything takes place away from any altar. Certainly, one must admit that when the Israelites were semi-nomads, they slaughtered beasts as sacrifices: it is a shepherd custom, and there is evidence of such sacrifices in Arabia in far distant times. But we shall never know exactly what rites the Israelites followed in those early days.

4. *Expiatory sacrifices*

The critical school acknowledged that at least holocausts and communion-sacrifices were offered from the time of the settlement in Canaan; but it claimed that sacrifice for sin (*ḥaṭṭa'th*) and the sacrifice of reparation (*'asham*) were unknown before the Exile. They are first mentioned, it is claimed, in Ezechiel, who refers to both of them several times (Ez 40: 39; 42: 13; 44: 29; 46: 20) and gives some details about the sacrifice called *ḥaṭṭa'th* (Ez 45: 19-20, 23).

Nevertheless, it would be rather odd to find new types of sacrifice, for which there was no precedent, invented during the Exile, when there was no external cult at all. Secondly, it is noteworthy that Ezechiel does not explain what he means by *ḥaṭṭa'th* and *'asham*; in other words, he presumes that the terms are known. Thirdly, the ritual in Leviticus is full of obscurities when it is describing these sacrifices and the way in which they are distinguished from each other: the best explanation of this confusion is that the authors of this ritual piece together ancient elements whose precise meaning they did not understand.[1] Fourthly, if the Law of Holiness in Leviticus is, as was claimed above,[2] older than the book of Ezechiel, then Lv 19: 20-22 implies that at least the sacrifice of *'asham* was known in the last years of the monarchy. We can also appeal to two more ancient documents, but their value is contested.

In the passage containing Joas' commands about the Temple, 2 K 12: 17 says that 'the money from the *'asham* and the money from the *ḥaṭṭa'th*

1. Cf. p. 421. 2. Cf. pp. 144 and 425-426.

(reading the singular, with the Greek) were not given to the Temple of Yahweh, but were given to the priests'. It is difficult to say whether this text refers to faults similar to those which were expiated by sacrifices of *'asham* and *ḥaṭṭa'th*, or to taxes which had to be paid on the occasion of these sacrifices, or to payments of money which might be made instead of the sacrifices. Nevertheless, it is significant that this money reverts to the priest, like the meat of victims offered in these sacrifices for sin, according to the ritual in Leviticus: and the terms used here in the Book of Kings are certainly technical terms in liturgical language. Now, in the evolution of worship, it is not normal for a custom of paying money to be replaced at a later date by the offering of a victim; in fact, it is quite the contrary process which takes place. Thus this text in the Book of Kings implies that the sacrifices themselves are of ancient origin. (If the text refers to payments in addition to the sacrifices, as in the laws of Lv 5: 14-16; Nb 5: 8, then it evidently presupposes that the sacrifices themselves were offered.)

The text in Os 4: 8 is equally difficult: 'They feed on the sin (*ḥaṭṭa'th*) of my people, and are greedy for its wickedness (*'awon*)'. It is tempting to take this as meaning that the priests feed on the *hatta'th* of the people because they receive all the meat offered in a sacrifice of *ḥaṭṭa'th*. But the parallel term, 'wickedness' (*'awon*), is not a word used for sacrifice, and this justifies a different interpretation: the priests and the people are practising a cult which God does not accept (cf. the immediate context, Os 4: 4-7, 12-13), and all the sacrifices, which are eaten by the priests, are a 'sin' and a 'wicked thing'. All the same, it is possible that the word *'awon* ('wickedness') is used here only to make a kind of parallel, and that *ḥaṭṭa'th* is a technical term meaning a sacrifice for sin.

There are, then, a certain number of converging arguments in virtue of which one may admit that expiatory sacrifices existed under the monarchy; but it must be granted that they were less common than the holocaust or the communion-sacrifice.

5. *Vegetable offerings and incense-offerings*

In the liturgical language of Ezechiel and the Pentateuch, the word *minḥah* always refers to offerings of vegetable produce as distinct from sacrifices in which blood is shed. It is commonly held that in pre-exilic texts the term is used indifferently of all kinds of sacrifice, including sacrifices in which blood is shed. This does not seem precise enough: when *minḥah* is mentioned alongside *zebaḥ* in 1 S 2: 29; 3: 14; Is 19: 21, alongside *'olah* in Jr 14: 12; Ps 20: 4, and alongside *shelem* in Am 5: 22, it must bear the more precise meaning of a vegetable offering. There are other texts in which it is impossible to decide whether it refers to an animal or a vegetable offering. And, finally, there are some texts where it must refer to a sacrifice of animals (thus 1 S 2: 17; 26: 19), but the reason is that *minḥah* is then used in its general sense of a 'gift' (or, a 'tribute'),[1] which is true of every sacrifice.

We have already pointed out that the shewbread was rather similar to vegetable offerings, and these loaves are mentioned in the ancient story preserved in 1 S 21: 3-7. They are contrasted with 'profane' bread, and are called the 'holy bread of the face' (of Yahweh); they were regularly replaced 'before Yahweh'. The word *q'ṭoreth*, meaning 'that which goes up in smoke', could also be used in a general sense for any sacrifice which was burnt upon the altar: this is probably the meaning of 1 S 2: 28 and Is 1: 13, and the cognate verb certainly means 'to sacrifice animals' in 2 K 16: 13, 15. The special sense of 'perfume-offerings', which is the meaning of *q'ṭoreth* and of *q'ṭoreth sammîm* in the Priestly writings,[2] is not found in any pre-exilic text, and it has therefore been argued that the custom did not exist before the Exile.

Nevertheless, there is evidence of an equivalent rite in some ancient texts: it is the offering of incense (*l'bonah*) mentioned in Jr 6: 20; 17: 26 (the authenticity is questioned); 41: 5. We have shown above that there was in Solomon's Temple an altar which was used for these offerings.[3] In 1 K 3: 3, the Deuteronomic redactor condemns a certain cult as illegitimate simply because it is practised outside the Temple: he describes this cult by using the verbs 'to make to smoke' and 'to slaughter'; it is quite probable that the first verb refers to offerings of incense, and that the second refers to sacrifices of beasts (cf. 1 K 11: 8).

A recent discovery may confirm this: at Bethel, a seal from South Arabia has been discovered, and this seal may have been used to mark the bags of incense which were imported for the use of the sanctuary there. Again, the papyri from Elephantine state that in the temple there (built before 525 B.C.),[4] the Jews offered sacrifices of animals, of vegetable produce and of incense: and these men followed the customs which obtained in the last years of the monarchy.

The custom of offering incense certainly existed in Israel from ancient times: it was a custom of other nations, too, and especially of the Egyptians, but the rites changed as time went on. Perhaps to begin with, portable censers were used, and there may be some record of them in certain stories about the desert (Lv 10: 1f.; Nb 16: 1f.) and in the instruments, the shovel (*maḥtah*) and the scoop (*kaph*), which were later used to carry the burning coals and the perfume on to the altar. This altar is mentioned for the first time, we said, in Solomon's Temple, and altars dating from the same period have been found in excavations.[5] It seems that for a long time pure incense was used, without any other additional perfumes, and this custom is laid down in the ritual for the *minḥah* (Lv 2: 1f.), for first-fruits (Lv 2: 15) and for the

1. Cf. p. 255. 2. Cf. p. 301. 3. Cf. p. 411.
4. Cf. p. 340. 5. Cf. p. 411.

shewbread (Lv 24: 7): all three are ancient rites. For the special offerings of incense which were instituted after the Exile, the mixture prescribed by Ex 30: 34–38 was used, and the rite was called *q'ṭoreth sammîm*, an 'offering of aromatics', in the plural.

6. *Conclusion*

In offerings of perfume and of vegetable produce, and for the different types of animal sacrifice, there is, then, a real continuity between the cult practised in the monarchic period and that followed after the Exile: the essential forms of the post-exilic cult are found also in the days before the Exile. But there was a development: before the Exile, communion-sacrifices were more frequent than holocausts, but after the Exile holocausts became the more important kind of sacrifice. After the Exile, the special sacrifices for the expiation of sin developed further and in the end an expiatory value was ascribed to the holocaust itself (Lv 1: 4); the relation of vegetable offerings to communion-sacrifices was more clearly defined; and for the offering of perfumes, a new mixture was prescribed, a new name was given to the rite, and a new ritual for the offering came into force. This is not to be wondered at, and it would have been astonishing if the ritual had not changed throughout the many centuries in which we have followed its history. But these changes should not lead us to forget the antiquity and the fundamental unity of the ritual followed in the sacrifices of Israel.

Chapter Twelve

THE ORIGIN OF ISRAELITE RITUAL

THE last chapter argued from the evidence of biblical texts to the conclusion that the rites used in Israelite sacrifices were of ancient origin. This conclusion can be confirmed by comparing Israelite ritual with the rituals of other Oriental religions, in which there are similar practices. But this similarity raises another question: did Israel borrow its rites from the cultural background of the neighbouring Semitic peoples; for the connections with other nations, belonging to more distant races or lands, are either accidental or of secondary importance.

1. *Mesopotamian sacrifice*

The normal term for sacrifice in Akkadian is *nequ*; the Akkadian equivalent of the Hebrew *zebaḥ* is *zîbu*, but it is rarely used and may be borrowed from West Semitic. The literal meaning of *nequ* is a 'libation' of water, of wine or of beer and so on, which is made along with a sacrifice. The sacrifice was first and foremost a meal offered to a god. The altar was the table of the god, and every kind of food which men eat was laid upon it: meat (especially mutton, but also beef and gazelle), poultry, fish, vegetables, fruit, sweets, and, of course, drink and bread. In rituals or in descriptions of sacrifices, we sometimes find mention of twelve, twenty-four or thirty-six loaves (the figures are bound up with the sexagesimal system of counting used by the Mesopotamians). The god's table was laid twice a day (four times in the latest ritual), and the priest arranged the feast. Alongside the altar table stood a perfume-brazier upon which fragrant wood and aromatic substances burned in order to delight the gods and to attract them to the feast. In the Babylonian story of the Flood, Utnapishtim, the Babylonian Noah, offered a sacrifice: 'I set up seven and seven incense-burners, and laid upon them reeds, cedar-wood and myrtle; the gods scented the fragrance, the gods scented the lovely fragrance, the gods collected like flies around the sacrificer.'

In Mesopotamia, the blood of victims was used only in a very minor way: it is doubtful whether it was ever used in the ritual, for there is no explicit reference to libations of blood in normal sacrifices. There was an official called 'the sword-bearer', but he merely cut the throat of the animal which was destined to be the food of the god. The food was shared between the gods, the priest-king, the clergy and the staff of the temple, and the part due to each one was prescribed in liturgical texts. It would be inaccurate, however, to call these sacrifices 'communion-sacrifices', for the man who offered the sacrifice received nothing back: those who conducted the cult took it all as their share. The liturgical texts do not say what became of the food set out on the table of the god, but Dn 14: 1-22 gives a satirical explanation of how it disappeared.

In ordinary sacrifices, no part of the victim was burnt upon the altar, and the essential forms of Israelite sacrifice, *viz.* the holocaust and the communion-sacrifice, did not exist in Mesopotamia. Similar customs are mentioned only for particular occasions: an animal was wholly or partly burnt in certain ceremonies of purification, of consecration and of conjuration, and these ceremonies sometimes included an anointing with blood. These two rites, burning an animal and anointing with its blood, are foreign to normal Mesopotamian ritual, and they may have been adopted from West Semitic peoples, among whom there is ample evidence of their use.

There were no expiatory sacrifices either. The nearest parallel to them is what has been called, rather inaccurately, the 'substitution-sacrifice'. Gods might seek revenge, and demons sought to hurt men; and how was man to avert an evil destiny which had fallen to him by lot? The peoples of Mesopotamia took an animal (often a different type of animal from those offered to the gods as food), or made a model of an animal out of reeds, mud and paste: this animal or model was the *puḫu* or the *dinânu*, *i.e.* the 'substitute' of the man offering it. A priest who acted as an exorcist then killed the victim, destroyed or mutilated the model with appropriate formulas, and the anger of the gods or demons was thus turned against the 'substitute'. The sick man was cured, the danger was averted. One text is extremely clear: 'He gave a lamb for his life, he gave a lamb's head for a man's head, he gave a lamb's neck for a man's neck, he gave a lamb's breast for a man's breast!' The same rite could be used to ward off evil. In one Assyrian treaty, the agreement is confirmed by the immolation of a ram, during which the following words were recited: 'This head is not a ram's head, it is the head of Mati'ilu, the head of his sons, of his nobles, of his people and of his country. If the undermentioned person sins against the clauses (of this treaty), may the undermentioned person's head be wrenched off . . . just as this head is wrenched off. This leg is not a ram's leg, it is the leg of the undermentioned person . . . etc.'

Lastly, we must mention a custom known as the 'substitute king' or the 'royal substitute', for several rather adventurous theories have been based upon it. Often enough, these theories are based upon wrong translations of certain texts, and the way in which the texts are then combined leaves much to be desired. It is suggested, then, that each year, at the New Year feast, a man was chosen to take the place of the king and was put to death: the purpose of the ceremony was to ensure a renewal of life for the king and of prosperity for the country. In fact, however, a more sober interpretation of the texts leads to a different conclusion: when particularly dangerous omens were seen, such as an eclipse of the moon or sun, a substitute exercised the royal power for all outward purposes, in order to ward off the danger from the real king and to draw the dangers upon himself. The critical period was held to last one hundred days, and at the expiration of this period the real king began to rule again in the normal way. Most scholars admit that the substitute was put to death at the end of his 'reign', but the texts do not say so explicitly: only once is the death of a substitute king mentioned, and it may have been due to natural causes.

Whether or not the substitute was put to death after his task was over, this custom of replacing the king by a substitute does not prove that human sacrifice was offered in Mesopotamia. Similarly, the magic rites for transferring the vengeance of the gods to an animal or to a model of an animal cannot be called 'substitution-sacrifices' except by a misuse of language. There is no place in them for that religious sentiment which seeks to make reparation to the deity, and they cannot be compared with the expiatory sacrifices practised in Israel.

In the last generation, some scholars thought that the late Jewish ritual which was composed during the Exile had been influenced by Babylonian ritual. It is quite possible that certain secondary terms (*t'nûphah* and *t'rûmah*) were borrowed from the juridical (but not from the liturgical) language of Babylon, and that the occasional references to the altar as a 'table' (Ez 44: 16; Ml 1: 7, 12; Is 65: 11 refers to the table of false gods), and the very common references to the 'table' of the shewbread reflect the language used in Babylonian worship (cf. Dn 14: 12, 18); but the shewbread itself is mentioned in the old, pre-exilic text of 1 S 21: 4-7, at a time when it is most unlikely that Israel was adopting customs from Mesopotamia. In short, there may be some tenuous and secondary contacts between the sacrificial system followed in Israel and that followed in Babylonia, but, these apart, the two systems are very different from each other and certainly independent of each other.

2. *Sacrifice among the ancient Arabs*

Our information about sacrifice among the ancient Arabs comes from various sources: the relics of pagan practices which survive in Islam, allusions in the Koran, information contained in the rare pre-Islamic writings which have survived, pre-Islamic inscriptions, and above all, old traditions which have been collected by later Arab authors. But all these sources together do not enable us to construct a complete and satisfactory picture: the most modern texts have to be approached in a severely critical way, and the oldest texts (the inscriptions) are very laconic.

One text, which is very often quoted as a description of an Arab sacrifice, must be definitely rejected, though it is frequently cited to prove or to confirm a particular theory about Semitic sacrifice. It is a story written by a monk of Sinai about 400 A.D., and published under the name of St. Nilus. It tells how St. Nilus' son was made prisoner by the Saracens, who decided to offer him as a sacrifice to the Morning Star, as was their practice when they captured handsome young men. Everything was prepared—the altar, the sword, the libation and the incense—but the barbarians woke up too late, for the planet (which had to be visible) was no longer to be seen, and so the young man was saved. The author adds that when the Arabs had no men to offer in sacrifice, they used to kill a camel instead; the man performing the sacrifice first stabbed it and tasted its blood, and then all the others fell upon the beast to tear off a piece of the flesh, which they ate raw: everything, including the intestines, the bones and the marrow, had to disappear before sun-rise. Almost everything in this fantastic story is false, and almost every detail is contradicted by other documents.

A further difficulty is that, before the coming of Islam, the Arabs had not one religion but several: the religions varied from place to place, and we have little information about the ritual practised by any of them. We must restrict our statements to what seems most probable.

The most direct contact the Israelites had was with Northern Arabia, and this is the very region in which information is most scanty. We know that the inhabitants of this area made offerings to the gods, and one Liḥyanite inscription may refer to a human sacrifice, though its meaning is not certain. The Safaites certainly killed animals for sacrifice, but none of the sacrifices mentioned in inscriptions were offered at a sanctuary: they were all offered at a camping-spot, on the occasion of an event in which all the family was concerned.

We have no inscriptions from Central Arabia, and are therefore dependent upon what Arab authors tell us. Offerings of flour and libations of milk were known, but they were rare. In certain ceremonies a man's hair was cut off and offered up; this offering, however, was not a sacrifice, but a rite of de-consecration, like the rite used in Israel for the *nazir* (Nb 6: 18).[1] An extra share of booty and the first-fruits of the harvest were normally offered to the gods. These poor nomadic tribes did not make offerings of incense or perfumes, but they did sacrifice animals. No part of the victim was ever burnt upon an altar; the sacrifices, therefore, were not the equivalent of the *'olah* and *zebaḥ* sacrifices of the Israelites.

Indeed, there was not even an altar in the sense of the Hebrew *mizbeaḥ*: what corresponded to it was the *nuṣub* or *manṣab*, which is the *maṣṣebah* of the Bible, *i.e.* an upright stone which could have a roughly human form. It stood for the deity, and the sacrificial rite consisted in cutting the throat of the

1. Cf. p. 466.

victim in front of this stone, and in rubbing the stone with the blood, which flowed into a ditch out near the stele. The victims were domestic animals, sheep, cattle and camels: to offer a gazelle instead of a sheep was considered to be defrauding the deity. The throat was cut by the man offering the sacrifice, and then, he, along with his family and any guests he had invited, ate the meat. Human sacrifices are mentioned only by Christian writers, and there is no means of checking their testimony.

In Southern Arabia, civilization was far more advanced, and the kingdoms of Ma'an, Saba, Qataban and Hadramut all had both sanctuaries and rituals. Dues and all kinds of offerings were presented to the temples, and sacrifices properly so called were offered upon altars. There were altars for libations and altars for perfumes: they are referred to in inscriptions, and many of them have been found by archaeologists. Both in public and in private worship, the use of aromatics was widespread. Animals were everywhere offered in sacrifice, and the victims chosen were usually sheep or bulls, though wild animals, such as gazelles and leopards, were also used. There is not a single text which certainly refers to human sacrifice. The immolation took place on the altar itself, which is called *mḏbht*, the equivalent of the Hebrew *mizbeaḥ*. It is commonly claimed that the holocaust was one form of sacrifice in Southern Arabia, but this not at all certain. There is a word *mṣrb* which refers to an object used in worship, and which comes from a root meaning 'to burn', but the only inscription in which details are given about this *mṣrb* refers to a *mṣrb* of myrrh and a *mṣrb* of fragrant wood; it may mean, then, an altar for perfumes. There is also a verb *hnr*, meaning 'to burn, to offer a burnt sacrifice', but the contexts in which it is found never mention an animal as victim, and every one of them can be taken as referring to an altar of incense.

To the extent to which it is known, the sacrificial system of Arabia has more in common with Israel than the system followed in Mesopotamia: we may cite, for example, the importance of animal sacrifices, the use of the same kind of animal (usually tame) for sacrifice, the way in which those offering it share in the meat of the victims, the use to which blood is put in Central Arabia, the name of the altar in Southern Arabia, and the widespread use of perfume-offerings in the South. These common features confirm the view that Israelite rites were of ancient origin; the similarities are explained by the common origin of the two peoples, by the pastoral life which the ancestors of Israel led and which the Arab nomads still lead (shepherds normally offer sacrifice from their flocks), and lastly, by the contacts between the two peoples in their culture and their commerce (the perfumes of Arabia). But we cannot conclude that Israel adopted any of these rites from the ancient Arabs, for essential features of the Israelite system are lacking in Arabia: the total or partial burning of the victim upon an altar was a rite followed in every kind of Israelite sacrifice, but there was no such rite in Northern or

Central Arabia, and the assertion that it took place in Southern Arabia is based on a questionable proof.

3. *Canaanite sacrifices*

Our knowledge of Canaanite sacrifices comes from three different sources: the allusions in the Bible, or the condemnations which it utters against the cult of the Baals and the Astartes when the Israelites took part in them, inscriptions from the Phoenician homeland and from its colonies, and the texts of Ras Shamra.

Among the biblical references, we must first set aside all that is not strictly Canaanite, such as the late Assyrian cults, like the cult of stars (2 K 21: 3*b*; 23: 5*b*; Jr 44: 15-25), and the syncretist or mystery-rites mentioned in the late texts (Ez 8: 7-13; Is 65: 2-5; 66: 3). If we set aside sacrifices of babies also (we shall discuss them later to show that human sacrifice was never lawful in Israel),[1] then, according to the biblical evidence, Canaanite sacrifices do not seem to be materially different from those which were offered to Yahweh. Solomon had in his harem Moabites, Ammonites, and Sidonians, who offered incense and sacrifices to their gods (1 K 11: 8). Naaman offered holocausts (*'olah*) and communion-sacrifices (*zebaḥ*) to other gods, and vowed that he would in future offer them only to Yahweh (2 K 5: 17). The description of the sacrifice on Carmel (1 K 18) tells how the prophets of Baal and Elias himself prepared their holocausts in the same way, and the point of the story is lost if this was not the normal way of offering sacrifice to Baal. Jehu is supposed to be following the Canaanite ritual in the story about the temple of Baal (2 K 10: 18–27), and both *zebaḥ* and *'olah* are mentioned there. For the Deuteronomic redactor of the Books of Kings, the words sacrifice and perfume-offerings sum up that cult of the 'high places' which he condemns in the reign of almost every king of Judah (1 K 22: 44; 2 K 12: 4; 14: 4 etc.), and even in the reign of Solomon during the years before the Temple was built (1 K 3: 3). These were offerings meant for Yahweh, but Jeremias speaks in the same terms of the sacrifices and incense offered to Baal (Jr 7: 9; 11: 12, 13, 17; 32: 29). In all these texts, the verbal form used is the Pi'el (*qiṭṭer*), not the Hiph'il (*hiqṭir*), for the latter form is normally kept for the cult of Yahweh (but cf. 1 K 11: 8; Jr 48: 35; Os 2: 15); this nicety of writing, however, does not mean that the rite was different. The Bible does not condemn this cult because of the rites it entailed, but because it was offered in illegitimate sanctuaries or to deities other than Yahweh. According to the Bible, then, there was a fundamental similarity between Canaanite sacrifice and Israelite sacrifice; but biblical texts cannot prove that the technical terms used in connection with sacrifice were the same among the Israelites and among the Canaanites.

Canaanite terminology must be sought in Phoenician and Punic inscrip-

1. Cf. pp. 443-446.

tions. Among the Punic inscriptions, the most important for our purpose are two price-lists, called respectively the Carthage price-list, and the price-list of Marseilles (where the stone was taken from North Africa). The lists fix the amount of money to be paid for each kind of sacrifice, the part to be given to the priest and the part to be given to the man offering the sacrifice (the 'master of the sacrifice'); they do not, however, give a description of the rites, nor do they tell us the motives for which the various sacrifices are offered. In addition to the offering of vegetable produce (called *minḥah*, and in Hebrew), the price-list from Marseilles mentions three kinds of sacrifice, the *kalil*, the *ṣewa'at* and the *shelem kalil*. In the *kalil*, a very small part of the meat is given to the priest, and nothing to the man offering the sacrifice; in the *ṣewa'at*, the breast and the leg are given to the priest, and the rest to the man making the offering; no indication is given as to how the meat is to be divided in a *shelem kalil*, except when a fowl is offered in an exorcism or in taking auspices: the meat then belongs to the man bringing the sacrifice. By comparing these rules with Leviticus, some scholars identify the *kalil* with expiatory sacrifice, the *ṣewa'at* with communion-sacrifice, and the *shelem kalil* with the holocaust. We cannot be certain of these identifications: the clearest is the similarity between the *ṣewa'at* and the *zebaḥ* or *zebaḥ shelamîm* used in Israel, but it should be noted that the names are not the same. The question becomes more complicated still if we compare also the price-list from Carthage: this gives slightly different regulations for the *kalil* and the *ṣewa'at*, and never mentions the *shelem kalil*. There were, then, certain variations even within the Carthaginian system itself. We find yet other names used throughout the rest of the Punic world: in a Neo-Punic inscription of the Roman period, *'lt* is used alongside *mnḥt*, and these two words correspond to the Hebrew *'olah* and *minḥah*; *'zr* (a 'votive offering'?) is found in several inscriptions. The use of perfumes is attested by a fragment of a ritual which speaks of *qṭrt* and *lbnt*, *i.e.* the equivalent of the Hebrew *q'toreth* and *l'bonah*. The inscriptions date from different periods, but they are all later than Leviticus. In Phoenicia itself, there are inscriptions going back to the era before Israel went into Exile, but unfortunately they contain no information about sacrifices: for this period, we have to rely on the biblical texts cited above. By comparing these texts with the information given in later inscriptions, we can conclude only that the Canaanite system of sacrifice was similar to the Israelite system: they offered at least holocausts and communion-sacrifices, vegetable produce and perfumes, but the two systems developed independently of each other, and their terminology was not altogether the same.

At Ras Shamra, the ancient Ugarit, archaeologists have discovered some texts dating from the fourteenth century B.C., *i.e.* before the Israelites settled in Palestine. Scholars have compiled lists of Ugaritic sacrificial terms and tried to find the corresponding Hebrew terms. Many of these identifications are uncertain, because the meaning of the Ugaritic terms is not beyond dispute. The most significant are those terms which appear in ritual texts: *dbḥ* (sacrifice)—*zebaḥ*; *shlmm* (peace-offering)—*sh'lamîm*; *shrph* (burnt-offering) may correspond to those sacrifices which were wholly or partially burnt upon the altar. The word *'ṯm* has also been cited as the equivalent of the Hebrew *'asham*, but the meaning of the word is not at all certain, and we are not even sure that it belongs to the Semitic language of Ugarit. Perhaps the descriptions of certain actions in the great poems of Ras Shamra are of greater value than this handful of terms from brief and mutilated texts. We read in the story of the sacrifice offered by the hero Keret. 'He rose and painted his face (not: 'put blood on his face'), 'washed his hands to the elbow, his fingers to the shoulder; he entered into the shadow of the tent and took a lamb of sacrifice into his hand, a young beast into his two hands, all his best food, he took . . .? a bird of sacrifice; he poured wine into a silver cup, honey into a golden cup; he went to the top of the tower, he climbed up on to the shoulder of the wall, he raised his hands to heaven, he sacrificed to the Bull El, his father, he honoured Baal with his sacrifice, the son of Dragon with his offering'. Keret then came down again and got food ready for the town: this food was, it appears, unconnected with the sacrifice, so that the sacrifice would have been a holocaust. It would, however, be imprudent to regard this poetic description as a ritual. We may note, too, that the Ras Shamra texts, like the Phoenician and Punic inscriptions, do not seem to attach any ritual importance to the blood of the victim.

The information gathered here comes from several places and from many different periods. In our opinion, it does not justify the conclusion that Israel took all its ritual for sacrifices from Canaan, but it does indicate that Israelite ritual is far closer to the ritual of Canaan than to that of Mesopotamia or Arabia. The relationship between Israelite and Canaanite ritual is probably more complex than is usually admitted, and we shall attempt to define it.

4. *The origin of the sacrificial ritual of Israel*

The feature which distinguishes Israelite and Canaanite rituals from those of other Semitic peoples is that, when an animal is sacrificed, the victim, or at least a part of it, is burnt upon an altar. This rite did not exist in Mesopotamia or in Arabia, but it did exist among the Moabites and the Ammonites, according to the allusions in the Bible. The rite is thus peculiar to the West Semitic peoples, but it is also a Greek rite. The typical sacrifice (θυσία) is closely connected with the *zebaḥ*: part of the victim is burnt upon the altar, part is given to the priests, and the rest is eaten in a sacred meal. The sacrifice *'olah*, in which the whole victim is burnt upon the altar, corresponds to the Greek holocaust, which was much rarer than the θυσία (as the *'olah* was at first rarer than the *zebaḥ*), and which was confined to the worship of the gods of the underworld, and of dead heroes. One could extend this range of contacts to include other facts in the cult and point out, for example, that βωμός, meaning both a 'platform' and 'altar', may correspond to *bamah* the 'high place' which served as an altar.[1] These kindred customs must have originated in a civilization which preceded both the Hellenes and the Canaanites along the shores of the Eastern Mediterranean. The custom of burning either the whole or part of the victim upon an altar obtained in Canaan before the Israelites came to Palestine. On the other hand, there is no certain proof that the Israelites practised the custom when they were semi-nomads, and perhaps the oldest form of sacrifice they practised is the type which survived in the offering of the Paschal lamb. This sacrifice was closely linked with the history of their sojourn in the desert: no part of the victim was burnt, blood played an important rôle and the meat was eaten by the faithful: we have seen how all these characteristics are found in the sacrifices of the ancient nomadic Arabs. When they settled in Canaan, they adopted from the Canaanites the sacrifices called *'olah* and *zebaḥ*, which were burnt upon the altar; they then combined these sacrifices with the ancient rites about the use of blood—rites, then, which retained their efficacy and which were not found among the Canaanites—and the two rituals, Israelite and Canaanite, afterwards developed independently of each other. We suggest this explanation of the origin of Israelite ritual only as a hypothesis which attempts to take into consideration all the information at present available.

5. *Human sacrifice in Israel*

One theory which is put forward by historians of comparative religion is that animals were sacrificed as substitutes for men, and from this many writers conclude that originally men were put to death in sacrifice. We have already stated that the 'substitution-sacrifices' in Mesopotamia were connected with magic rather than with religion, and that the Israelite custom of laying one's hands on the victim did not mean that the victim was a substitute for the person offering the sacrifice. We shall return to these issues in the next chapter, where we shall put forward a theory of sacrifice.

In fact, however, human sacrifice was known in the ancient Oriental religions, but such sacrifices were so exceptional that one hesitates to call them true sacrifices. At the dawn of Egyptian history, prisoners or foreigners were sometimes put to death, but very soon the practice gave way to a symbolic execution carried out on little clay models. In Mesopotamia, there is the instance of the substitute-king which we have already mentioned[2]; and we know from the large numbers of skeletons found in the royal tombs of Ur that in this distant epoch wives and servants of the kings were buried with them; but this does not mean that these people were put to death as a

1. Cf. pp. 284-285.

2. Cf. pp. 434-435.

sacrifice. In Arabia, there is only the evidence, itself suspect, of a few late authors.

The clearest texts comes from the Phoenician world, and they concern the sacrifice of babies: we shall discuss this point in a special paragraph. There are also the so-called 'foundation-sacrifices', which are often mentioned in the reports of Palestinian archaeologists about the excavations of Canaanite towns: as a general rule, these skeletons merely show that the normal practice was to bury children who died in infancy under the ground in the house, but there are some examples which are more decisive (like the one referred to in 1 K 16: 34). We have already stated that the theory of human sacrifice is scarcely tenable for Oriental cultures other than of Israel, but it has been asserted that even Israel practised it. Some writers hold that apostate Israelites offered human sacrifice to foreign deities, that some of them even offered such sacrifices to Yahweh (whom they identified with these foreign deities), and even that at some distant era Yahwism gave official recognition to, and actually prescribed, human sacrifice. Stated in this form, the thesis is, from a critical point of view, quite untenable.

(a) *Human sacrifices in historical texts.* Certain stories in the historical books of the Bible are claimed as evidence in favour of this thesis. We have just cited 1 K 16: 34: in the reign of Achab, Hiel of Bethel rebuilt Jericho: 'at the price of his first-born, Abiram, he laid the foundations, and at the price of his last-born, Segub, he set up its gates' (cf. Jos 6: 26). The meaning of the text is disputed, but even if it does refer to foundation-sacrifices, this could easily be explained, in Achab's reign, by the religious influence of Phoenicia. The execution of prisoners of war, even when it took place 'before Yahweh', was not a sacrifice, but the fulfilment of the *ḥerem*[1] (1 S 15: 33, cf. v. 3). The story of how Saul's descendants were handed over to the men of Gibeon and cut in pieces by them on the high place of Gibeon (2 S 21: 1-14) is presented, from the Israelite side, as the acquittal of a blood-debt; the Gibeonites gave their revenge the form of a fertility-rite (the poems of Ras Shamra throw light on this), but since the Gibeonites were not Israelites, this story teaches us nothing about the religion of Israel. This leaves only the story of Jephthah (Jg 11: 30-40): the obvious meaning of the text (and it should not be toned down) is that Jephthah had promised that, should he return victorious, he would offer as a holocaust the first person who came out of his house: it was his only daughter, and he offered her in sacrifice. But the story is told as a quite extraordinary and shocking incident: so, too, was the action of the king of Moab, when he immolated his only son upon the rampart of his capital while it was being invested by the Israelites (2 K 3: 27). The story of Jephthah cannot be used as evidence in the study of Israelite ritual.

Some authors cite the story of Abraham's sacrifice (Gn 22: 1-19). God asked Abraham to offer his only son as a holocaust, but stayed his hand when

1. Cf. pp. 260-261.

it was already raised to stab Isaac, and a ram was offered instead of the child. This, it is claimed, is an aetiological story, meant to explain and to justify the replacement of human sacrifice by the sacrifice of animals. Yet the meaning of the story in the mind of the editor of Genesis, and in its context of patriarchal history, seems to be quite different: when God commanded Abraham to sacrifice the son in whom the divine promises were centred, he was subjecting Abraham's faith to an extraordinary test, and Abraham's obedience was rewarded by a solemn renewal of the promise made to his posterity. Any Israelite who heard this story would take it to mean that his race owed its existence to the mercy of God, and its prosperity to the obedience of their great ancestor. There is also a liturgical intention, but it is secondary in the story: the Israelites do not offer children to Yahweh as the Canaanites do to their gods. Possibly there is behind the story an old account of the foundation of a sanctuary in which, from the very beginning, animals were sacrificed: the point would then be to contrast this sanctuary with other sanctuaries, Canaanite sanctuaries, in which human victims were killed. But this would only confirm the conclusion which the story is meant to assert, namely, that the religion of Israel rejected human sacrifice.

(b) *Prophetical texts.* Proofs drawn from the prophets are no more convincing either. The text of Os 13: 2 is most obscure and is translated in a number of ways; not everyone will admit that it refers to human sacrifice, but even if it does, it is speaking of sacrifices offered to idols, and it condemns the cult. Mi 6: 1-8 must be taken as one pericope, and there the people answer Yahweh by asking: 'Will Yahweh be pleased with thousands of rams, or with torrents of libations of oil? Must I offer my eldest son as the price of my forfeit, the fruit of my loins for my own personal sin?' (v. 7), but God replies (v. 8) that he asks them only 'to do justice'. The meaning is clear: in the eyes of the prophet, sacrificing one's children would be as absurd and as useless as sacrificing thousands of rams and torrents of oil. This does not mean that the Israelites had a custom of sacrificing their children to Yahweh, any more than that they poured out for him 'torrents of oil'. There is a disputed and late text in Is 66: 3 which does refer to the execution of a man as a ritual, but it contrasts it with the normal sacrifice, a bullock. This leaves only the text in Ez 20: 25-26, which we shall discuss in a moment.

(c) *The law concerning the first-born.* For some critics, certain texts about the first-born are decisive: 'Thou shalt give me the first-born of thy sons. Thou shalt do the same for thy livestock, big and small. The first-born shall be left seven days with its mother, and then, on the eighth day, thou shalt hand it over to me' (Ex 22: 28-29). The command is unqualified, and the texts which state that the first-born of men are to be ransomed, whereas the first-born of beasts are to be sacrificed (Ex 13: 11-15; 34: 19-20) are, it is claimed, of later origin, enacted to mitigate an ancient and cruel custom. Against this view, it should be noted that the last two texts are attributed by literary critics to the ancient sources of the Pentateuch, and are regarded as almost contemporary with Ex 22: 28-29. Conversely, Ex 13: 1-2, which is the work of the later Priestly redactors, is just as unqualified as Ex 22: 28-29: 'Consecrate to me every first-born, the first-fruits of the mother's womb among the children of Israel. Man or tame animal, it belongs to me.' Both texts simply take for granted that the first-born of men are not treated in the same way as the first-born of beasts: all the first-born belong to Yahweh, but men are redeemed and beasts are sacrificed. It seems certain that no Israelite ritual ever prescribed the sacrifice of the first-born.

The critics in reply bring forward the text of Ez 20: 25-26: 'I went so far as to give them laws which were not good, and customs by which they could not live, and I defiled them by their offerings, making them sacrifice all their first-born, to punish them, that they might know that I am Yahweh'. This text seems to say that the custom was normal in Israel, and that it was sanctioned by a command of God. But it is absurd to say that Israel ever sacrificed 'all its first-born' at any period in its history, and it is equally absurd to say that Ezechiel, who in other places condemns the sacrifice of infants (Ez 16: 20; 20: 31), could ever have thought that this custom had been positively enjoined by God. Consequently, the words of the prophet cannot be taken literally. He is attributing to divine causality all the actions, good and bad, of men; he is referring to the permissive will of God, as is the writer of Ex 4: 21; 7: 3, etc. and especially of Is 6: 9-10 (a text cited with reference to the parables of Jesus, Mt 13: 13-15, and by Paul to the Jews of Rome, Ac 28: 26-27). Yahweh had ordered the Israelites to consecrate to him all the first-born: the Israelites, led astray by the example of the Canaanites, killed their children for sacrifice. God let them do so, let them defile themselves 'to punish them, that they might know that I am Yahweh'. The sin was foreseen by God and punished by God, and thus entered into the mysterious plan of salvation. Ezechiel states the fact without nuances, but we have an explicit statement of Jeremias on the same point: 'They built the *bamah* of Tophet in the valley of Ben-Hinnom to burn their sons and their daughters; this I had never prescribed, this I had never dreamt of' (Jr 7: 31; cf. 19: 5).

(d) *Sacrifices to Moloch*. The ground is thus cleared for another question, on which much ink has flowed in the last few years. The word *molek* (Moloch in the Greek and Latin versions) is found five times in the Law of Holiness (Lv 18: 21; 20: 2-5) and then in 2 K 23: 10 and Jr 32: 35; it should be corrected in 1 K 11: 7 and (probably) restored in Is 30: 33. The word is always used in connection with the sacrifice of a child, male or female, who was said to 'pass through the fire': according to 2 K 23: 10 and Jr 32: 35, this took place in the 'roaster' (*topheth*) of the valley of Ben-Hinnom near Jerusalem. Though the word *molek* is not used, the same rite is mentioned in 2 K 16: 3; 17: 31; 21: 6; Jr 3: 24 (?); 7: 31; 19: 5; Dt 12: 31 and presumably Ez 23: 39.

Note that these sacrifices are not related to the ordinary worship practised on the high places, and that the high places are often mentioned without reference to this cult; the use of the word *bamah*, therefore, to describe the 'roaster' in the valley of Ben-Hinnom is somewhat surprising. It should be noted, too, that among the texts cited, those which are in any way detailed appear to restrict the practice to the region around Jerusalem; the nearness of the Temple presumably accounts for the insistence of the Law of Holiness, and this law, as we have said, reflects the teaching of the priests in Jerusalem towards the end of the monarchy. These sacrifices were practised, too, only during a certain period: they are first mentioned under Achaz (2 K 16: 3), when foreign influences were encroaching upon the cult, and 2 K 17: 31; Dt 12: 31 condemns them as a pagan custom. All the texts lead to the same conclusion: the practice was introduced late in the history of Israel and from outside, and it was condemned by all the spokesmen of Yahwism, by the Deuteronomist, the Prophets and the Priestly editors. It never formed part of the Israelite ritual for sacrifices.

Its origin must be sought, evidently, in Canaanite culture (in the broad sense). Punic and Neo-Punic inscriptions contain the expressions *mlk 'mr* (transcribed *molchomor* in Latin) and *mlk 'dm*. Very probably, these phrases mean respectively 'offerings of lamb' and 'offering of man', and refer to the sacrifice of an infant, or of a lamb as substitute. This interpretation is supported by a find in the sanctuary of Tanit at Carthage, where archaeologists have discovered urns containing burnt bones of lambs and goats, and, more often, of children. There is, too, a famous text of Diodorus Siculus (*Biblioth. Hist.* XX 14): in 310 B.C., when a disaster was threatening Carthage, the inhabitants of the town decided it was due to the anger of Kronos, to whom they had formerly sacrificed their finest children: instead, they had begun to offer sickly children, or children they had bought. Thereupon, they sacrificed two hundred children from the noblest families. There was a bronze statue of Kronos with outstretched arms, and the child was placed on its hands and rolled into the furnace. Whether the details be true or false, the story is evidence of a custom to which other classical authors also allude.

These inscriptions and texts are of late date, but the *molk* offering is mentioned in two steles from Malta belong to the seventh or the sixth century B.C. The sacrificial term has not so far been found in inscriptions from Phoenicia proper, but child-sacrifice was practised there: a fragment of Philo of Byblos cited in Eusebius (*Praep. Evang.* I 10) says that the Phoenicians had an ancient custom—'they offered their dearest children in a way full of mystery' when danger threatened the nation. Porphyry (*De abstin.* II 56) says that the Phoenician History written by Sanchuniaton and translated by Philo of Byblos was full of stories about child-sacrifices offered to Kronos in times of calamity. These texts furnish the connecting-link with the story told by Diodorus Siculus, and we may mention also the reference to the king of

Moab's offering his son as a holocaust when his capital was under siege (2 K 3: 27).

The sacrifice of children, then, by burning them to death probably made its way into Israel from Phoenicia during a period of religious syncretism. The Bible mentions only two specific instances, and they are motivated by the same exceptional circumstances as the Phoenician sacrifices: Achaz 'made his son pass through the fire' (2 K 16: 3) during the Syro-Ephraimite War, and Manasseh did the same (2 K 21: 6) when confronted with some Assyrian threat which is not mentioned in the Books of Kings but which may be alluded to in 2 Ch 33: 11f. Yet the custom must have been fairly widespread to have deserved the condemnations uttered by Deuteronomy, Leviticus and the Prophets. Though Phoenician texts properly so called do not mention the word, it is possible (we say no more) that the sacrifice was called *molk* in Phoenicia, as in Carthage, and that it came into Israel under this name.

But even if this is true, the sacrificial meaning of the word was soon forgotten in Israel; perhaps it was never taken in this sense at all. There was a god called Malik ('king') in the pantheons of Assyria and of Ras Shamra, and the god of the Ammonites was called Milkom (2 S 12: 30; 1 K 11: 5, 33; 2 K 23: 13), which is merely another form of the same word. More often, the word *melek* ('king') is an appellative of a god, used instead of the god's proper name. This appellative use is found in the Bible itself in Is 57: 9 (*Melek*) and in the Massoretic text of Is 30: 33 (in connection with the 'roaster' in the valley of Ben-Hinnom); it is also found in composition with divine names (Adrammelek and Anammelek, 2 K 17: 31, again in connection with the burning of infants for sacrifice). These offerings, then, were held to be offerings to a king-god, a Melek, who was an idol (Ez 23: 39), a Baal (Jr 19: 5; 32: 35), a Disgrace (perhaps Jr 3: 24). The form *molek*, which predominated in these texts, is to be explained by a change of vocalization telling the reader to say *bosheth* (disgrace, shame); this is in fact the reading of the consonants too in Jr 3: 24. (Compare the substitution of *bosheth* for Baal in Jr 11: 13; Os 9: 10 and in certain proper names.)

The question is clearly most complicated, and no final solution has yet been proposed. But whether these sacrifices were offered to a god Moloch or offered as *molk*, one thing is certain: the sacrifice of infants in fire was something foreign to the ritual of Israel.

Chapter Thirteen

THE RELIGIOUS SIGNIFICANCE OF SACRIFICE

SO we come to our last question: what was the purpose of sacrifice? What was its religious significance in the minds of the Israelites? What place did it occupy in their conception of man's relations with God? In seeking to answer these questions, we ought to beware of two dangers. Historians of comparative religion are tempted to misuse the comparative method, and to bring forward, as an explanation of Israelite sacrifice, the practices or the ideas of peoples with different religious concepts; in particular, they look for analogies between Israelite ritual and the customs of so-called 'primitive' peoples, for among these primitive peoples, they claim, we find the fundamental significance of ritual. Theologians, on the other hand, tend to use the sacrifice of the New Testament (and subsequent Christian doctrinal interpretations of it) in order to explain the true meaning of Old Testament sacrifice. Both parties tend to neglect or to underrate elements which may be proper to Israelite sacrifice. It is true, of course, that one must take into consideration the world in which Israel lived, and also inquire how the sacrifices of the Old Law are prolonged and fulfilled in the sacrifice of the New Covenant; but surely the first task is to examine the notion of sacrifice as presented in the Old Testament itself? We shall begin by setting aside a number of theories which are unsatisfactory.

1. *Was sacrifice a gift to a malevolent or a selfish deity?*

This theory was expressed in a particularly brutal way by Renan in his *Histoire d'Israel*: 'That state of madness through which humanity passed in the first ages of its existence has bequeathed to us many errors, but of them all, sacrifice is the oldest, the worst and the most difficult to uproot. Primitive man, whatever his race, thought that the way to quieten the unknown forces around him was to win their favour as one wins the favour of men, by offering them something. This was logical enough, for the gods whose favour he sought were malevolent and selfish. This appalling absurdity (which the first appearance of religious common sense ought to have swept away) had become an act of subjection, with man, as it were, the liege of the Deity. Patriarchal religion could not emancipate itself from this notion. The prophets of the eighth century B.C. were the first to protest against this error, and even they could not suppress it!' It is doubtful whether so materialistic an explanation is valid of any people, however 'primitive' or degraded they are presumed to be, and modern studies in religious ethnology come to very different conclusions. And it is quite certain that Renan's description does not apply to any period of Israel's religion: not a single biblical text can be cited, or even stretched, to justify it.

A less extreme view is that sacrifice is a gift given with the purpose of profiting both God and man, a kind of contract *do ut des*. It is certainly true that one of the reasons why man offers sacrifice is to receive some benefit (material or spiritual) from God; it is an offering made to God, but it is a gift of a particular kind. True, in every popular religion, including Israel's, man's desire to receive something from God may become the predominant motive for sacrifice; it is also true that in certain religions, the deity seems to be in equal need of something from man (we shall return to this when we discuss sacrifice considered as a meal for the god), but this cannot have been the notion of sacrifice in Israel. In the Bible, God is the sovereign lord of all things, of man and of all his possessions: God does not need to be given anything by men, for he can take everything.

2. *Did sacrifice achieve union with the deity by magic?*

This explanation of sacrifice is put forward under two forms: in the first, God and man are brought together by man's eating a divine victim; in the second, they are united by the immolation of a victim representing man.

(a) *Union with a god by man's eating a divine victim.* The presupposition of this theory is totemism: members of the tribe were related by kinship to the tribal god, who was the ancestor of the entire tribe, and whose life circulated in the animal (the *totem*) consecrated to him. The object of sacrifice was to strengthen this relationship, and to share in the god's life by eating his sacred animal. This idea—so it is claimed—was at the root of the sacrifice of the ancient Arabs, who attached particular importance to blood-ties, and Israelite sacrifice was a more highly developed form of the same idea. The faithful worshipper was the subject of the king-god, he farmed the land belonging to the god, and sat at his table: basically, it was the same outlook as prevailed in ancient Arabia. Now this is simply not proven. Totemism, however, is no longer a fashionable theory: everyone now recognizes that it is not a regular religious phenomenon. Moreover, it is quite exceptional for men to eat the totem animal, and even when they do so, their purpose is not to unite themselves with their god. The only evidence that the ancient Arabs practised totemism comes from the spurious story of St. Nilus,[1] and it is impossible to discern any traces of totemism among the early Israelites.

(b) *Union with a god by the immolation of a victim representing man.* The sacrificer substituted the victim for himself. By placing his hands upon it,

1. Cf. p. 436.

he transferred to the animal his sins and his life-principle. (The life-principle was in the blood.) When the animal was killed, the sins were carried away, and the life-principle was released. The blood which was shed incorporated the life-principle of the victim (and consequently of the sacrificer); when, therefore, this blood was poured out at the foot of the altar or sprinkled on something which represented the deity, it brought the life of the sacrificer into contact with the deity, and thus established, or re-established, the bond between God and his servant. In the previous hypothesis, eating the victim was the essential element; in this second hypothesis, it is immolation and the use of the blood, and the sacred meal is only a complementary rite. In both hypotheses, true sacrifice always demands the shedding of blood.

It is quite true that this use of blood in ritual was meant to bring about the closest possible contact between God and that part of the victim which, because it was held to contain the life-principle, belonged to him alone. But this does not mean that the life of the person offering sacrifice was brought into contact with the life of God. We have already shown[1] that the rite of laying hands on the victim does not symbolize the transference of the life or the sins of man to the victim: it merely testifies that this victim comes from this particular individual, and that it is being presented on his behalf.

3. *Was sacrifice a meal taken by the god?*

In answer to these theories, some writers assert that the whole problem is much simpler: sacrifice was a meal offered to God, for God was thought to be like men, needing food and enjoying the flavour of meat. Hence the altar is termed 'God's table', and the shewbread is called 'God's loaves'. Hence, too, the need to prepare a sacrifice as one prepares a meal: salt, cakes and wine had to be offered along with it. The supporters of this theory admit that in the texts of Leviticus and in the post-exilic worship, these terms are to be taken in a metaphorical sense, but, it is claimed, the terms bear witness to an older concept of sacrifice, materialist and anthromorphic.

In fact, the neighbours of Israel, especially the Mesopotamians, did strongly emphasize that sacrifice was a meal provided for the god,[2] and the banquets to which the gods invite each other in the poems of Ras Shamra show that the Canaanites, even if they did not have the same concept of sacrifice, at least believed that the gods needed food.

Our concern, however, is with Israel. Apart from a few exceptions (which we shall discuss later), the terms which seem to equate sacrifice with a meal provided for God are found only in late texts, and everyone admits that in these late texts they are not to be taken in the literal sense. What about the ancient texts? In Gn 8: 21, 'Yahweh inhaled the pleasant fragrance' of Noah's sacrifice; later on, this expression became a technical term and in the

1. Cf. p. 416. 2. Cf. p. 433.

late rituals it has lost all its literal meaning. In the text of Genesis, however, it is an echo of the Babylonian story of the Flood, with which the biblical story has so many contacts. We have already cited the text: 'The gods scented the fragrance, the gods scented the lovely fragrance, the gods collected like flies around the sacrificer'.[1] The biblical phrase is borrowed, but it is most discreetly re-phrased. A second text occurs in Yotham's fable, where the trees are trying to choose a king: mention is made of oil 'which brings honour to gods and men', and of must 'which brings joy to gods and men' (Jg 9: 9, 13). This is an old fable, but it may have been composed outside Israel; Ps 104: 15 (which is inspired by it) omits all mention of the gods, and refers only to men, whose hearts find joy in wine, whose faces shine with oil. Two other ancient stories about the sacrifices of Gideon (Jg 6: 18-22) and of Manoah (13: 15-20) reject the notion that Yahweh lives on the food of sacrifices: both Gideon and Manoah invite the Angel of Yahweh (whom they have not recognized) to a meal, and on both occasions, the sacrifice is transformed into a holocaust (cf. Jg 13: 16: 'Even if thou shouldst insist, I would not eat of thy meal'). In only one instance is the anthropomorphism taken to extremes: Abraham welcomed three mysterious visitors, among whom Yahweh was concealed: Abraham prepared a meal for these three 'men' and 'they ate it' (Gn 18: 8). But this meal was not a sacrifice.

One must, however, admit that certain features in Israelite ritual did tend to make sacrifice look like a meal in which Yahweh took part, and it may have been understood as such at the popular level. (We may cite, as examples of these features, the sacrificial meal which accompanied the *zebah*, and the offerings of cakes, of oil and of wine upon the altar: the custom of making these offerings may have been borrowed from Canaanite ritual.) We read in Ps 50: 12-13 a protest against this idea:

> 'If I am hungry, I shall not tell thee,
> for the world is mine, and all that it contains.
> Am I to eat the flesh of bulls,
> am I to drink the blood of goats?'

The Canticle of Moses asks where are the gods 'who used to eat the fat of their sacrifices, who used to drink the wine of their libations' (Dt 32: 38). In spite of these foreign influences and these deviations from orthodox Yahwism, we must insist that one cannot satisfactorily explain Israelite sacrifice by calling it a meal offered to a god.

The fault common to all the three theories which we have so far discussed is that they neglect the strictly religious significance of Israelite sacrifice, and that they all presuppose a cruder concept of the divinity, and of man's relations with God, than ever obtained in Israel.

1. Cf. p. 433.

4. *Outline of a theory of sacrifice*

Sacrifice is the essential act of external worship. It is a prayer which is acted, a symbolic action which expresses both the interior feelings of the person offering it, and God's response to this prayer. It is rather like the symbolic actions of the prophets. By sacrificial rites, the gift made to God *is* accepted, union with God *is* achieved, and the guilt of man *is* taken away. But these effects are not achieved by magic: it is essential that the external action should express the true inward feelings of man, and that it should be favourably received by God. Failing this, sacrifice is no longer a religious act.

On the other hand, sacrifice is one act with many aspects, and we must beware of simple explanations. Sacrifice is not merely a gift, nor merely a means of union with God, nor merely a means of expiating sin: there are several motives for it, which apply at one and the same time, and it satisfies several imperative instincts of the religious conscience.

Some of the rites, and some of the terms which describe these rites, date back to the pre-history of Israel, but we should not admit without proof that the meaning of these rites remained unchanged. Other rites, and other terms, were adopted by Israel from neighbouring peoples, especially from the Canaanites; but again, we should not admit without proof that these rites had the same meaning in Israel as they had among its neighbours. Israel's religion gave a new significance to the forms of worship which it inherited, or which it adopted from abroad. If we wish to discover what value Yahwism placed upon sacrifice, we must look for the answer in the Old Testament itself.

(a) *The gift.* God is the sovereign lord: everything belongs to him, and all man's possessions come from him. This is the theme of Ps 50: 9–12 (on sacrifices), and of the beautiful prayer which 1 Ch 29: 14 ascribes to David: 'Everything comes from thee, and even what we have given thee comes from thy hand'. Man owes everything to God, and it is therefore right that he should render tribute to God, as a subject pays tribute to his king, or a tenant to his land-owner. It is a kind of desecration: by giving a part to God, to whom all belongs, man 'desecrates' things and may use the rest as his own. This intention can be clearly seen in the offering of the first-fruits of the harvest and in the law about the first-born.

Yet sacrifice is something more than tribute. It is a gift, but a gift of a particular kind. More accurately, it is something which every gift ought to be in order to have ethical value: the victims (or the offerings) are domesticated animals (or vegetable produce) which man needs to support his life, and which are, as it were, part of his life and of himself. He deprives himself of them in order to give them away: by doing so he loses the gift, but he also gains something, for the acceptance of the gift involves God in an obligation.

God does not, of course, need the gift, but by accepting it, he binds himself in some way.

In this sense, every sacrifice is a gift, and it is not without significance that the term *minḥah* (meaning, literally a 'gift') is used not only for vegetable offerings, but also in the general sense of 'a sacrifice'.[1] Sacrifice is the means whereby men make gifts to God, and the offering is made in a way of its own: the gifts are wholly or partially destroyed; flour, bread and incense are burnt, liquids are poured out, and animals are slaughtered and burnt.

The purpose of this destruction is not merely to destroy. In opposition to the theory that sacrifice consists in annihilation, and in opposition to a certain modern school of spirituality, we must maintain that God, who is Lord of life and of all being, cannot be honoured by the destruction either of being or of life. In this context we may recall that animals were normally killed by the man offering the sacrifice, not by the priest; the essence of sacrifice, then, does not lie in the immolation. Immolation is only a preparation for the sacrifice, like the laying-on of hands.

Two reasons may be given for the destruction of the victim's carcase or of the vegetable offerings upon the altar, and they are complementary to each other. The first is that such destruction makes the offering useless, and makes it, therefore, an irrevocable gift. This idea harmonizes with a wider concept, that everything which is consecrated to God must be withdrawn from profane use; there are many analogies in other rites and in other religions, such as the custom of breaking vases which have been used for libations, or of throwing votive offerings into a spring, a well, or the sea.

The second reason is that destruction is the only way to give the offering to God, by transferring it into the realm of the invisible. This reason can be perceived first in the vocabulary used: 'to offer' a sacrifice is, in Hebrew, 'to bring near' or 'to make to rise up', and the sacrificial term *'olah* means 'that which goes up'. The rites themselves make this even clearer: sacrifice is essentially connected with the altar, for the altar is the symbol, or the reminder, of God's presence, an instrument of mediation between God and man.[2] That part of the offering which reverts to God is placed upon the altar. Blood, as the life-giving element, is particularly important: in every sacrifice it is poured out around the altar. In sacrifices of expiation it is rubbed upon the horns of the altar; in sacrifices offered for the sin of the high priest or of the people, it is sprinkled upon the veil which hides the Holy of Holies, the Dwelling of Yahweh; and on the great Day of Atonement it is taken inside the Holy of Holies itself, and there sprinkled over the mercy-seat, the throne of the divine Presence. All the other parts which are given back to God are destroyed upon the altar, and they take a spiritual form as they rise in smoke from the altar towards him. The offering is thus brought into contact with the symbols of God's presence, and brought as close as possible to him.

1. Cf. pp. 430-431. 2. Cf. pp. 413-414.

From this point of view, the holocaust may be considered the most perfect sacrifice, for man receives nothing of it, and all is burnt. But making a gift to God is only one aspect of sacrifice.

(b) *Communion*. Religion does not consist merely in expressing our dependence upon God: it includes also (as a consequence of this dependence) a quest for union with God. The Israelites never thought that they could be physically united with God by eating a divine victim, or by transferring into the realm of things divine a victim with which the man offering sacrifice had been identified. But there is another kind of union, which results from sharing the same possessions, from sharing a common life, and from the practice of hospitality. When Yahweh had accepted the victim and had received his part (upon the altar), the men who had offered the sacrifice then ate the rest in a religious meal, and so shared the sacrifice. St Paul is referring to the sacrifices of Israel when he writes 'Are not they who eat the victims in communion with the altar?' (1 Co 10: 18). Just as a contract between men was sealed by their taking a meal together (cf. Gn 26: 28–30; 31: 44–54), so the covenant between the worshipper and his God was established or strengthened by this sacrificial meal. Hence it is called the *zebaḥ sh'lamîm*, the sacrifice of communion, the sacrifice of covenant. It was a joyful sacrifice in which the two ideas of a gift and of communion were both included; the offering was made by man, and it achieved its effect in maintaining friendship with God. Hence it was regarded as the most complete kind of sacrifice, and at the beginning of Israel's history, it was the most frequent kind offered.

(c) *Expiation*. Since in every sacrifice man deprived himself of something useful in order to present it to God, and since all sacrifice tended to establish good relations between God and man, every sacrifice had some expiatory value. When the writer wished to underline the gravity of Eli's offence in 1 S 3: 14, he wrote that 'neither sacrifice (*zebaḥ*) nor offering (*minḥah*) will ever efface the fault of Eli'. The sacrificial code in Leviticus ascribes an expiatory value to the holocaust. Blood played an important part in all animal sacrifices, and, according to Lv 17: 11, the blood was given to men 'to perform the rite of expiation upon the altar'.

But there were circumstances in which the need for expiation was more acutely felt. When a man had sinned, he needed to find grace again, and he had to ask God to re-establish the covenant whose terms he had broken. This was the purpose of sacrifices for sin and of sacrifices of expiation: the ritual use of blood was of special importance, and there was no sacrificial meal, for the sinner could not share the company of God until the covenant had already been re-established. We tried to show above[1] that expiatory sacrifice was of ancient origin in Israel, but this kind of sacrifice was developed from the other kinds, and it became much more important when great national

1. Cf. pp. 429–430.

calamities brought home to the people the sense of its own guilt, and when the nation developed a more acute sense of sin and of Yahweh's demands.

5. *Polemic against sacrifices*

The pre-exilic Prophets uttered some violent attacks on sacrifices: Is 1: 11-17; Jr 6: 20; 7: 21-22; Os 6: 6; Am 5: 21-27; Mi 6: 6-8. They contrast the futility of sacrifices with obedience to Yahweh, and with the doing of right and of justice (Is 1: 16-17; Jr 7: 23; Am 5: 24; Mi 6: 8). Some authors have therefore drawn the conclusion that the Prophets condemned sacrifices of every kind. Since several of these passages mention sacrifices along with pilgrimages and feasts, the same authors admit that the Prophets condemned all exterior worship. But these Prophets do not condemn the Temple itself[1]; hence they are regarded as advocates of a Temple without altar and without sacrifices; they would thus be the Protestants of the Old Testament. If this attitude is adopted, then one should go further, for Is 1: 15 mentions, along with sacrifices and feasts, prayer itself: 'No matter how many prayers you say, I shall not listen.' Now since no one holds that the Prophets condemned prayer, the whole argument leads to an absurd conclusion and simply falls to pieces. These biblical texts, therefore, cannot mean that the Prophets uttered condemnations of sacrifice itself.

Yet the texts must be explained. It is not enough to say that the Prophets are condemning the cult because, in their day, it had been contaminated with pagan practices or ideas. They do, of course, condemn such worship, but in other texts (Os 2: 13-15; 4: 11-13; 13: 2; Am 4: 4-5; Jr 7: 17-18, etc.); in the preceding paragraph we have retained only those texts which appear to be directed against external worship offered to Yahweh in accordance with the rites prescribed. We have already attempted to give an explanation of Am 5: 21-27 and of Jr 7: 21-22 when we were treating of the cult in the desert,[2] and the same principle should be applied to the other texts also. Though the expression of condemnation is unconditional it should be taken in a relative sense: it is a 'dialectical negation', of which several other examples can be cited in Hebrew and in New Testament Greek. 'Not this but that' is a way of saying 'Not so much this as that'. The literal rendering of Os 6: 6, for example, is: 'It is love that I want, not (*lo'*) sacrifices, and the knowledge of God rather than (*min*) holocausts', and the parallelism demands that the first formula should be comparative, like the second (cf. Pr 8: 10). This is clearer still in the words of Samuel, who was a prophet and who nonetheless offered sacrifices: 'Does Yahweh take pleasure in holocausts and in sacrifices, as in obedience to the word of Yahweh? Yes, obedience is more than the best sacrifice, and docility more than the fat of rams' (1 S 15: 22). The Prophets are opposed to the formalism of exterior worship when it

1. Cf. p. 326. 2. Cf. p. 428.

has no corresponding interior dispositions (Is 29: 13): in these texts they are speaking as preachers. The priestly texts, which are rituals, do not have occasion to say this, but they obviously presuppose that the religious act of sacrifice is of no avail unless the man offering it has sincere dispositions.

The Wisdom books repeat the same lesson: 'The sacrifice of the wicked is an abomination to Yahweh, but the prayer of upright men is his delight' (Pr 15: 8; cf. 21: 27), and 'To put into practice justice and right is, in Yahweh's eyes, of more value than sacrifices' (Pr 21: 3). There are certain Psalms which seem to reject the principle of sacrifice (Ps 40: 7–8; 50: 8–15; 51: 18–19), but these texts should be interpreted in the same way as the texts of the Prophets.

There is another factor also which explains why the Prophets rejected sacrifices: they mention it in their oracles of condemnation. The judgment of God is imminent and will not be averted by outward acts of worship, because the people's sins are too grave (cf. Jr 6: 19–20; 14: 12; Mi 3: 4 and also 1 S 3: 14).

The Prophets, the Wisdom Books and the Law all speak of sacrifice from different angles, but they do not contradict each other, as is sometimes claimed. Nor is there any break between the period before the Exile and the period after the Exile. There is continuity, and Ezechiel is the link. He was a prophet and a priest; he certainly did not reject as illegitimate the whole liturgy of the monarchic period, and he outlined a programme for the future liturgy with all its exterior acts. The post-exilic prophets preached this idea in a restored Israel. During the same years, the ritual became more precise, and it was accepted by everyone as an institution coming from God. After this, there was no further polemic against sacrifices.

But, it will be said, what about the Essenes? According to Philo (*Quod omnis probus liber sit*, 75), they did not offer animals in sacrifice, and according to Josephus (*Ant.* XVIII i, 5), they offered sacrifice only in private, away from the Temple. New light has been thrown on this evidence by the discoveries and the texts which have emerged from Qumran: these texts certainly come from a community which must be called, in some way or other, an 'Essenian' society. These sectaries broke off relations with the priests of Jerusalem and took no part in the official worship, but they still claimed to be scrupulous observers of the Law. Consequently, they did not offer sacrifice, for, outside the Temple, sacrifice would have been unlawful. Excavations at Qumran have brought to light heaps of animal bones which were buried in a ritual way, and some authors have therefore claimed that these bones are the remains of sacrifices: these finds would therefore confirm the statement of Josephus that the Essenes offered private sacrifices. It is more likely, however, that these bones are the remains of religious meals which did not have a strictly sacrificial character. Yet our uncertainty about the text of Josephus and about the finds at Qumran makes no difference to the essential point:

the Essenes did not reject the cult itself which was practised in the Temple. They merely cut themselves off from the priesthood which presided in the Temple at the time, for they considered the men unworthy of that office. The Qumran texts extol the value of sacrifice, and give it a place in the ideal regulations which they lay down for the Community.

The Prophets condemned formalism in worship; Jeremias preached a religion of the heart; Ezechiel demanded sublime holiness; and all the most authentic spokesmen of Judaism repeat the message down to the age when the community of Qumran set before its members an ideal of piety, of penance and of moral purity. All these witnesses contributed to make the cult more interior and more spiritual; the cult was more and more considered as the outward expression of interior dispositions, and it was the inward spirit which gave it all its value. The way was thus prepared for the New Testament. Jesus did not condemn sacrifice; indeed, he offered himself as a sacrifice (Mk 10: 45; Eph 5: 2); he is the Paschal victim (1 Co 5: 7) and his sacrifice is the sacrifice of the New Covenant (Lk 22: 20; 1 Co 11: 25). This is the perfect sacrifice, by reason of the nature and of the dispositions of the victim: he offered himself of his own free will, in an act of obedience. It is perfect also by reason of the manner in which it was performed: it was a total gift, in which the victim returned wholly to God; a communion-sacrifice more intimate than man could ever have suspected; an expiation-sacrifice sufficient to atone for all the sins of the world. And precisely because it was a perfect sacrifice which at one stroke exhausted all the possible aspects of sacrifice, it is unique. The Temple could disappear, and animal sacrifices had to end, for they were merely the imperfect figure, indefinitely repeated, of the sacrifice of Christ who offered himself 'once for all' in a 'unique offering' for our redemption and our sanctification, as the Epistle to the Hebrews repeatedly insists (He 7: 27; 9: 12, 26, 28; 10: 10, 12, 14). And the Church which Jesus has founded will continue, until the end of time, to commemorate this perfect sacrifice and to live by its fruits.

CHAPTER FOURTEEN

SECONDARY ACTS OF THE CULT

1. *Liturgical prayer*

PRAYING means 'speaking to God'; prayer, therefore, establishes a personal relationship between man and God, and it is the basic act of religion. The reason why we are treating it here among the secondary acts of worship is because our theme is the institutions of Israel, and prayer is relevant only in so far as it forms part of exterior worship. In the Old Testament, liturgical prayer was not an institution independent of other cultic acts, as it has come to be in synagogue services. There are, it seems, only two references in the Old Testament to liturgies which consisted entirely in singing or reciting prayers, and they were both penitential services (Ne 9 and Jl 1-2).

(a) *Prayer and the cult.* It is quite certain, however, that in Israel cultic actions were accompanied by words; this was so in all Oriental religions, and indeed, it is true of every religion in the world. The Bible contains some formulas for blessings (Nb 6: 22-27) and for cursing (Dt 27: 14-26: the people joined in these curses); it also gives the formula to be used in the ritual of the 'bitter water' (Nb 5: 21-22), the words to be pronounced when the person responsible for a murder could not be discovered (Dt 21: 7-8), the formulas for the offering of the first-fruits (Dt 26: 1-10) and of the three-yearly tithe (Dt 26: 13-15), and the 'lesson' for the feast of the Passover (Dt 6: 20-25, cf. Ex 12: 26-27).

Sacrifice was the central act of the cult, and the very action of sacrifice was itself a prayer; but it was accompanied by vocal prayer. The code in Lv 1-7 does not mention vocal prayer in connection with sacrifice, because it is concerned only with the actual rites to be followed, but Am 5: 23 says that hymns were sung to the accompaniment of instruments while sacrifice was being offered. And in fact, public prayer naturally tends to become rhythmic hymn-singing. Liturgical singing made its appearance once the cult and the priesthood were organized in a public sanctuary, and Solomon's Temple had a group of singers attached to it from its earliest days.[1] After the Exile, the members of this Temple choir became more important and more highly esteemed, and the Chronicler's interest in sacred music is well-known.[2]

The hymn-book, or the prayer-book, of the second Temple is the Psalter,

1. Cf. p. 382. 2. Cf. pp. 391-392.

and it contains some liturgical hymns dating from the time of the monarchy. The text of the Psalter makes it clear that the psalms were used in connection with worship: some of them make reference to a rite (usually sacrifice) which is to be performed as they are sung (Ps 20: 4; 26: 5; 27: 6; 66: 13–15; 81: 4; 107: 22; 116: 17), and others speak of the Temple in which they were sung (Ps 48; 65; 95; 96; 118; 134; 135). The 'Gradual Psalms' (Ps 120–134) and Ps 84 were songs for pilgrimages. On the other hand, it is often hard to distinguish between individual and collective prayers, or between private and liturgical prayers: psalms which are placed in the mouth of an individual were sometimes written to be used in the Temple services, and others were adapted for liturgical use by the addition of doxologies. In general, we do not have sufficient information to decide at which ceremonies or feasts psalms of this kind were sung. We can, of course, work out hypotheses from the general content of the psalms, but this is still guess-work; and we can use the information given in the titles of psalms, but this information is valid only for a very late period. The Hebrew title of Ps 92 says it is a psalm for the Sabbath, and the Greek titles of Ps 24, 48, 93, 94 say they are to be sung on other days of the week. Ps 30 was a psalm for the feast of the Dedication (according to the Hebrew text), and Ps 29 was sung at the feast of Tents (according to the Greek).

Any discussion about people's motives for praying or the themes of their prayer is part of biblical theology, but a study of Old Testament institutions must discuss the rules which governed the place, the time and the posture to be adopted in prayer.

(b) *The place and time of prayer, etc.* The Israelites normally prayed in the Temple, *i.e.* in the Temple courts, facing the sanctuary (Ps 5: 8; 28: 2; 138: 2). After the Exile, the Jews outside Jerusalem turned towards the Holy City and towards the Temple (1 K 8: 44, 48). Daniel prayed in his high room from a window facing Jerusalem (Dn 6: 11). The custom was sanctioned by later Judaism, and it governed the orientation of synagogues.

Ps 4 is an evening prayer, and Ps 5 a morning prayer; Judith prayed at the hour when the evening sacrifice of incense was being offered in the Temple (Jdt 9: 1). Daniel prayed three times a day (Dn 6: 11), and Ps 55: 18 tells us that the Israelites prayed 'in the evening in the morning and at noon'. These texts, however, are late texts, and concern private prayer. Now, in this later age, only two services were held each day in the Temple, in the morning and in the evening; the rules for private prayer, therefore, had ceased to be connected with the cult in the Temple.

Certain texts seem to indicate that the Israelites prayed standing upright: *e.g.* 1 S 1: 26; 1 K 8: 22; Jr 18: 20 all use the verb *'amad*, the ordinary meaning of which is 'to stand erect'. There are many texts to show that this was the custom in New Testament times. The verb *'amad* can, however, mean simply 'to be' in front of God, without implying that one is actually standing. In

2 Ch 6: 13, we read that Solomon built a platform, 'went up onto it, stopped (*'amad*) and knelt down'. Perhaps, too, the Israelites changed their attitude during prayer, according to the different intentions for which they were praying. The penitential liturgy of Ne 9: 3-5 (re-edited by the Chronicler) began with a reading from the book of the Law, during which the people stood (*wayyaqûmu*); then they knelt down (*mishtaḥawîm*) to confess their sins, until the Levites gave the order to rise ('Stand up!'—*qûmu*); thereupon they sang a psalm (cf. also 1 K 8: 54-55). But the ordinary attitude of prayer was meant to express humility and submission before God; 'Bow down, prostrate yourselves, kneel down before Yahweh' (Ps 95: 6). Men prayed on their knees (1 K 8: 54; Is 45: 23; Dn 6: 11), with their hands raised to heaven (1 K 8: 22, 54; Ps 28: 2; Is 1: 15; Lm 2: 19). Sometimes they prostrated themselves, kneeling and bowing their foreheads to the ground (Ps 5: 8; 99: 5, 9, etc.). The pagans adopted the same attitudes when praying to their gods (Ex 20: 5; Dt 4: 19; 1 K 19: 18; 2 K 5: 18, etc.), and the gestures were part of the normal courtesies towards the king or towards a person whom one wished to honour (1 S 24: 9; 2 S 9: 8; 1 K 2: 19; 2 K 1: 13; 4: 37; Est 3: 2, etc.).

The terms most commonly used for prayer are the verb *hithpallel* and the noun *t'pillah*. The same root in Arabic means 'to make a hole in', 'to cut', and it has therefore been suggested that the Hebrew terms are the relics of an ancient custom: in other words, that the Israelites used to make gashes on their bodies (as the prophets of Baal did on Carmel, 1 K 18: 28) in order to make their prayer more urgent and more effective. Against this, we may point out that the text in Kings uses a different verb, and that the meaning of the root, even in Arabic, is far wider. In Hebrew, the root seems to mean 'to decide, to arbitrate, to intercede' (cf. especially Gn 20: 7; 1 S 2: 25). Prayer, then means making intercession, and the person who pronounces a prayer on behalf of the people or of an individual is a mediator: he may be a holy person, or a consecrated person, such as a king, a prophet or a priest. But whatever be the basic meaning of the root, *hithpallel* and *t'pillah* came to mean respectively 'to pray' and 'prayer'. In the Old Testament, prayer was addressed directly to God, without reference to any heavenly mediator. The notion of angelic intercession for men appeared only after the Exile, when the doctrine of angels began to develop: at first the idea is expressed only timidly (Jb 5: 1; 33: 23-24; Za 1: 12), but it is clearer in Tobias (Tb 12: 12), where Raphael says: 'When you were at prayer, you and Sarra, it was I who presented your requests before the Glory of the Lord, and it was I who read them out' (cf. also 12: 15, according to one of the Greek recensions). This doctrine was stressed in the apocryphal books of Judaism, and was repeated in the New Testament (Ap 8: 3). There is only one mention of intercession by a saint, in 2 M 15: 14, where we read that Jeremias 'prays much for the people and for all the holy city'.

2. *Rites of purification and of de-consecration*

In the minds of the ancients there was a close connection between the notion of ritual impurity and the notion of being consecrated to God. There was a mysterious and frightening force inherent in things which were impure and in things which were sacred, and these two forces acted on everything with which they came into contact, placing the objects or persons which touched them under a kind of interdict. Both what was impure and what was consecrated were alike 'untouchable', and any person who touched them became himself 'untouchable'. These primitive notions are found in the Old Testament: one law forbade men to touch the Ark of the Covenant, and another law forbade men to touch a corpse; a mother had to purify herself after childbirth, because it made her impure, and a priest had to change his clothes after a sacrifice, because it had made him a consecrated person. Yet this impurity is not to be understood as a physical or moral defilement, and this kind of holiness is not to be understood as a moral virtue: they are rather 'states' or 'conditions' from which men must emerge in order to re-enter normal life.

The Bible described the extent of these interdicts, and the rituals for purification and de-consecration; and here, perhaps more than anywhere else, the religion of Israel preserved some very archaic customs. It is strange that these customs were integrated into the Priestly legislation, the very latest part of the Pentateuch; yet, though the rites were retained, they were given a new meaning. They served to separate Israel from the pagan world around it, and to inculcate the idea of Yahweh's transcendent holiness and of the holiness which his chosen people ought to preserve. Hence, in the final synthesis of Leviticus, the Law of Purity (Lv 11-16) was put beside the Law of Holiness (Lv 17-26): they are the two aspects, negative and positive, of that holiness which is demanded by God.

(a) *Sacrifices and ablutions.* Sacrifices held an important place in rituals of purification and of de-consecration: after childbirth, women had to offer a holocaust and a sacrifice for sin (Lv 12: 1-8); lepers, on the occasion of their purification, had to offer a sacrifice of reparation (or a sacrifice for sin) and a holocaust (Lv 14: 10-32); men and women had to offer a holocaust and a sacrifice for sin whenever they contracted sexual impurity (Lv 15: 14-15, 29-30). A Nazirite who had become impure through contact with a corpse was obliged to offer a sacrifice for sin, a holocaust and a sacrifice of reparation (Nb 6: 9-12), and, when the period covered by his vow was ended, a holocaust, a sacrifice for sin and a sacrifice of reparation (Nb 6: 13-20).

But there were other rites, too, for purification or de-consecration: some of them were combined with sacrifices, others were not. We have already stated that both what was impure and what was consecrated affected everyone who came into physical contact with it: it was natural to 'wash' themselves clean from the effects of this contact. Thus, for example, the priest who was to conduct worship might have contracted some impurity: consequently, he had to wash himself before beginning the service so that he might safely enter the realm of things sacred (Ex 29: 4; 30: 17-21; Lv 8: 6; 16: 4). The laws about purity prescribed that vessels, clothes or persons which had been defiled by contact with something unclean should be washed in water (Lv 11: 24-15, 28, 32, 40; 15 *passim*; 22: 6). But water was also used to wash things which had been in contact with something sacred: meat which had been offered in sacrifice was a most holy thing, and therefore the metal vessel in which it had been boiled had to be scoured and rinsed in water; if it was an earthenware vessel, it was to be broken (Lv 6: 21). On the Day of Atonement, the high priest had to change his clothes and to wash his entire body after he had come out of the Holy of Holies; similarly, the man who led the scapegoat out into the desert, and the man who burnt the victims offered in sacrifice for sin, both had to change their clothes and to wash themselves (Lv 16: 23-28). Those who took part in the ritual of the red heifer were obliged to follow these rules too (Nb 19: 7-10, 21). Those who took part in a holy war[1] were 'sanctified' by taking up arms in such a cause, and even the booty which they captured was holy; before they could return to normal life, the fighting men and the booty alike had to be de-consecrated, and the period prescribed for this rite was seven days. The fighting men and the prisoners stayed outside the camp for seven days; they washed their clothes and purified themselves. They washed, too, all the leather materials, all the textile and wooden objects, but metal objects were first passed through fire before being washed (Nb 31: 16-24).

(b) *The ashes of the red heifer.* In the text just cited (Nb 31: 16-24), the metal had to be washed in 'lustral water' (*mê middah*, meaning literally 'water to take away defilement'); there was a special ritual for preparing it (Nb 19: 1-10). A red heifer, without blemish and one which had never borne the yoke, was slaughtered outside the town ('outside the camp', the text says, because it is attributing the institution to the desert period); it was slaughtered by a lay person in the presence of a priest. The whole carcase was then burnt, and as it was burning, the priest threw into the fire cedar-wood, hyssop and red cochineal; the ashes were then collected and kept in a ritually pure place. Lustral water was prepared by putting some of these ashes into a vessel and pouring upon them running water, *i.e.* water coming directly from a spring or from a stream. This rite certainly originated in pagan practices, and it must have been originally a magic rite: many peoples regard red as a protective colour to avert evil and to put demons to flight, and the ashes of animals are often used for lustrations, as running water is used to take away defilement. The rite, then, must be of ancient origin; it was accepted by Yahwism, and the rôle of the priest made it a

1. Cf. pp. 258-259.

legitimate ceremony; originally, it had nothing to do with sacrifice, but it was likened to a sacrifice for sin (the very term is used in Nb 19: 17, cf. v. 13, and compare Nb 19: 4 and 8 with Lv 16: 27–28).

This water was used for purification: it was sprinkled on anyone who touched a corpse, or bones, or a tomb; it was also used to purify the house of a dead man and its furniture (Nb 19: 11–22). Outside this text, this kind of water is mentioned only once, in the text previously cited (Nb 31: 23), where it is prescribed for the purification of plunder taken in a holy war: but here it seems to be an addition, which adds nothing significant to the context. Curiously enough, this lustral water is not mentioned in other texts which refer to impurity contracted by contact with a dead body: the Law of Holiness prescribes washing, but with ordinary water (Lv 22: 4–6) and the law about Nazirites lays down a complicated ritual but makes no mention of lustral water (Nb 6: 9–12). On the other hand, the ancient texts which describe funeral rites do not remotely suggest that contact with a corpse brings on defilement (cf. especially Gn 46: 4; 50: 1). Thus the rite concerning the ashes of the red heifer and the use of lustral water is rather paradoxical; it appears to have been an archaic rite which lived on side by side with the official religion; it was not even part of the ordinary life of the people, and yet, in the end, it was incorporated, at a very late date, into the Priestly legislation.

(c) *The ritual for leprosy*. The ritual for leprosy (which takes up two long chapters of the Law of Purity, Lv 13–14) raises a similar problem. The Hebrew word which modern translations render as 'leprosy' is *sara'ath*, but the disease it specifies is not—or not merely—what we nowadays term leprosy. *Ṣara'ath* is applied to different skin diseases, the symptoms of which are described in Lv 13: 1–44: the symptoms are not those of what we call leprosy (*Elephantiasis Graecorum*), and the diseases described can be cured. Though the priest had to decide whether a particular man was infected with this 'leprosy', he made his decision not as a physician, but as an interpreter of the Law: the 'leper' was declared impure, cut off from the community and compelled to live at a distance from the town (cf. the relatively early text of 2 K 7: 3) until he was cured.

The priest also decided when a man was cured (Lv 14: 3; cf. Mt 8: 4 and parallels; Lk 17: 14). But before the 'leper' could return to ordinary life, he had to undergo a ceremony of purification. A vessel was filled with water from a spring or from a stream, and a bird was then slaughtered over this vessel, so that its blood dripped into the water. Next, another bird was thrust into the water alive; cedar-wood, red cochineal and hyssop were put into the water; then the live bird was released in the open country, the leper was sprinkled with water and he was pronounced clean. Seven days later, he shaved all the hair off his body, washed his clothes and took a bath; and then he was clean (Lv 14: 2–9).

But the text continues: on the eighth day, he is to offer a sacrifice of reparation, a sacrifice for sin and a holocaust. The priest took the blood from the sacrifice of reparation and smeared it on the right ear, the right thumb and the right big toe of the man who had been cured; next, he anointed the same parts with oil and poured the remainder of the oil on the head of the ex-leper (Lv 14: 10–32). Similar rites are prescribed for the investiture of the high priest (Ex 29: 20–21; Lv 8: 12),[1] but in Lv 14 the purpose of the ceremonies is purification, not consecration. Blood was used in the same way as in expiatory sacrifices,[2] and the rites of anointing may be compared with the rite for the 'purification of the forehead' which is mentioned in Mesopotamian contracts for the liberation of slaves: there is also a particularly striking parallel in a text from Ras Shamra which records the emancipation of a female slave: 'I have poured oil upon her head, and I have declared her pure'.

Chapter 14 of Leviticus is a combination of two rituals. One of them (vv. 2–9) is of archaic origin: skin diseases, which are so loathsome and so contagious, are caused by a demon, and this demon must therefore be chased away. Here we meet again certain features of the ritual for the red heifer: since red is a colour which frightens evil ones away, reddened water and red cochineal are used; cedar-wood, hyssop and running water have a cleansing power; as the bird flies away in the open country, it carries the evil away with it; and all hair must be shaved off because it bears signs of the disease (Lv 13: 2–44 *passim*). The second ritual (Lv 14: 10–32) applies to lepers the levitical rules about expiatory sacrifices; it contains, however, one element which does not come from the ritual of expiation, namely, the anointing with oil, but we have seen that this rite was practised in parallel circumstances among the neighbours of Israel.

Not only human beings were subject to 'leprosy': mildew on clothes, on textile or leather-work was called 'leprosy', and the objects became thereby impure. Again, it was the priest's duty to make the decision and to isolate the object. If the corruption showed signs of spreading, or did not disappear after washing, then the thing had to be burnt; if the marks disappeared after a washing, then the object was washed a second time and declared 'pure' (Lv 13: 47–59). Houses, too, could be infected with 'leprosy': if the walls became covered in saltpetre or moss they might well seem to have 'leprosy' (Lv 14: 33–53); if the priest decided that this was so, the affected stones were taken out and the walls were scraped; if the signs of leprosy continued to spread, the house was demolished, but if they disappeared, the house was declared pure. In either case, however, the 'sin of the house' had to be expiated, and the ritual was the same as for the purification of a leper (Lv 14: 2–9).

All these various prescriptions are evidence of very primitive ideas; they are the remains of old superstitious rites. And yet there is no reference to

1. Cf. p. 414. 2. Cf. p. 419.

them in the pre-exilic texts, just as there is no reference to the ashes of the red heifer or to the use of lustral water in the years before the Exile. There is only one possible conclusion, and it must apply to all the laws about purity in Lv 11-16: after the Exile, the Jews became increasingly conscious of the need for purity, and the fear of impurity eventually became an obsession with them; hence the writers of the Priests' Code multiplied the instances of impurity and prescribed all the correct remedies for it; they borrowed material on every side, integrated popular superstitions into the Levitical system and imposed so many prescriptions that the law became too complicated to be practical. Post-biblical Judaism travelled even further in the same direction. The ritual had at first served to give expression to the holiness of God and of his people, but it changed into a narrow system of formal observance, a yoke too heavy to be borne; what had once been a protection became an iron collar. Jesus condemned the scribes and the Pharisees for putting heavy loads upon the necks of other men (Mt 23: 4) and thereby preventing them from entering the Kingdom of Heaven (Mt 23: 13). He proclaimed that the only uncleanness which brings defilement is moral uncleanness (Mt 15: 10-20), and St Paul laid down that 'nothing is of itself unclean or impure' (Ro 14: 14).

3. *Rites of consecration*

(a) *General remarks.* In the minds of the Israelites, the notion of purification was closely connected with the idea of sanctification, and the words which express the two ideas can be used as synonyms. Yet there is a difference: purification meant removing the obstacle which hindered a man from coming near to God, whereas sanctification either prepared a man to meet God or resulted from close contact with God. Purification expressed the negative, sanctification the positive, aspect. Everything which was related to God was holy, and therefore nothing could penetrate within the realm of the divine unless it had first been 'sanctified', *i.e.* unless it had been withdrawn from the realm of things profane. Hence the verb *qiddesh*, meaning literally 'to sanctify, to hallow', can often be translated 'to consecrate'.

This consecration did not necessarily entail the performance of a special rite: any action which brought a person or a thing into close relationship with God or with divine worship automatically consecrated that person or thing. Those who took part in a holy war were 'sanctified', and the plunder they captured was consecrated to God[1]; priests were sanctified simply by beginning to exercise their office[2]; the desert Tent and the Temple were holy, merely because God dwelt inside them; their furnishings were holy because they served for divine worship; the victims and the offerings were holy because they had been presented to God. Certain interdicts, however,

1. Cf. pp. 257-261. 2. Cf. pp. 347-348.

resulted from this consecration: but these interdicts did not bring about consecration—they were the result, not the cause, of consecration. Things and persons which had been consecrated to God might not be profaned. Fighting men were bound to observe continence (1 S 21: 6; 2 S 11: 11); no one could profit from plunder taken in a holy war (Jos 6: 18f.; 1 S 15: 18-19); the priests were subject to strict rules concerning purity (Lv 21: 1-8); sacrificial victims, offerings and tithes were 'holy things', or even 'most holy things', which had to be destroyed or eaten under special conditions and by particular persons (Lv 2: 3, 10, etc.; Nb 18: 8-9; Ez 42: 13).

In the instances just mentioned, consecration resulted from some contact with the realm of the divine; but late in Israel's history, particular rites were prescribed for certain occasions, with the object of bringing about consecration. We have already studied the post-exilic rite for the consecration of the high priest, and shown how it included purification, clothing and anointing with a specially prepared chrism.[1] The same late texts prescribe that the sanctuary, the altar and all the sacred furniture are to be anointed with this holy oil (Ex 30: 26-29; 40: 9-11; Lv 8: 10).

Under the monarchy, this anointing was the essential feature in the coronation ritual; it was the anointing which made the king a sacred person.[2] The sign of this consecration was the *nezer* which the king wore (2 S 1: 10; 2 K 11: 12; Ps 89: 40); it was also an ornament of the high priest's headdress, an ornament which was identical with the *ṣiṣ*, the golden flower he wore above his forehead (Ex 39: 30; Lv 8: 9).[3] We may also recall that the correct translation of *nezer* is not 'diadem' but 'sign of consecration'.

The basic meaning of the root *nzr* is 'to separate' or 'to keep separated' from profane use; it means also 'to place under interdict' in the sense of 'to consecrate'. From this verb comes the noun *nazir*, meaning a person consecrated to God. And there is a synonym of *nzr* which is written *ndr*, from which comes the noun *neder*, meaning a 'vow', *i.e.* the consecration of a thing or of a person to God. Since these terms are so closely related, we shall treat here of vows and of the Nazirites.

(b) *Vows*. A vow (*neder*) is a promise to give or to consecrate to God a person or thing, *e.g.* a tithe (Gn 28: 20-22), a sacrifice (2 S 15: 8), plunder taken in war (Nb 21: 2), a person (Jg 11: 30-31; 1 S 1: 11). In all the instances cited, the vow was a conditional promise to give something to God, if God first granted a favour: Jacob promised to pay a tithe if Yahweh brought him home safe and sound; Jephthah promised to sacrifice someone if he won a victory; Anna promised to consecrate her child to God if he would grant her a son and so forth. The purpose of these vows was to add force to a prayer by making a kind of contract with God. All the vows in the Old Testament seem to have been of this kind, even when the condition was not openly expressed, and this justifies the distinction we made above between

1. Cf. pp. 398-400. 2. Cf. pp. 103-106. 3. Cf. p. 399.

'votive' sacrifices and 'voluntary' sacrifices.[1] Some texts of Leviticus, however (Lv 7: 16-17; 22: 18-23), and even of Deuteronomy (Dt 12: 6, 11, 17) are not too clear about this distinction; there are, too, some general expressions in the Psalms (Ps 50: 14; 61: 9; 65: 2) which indicate that, as time went on, vows were becoming more like simple promises, and that they were not dependent on the granting of a favour of God. We are going to discuss, in a moment, the vow of the Nazirite, and this, in its final form, was certainly an unconditional promise.

Once a vow had been taken, man was bound to stand by it (Nb 30: 3; Dt 23: 22-24); it was better not to take vows at all if one could not fulfil them (Qo 5: 3-5). Yet certain vows were unlawful: the first-born of cattle could not be consecrated to Yahweh because they belonged to him by right (Lv 27: 26); because God was holy, any vow to consecrate to him the revenues from sacred prostitution was null and void (Dt 23: 19). The Law contained certain special provisions for vows taken by women: any vow taken by an unmarried woman could be annulled by her father; any vow taken by a married woman could be annulled by her husband, but a widow or a woman who had been divorced could take vows validly (Nb 30: 4-17). A vow imposed a grave obligation, but eventually this obligation was not so rigidly enforced, and men were allowed to commute the obligation into a payment of money: the tariffs were fixed down to the smallest details by the late law of Lv 27: 1-25.

(c) *The Nazirites.* Any person, man or woman, could consecrate himself or herself to God for a limited period: this was called taking the vow of a Nazirite, and the rules for it are given in Nb 6: 1-21. During this period of consecration, the *nazir* was to abstain from wine and all fermented drinks, to allow his hair to grow and to avoid all contact with any dead body. Should anyone die unexpectedly in his presence, he became impure: he had to shave himself, to offer one pigeon as a sacrifice for sin, another as a holocaust, and a lamb as a sacrifice of reparation; then he had to begin once more to live as a Nazirite, and to complete the whole period anew, without counting the time that had already passed. At the end of the period, he had to offer a holocaust, a sacrifice for sin and a communion-sacrifice; he shaved his head and burnt the hair along with the communion-sacrifice; after this ceremony the Nazirite was 'desecrated'. He could then return to normal life and was once more allowed to drink wine.

The practice was certainly known in New Testament times. St. Paul completed a vow of this kind at Cenchreae (Ac 18: 18), and again, along with four other Nazirites, at the Temple in Jerusalem (Ac 21: 23-24). Under the Maccabees, one of the problems was that the Nazirites could not observe the rites which were prescribed for the ending of their vow, since the Temple was profaned (1 M 3: 49-51).

1. Cf. p. 417.

The law in Numbers, however, merely codifies a very ancient custom and adapts it to the Levitical ritual. It also reduces to a temporary vow something which had originally been a consecration for life. According to Am 2:11-12, God raised up prophets and Nazirites in Israel, but the people made the Nazirites drink wine, and forbade the prophets to speak. In this text, the Nazirite is not a person who has taken a vow, but a man possessed of a God-given charisma: it is a life-long state resulting from a call by God. The Nazirite is a man whom God has consecrated to himself, *i.e.* (according to the basic meaning of the word) a man whom God has separated from the realm of things profane. The external symbols of this separation lie in the various things forbidden to the Nazirite; here in Amos, only abstaining from wine is mentioned, but Nb 6: 3-4 extends the prohibition to everything produced from the vine.

The only ancient story which speaks of a Nazirite is the story of Samson, and here, too, the consecration is life-long, and results from a divine call. Even before he was born, his mother had to abstain from wine and fermented drink, because the child she was to bear would be a '*nazir* of God'; Samson himself was to follow the same rule, no razor was ever to 'pass over his head', but he was to be 'a *nazir* of God from his mother's womb to the day of his death' (Jg 13: 4-5, 7, 13-14). His long hair was the sign of his consecration (cf. Nb 6: 9, 18) and the source of his miraculous strength (Jg 16: 17); God had chosen Samson and given him this extraordinary strength to make him his champion. This, too, is the meaning we should give to the adjective *nazir* when it is applied to Joseph in the Blessings of Jacob (Gn 49: 26) and in the Blessings of Moses (Dt 33: 16). The first text implies, and the second expressly states, that uncut hair is the characteristic mark of the Nazirite, and this remained true down to the last examples mentioned in the Bible (Ac 18: 18; 21: 23-24). An extension of this usage can be seen in the application of the word *nazir* to vineyards which were not pruned in sabbatical or jubilee years, *i.e.* in which the seeds were allowed to grow without hindrance (cf. Lv 25: 5, 11).

Possibly we ought to combine with this story of Samson the old rituals concerning the holy war: the combatants were consecrated to God, and from Jg 5: 2 (cf. Dt 32: 42) we are justified in asserting that they wore their hair long. If this was the origin of the institution, it quickly evolved into something different. Samuel was given to God for the whole of his life, and the razor would never pass over his head (1 S 1: 11); though the word *nazir* is not used, this is evidently what is meant. Samuel, however, was consecrated for the service of God, not for war (unless one chooses to link this feature with the description of Samuel as Judge and as the conqueror of the Philistines, 1 S 7: 2-14). Moreover, Samuel's consecration resulted from a vow made by his mother, not from a choice made by God; thus we can already glimpse the first appearance of the idea of a vow, which later became the characteristic feature of Naziritism.

CHAPTER FIFTEEN

THE LITURGICAL CALENDAR

IN Israel, as among all nations, there was a host of feasts which, though they did not celebrate a religious event, had a religious character. The Bible mentions some of them, though usually it gives no details about the way in which these feasts were observed. The family or the clan held a feast to celebrate the various events of human life: *e.g.* the weaning of a child (Gn 21: 8),[1] a marriage (Gn 29: 22f.; Jg 14: 10f.),[2] a funeral (Gn 23: 2; 2 S 1: 11-12, 17f.; 3: 31f.)[3] and so forth. Life in the country provided other occasions for rejoicing (*e.g.* sheep-shearing, 1 S 25: 2-38; 2 S 13: 23-29; cf. Gn 38: 12), and we shall see in a moment how the three great feasts of the year were connected with events of pastoral or agricultural life. Public events were also occasion for feasts: *e.g.* the coronation of the king,[4] or a victory in war, which would be celebrated with singing and dancing (Ex 15: 1-21; 1 S 18: 6-7); and on the occasion of national calamities the people would fast (Za 7: 1f.; 8: 19) and sing lamentations (Jl 1-2 and the Book of Lamentations). Many feasts of which we have now no record must have been observed in the sanctuaries of Israel (cf. Os 4: 15; 12: 12; Am 4: 4-5), for it is only rarely that a really ancient story alludes to one, *e.g.* there was a pilgrimage from Shechem to Bethel (Gn 35: 1-4), and a feast of Yahweh at Shiloh (Jg 21: 19-21; cf. 1 S 1: 3f.). In this book we shall discuss only those feasts which were of importance for a considerable period; we are better informed about these, because they were incorporated into the Temple worship in Jerusalem. We shall begin by describing the ordinary services which were conducted in the Temple, and then pass on to discuss the religious calendars which give the order of the great annual feasts.

1. *The ordinary services of the Temple*

(a) *The daily services.* The laws in Ex 29: 38-42 and in Nb 28: 2-8 lay down that two lambs should be offered daily as holocausts, one in the morning and one in the evening 'between the two evenings', *i.e.* at twilight.[5] An offering of flour kneaded with oil, and a libation of wine were made along with this sacrifice. Lv 6: 2-6 also assumes that two holocausts were offered daily, one in the morning and one in the evening (cf. Si 45: 14).

1. Cf. p. 43. 2. Cf. p. 34. 3. Cf. pp. 59-61.
4. Cf. pp. 102-107. 5. Cf. p. 182.

Ex 30: 7–8 adds that these sacrifices must be accompanied by an offering of incense upon the altar of perfumes, and Judith is said to have prayed at the hour when the evening offering of incense was rising from the Temple (Jdt 9: 1). This daily service was termed the 'perpetual' (*tamîd*) sacrifice (Ex 29: 42; Nb 28 and 29 *passim*; Esd 3: 5; Ne 10: 34); when Daniel says it was interrupted, the writer is referring to the persecution of Antiochus Epiphanes (Dn 8: 11, 13; 11: 31; 12: 11), and the Books of Maccabees tell how it was re-established by Judas Maccabee. The ritual is ascribed by the Chronicler to the monarchic period (1 Ch 16: 40; 2 Ch 13: 11; 31: 3), but it is certainly of post-exilic origin. Ezechiel makes no provision for a holocaust in the evening (Ez 46: 13–15), and this ruling is in accordance with pre-exilic usage: 2 K 16: 15 (under Achaz) distinguishes the morning holocaust (*'olah*) from the evening offering (*minḥah*). This evening offering (still called *minḥah*) is an indication of time in Esd 9: 4–5 and Dn 9: 21. These texts prompt us to take *minḥah* in its strict sense, *i.e.* as a vegetable offering, when it is used to denote a time in the afternoon: this must be its meaning in 1 K 18: 29, 36, but the time must have been well before dusk because the story (1 K 18: 40–46) places the massacre of the prophets of Baal, the prayer of Elias, the rainstorm, and the return of Achab to Yizreel, on the same day. We have already noted that in the post-exilic ritual, the time for the evening sacrifice was fixed at twilight, but in New Testament times, the lamb was sacrificed in the middle of the afternoon, about three o'clock (according to Josephus and the Mishnah), the hour at which Jesus died on the cross (Mt 27: 46–50 and parallels).

(b) *The sabbath.* We shall devote a special chapter to the study of the sabbath.[1] Here we are concerned only with the changes it involved in the daily services of the Temple. According to Nb 28: 9–10, every Sabbath day two other lambs were to be offered, with a *minḥah* and a libation, in addition to the daily holocausts. Since the victims, the offerings and the libations are exactly the same as in the daily sacrifices, it seems that the daily holocaust was simply doubled in quantity on the sabbath; presumably the offerings were made at the same hours. Ezechiel had looked forward to a more costly ritual: the prince would enter by a porch which would remain closed for the rest of the week, and the sabbath holocausts would consist of ten lambs and a ram (Ez 46: 1–5). We do not know what was the practice in the days of the monarchy, but the story of Athaliah shows that on the sabbath the Temple guard was doubled: this would imply that more people came to worship (2 K 11: 5–8; cf. Ez 46: 3).

(c) *The new moon.* The ritual in Nb 28: 11–15 prescribes that on the first day of each new lunar month a holocaust should be offered which consisted of two bulls, a ram and seven lambs; offerings and libations were to be made along with it, and a goat was to be offered also, as a sacrifice for sin.

1. Cf. pp. 475–483.

Ezechiel had hoped that on this day the prince would offer a bull, a lamb and a ram (Ez 46: 6-7).

This feast, to celebrate the first day of the new moon, was a very ancient one. It is mentioned, along with the sabbath and other feasts, in Is 1: 13-14; Os 2: 13. Like the sabbath, it was a day of rest (Am 8: 5)—a good day, therefore, to visit a 'man of God' (2 K 4: 23). King Saul invited guests to dine with him at the new moon, and the meal had a certain religious character, for the guests had to be 'pure' to take part (1 S 20: 5, 18, 26); the same text may imply that the feast lasted two days (1 S 20: 19, 27). Possibly, too, the first day of a month was chosen for the annual sacrifice on behalf of the clan (cf. 1 S 20: 6, 29). New moons continued to be festal days down to the end of Old Testament times (cf. Esd 3: 5; Ne 10: 34; 1 Ch 23: 31; 2 Ch 2: 3; 8: 13; 31: 3), and even in New Testament days (Col 2: 16); but all except that of the seventh month lost much of their importance (Lv 23: 24-25; Nb 29: 1-6).[1]

2. *The religious calendars*

Against this background of daily, weekly and monthly worship, the great annual feasts stood out in relief. The general word for a 'feast' is *mô'ed*: the term means a fixed place or a fixed time—a rendezvous—and the desert Tent was called *'ohel mô'ed* or 'The Tent of Meeting'. Thus the word came to mean a meeting or an assembly, and finally an assembly or meeting to celebrate a feast. The term *mô'ed* is mentioned alongside sabbath-days or new moons in Nb 10: 10; 1 Ch 23: 31; Is 1: 14; Lm 2: 6; Os 2: 13, etc., as if it were expressly reserved for annual feasts (cf. Lv 23: 37-38). But it is also found (Os 2: 13; Ez 46: 11) alongside *ḥag*, which is applied particularly to the three great annual feasts, as we shall see. In Nb 29: 39, *mô'ed* occurs at the end of a ritual which begins by speaking of daily sacrifices, of sabbath-days and of new moons, and which then goes on to speak of the annual feasts. The word must therefore have had a rather wide meaning, and it seems to have been used for all kinds of religious assemblies.

The word *ḥag*, on the other hand, was reserved for the three great feasts of pilgrimage: the root means 'to dance, to turn around' (cf. Ps 107: 27), and the noun alludes to the processions and the dances which, in olden times, were part of the ritual of a pilgrimage. Even to-day, the Moslems call the pilgrimage to Mecca the *ḥaj*.

The Old Testament contains several lists of feasts which are spread out over the year: these lists are religious calendars, and it is interesting to compare them with one another, taking them in the probable order in which they were composed. This general review is necessary before we can begin to study each feast on its own: here we take for granted only a general acquaintance with the Israelite calendar.[2]

1. Cf. p. 503.
2. Cf. pp. 188-193.

(a) *The Elohistic Code of the Covenant.* The shortest calendar is that in Ex 23: 14-17: 'Three times a year thou shalt make the *ḥag* for me', *i.e.* the *ḥag* of the *maṣṣôth* (unleavened bread), which lasted seven days in the month of Abib; the *ḥag* of the *qaṣîr* (harvest); the *ḥag* of the *'asîph* (ingathering). The 'harvest' (*qasir*) represented the harvesting of the first cereal crops, whereas the *'asîph* represented the collecting of fruits from the fields and orchards and the storing in barns; the *'asîph* took place *b*e*ṣe'th hashshanah*, 'at the turn of the year', *i.e.* at the beginning of the year, which, at this period fell in the autumn.[1] The text concludes: 'Three times a year, all thy menfolk shall present themselves before the Lord Yahweh'. It has recently been suggested that this text lays upon each individual the obligation of making a pilgrimage three times a year, at dates of his own choosing; he would not have been bound to attend at the three great annual feasts, and these feasts would not have been occasions of pilgrimages. But this does not follow from the text: v. 17 merely repeats v. 14, in which *r*e*galîm* means 'times' and is a synonym of the word *p*e*'anîm* in v. 17 (cf. Nb 22: 28, 32, 33).

(b) *The Yahwistic Code of the Covenant.* Ex 34: 18-23 gives the same prescriptions under a slightly different form: it mentions the *ḥag* of the *maṣṣôth*, which lasts seven days in the month of Abib, the *ḥag* of the *shabu'ôth* ('weeks') for the 'first-fruits of the harvest' (*qasir*) of the corn, and the *ḥag* of the *'asîph* ('ingathering'), which takes place at the *t*e*qûphath hashshanah*, *i.e.* at the end of the year.[2] This text contains the same conclusion as Ex 23: 17: 'Three times a year all thy menfolk shall present themselves before the Lord Yahweh, God of Israel.' But this calendar includes also the law about the first-born (vv. 19-20) and the law concerning the Sabbath (v. 21): both these laws are given separately in the Elohistic Code (Ex 22: 28-29 and 23: 12).

It is noteworthy that both these calendars speak of the *maṣṣôth* and yet make no reference to the Passover: it is only mentioned afterwards, and then only incidentally, in Ex 34: 25; it is never mentioned at all in Ex 23 (unless there is a reference to it in Ex 23: 18, though this is not part of the calendar). The feasts are obviously agricultural feasts, and they are not fixed for a certain day; the date depends on the work in the fields, and will vary a little from year to year according to the weather. The 'beginning of the year' mentioned in Ex 23: 16 and the 'end of the year' mentioned in Ex 34: 22 are, in spite of the apparent contradiction, synonymous terms: they stand for the transition-period from one year to the next, and in these early days the year began in autumn, when the fruit was gathered from the trees. No precise date was fixed, but, since both calendars date back long before the centralization of worship, the feasts would be kept in local sanctuaries; it would therefore be easy enough for a community to fix dates for the feasts,

1. Cf. p. 190.
2. Cf. *ibid.*

while taking into consideration the state of work in the district. When the texts of the historical books mention a feast for which 'all Israel' ought to assemble at a particular sanctuary, they expressly state that royal messengers were sent round to make this known (1 K 8: 1-2, under Solomon; 2 K 23: 1, 21, under Josias; 2 Ch 30: 1-6 presumes that it happened under Ezechias too).

(c) *Deuteronomy*. The law in Dt 16: 1-17 retains the same calendar, and the same conclusion as in Ex 23: 17 and 34: 23: 'Three times a year all thy menfolk shall present themselves before Yahweh thy God'. The only difference is that it immediately adds 'in the place which he will choose' (v. 16), and this addition is inserted after each of the three feasts (vv. 2, 11, 15): it is an assertion of the centralization of the cult which Deuteronomy wishes to impose. The three feasts are: the Passover, which is henceforth linked with the *maṣṣôth* in the month of Abib (vv. 1-8 and 16); the *ḥag* of the *shabu'ôth* (of 'weeks'), and the meaning of this name is here explained: it is to be held seven weeks after the cutting of the first ears of corn (vv. 9-12); thirdly, the *ḥag* of the *sukkôth* ('tents'), which is to take place when the produce of the threshing-floor and of the presses is gathered in (vv. 13-15).

The word *sukkôth* is first mentioned at the feast of Ingathering, but its meaning is not explained. This calendar still assumes that the year begins in autumn (cf. its reference to the month Abib, a Canaanite name). The dates were still only vaguely fixed.

(d) *The Law of Holiness*. The first text which mentions precise dates is Lv 23, and these dates are given according to a calendar which begins in spring: the months, too, are called by an ordinal number, because at some period between Dt 16 and Lv 23 the Babylonian calendar was adopted.[1] Lv 23, however, raises a difficult problem of literary criticism. It certainly stems from more than one source: there are two titles (vv. 2 and 4), two conclusions (vv. 37 and 44), two rulings for the feast of Tents (vv. 34-36 and 39-43) and the latter ruling is not homogeneous. We must therefore distinguish at least two strata in the chapter, one of which represents the first Law of Holiness, which (in our opinion) dates from the last years of the monarchy, and another which represents the exilic and post-exilic additions. We cannot say for certain to which of the two editions each verse belongs, but we may propose (with due reservations) that the following verses should be ascribed to the ancient form of the Law of Holiness: Lv 23: 4-8, which treats of the Passover, to be held on the 14th day of the first month, and to be followed by the Feast of Unleavened Bread, which lasts seven days; Lv 23: 16-21*a*, which treats of the feast of Weeks, fifty days after the feast of Unleavened Bread; Lv 23: 34*b*-36, which treats of the feast of Tents, to be held on the 15th day of the seventh month, to last seven days, and to be

1. Cf. pp. 191-192.

followed by a solemn day of rest; Lv 23: 37-38, the conclusion. The additions (which may perhaps contain some ancient elements) concern: the Sabbath (v. 3—which is excluded by the original conclusion, v. 38); the feast of the first sheaf (vv. 10-15); the feast held on the 1st day of the seventh month (vv. 24-25); the Day of Atonement, to be held on the 10th of the same month (vv. 27-32); a different ritual for the feast of Tents (vv. 39-43); a new conclusion (v. 44).

(e) *Ezechiel.* A religious calendar can be drawn up from the prescriptions laid down in Ez 45: 18-25 for feast-days: on the 1st day of the first month (of a year beginning in spring) a sacrifice is to be offered for the sin of the sanctuary; on the 7th of the same month, the sacrifice is to be repeated, for the sins committed inadvertently by individuals. The Greek version gives the 1st of the seventh month as the date of this second sacrifice; this would harmonize with the text of Nb 29: 1, and would assign one sacrifice to each half of the year. The Hebrew reading is to be preferred, however: the second sacrifice marks the 'octave' and the two sacrifices taken together constitute 'the expiation for the sanctuary' (Ez 45: 18-20). The Passover (here called a *hag*) is to be kept on the 14th of the first month; it is to last seven days, during which holocausts and sacrifices for sin are to be offered (vv. 21-24). A sacrifice for sin and a holocaust were also to be offered for the 'feast' of the seventh month, and for the seven following days.

This insistence on sacrifices of expiation is characteristic of Ezechiel; and we may note also that he does not mention the feast of Weeks, and that he does mention ceremonies of purification at the beginning of the year. This latter ritual is not mentioned anywhere else, and it would seem that it was never put into practice: Ezechiel's prescriptions were replaced by those of the Priests' Code (Lv 23, in its final edition, and Nb 28-29).

(f) *The rules for sacrifices given in Numbers.* In fact, Nb 28-29 is a commentary on the liturgical cycle of Lv 23 (with the additions to that chapter). It neglects entirely Ez 45: 18-25, and stipulates what sacrifices are to be offered in particular circumstances: for the daily ritual (Nb 28: 3-8); the Sabbath (Nb 28: 9-10); the new moon (Nb 28: 11-15); the Passover and the Feast of Unleavened Bread (Nb 28: 16-25); the Feast of Weeks (Nb 28: 26-31); the 1st of the seventh month, called the 'Day of Acclamation' (Nb 29: 1-6); the Day of Atonement (Nb 29: 7-11); the feast of Tents (Nb 29: 12-38).

This text gives the complete list of the sacrifices offered in the second Temple after the time of Esdras.

(g) *Later feasts.* Later still, other feasts were inserted into the liturgical calendar. The months to which these feasts are assigned are called by their Babylonian names, and this only serves to stress that they were instituted at a late date. Some of them were observed only for a short period: *e.g.* the feast which celebrated Simon Maccabee's capture of the citadel of Jerusalem on the 23rd Iyyar; the feast of the wood destined for the altar, on the 14th

Ab; the feast of Nicanor, on the 13th Adar. Others, however, have been observed down to modern times, namely, the feast of Purim, on the 14th and 15th Adar, and the feast of the Dedication, on the 25th Kisleu. These feasts will be studied along with the post-exilic feasts.[1]

1. Cf. p. 507ff.

Chapter Sixteen

THE SABBATH DAY

We have already studied the week, in the chapter on divisions of time[1]; here we are concerned with the religious institution which marked the seventh day of the week, the sabbath day.

1. *The name: its etymology*

The English word 'sabbath' is a transcription of the Hebrew *shabbath.* This noun is used only in religious contexts: it is used for the seventh day of the week (frequently), for the entire week (once, in Lv 23: 15, though this instance is itself doubtful) and for the sabbatical year which occurred every seven years (Lv 25: 2, 8, 34, 35, 43). A longer form (*shabbathôn*) is used for certain feast days and days of rest, but these days did not necessarily fall on a sabbath.

Some ancient writers (Theophilus of Antioch and Lactantius) say that the Hebrew word is derived from *sheba'*, meaning seven; but *'ayin* is a strong consonant, and this etymology is therefore impossible. A number of modern writers have put forward a corrected version of this hypothesis: they, too, maintain that *shabbath* is derived from 'seven', but via the Akkadian. In Akkadian, *'ayin* was not pronounced; *shibittu* means 'sevenfold, seven', and *shapattu* (which means, as we shall see, the day of the full moon) is said to be a dual form, meaning 'twice seven'. The latest suggestion is that a hypothetical Akkadian form *shab'atâni* ('twice seven') gave rise to the Hebrew *shabbathôn*, and that this Hebrew word was afterwards shortened to *shabbath.* But, as we shall show, it is most unlikely that the Hebrew institution was adopted from Mesopotamia, and the form *shabbathôn* is derived from *shabbath*, not vice versa.

The simplest etymology is from the Hebrew verb *shabath*, which often means 'to cease working, to rest', and which may therefore be rendered 'to keep a sabbath'. The basic meaning of this verb is, however, quite independent of the institution of the sabbath, and is simply 'to stop (*intransitive*), to cease' (Gn 8: 22; Jos 5: 12, etc.); in the active form, it means 'to make to cease, to stop (*transitive*)' (Ex 5: 5; Is 13: 11; Jr 7: 34, etc.). This is the etymology which the Bible itself puts forward in Gn 2: 2-3. Nevertheless, if the

1. Cf. pp. 186-188.

noun is derived from the verb *shabath*, and if it is a stative word, meaning 'a day on which men cease to work', then the formation of the noun (*shabbath*) is irregular: the regular form would be *shebeth*. The form *shabbath* ought to have an active meaning, signifying 'the day which stops (*transitive*), which marks a limit or a division', and we shall have to ask whether this was not its first meaning.

2. *Was the sabbath of Babylonian origin?*

If the etymology of the word is debated, the origin of the institution is even more so. Some writers have argued that the sabbath came from Mesopotamia. Certain Babylonian texts prescribe as 'evil' days the 7th, 14th, (19th), 21st and 28th days of a month, and say that on these days 'the shepherd of the peoples (*i.e.* the king) must not eat cooked meat or baked bread, must not change his clothes or put on clean clothes, must not offer sacrifice, must not go out in his chariot or exercise his sovereign power. The priest must not deliver oracles, and the physician must not touch the sick. It is an unsuitable day for any desirable action.' (There are slight variations among the texts.) On the other hand, the Akkadian word *shapattu* stands for the middle day of the month, *i.e.* the day of the full moon, which was a 'day when the gods' heart was appeased', and therefore a day of good omen.

Now certain texts of the Old Testament draw a parallel between the sabbath day and the day of the new moon, because both of them are days of rest (2 K 4: 23; Is 1: 13; 66: 23; Os 2: 13; Am 8: 5). In these texts, therefore, *shabbath* could mean the full moon, and Ps 81: 4 does actually use the rare word *kese'* ('full moon') in the same way: 'Sound the trumpet at the new moon, at the full moon, on the day of our feast.' Furthermore, the two principal Israelite feasts, the Passover and the feast of Tents, were kept at the full moon of the first and seventh months respectively, and in later times the feast of Purim was fixed for the full moon of the twelfth month.

From this, these writers argue that in ancient times, Israel kept only one sabbath day each month, at the full moon, and that this day was a joyful feast. Ezechiel, it is said, was the first to introduce the idea of a day of rest after six days of work (Ez 46: 1), and he made the weekly sabbath day the sign of the Covenant with Yahweh (Ez 20: 12, 20). He was inspired by the Babylonian custom of regarding the 7th, 14th, 21st, and 28th days of the month as 'evil' days, and this Babylonian influence changed the Israelite sabbath from a joyful feast into a day surrounded by prohibitions. The Israelites, however, were anxious to avoid any contamination with the cult of the sun, moon and stars; the Jewish sabbath was therefore held every seven days irrespective of the phases of the moon, and it thus introduced a continuous series of weeks which were independent of the lunar months.

There are serious objections to this theory. The days specified in Babylonian calendars (7th, 14th, etc.) were 'evil' days, of ill omen; the Israelites never looked upon their sabbath in this way, not even when later legislation forbade them to perform so many actions on this day; any resemblances with the Babylonian text cited above are quite superficial. The Akkadian *shapattu* was simply the day of the full moon, the middle day of the month, and there is no evidence whatever that this was a day of rest on which no work was done; it was even used for closing the accounts in financial transactions. The days of 'evil omen' are never called *shapattu* and the calendars and almanacks are themselves far from clear as to how the 'evil days' should be fixed. It is hard to imagine that the *shapattu*, a day of good omen, could have lost this meaning and have come to signify the days of evil omen; and it is equally difficult to see how these days of evil omen could have lost their connection with the phases of the moon, and have become the weekly sabbath of the Jews. One of the supporters of this theory is forced to admit that 'the Hebrews seem to have borrowed this word because of their utter failure to understand the Babylonian calendar'. This statement is itself an admission that the solution proposed rests on very feeble arguments.

Some biblical texts mention the sabbath along with the new moon; but this does not necessarily mean that the sabbath marked the full moon. In Is 66: 23 (a post-exilic text), the reference is certainly to a weekly sabbath; this, and all the other texts where the sabbath and the new moon are mentioned together, can be sufficiently explained by the fact that both were feast-days which recurred regularly and frequently. Nor can Ps 81: 4 be cited to confirm the theory: the reference there is to the feast of Tents, 'our feast': the horn was blown on the new moon of the seventh month (Lv 23: 24), and on the full moon, the 15th, the feast began (Lv 23: 34).

Yet it is obvious that there is some similarity between the Hebrew word *shabbath* and the Akkadian word *shapattu*. And perhaps they are related, but this connection need not be explained by saying that the Israelites borrowed their word from the Akkadian. If we take the basic meaning of the root *shbth* or *shpth* in Akkadian and Hebrew, then the Akkadian *shapattu* can mean that day in the middle of the month which marked a definite boundary, for it divided the month in two; and the Hebrew *shabbath* may have meant, originally, the day which marked a definite boundary, because it separated the weeks from one another; the two words would then be close to each other in meaning because of their common etymology. But everyone must allow that the Israelite sabbath was not dependent on the Babylonian calendar, or on any lunar calendar at all.

Lastly, the biblical texts themselves contradict the history which this theory presupposes. Ezechiel did not invent the sabbath, for he does not present it as something novel; on the contrary, he accuses the Israelites of having been unfaithful to it (Ez 20: 13; 22: 26; 23: 38). We shall show further on that the Israelite sabbath was of very ancient origin; it existed long before the Babylonian calendar was adopted in the period immediately preceding the Exile.

3. *Was the sabbath of Canaanite origin?*

Other writers recognize that the sabbath was of ancient origin, and that it is most unlikely that the Israelites adopted it directly from the Babylonians; but they are impressed by the similarity of the names, and by the Babylonian calendars (which, they believe, are themselves the product of a very old tradition). Consequently, they assert that the sabbath must have reached Israel via the Canaanites, from whom the Israelites would have copied it when they settled in Palestine.

This hypothesis does not provide a satisfactory answer to the objections raised against the first theory: *i.e.* it does not explain the difference between the sabbath and the *shapattu*, or between the sabbath and the days of evil omen in Babylonia; nor does it explain how a system which was bound up with a lunar month became disconnected from it. And even if we admit that these most unlikely changes were made by the Canaanites, we should still have to prove that the Canaanites knew of the week and of the sabbath. Now there is no evidence whatsoever to prove this, either in Phoenician inscriptions or in the older texts (from Ras Shamra). It is true that some of the poems from Ras Shamra mention periods of seven days and of seven years, but these periods do not form part of a continuous cycle, and the seventh day has none of the characteristic features of the sabbath. All the evidence which we so far possess indicates that the Canaanites were not familiar with the division of time into weeks, and under Nehemias, the Phoenician merchants did not observe the sabbath (Ne 13: 16). Moreover, how could the sabbath have been a characteristic sign of the Covenant between Yahweh and Israel (Ez 20: 12, 20; Ex 31: 12-17), if it was also observed by the Babylonians in the land of Exile, or by the Canaanites in the Palestinian home-land?

4. *Was the sabbath of Qenite origin?*

We must, then, look for the origin of the sabbath at some period before the Israelites settled in Canaan. The Bible does not record the institution of the sabbath: the story of the quails (Ex 16: 22-30) implies that it was in existence before the legislation at Sinai, and the story of creation (Gn 2: 2-3) says that it came into existence at the beginning of the world. The Israelites believed, therefore, that the institution was known before they accepted the Yahwistic religion; since, however, the sabbath was inseparably linked with Yahwism, we should conclude that the Israelites adopted the sabbath when they accepted this religion.

Here we encounter the Qenite hypothesis, which some writers use to explain the origins of Yahwism itself. Yahweh's revelation came to Moses in a land where the Qenites lived; the Qenites were related to the Midianites (Nb 10: 29 and Jg 1: 16), and they afterwards kept up their connections with Israel (Jg 1: 16; 4: 11, 17; 1 S 15: 6). Even the Rekabites, those uncompromising Yahwists, were said to be of Qenite stock (1 Ch 2: 55 and 4: 12).[1] Now, 'Qenite' can mean 'a blacksmith', and the fact that Sinai was in ancient times a mining area would be sufficient to justify their presence in the region, and their contacts with the Israelites in the desert. If we now ask what particular work was forbidden on the sabbath, there is only one hint in an ancient text: 'You shall not light a fire on the sabbath day in any of your dwellings' (Ex. 35: 3). We may recall, too, the story in Nb 15: 32-36, where a man is stoned to death for having collected wood for a fire on the sabbath day. For blacksmiths, the command not to light a fire would mean that they were not to do their ordinary work. Lastly, in much later times, and outside Israel, the seventh day of the week was the day of Saturn, the dark planet: it was, then, a day when the fire in forges could appear to be of ill omen. Now, a difficult and corrupt text in Amos (Am 5: 26) seems to allude to the Israelites' having worshipped in the desert a certain Kevan: and Kevan is one of the Assyrian names of Saturn.

The hypothesis is both ingenious and fragile. We should beware of attributing too many things to the Qenites, of whom we know almost nothing; in particular, we do not know whether they really were blacksmiths, or whether they knew of the week, or whether they venerated Saturn. It is certainly true that the sabbath goes back to the very origins of Yahwism, and perhaps to even earlier times; but, whatever its origin, in Israel it took on a religious significance which it did not possess before. This is what we are now going to show.

5. *The antiquity of the sabbath*

In Israel, the weekly sabbath was certainly of great antiquity. It is mentioned in the Elohistic Code of the Covenant (Ex 23: 12), in the Yahwistic Code (Ex 34: 21) in the two redactions of the Ten Commandments (Dt 5: 12-14 and Ex 20: 8-10), and in the Priests' Code (Ex 31: 12-17), *i.e.* in all the traditions of the Pentateuch. And everywhere it is described in the same way, as a seventh day on which men rest after six days of work. The two Codes of the Covenant take us back to the early days of the settlement in Canaan, and the Ten Commandments, in their original form, go back to the time of Moses. The law about the sabbath is given in both redactions of the Decalogue, and there is no reason for saying that in both cases it is a later addition, inserted into the primitive texts. True, the motives for observing it are not

1. But cf. p. 15.

the same in the two forms of the Ten Commandments, but we shall return to this point later. For the present, it is enough to have shown that the weekly sabbath goes back to the first origins of Yahwism.

Should we go further back still? None of the theories we have examined has brought forward sufficient evidence to prove that the sabbath originally came from Mesopotamia, or from Canaan, or from the Qenites; if the Qenite hypothesis looks the least unlikely, this may be merely because we have no documents at all which contradict it. Obviously, the sabbath day may have originated outside Israel, but we cannot prove this.

One thing, however, is certain: it is useless to try to find the origin of the sabbath by connecting it in some way with the phases of the moon: a lunar month of 29 days, 12 hours and a fraction cannot be divided into periods of seven full days. A far more satisfactory explanation is to be found in the almost universal custom of keeping days of rest, or feast days, or market days, at regular intervals: *e.g.* the Romans held their *nundinae* every ninth day, and the Lolo women of South West China refrain from sewing and washing every sixth day. The reasons for picking particular days vary considerably, but they are generally religious, and there are usually laws commanding certain things to be done, and others not to be done, on these 'reserved' days.

6. *The religious significance of the sabbath*

Whatever its origin was, the sabbath took on a particular meaning which made it an institution peculiar to Israel. Its characteristic feature lies not in the regularity with which it recurs, nor in the cessation of work, nor in the various prohibitions which the cessation of work implies: all this is found, more or less, in other civilizations. Its distinctive trait lies in the fact that it is a day made holy because of its relation to the God of the Covenant; more, it is an element in that Covenant. Other religions had a day which was *tabu*; in Israel, this became a day 'consecrated to Yahweh', a tithe on time, just as the first-born of the flock and the first-fruits of the harvest were a tithe on the work of the other days. This is why a clause about the sabbath appears in the various pacts inaugurating the Covenant,[1] in the original pact at Sinai, *viz.* the Ten Commandments, and in the pact of the tribal federation, *viz.* the Code of the Covenant (Ex 23: 12, and its parallel, Ex 34: 21). Neither the sabbath nor the new moon is mentioned in the Code of Deuteronomy (Dt 12-26), but the reason is probably that this Code is concerned only with those feasts for which the people had to come to the one central sanctuary. The sabbath is mentioned, however, in the Law of Holiness (Lv 19: 3, 30; 23: 3; 26: 2) and in the Priests' Code (Ex 31: 12-17; Nb 28: 9-10).

In the original form of the Decalogue, the commandment about the sabbath was given without commentary. At some later dates, motives were

1. Cf. pp. 147-148.

inserted, but these motives reflect two different backgrounds of thought, and they can be perceived in the two longer forms of the Commandments:

(1) In Dt 5: 14*b*-15, the human and the social aspects stand out: a man, and his servants too, male or female, must have an opportunity to rest. (This attitude is found in Ex. 23: 12 also.) All the same, the sabbath is connected with the history of salvation: 'You shall remember that you were a slave in the land of Egypt, and that Yahweh your God brought you out with a strong hand and an outstretched arm; *that is why* Yahweh your God has commanded you to observe the sabbath day' (Dt 5: 15). This mention of the Israelites' sufferings in Egypt is found in Dt 6: 20-25; cf. 10: 19 also; it is mentioned, too, in connection with the social laws in Dt 24: 18, 22, in the Code of the Covenant (Ex 22: 20; 23: 9) and in the Law of Holiness (Lv 19: 34). But there is more than this in Deuteronomy: God's great actions delivered Israel (Dt 5: 15) and brought it into the Promised Land (Dt 6: 23); there the people found their *m'nûḥah*, *i.e.* their 'place of rest' after the trials they had suffered in Egypt and in the desert (Dt 12: 9; cf. Ps. 95: 11). In memory of this, the Israelites were commanded to rest on the sabbath day.

(2) Ex 20: 11 adds to the original form of the commandment these words: 'For Yahweh took six days to make the sky, the earth, the sea and all that they contain, but on the seventh day he rested; *that is why* Yahweh blessed the sabbath day and consecrated it.' This is the remark of an editor who drew his inspiration from the Priestly account of creation: the work of creation was spread over the six days of the week, and on the seventh day, God 'rested after all the work he had done. God blessed the seventh day, and sanctified it' (Gn 2: 2-3). The connection between creation and the sabbath is developed in the law in Ex 31: 12-17, which also comes from the Priests' tradition: the sabbath is an 'everlasting sign' between Yahweh and his people, an 'unbreakable covenant'. It is a day of rest after six days of work; it is a day consecrated to Yahweh 'because Yahweh took six days making the sky and the earth, but on the seventh day he rested, and paused for breath'. This idea of God's resting is not an anthropomorphism, but the expression of a theological idea: creation is the first action in the history of salvation; once it was over, God stopped work, and he was then able to make a covenant with his creature. (Similarly, the end of the Flood makes possible the covenant with Noah, and the rainbow is the sign of the covenant: Gn 9: 8-17.) The 'sign' of the Covenant made at the dawn of creation is the observance of the sabbath by man (cf. Ez 20: 12, 20): it is a reminder of the first sabbath when God himself rested after creating the world.

Both motives, therefore, are connected with the Covenant: the only difference is that whereas Deuteronomy has in view the people of the Covenant, the Priestly texts place the emphasis on the God of the Covenant. This latter position is more theological, and consequently the Priests' tradition underlines the religious character of the sabbath: it is 'for Yahweh'

(Lv 23: 3), it is the 'sabbath of Yahweh' (Lv 23: 38), the day 'consecrated to Yahweh' (Ex 31: 15), consecrated, in fact, by Yahweh himself (Ex 20: 11). Since, then, the sabbath was a sacred sign of the Covenant, to observe it was a guarantee of salvation (Is 58: 13-14, cf. 56, 2; Jr 17: 19-27 [post-exilic]); if an individual failed to observe it, he ceased to belong to the community (Ex 31: 14; 35: 2; Nb 15: 32-36), and if the people failed to observe it, they would bring upon themselves the punishment of God (Ez 20: 13; Ne 13: 17-18).

7. *The history of the sabbath*

This theological interpretation was only gradually developed. The old historical and prophetical texts present the sabbath as a day of rest, a joyful feast-day (Is 1: 13; Os 2: 13) on which men visited sanctuaries (same texts) or went to consult a 'man of God' (2 K 4: 23). Normal heavy work was interrupted (Ex 20: 9-10 and Dt 5: 13-14, Ex 23: 12 and 34: 21), and so were commercial transactions (Am 8: 5); but short journeys were allowed (2 K 4: 23), and it was the day for the changing of the guard at the Palace and in the Temple (2 K 11: 5-8).

After the destruction of the Temple, and during the Exile, the other feasts could no longer be observed; hence the sabbath acquired a new importance, for it then became the distinctive sign of the Covenant (cf. Ezechiel, and the Priestly texts cited above). After the Return, the Jews looked upon the sabbath as a 'pleasant and venerable' day (Is 58: 13): special sacrifices were offered in the Temple,[1] but rigid prohibitions were also introduced: no one was to do business or to travel on the sabbath day (Is 58: 13); no one was to carry a load on that day, or to bring loaded beasts into Jerusalem; nothing was to be taken out of the house, and no work was to be done (Jr 17: 21-22, which is an addition to the collection of Jeremias' prophecies). When Nehemias returned for his second mission, he found that these laws were not being observed: men were treading the presses on the sabbath day, and bringing farm produce into Jerusalem; and Phoenician traders were selling their wares (Ne 13: 15-16). To prevent these infringements of the Law, Nehemias had the gates of Jerusalem closed (Ne 13: 19-22), and the community solemnly promised that they would, in future, respect the sabbath law (Ne 10: 32).

The rules became stricter and stricter. Under the Maccabees, a group of Jews let themselves be slaughtered by the Syrians rather than violate the sabbath rest by active resistance (1 M 2: 32-38, cf. 2 M 6: 11, 15: 1-3). Mattathias decided that the Jews could defend themselves if they were attacked on a sabbath day (1 M 2: 39-41; cf. 9: 43-49), but according to 2 M 8: 25-28, the Jews who had defeated Nicanor halted the pursuit when the sabbath began, and did not begin to share the booty until the day after

1. Cf. p. 469.

the sabbath. The Jewish group which adopted a calendar based on the week[1] laid particular stress on the sabbath: the Book of Jubilees (50: 8-12) forbids the use of marriage, the lighting of a fire or the preparation of food on this day; the Document of Damascus, which comes from the Qumran sect, lists a dozen prohibitions, and, according to Josephus (*Bell.* II, viii, 9) the Essenes 'refrain from working on the sabbath more strictly than any Jew: not only do they prepare their food the day before, so that they will not have to light a fire, but they do not dare to move any household object whatsoever, or even to relieve nature'.

In New Testament times, the Pharisees forbade men to carry a bed (Jn 5: 10), to nurse a sick person (Mk 3: 2; Lk 13: 14), to pick a few ears of corn (Mt 12: 2) or to walk further than a 'sabbath day's journey' (cf. Ac 1: 12), which was about two thousand paces or cubits. Jesus did not condemn the sabbath itself (Lk 4: 16; Mt 24: 20) but he did reject narrow-minded interpretations of the laws about it. He preached that the sabbath obligation yielded before the precept of love of one's neighbour (Mk 3: 4; Lk 13: 15-16) that the 'sabbath was made for man, not man for the sabbath' (Mk 2: 27). The Rabbis of the second century after Christ have left behind a similar formula in their gloss of Ex 31: 14: 'The sabbath was given to you; you were not given to the sabbath'; but they did not allow any derogation from the law except in danger of death, or in cases of very special urgency. In the end, the Mishnah codified thirty-nine kinds of work which were forbidden on the sabbath day, and the list became even longer and more complicated in succeeding centuries.

Jesus claimed that 'the Son of Man is lord of the sabbath' (Mk 2: 28); he could therefore abolish the sabbath, and he did in fact do so, for the New Covenant which he brought abrogated the Old Covenant, of which the sabbath was the sign. The Christian Sunday is not in any sense a continuation of the Jewish sabbath. The latter closed the week, but the Christian Sunday opens the week in the new era by commemorating the Resurrection of our Lord, and the appearances of the risen Christ, and by directing our attention to the future, when he will come again. And yet Sunday does symbolize the fulfilment of those promises which the sabbath foreshadowed. Like all the other promises of the Old Testament, these promises too are realized not in an institution, but in the person of Christ: it is he who fulfils the entire Law. Sunday is the 'Lord's Day', the day of him who lightens our burdens (Mt 11: 28), through whom, with whom and in whom we enter into God's own rest (He 4: 1-11).

1. Cf. p. 188.

Chapter Seventeen

THE ANCIENT FEASTS OF ISRAEL

In ancient Israel, the great annual feasts were the three feasts of pilgrimage (*ḥag*), *i.e.* the feasts of Unleavened Bread, of Weeks and of Tents, and the feast of the Passover, which was eventually combined with the feast of Unleavened Bread.

1. *The feasts of the Passover and of Unleavened Bread*

In New Testament times, the Passover was the principal feast in the Jewish year, and it has remained so ever since; but it was not always the main feast, and several points in its long history are still obscure. It is not our intention to discuss here the form which the feast has taken in post-biblical Judaism (this is the subject of the treatise in the Mishnah entitled *Pesaḥim*), nor the feast which the Samaritans still keep to-day, in accordance with their own ancient rites; we shall restrict ourselves to what we learn from the Old Testament. The information it contains is not very plentiful, and it is sometimes difficult to interpret. First we have liturgical texts: the ritual for the Passover contained in the story of the Exodus from Egypt (Ex 12); the religious calendars in Ex 23: 15; 34: 18 and 25; Dt 16: 1-8; Lv 23: 5-8; the rituals in Nb 28: 16-25 and Ez 45: 21-24; and the story in Nb 9: 1-14, which provides a justification for keeping the Passover in the second month. Secondly, certain historical texts mention or describe the celebration of a particular Passover: the first Passover, at the Exodus (Ex 12); the first Passover in Canaan (Jos 5: 10-12); the one celebrated by Josias (2 K 23: 21-23= 2 Ch 35: 1-18); that celebrated after the Return from the Exile (Esd 6: 19-22); to these we should add the Passover under Ezechias, which is described at length in 2 Ch 30, though it has no parallel in the Books of Kings. Lastly, we must take into account three important non-biblical documents, a papyrus and two ostraka, from the Jewish colony at Elephantine.

(a) *The historical development.* The legislative texts (apart from the one in Ezechiel) all come from the Pentateuch, and they belong to different traditions. Hence they enable us to trace the historical development of the feast; this development is confirmed by the more laconic information in the historical books and in the documents from Elephantine. Since the latest texts are the most detailed and the clearest, the best approach is to start with them and then to trace the history of the feast further back, to see if we can decide anything about its origin.

1. *The Priestly tradition.* This tradition is contained in Lv 23: 5-8; Nb 28: 16-25, cf. Nb 9: 1-14 and, in Ex 12, by vv. 1-20 and 40-51. In fact, these texts speak of two successive feasts, the feast of the Passover and the feast of the Unleavened Bread. The Passover was to be celebrated at the full moon in the first month of a year beginning in spring. According to this account, on the 10th day of the month, every family chose a one-year old lamb, a male and one without blemish; this lamb was killed at twilight on the 14th, and its blood was sprinkled over the lintel and the stiles of the door of the house. This was a *zebaḥ* sacrifice,[1] the meat of which had to be roasted and eaten on this same night of the full moon; not a bone of the victim was to be broken, and the remains of this religious meal were to be burnt. Unleavened bread and bitter herbs were eaten at the meal, and all who took part in the ceremony were in travelling dress. If the family was too small to eat a whole lamb, it joined with some neighbouring family. Slaves and *gerîm* (resident aliens) could share in the meal, provided they were circumcised.

On the following day, the 15th, the feast of Unleavened Bread (*maṣṣôth*) began. All the old, leavened, bread was destroyed, and for seven days, from the 15th to the 21st, only unleavened bread was eaten; the first and the seventh day were days of rest from work, and a religious meeting was held.

This ritual is in harmony with the brief injunction in Ez 45: 21, with the description of the Passover celebrated upon the Return (Esd 6: 19-22), and with the information supplied by the 'Passover Papyrus' from Elephantine. This last document, dating from 419 B.C., lays great stress on the dates to be followed for the Passover and the feast of Unleavened Bread; and the reason for this insistence is that the prescription was new to this Jewish colony.

2. *Deuteronomy.* At first reading, the passage in Dt 16: 1-8 seems to combine the Passover and the feast of Unleavened Bread even more closely than the Priestly texts do. The passage, however, is not a literary unity. Verses 1, 2, 4*b*-7 refer to the Passover: it was to be celebrated in the month of Abib, but the day was not fixed. (In the ancient calendar, where the year began in autumn, the month of Abib corresponded to what was, in the later calendar, the first month of the year, in the spring.) The text then says that the victim could be a head of cattle or a sheep or a goat; it was to be killed at sundown, not wherever a man lived, but 'in the place chosen by Yahweh for his name to dwell there', *i.e.* in Jerusalem. The victim was to be cooked, and eaten during the night, at this sanctuary; in the morning everyone was to return home.

Verses 3, 4*a*, and 8, however, refer to the feast of Unleavened Bread: for seven days, the Israelites were to eat *maṣṣôth*, *i.e.* 'bread of misery'. On the seventh day, no work was to be done, but a religious meeting was to be held.

1. Cf. p. 427.

Passover at full moon first month of year in spring

Unleavened Bread

The connection of the two feasts is clearly artificial, for if the people went home on the morning after the Passover, they did not stay until the final meeting on the seventh day to eat unleavened bread.

The Passover under Josias (2 K 23: 21–23) was celebrated according to this Deuteronomic ritual, and this text makes no mention of any feast of Unleavened Bread. On the other hand, the novelty of this feast is strongly underlined: 'No Passover like this had ever been celebrated since the days of the Judges who ruled Israel, or during all the time of the kings of Israel and of Judah.' There is a much longer account of this Passover in 2 Ch 35: 1–18 but it tells us nothing more about the customs followed in the time of Josias: the additional information is inspired by practices in vogue during the Chronicler's day: the feast of Unleavened Bread is mentioned (v. 17) and the contradiction between the rules for the Passover and for the feast of Unleavened Bread (cf. Dt 16: 7–8) is suppressed. The Chronicler, too, insists that this feast was of quite a new kind: no Passover like that had ever been celebrated since the time of Samuel (2 Ch 35: 18).

In order to discover precisely how this was a new kind of feast, we must compare it with more ancient customs.

3. *The ancient religious calendars*. Of the religious calendars listed on pp. 471–473, the two most ancient ones speak of the feast of Unleavened Bread (Ex 23: 15; 34: 18), but not of the Passover. *Maṣṣôth* were to be eaten for seven days in the month of Abib, and this was one of the three feasts of pilgrimage, *ḥag* (cf. Ex 23: 14, 17; 34: 23). These were the three feasts on which Solomon officiated in person at the Temple (according to 1 K 9: 25), and they are mentioned by name (Unleavened Bread, Weeks, Tents) in the parallel passage in 2 Ch 8: 13; cf. Dt 16: 16.

The Passover is mentioned in Ex 34: 25, but this is not part of a calendar for pilgrimage feasts; the parallel cited in this verse would suggest that we ought to see a reference to the Passover in Ex 23: 18 as well; but the context of this verse, too, is not concerned with the three pilgrimages. However, since the word *ḥag* occurs in both verses, both must have been edited after Deuteronomy, when the Passover had become a pilgrimage (*ḥag*).

And this is precisely where the innovation of Deuteronomy and of Josias lay: they made the Passover a pilgrimage, for which men came to the one central sanctuary. It was a consequence of the centralization of worship. The Passover had previously been a family feast kept in each town and in each home (cf. Ex 12: 21–23 and Dt 16: 5); it was quite distinct from the pilgrimage of the *maṣṣôth*. The two feasts, however, fell at the same time and had (as we shall see) several features in common: hence they were eventually combined. But they were not combined in the time of Josias, and the first mention of them as one feast is to be found in Ez 45: 21 and in the Priests' traditions.

Yet, according to another text of Chronicles, Josias' feast was not so very novel an idea. A similar Passover had been held under Ezechias; under him, however, the time needed for the purification of the priests and for gathering all the faithful from the former Northern kingdom led to the postponement of the feast, and it was celebrated, by way of exception, on the 14th of the second month. It was, says 2 Ch 30: 26, a feast such as had not been seen in Israel since the time of Solomon. Attempts have recently been made to defend the historicity even of the details in this story, and the observance of the feast in the second month has been attributed to a discrepancy between the calendars followed in Ephraim and in Judah. It seems, however, that the reform of Ezechias is a product of the Chronicler's imagination: the Books of Kings make only a passing allusion to this reform, but the Chronicler has described it on the pattern of Josias' reform. He has even stated that it ended with a solemn Passover; his description of this feast, however, follows the rules laid down by the Priests' Code rather than those of Deuteronomy, for the feast of Unleavened Bread is unhesitatingly connected with the Passover. The idea of a Passover in the second month is also taken from the Priests' Code; it is inspired by Nb 9: 1-14, which mentions the two excusing causes advanced by the Chronicler (lack of purity, and a long journey). This rule in Nb 9: 1-14 is to be explained by the conditions in which the Jews found themselves after the Exile, and in particular by the relations between the community in Palestine and those who had stayed in Babylonia, or who were living in the Diaspora.

It must be granted, then, that the Passover celebrated under Josias according to the prescriptions of Deuteronomy was something new; but had it never been heard of before? Certain texts in the Bible would indicate rather that it was a return to an older custom which had long been neglected: 'since the time of the Judges' says 2 K 23: 22; 'since the time of Samuel', says 2 Ch 35: 18 (which comes to the same thing). But we must distinguish two questions, namely, the combination of the Passover with the feast of Unleavened Bread, and the obligation to celebrate the Passover (alone) at Jerusalem.

The text of Jos 5: 10-12 has been used to prove that these two feasts were already combined in ancient times: when the Israelites pitched their first camp in the Promised Land, at Gilgal, they celebrated the Passover on the evening of the 14th of the month; on 'this same day', 'the day after the Passover', they ate produce of the land, *maṣṣôth* and parched corn, and then the manna ceased to fall. This story, it is claimed, represents a tradition of the sanctuary at Gilgal, and both the Passover and the *maṣṣôth* commemorated the end of the Exodus and the entry into the Promised Land. To this, other writers object that since the feast of Unleavened Bread is placed on the day after the Passover, the narrative must depend on the Priestly tradition, and must therefore be a late account. This objection, however, is not valid, for the words 'the day after the Passover' are missing from the best witnesses of the Greek version, and they contradict the phrase next to them, 'this same day'; in all probability, they are a gloss. On the other hand, it is by no means certain that the text is referring to that feast of *maṣṣôth* which is described by the liturgical texts: the oldest liturgical texts say that the feast lasted seven days, and they do not mention parched corn. Rather, the general impression is that Jos 5: 10–12 represents an independent tradition which reflects a custom of the sanctuary at Gilgal; but this does not prove that, from the moment the Israelites settled in Canaan, the Passover and a feast of Unleavened Bread like that described in the other texts were combined. The earliest religious calendars mention the feast of Unleavened Bread, but not the Passover; the two feasts had not been combined when Deuteronomy was first made known; and the story of Josias' reform mentions only the Passover.

The other question concerns the obligation of keeping the Passover at Jerusalem, and here Deuteronomy does introduce something new. Before the institution of the monarchy, the Passover may well have been a common feast celebrated at the central sanctuary of the tribal federation,[1] as 2 K 23: 22 and 2 Ch 35: 18 assert; it certainly had been a tribal feast before the settlement. But the settlement led to a loosening of tribal bonds, and to a decentralization of cultic worship[2]; and so the Passover became a family feast. This would explain why it is not mentioned in the calendars of Ex 23 and 34, and it would also explain why such stress is placed on the details by the old Yahwistic ritual in Ex 12: 21–23. The feast of Unleavened Bread, on the other hand, would be one of the annual pilgrimages to the local sanctuaries. Deuteronomy, and Josias' Reform, made Jerusalem the centre for both feasts, and in the end they were combined.

Whatever one may think of the details of this history, the two feasts were certainly of different character and of different origin.

(b) *The origin of the Passover.* The Hebrew word for the Passover is *pesaḥ*. It seems impossible to draw any conclusions from the meaning of the word, for its etymology is warmly debated. The Bible connects it with the root *psḥ*, meaning 'to limp' (2 S 4: 4), 'to limp, to hobble, to jump' (1 K 18: 21); in the last plague of Egypt, Yahweh 'jumped over, left out' the houses where the Passover was being observed (Ex 12: 13, 23, 27); this is not the primary meaning, but an explanation added in later times. Others have compared it with the Akkadian word *pashâḫu*, meaning 'to appease'; but the Israelite Passover never had any expiatory purpose. According to a more modern theory, it is to be explained by the Egyptian: it is said to be a transcription of an Egyptian word meaning 'a stroke, a blow': the Passover would then be the 'blow' of the tenth plague (Ex 11: 1), in which Yahweh 'struck' the first-born of Egypt (Ex 12: 12, 13, 23, 27, 29). This too is not convincing: it is easy to allow that the Israelites gave an Egyptian name to a

1. Cf. p. 331. 2. Cf. p. 332.

custom borrowed from Egypt, but it is hard to admit that they gave an Egyptian name to a custom which was strictly their own and which was actually instituted against the Egyptians. In addition, this explanation looks for the origin and the meaning of the Passover in the plague of the first-born of Egypt, and this is a secondary feature of the feast.

If we leave etymology aside, the Passover is seen to be a rite practised by shepherds. It is the kind of sacrifice which nomads or semi-nomads offer, and no other sacrifice in all Israelite ritual is more like the sacrifices of the ancient Arabs: there is no priest, no altar, and the use of the blood is most important.[1] The Passover was the spring-time sacrifice of a young animal in order to secure fecundity and prosperity for the flock. The purpose of putting blood upon the stiles of the door (originally, on the tent-poles) was to drive away evil powers, the *mashḥît* or Exterminator, who is mentioned in the Yahwistic tradition (Ex 12: 23), and also perhaps, in a disfigured text, in the Priestly tradition (Ex 12: 13). As we have suggested, it may have been a feast celebrated when the tribe struck camp before setting out for the spring pastures, but this is not the whole explanation: it was, in a more general way, an offering for the welfare of the flock, like the old Arab feast which fell in the month of Rajab, the first month of spring. The other details of the Passover stress still more that it was essentially a feast for nomads: the victim was roasted over a fire without any kitchen utensils; it was eaten with unleavened bread (which is still the normal bread of Bedouin to-day), and with bitter herbs (which does not mean vegetables grown in the garden, but the desert plants which Bedouin pick to season their food). The ritual prescribed that those eating it should have their belts already fastened, sandals on their feet (as if they were going to make a long journey on foot), and a shepherd's stick in one hand.

This pastoral feast was not an offering of the 'first-born' of the flock; this is nowhere stated, even in the most detailed texts about the choice of the victim or about the rites to be followed at the feast. Nevertheless, Ex 34: 19-20 has put the law about the first-born in between the regulation for the feast of Unleavened Bread and its natural conclusion in 20*b* (as a comparison with Ex 23: 15 shows): and Ex 13: 1-2, 11-16 connects the law about the first-born with the law about the Passover and Unleavened Bread. It is an artificial connection, to establish which the tenth plague is used; during the night of the Passover, God struck the first-born of Egypt and spared the houses marked with the blood of the Passover victim; and, says Ex 13: 15, that is why the first-born of animals are killed, and the first-born of men are redeemed. This connection, however, is not mentioned in the basic account: there is no reference to it in the Passover ritual, and the law about the first-born is given separately in the old Code of the Covenant (Ex 22: 28-29).

The only texts which fix the date of the Passover are the Priestly texts and

1. Cf. pp. 435-438.

Ez 45: 21: they fix it for the 14th-15th of the first month, *i.e.* at the full moon. This must have been the date of the Passover from the very beginning. Since it was kept in the night-time, and in the desert, it would be observed at the full moon, not necessarily because it was connected with the cult of the stars, but simply because it was the brightest night of the month. This common-sense explanation is itself sufficient to refute the suggestion that the Passover was at first celebrated on the night of the new moon. Since *ḥodesh* meant the 'new moon' before it came to mean 'a month', the following rendering of Dt 16: 1 has recently been suggested: 'Take care to observe the new moon (*ḥodesh*) of Abib, and to celebrate then a Passover for Yahweh thy God'; the rest of the verse, in which *hodesh* occurs again (this time certainly with the meaning 'month') would be an addition by the Priests. There is, however, a more serious objection against the idea that from ancient times the Passover was kept at the full moon: an ostrakon found at Elephantine has on it a letter which, it is suggested, should read: 'Let me know when you celebrate the Passover.' If this is the correct interpretation of the text (and it is a most attractive rendering), and if this document is earlier than the Passover Papyrus mentioned above (which is probable), it still does not necessarily mean that the Passover was not previously kept at the full moon in the Jewish colonies of Egypt: the writer might be in doubt as to the month in which the feast was to be held, if the year could have had an intercalary month.[1]

One fact, however, is certain: the Passover was a most ancient feast. It dated back to the time when the Israelites were still semi-nomads. It dated back even before the Exodus, if the feast which the Israelites wanted to celebrate in the desert (Ex 5: 1) was itself a Passover. It was the Israelite version of the spring-time feast which all the Semitic nomads kept, but in Israel it acquired a particular meaning, which we shall explain in a moment.

(c) *The origin of the feast of Unleavened Bread.* The word *maṣṣôth* means 'unleavened, or unfermented, bread'. The feast of the *maṣṣôth* marked the beginning of the barley harvest, which was the first crop to be gathered. The seven weeks to the Harvest feast (or 'the feast of Weeks') were counted 'from the moment when the sickle begins to cut the grain' (Dt 16: 9). For the first seven days of the barley harvest, only bread made with the new grain was eaten: it was eaten 'without leaven', *i.e.* without anything from the harvest of the previous year in it. It represented, therefore, a new beginning. Further, it was wrong to present oneself before Yahweh with empty hands (Ex 23: 15 and 34: 20, where this rule is separated from the rule about Unleavened Bread by the insertion of the law about the first-born). The characteristic feature of this feast lay, therefore, in a first offering of the first-fruits, and this trait was accentuated in the later ritual giving details for the offering of the first sheaf (Lv 23: 9-14). But the real feast to celebrate the

1. Cf. p. 189.

first-fruits of the harvest was the feast of Weeks, which marked the end of the cereal harvests; the feast of Unleavened Bread was merely a preparation for this second feast, and the two together marked the beginning and the end of harvest-time.

The feast of Unleavened Bread was, therefore, an agricultural feast, and was not observed until the Israelites had settled in Canaan (Lv 23: 10 states this explicitly when referring to the first sheaf). It is quite possible, then, that the Israelites adopted this feast from the Canaanites. In this context, we may recall the execution of Saul's descendants at the high place near Gibeon (2 S 21: 9–11): it took place 'at the beginning of the barley harvest', and the Gibeonites took their revenge in the form of a fertility rite (as a passage in the poems of Ras Shamra shows).[1] The two rituals have nothing in common, however, except the date, and, in Israel, the feast of Unleavened Bread was always bound up with the week: the feast lasted seven days (Ex 23: 15; 34: 18), from one sabbath to the next (Ex 12: 16, Dt 16: 8; Lv 23: 6–8). This is the justification for the insertion of the law about the sabbath after that about the *maṣṣôth* in Ex 34: 21, and for the added detail 'even at harvest-time' (which began with the feast of Unleavened Bread). This connection with the sabbath shows that the seven days consecrated to the feast were not reckoned haphazardly, though seven-days feasts are found outside Israel; in Israel, this feast was essentially tied up with the system of the week, and this is confirmed by the fact that the Harvest feast was fixed for seven weeks after the feast of Unleavened Bread (Lv 23: 15; Dt 16: 9). The feast of Unleavened Bread may have been adopted by the Israelites from the Canaanites; but since the week and the sabbath are not found outside Israel, this feast must have taken on, apparently from the moment of its adoption, a strictly Israelite character. Since it was an agricultural feast, it depended on the condition of the crops, and could not be dated more precisely than in 'the month of the ears of corn', *i.e.* the month of Abib; this is the only regulation in the calendars of Ex 23 and 34 and in Deuteronomy.

We have seen that the Passover was kept during this same month, and at the full moon. Deuteronomy and the reform of Josias made the Passover a pilgrimage feast, as the feast of Unleavened Bread already was, and the obvious move was to combine the two feasts. The old rubric about eating unleavened bread at the Passover (a rubric which has nothing to do with the feast of Unleavened Bread) favoured the combination, and so perhaps did local usages, like that followed in the sanctuary at Gilgal (Jos 5: 10–12). The date of the Passover was already fixed for the full moon, and this was left unchanged; the feast of Unleavened Bread was attached to it, and ordered to be kept during the following seven days. This is the rule laid down in Lv 23: 5–8. Now, if the date we suggested for the Law of Holiness is correct,

1. Cf. p. 442.

this took place after Josias' reform, but before the Exile; this would then explain why Ezechiel knew of and accepted these dates (Ez 45: 21). Unfortunately, the Passover was reckoned by the phases of the moon, and the Unleavened Bread by the days of the week; this led to an insoluble problem, for the Passover would not necessarily fall on the day before a sabbath, and the feast of Unleavened Bread had to begin on a sabbath. In practice, the connection of the feast of Unleavened Bread with the week was abandoned, and both feasts were fixed by the moon, with the feast of Unleavened Bread following immediately after the Passover, whether it was a sabbath day or not. But in later times, the Pharisees and the Boethuseans (a group of the Sadducees) argued, without reaching any conclusion, as to how one should interpret the sabbath of the *maṣṣôth* and the 'day after the sabbath' in Lv 23: 11, 15. This was the day on which the first sheaf was to be offered, and from which the seven weeks were to be counted before the feast of Weeks; the Boethuseans said it was the sabbath which fell during the week of the *maṣṣôth*, whereas the Pharisees claimed that it was the very day of the Passover.

(d) *Their connection with the history of salvation.* All the traditions of the Pentateuch connect the feast of Unleavened Bread (Ex 23: 15; 34: 18; Dt 16: 3), or the Passover (Dt 16: 1 and 6), or both the Passover and the feast of Unleavened Bread (Ex 12: 23-27 and 39 [Yahwistic tradition]; Ex 12: 12-13 and 17 [Priestly tradition]), with the Exodus from Egypt. The text which connects them most closely is Ex 12, in which the rites for both feasts are incorporated into the story of the Exodus; and the theme of this chapter is that the two rites were instituted to help in setting Israel free, and to commemorate this deliverance.

Some scholars, who see in cult the actualization of myths, look upon the first sixteen chapters of Exodus (Ex 1-15) as the 'legend' of the Passover feast, and claim that it is useless to try to find historical events behind them: these chapters, they hold, are nothing more than the cultic expression of a myth about Yahweh's struggle with his enemies. The culminating point of the story is that night which is relived on the Passover night, on which men keep vigil as Yahweh himself 'kept vigil' (Ex 12: 42). In the morning (Ex 14: 24) the Egyptians are defeated: this is Yahweh's triumph, celebrated in a victory hymn; and this hymn ends with the glorification of the Temple at Jerusalem, in which the feast is held, and in which Yahweh dwells for evermore (Ex 15: 17).

No one will deny that there are cultic elements in the story of Ex 12, for the text itself stresses them; and everyone admits that the rites for the Passover and for the feast of Unleavened Bread have influenced the presentation of history. But this does not mean that Ex 12 (much less Ex 1-15) is merely a sacred commentary on certain rites. There are other elements in these chapters besides ritual ones, and the entire section forms part of a larger whole, which claims to be an historical work. Once more we must insist that Israel's religion was an historical religion, and that the faith of Israel was based on God's interventions in the history of his people. There was a feast called the Passover, probably even before Israel became a people; there was also a feast of Unleavened Bread, adopted perhaps from the Canaanites, but adopted in the fullest sense by the Israelites; and these two feasts were celebrated in the spring-time. One spring-time there had been a startling intervention of God: he had brought Israel out of Egypt, and this divine intervention marked the beginning of Israel's history as a people, as God's Chosen People: this period of liberation reached its consummation when they settled in the Promised Land. The feasts of the Passover and of Unleavened Bread commemorated this event, which dominated the history of salvation. Both feasts soon took on this meaning, but in the older traditions there are two separate feasts which commemorate the event independently; their common feature, however, made it almost inevitable that they should one day be combined.

2. *The feast of Weeks*

The second great feast of the year is called, in Ex 23: 16, the Harvest feast (*qaṣîr*), or, more strictly, the feast of the wheat harvest (as in Ex 34: 22). It was one of the main periods in the agricultural calendar of Palestine (Gn 30: 14; Jg 15: 1; 1 S 6: 13; 12: 17) and in the calendar of Gezer.[1] In Ex 34: 22, the feast is also called the feast of Weeks; the phrase is perhaps a gloss to underline the fact that it was the same feast as that mentioned in Dt 16: 9–10 (the *ḥag* of the *shabu'ôth*, *i.e.* the 'pilgrimage' of the 'weeks'). This last text gives an explanation of the name, and fixes the date precisely: the feast was celebrated seven weeks after the first cereals had been cut, *i.e.* seven weeks after the feast of the *maṣṣôth*. In Nb 28: 26 it is called both the 'feast of Weeks' and the 'feast of the first-fruits' (*bikkûrîm*). This was the real feast for the first-fruits of the harvest, and it was a joyful feast (cf. Dt 16: 11; Is. 9: 2).

The most detailed account of its ritual is found in Lv 23: 15–21: starting from the day after the sabbath on which the first sheaf was presented to Yahweh,[2] seven complete weeks were reckoned, which brings us to the day after the seventh sabbath, making fifty days in all. (Hence the Greek name for the feast: Πεντηκοστή, the 'fiftieth' day or Pentecost; it is first mentioned in 2 M 12: 31–32 and Tb 2: 1, along with the name 'feast of Weeks'.) These 'fifty' days between the beginning of the barley harvest and the end of the wheat harvest are probably connected with the periods given in an old system of reckoning for the use of farmers.[3] The ceremony was marked by the offering of two loaves made out of the new flour, baked with leaven, and this is the only instance in which the use of yeast is ritually prescribed

1. Cf. p. 184. 2. Cf. p. 492. 3. Cf. pp. 180 and 184.

for an offering to Yahweh. The unusual nature of the offering underlines the fact that it was a farmers' feast, and closely connected with the feast of the *maṣṣôth*: at the beginning of the harvest, unleavened bread was eaten as a sign that here was a new beginning; at the end of the wheat harvest, leavened bread was offered in sacrifice, because it was the ordinary bread of a farming population. It meant that the harvest-time was over; with this offering, ordinary customs were again observed. This connection with the feast of Unleavened Bread (and later with the Passover) explains why the Rabbis called this feast the closing '*aṣereth* (assembly) and even 'the '*aṣereth* of the Passover'.

The feast of Weeks was a feast for farmers living a settled life; Israel adopted it only after its entry into Palestine, and must have taken it from the Canaanites. (The custom of presenting to a god the first-fruits of the harvest is very widespread.) At first the date of the feast was not fixed (Ex 23: 16; 34: 22); the earliest text which states anything with precision is Dt 16: 9-10, but the dating is only relative, for it is reckoned from the feast of Unleavened Bread; and this latter feast was, at that period, dependent on the condition of the crops. Hence the date of Pentecost was not fixed until the Priests connected the feast of Unleavened Bread with the Passover. We have seen, however, that the interpretation of this ruling gave rise to disputes.[1] In the calendar followed by the Book of Jubilees and by the Qumran sect, in which the same feasts fall every year on the same days of the week,[2] the first sheaf, which had to be offered 'on the day after the sabbath', was presented on the Sunday following the octave of the Passover, *i.e.* on the 26th of the first month; the feast of Weeks fell, consequently, on the 15th of the third month.

Like the Passover, the feast of Weeks was eventually related to the history of salvation, but this connection was made at a far later date. Ex 19: 1 says that the Israelites reached Sinai in the third month after they had left Egypt: and since they had left Egypt in the middle of the first month, the feast of Weeks became the feast commemorating the Covenant at Sinai. 2 Ch 15: 10 mentions that under Asa, a religious feast was held in the third month to renew the Covenant, but it does not expressly state that this was the feast of Weeks. The first time the connection is openly mentioned is in the Book of Jubilees, which puts all the covenants it can discover in the Old Testament (from Noah to Sinai) on the day of the feast of Weeks. The Qumran sect, too, which called itself the community of the New Covenant, celebrated the renewal of the Covenant on the feast of Weeks, and this was the most important feast in its calendar.

Among orthodox Jews, however, the feast of Weeks always remained of secondary importance. It is omitted from the calendar of Ez 45: 18-25, and (apart from liturgical texts) it is mentioned only in late books of the Old

1. Cf. p. 492. 2. Cf. p. 188.

Testament, and only in connection with something else (2 M 12: 31–32 and Tb 2: 1). The Mishnah gives a complete treatise to all the annual feasts except this one, and the idea that it commemorated the day on which the Law was given on Sinai was not accepted by the Rabbis until the second century of our era.

The Christian feast of Pentecost had, from the first, a different meaning. According to Ac 2, it was marked by the gift of the Holy Spirit and by the calling of all nations into the new Church. The fact that it coincides with a Jewish feast shows that the old system of worship has passed away, and that the promises which that system foreshadowed are now fulfilled. But there is no connection between the Christian feast of Pentecost and the feast of Weeks as understood by the Qumran community or, in later days, by orthodox Judaism. The story in Acts contains no allusion to the Sinaitic Covenant nor to the New Covenant of which Christ is the mediator.

3. *The feast of Tents*

(a) *The names of the feast: its importance.* The third great feast of the year is called, in the English versions of the Bible, the feast of Tabernacles or Booths. 'Tabernacles' is a transliteration of the word used by the Vulgate, and means little to a modern reader. 'Booths' is just as meaningless, and it is not quite so familiar. 'Tents', which is a literal translation of the Latin *tabernacula*, tells the reader more, but it may also lead him into error: the feast never involved the erection of 'tents'. We shall, however, keep this term, for want of a more suitable word. In Hebrew, the feast is called *sukkôth*, and the correct translation of this is 'Huts'; but 'the feast of Huts' is not a very pretty phrase, and is just as likely to give a wrong impression as the rendering 'Tents', though for different reasons.

The name *sukkôth* first appears in the later religious calendars (Dt 16: 13, 16; Lv 23: 34) and in those later texts which depend on them (Esd 3: 4; Za 14: 16, 18, etc.); but the feast itself is certainly the same one as that referred to, in the two oldest calendars (Ex 23: 16 and 34: 22), as the 'feast of Ingathering' (*'asîph*).

It was the most important and the most crowded of the three annual pilgrimages to the sanctuary. Lv 23: 39 calls it 'the feast of Yahweh' (cf. Nb 29: 12). In Ez 45: 25 it is *the* feast, without further qualification, *i.e.* the feast *par excellence*, as it is in 1 K 8: 2, 65. It can be recognized too, in 'the feast of Yahweh which was held each year at Shiloh' (Jg 21: 19), and this, no doubt, was the occasion of Elqanah's annual visit to Shiloh (1 S 1: 3). Zacharias foretold that all the nations would come each year to worship Yahweh in Jerusalem, at the feast of Tents (Za 14: 16). Even in Josephus' time, it was 'the holiest and the greatest of Hebrew feasts' (*Ant.* VIII, iv. 1), and a pagan, Plutarch, uses an almost identical formula (*Quaest. conv.* IV, 6).

(b) *Its historical development.* The oldest texts leave us in no doubt about the character of the feast: it was a farmers' feast, the feast of Ingathering, when all the produce of the fields (Ex 23: 16), and all the produce of the threshing-floor and of the presses (Dt 16: 13), had been gathered in. When all the fruits of the earth had been gathered, and the olives and the grapes had been pressed, the farmers assembled to give thanks to God. It was a joyful feast, and Eli's suspicion that Anna was tipsy (1 S 1: 14-15) shows that heavy drinking of the new wine was not unknown.

Naturally, it was an occasion for popular rejoicing. Jg 21: 19-21 tells how the Benjamites, when they had been decimated, carried off young girls from Shiloh while they were dancing in the vineyards at the feast of Yahweh. A similar tradition is preserved in the Mishnah (*Taanith* IV, 8): on the 15th day of Ab (July-August), and on the Day of Atonement, the young girls of Jerusalem went out in white clothes, newly washed, to dance in the vineyards and to sing: 'Young man, raise your eyes and see whom you are going to choose. Do not look for beauty, but for good family.' We need not consider the dance in the month of Ab. The other could not possibly have taken place, as the text says, on the Day of Atonement, for this was the great day of penance. If (as it seems) the story records an ancient tradition, then it must refer to the feast of Tents, which was held a few days later. Dancing still took place at this feast even in New Testament times: good-living men, the leading figures in the community, would dance in the Temple courtyards, singing and brandishing lighted torches. It was a gala occasion, and the saying went: 'The man who has never seen the joy of the night of this feast has never seen real joy in all his life.'

Among the ancient liturgical texts, the first details about the ritual are to be found in Dt 16: 13-15, where the feast is called the feast of 'Huts' (*sukkôth*) without further explanation; it is described as a pilgrimage to the one central sanctuary, Jerusalem, and it lasted seven days. If we leave aside the mention of huts, this is exactly how the dedication of Solomon's Temple is described (it coincided with the feast of Tents): the faithful, we are told, came from all over the kingdom, kept a feast for seven days, and on the eighth day, at the command of the king, returned home (1 K 8: 65-66): the whole passage comes from the Deuteronomic editors.

The ritual outlined in Lv 23: 33-43 is far more precise, but it also raises questions of literary criticism.[1] Verses 34-36 repeat the prescriptions of Deuteronomy, but they mention an eighth day after the seven days of feasting; on this eighth day, a day of rest from work, the people were to assemble for worship and sacrifice. Nb 29: 12-34 lays down what sacrifices were to be offered during the seven days (the number of the main victims, bulls, grows steadily less), and Nb 29: 35-38 lays down the sacrifices for the eighth day, which were far less numerous. This eighth day is everywhere

1. Cf. pp. 472-473.

mentioned apart from the seven days of the feast, and is obviously a conclusion or appendix. In the later ritual contained in the Mishnah, there is no mention of living in huts or keeping a feast at night; the only rule is that the people are to remain in Jerusalem; the eighth day then, the day after the feast, was a day of transition before the return to normal life. It is wrong, therefore, to emphasize the silence of Ez 45: 25, for this verse is a very concise text which is dealing only with the sacrifices offered by the prince during the seven days of the feast of Tents (just as the previous two verses deal with the sacrifices to be offered during the seven days of the Passover and the feast of Unleavened Bread, Ez 45: 23-24). This is how 2 Ch 7: 8-10 presents the celebration of the feast in Solomon's day, but it puts the feast of Tents after the feast for the dedication of the Temple; the writer imagined that there had been seven days' celebration for the dedication of the Temple, followed by a further seven days for the feast of Tents. This way of looking at the dedication has been introduced into 1 K 8: 65 by a gloss in the Hebrew text which is not found in the Greek version.

The account of the celebration of the feast under Esdras (Ne 8: 13-18), in connection with the reading of the Law, is obviously inspired by the text of Lv 23; but this chapter was by then in a second (though not the final) stage of its redaction. Ne 8: 14 refers to Lv 23: 42-43: for seven days, men are to live in huts, in memory of the huts in which Israel dwelt after the Exodus from Egypt. When the people heard this text read out, they went off to cut branches and to erect huts for their families, either on the roof-tops or in the Temple courts or in the squares of Jerusalem: the text adds 'The Israelites had never done anything like this since the days of Josue (Ne 8: 17). It is hard to say what was so new about this action. It cannot have been the building of the huts themselves, for this must have been a feature of the feast in ancient times, since the feast had this name before Deuteronomy; it seems rather that, for the first time, these huts were erected at Jerusalem itself (which Dt 16: 15 does not mention).

Nor is this contradicted by Os 12: 10: 'I shall make thee live under tents once again, as on the day of Meeting (*mô'ed*)'. *Mô'ed* can also mean 'a solemn feast' (so the argument runs). Osee, however, lived before the centralization of worship, and therefore he could only be referring to a feast celebrated at a local sanctuary. Yet even this is not the true interpretation for the text speaks of 'tents', not of 'huts', and it is referring to the golden age of the desert period, when Yahweh 'met' Israel.

Lv 23: 40-41 represents a third, and last stage in the redaction of the passage: men are to take 'good fruit' and branches and to rejoice for seven days. There is no mention of fruit in Ne 8: 13-18, and the fruit had nothing to do with the erection of the huts; rather it was carried round in a joyous procession. This we know from later historical texts: in 2 M 10: 6-8, the renovation of the Temple is said to have been celebrated 'like the feast of

Tents', and for eight days the Jews carried around thyrsus, green branches and palms; Josephus, too, tells a story about Alexander Jannaeus, that high priest and king who was so hated by the Pharisees and the people: at the feast of Tents, he was pelted with the citrons which the people had in their hands (Ant. XIII, xiv, 5). The ritual in the Mishnah says that a citron (*'etrôg*) was carried in one hand, and a *lûlab* (a supple palm) in the other; branches of myrtle and of willow were tied to the *lûlab*.

(c) *Its dates*. If we take the literal sense of the terms used,[1] the feast was celebrated at the beginning of the autumnal year (according to Ex 23: 16), or at the end of this year (according to Ex 34: 22). There is no need to see in these two texts either a contradiction or an evolution in the way the feast was fixed. They simply mean that the exact date was not fixed at the time when these two texts were written: it depended on how the crops were ripening, for it was the 'Feast of the Ingathering', and was therefore held when all the crops had been gathered in, just before, or just after, the beginning of the year. The old agricultural calendar from Gezer begins with two months of harvesting.[2] Nor is this contradicted by Dt 31: 10-11, which commands that the law be read out on the feast of Tents 'at the end (*miqqeṣ*) of seven years', in the sabbatical year; the text should not be translated 'at the end of the seventh year', but 'every seven years', and the reference to the feast of Tents is of secondary importance: it merely indicates the occasion when this reading is to take place. In Dt 16: 13, the date of the feast is determined only by the progress of work in the fields: it is to be held when the produce of the threshing-floor and of the presses has been gathered in.

Incidental references in the Books of Kings give more precise indications, but these same texts also raise difficult problems. The dedication of Solomon's Temple (which coincided with the feast of Tents) took place in the month of Ethanim, according to the Canaanite calendar: a later insertion has explained that this was the seventh month of the Babylonian calendar introduced by Josias (1 K 8: 2). But, according to 1 K 6: 38, the Temple was completed in the Canaanite month of Bul; and another later insertion explains that this was the eighth month of the later Babylonian calendar. If we grant that these identifications are correct (and there is no reason to doubt it), then we must admit either that the dedication took place a month before work on the building was finished, or that it did not take place until eleven months afterwards. If the second alternative is correct, then the delay could be explained by the fact that all the bronze furnishings were still being cast: the story of how they were made is, in fact, contained in 1 K 7: 13-51, *i.e.* between the time when the Temple building was finished (1 K 6: 38) and the day of its dedication (1 K 8: 2). A third possibility is that the feast of the dedication and of Tents fell in the last week of Ethanim, and that the eighth day was the 1st of the month Bul: this reconciles the two data, but it is

1. Cf. p. 190. 2. Cf. p. 184.

scarcely convincing. It is essential to remember that in those days the date of the feast depended entirely on the condition of the crops: in that particular year, the harvest was gathered in before the work on the Temple was completely finished. Hence, the feast of Tents, and the dedication, were held in the month of Ethanim, but it was not until the following month, Bul, that the Temple was finished 'in all its plan and all its arrangement' (1 K 6: 38).

The question becomes more complicated, however, if we take into account the short note in 1 K 12: 32-33 about the inauguration of the new sanctuary at Bethel by Jeroboam I: 'Jeroboam celebrated a feast in the eighth month, on the fifteenth day of the month, like the feast they kept in Judah, and he went up to the altar . . . on the fifteenth day of the month, the month which he had arbitrarily chosen.' Two interpretations of this text have been put forward. One says that the feast was originally held in the eighth month, even in Jerusalem itself, and the arguments in its favour are these. First, Jeroboam celebrated a feast 'like the one they kept in Judah'; secondly, he must have held his feast at the same time, since his object was to prevent his subjects from going up to the Temple at Jerusalem (cf. 1 K 12: 38); thirdly, this would harmonize with the statement of 1 K 6: 38 that the Temple was finished (and dedicated) in the eighth month. The accusation that Jeroboam chose this date arbitrarily would be a tendentious note of a redactor, inserted after the time when the feast in Jerusalem had been put forward from the eighth to the seventh month; and this note of his would be in harmony with the date given (the seventh month) in 1 K 8: 2. The other interpretation says that Jeroboam did in fact alter the liturgical calendar, or, more precisely, that he reintroduced an old North-Israelite calendar, in which the feasts were determined by the agricultural conditions in Ephraim, where the harvest was later than in Judah. His purpose was, of course, to introduce a rival calendar to the one followed in Jerusalem. To this we must object that there is no difference in the time of harvest between Bethel and Jerusalem, that there is no noticeable difference between Ephraim and Judah, and that, if there was any difference, Ephraim would be rather in advance of Judah: at the present day, the cereals, olives and grapes around Nablus ripen earlier than those around Bethlehem and Hebron.

The following remarks, however, tell against both interpretations. First, the passage was edited at a comparatively late date, and certainly after Deuteronomy, for the month is denoted by an ordinal number; indeed, it is later than Lv 23, for the feast is fixed for the 15th of the month. Secondly, the date of the feast would not be more precisely fixed under Jeroboam than it was under Solomon. Thirdly, if the feast really was held in the eighth month, this merely means that in that particular year the feast was celebrated in the eighth month, both at Bethel and at Jerusalem. Lastly, we may note that there is no evidence to show that this date was afterwards observed for the feast of Tents in the Northern kingdom.

The date was not fixed before Lv 23: 34 (cf. Nb 29: 12), which says that the feast is to begin on the 15th of the seventh month of a year beginning in spring, that it is to last seven days, and that it is to end on the eighth day. Ez 45: 25 gives the same date. Attempts have been made, however, to show that this calendar was not yet observed in the time of Esdras. Ne 8: 13-18 does not state on which days of the month the feast was held, and from this some authors argue that the reference in v. 14 alludes to a law not contained in the Pentateuch. Some have even tried to calculate the date on which Esdras' feast was held: on the 1st of the seventh month, he read the Law before the whole people until midday (Ne 8: 2); on the 2nd, the heads of families met to study the Law under Esdras' guidance (Ne 8: 13); there they found a law telling them to live in huts during the feast of the seventh month, and this ruling was at once put into force (Ne 8: 14f.). Therefore, it is said, the feast was observed from the 3rd to the 10th. This reasoning, however, is incorrect. The text states quite clearly that the people dispersed after the 1st of the month, and that only a limited number attended the meeting on the 2nd; it also states that they had to call together all the people of Jerusalem and of the other towns in order to prepare for the feast (Ne 8: 15). Consequently, the feast could not possibly have begun on the 3rd. Moreover, since the references in vv. 14 and 18 correspond with Lv 23: 36 and 42, they undoubtedly refer to these laws; therefore the feast must have been celebrated from the 15th to the 22nd, as Lv 23: 34 prescribes.

(d) *The origin of the feast*. Plutarch (*Quaest. conv*. IV, 6) saw a similarity between the Jewish feast of Tents and the cult of Bacchus at vintage-time. This unhappy suggestion has from time to time been taken up by a few modern writers. Another writer has seen a connection with the feast of Adonis-Osiris; the *sukkôth* would then be the equivalent of the arbour erected over the bier of Adonis. There is, however, only one reference to the practice of this rite, and it comes from Alexandria, at the Greek period: Theocritus (*Idyll*. XV) is the source, and he says that the arbour was erected over the (dead) god, not over his devotees: there is, therefore, no possible connection.

An idea which has met with a more favourable welcome is based on the notion that at certain times, and especially at the turn of the year, evil powers are active, and attack homes: to cheat them, and to escape these attacks, the people would pass these days in temporary shelters. This would explain both the feast and the rites followed. In particular, nomads who had just begun to live as farmers would look upon their new way of life as fraught with all kinds of dangers. Hence, it is said, the feast must date from the early years of the settlement in Canaan, and must have been influenced by these primitive notions. The texts in the Bible itself offer no support whatever to this hypothesis; on the contrary, they provide all the elements of a far simpler and far more convincing solution. The ancient feast of Tents was an agricultural feast, as its other name (Ingathering) implies, and as the details added in Ex 23: 16 and 34: 22 show. Even when it had come to be known as the feast of Tents, it did not lose its agricultural character: the vague date in Dt 16: 13 and the precise date in Lv 23: 34 are both witnesses to this, and these features can be seen even in the most recent ritual, that ordering fruit to be carried in procession at the feast (Lv 23: 40). The feast, then, could not have been instituted until after the settlement in Canaan, and the presumption is that it was adopted from the Canaanites. This presumption is confirmed by Jg 9: 27: after the vintage, the people of Shechem held a joyful feast in the temple of their god. The story in Jg 21: 19-21, which is of ancient origin, shows the connection between the two feasts.

It is by no means so certain that we ought to connect it (as some authors do) with the story in Nb 25: 1-18: in the Plains of Moab, the Israelites took part in a licentious feast of Baal-Peor, and one of them was put to death for having taken a Midianite woman into his *qubbah*.[1] The word means 'a tent or an alcove' and it has been suggested that it is very like *sukkôth*. But this 'tent' was not a 'hut'; the word *qubbah* is found nowhere else in the Bible; and there is no proof that the feast in question was celebrated in the autumn, nor that it had any connection with the feast of Tents.

We can be certain that the feast of Tents was an agricultural feast: the rite about the *sukkôth* ought to find its explanation, then, in some present custom. Now from time immemorial until the present day, it has been the custom in Palestine to erect huts made out of tree-branches in the vineyards and orchards while the grapes and fruit are being gathered in: and this is still the most satisfactory explanation. Originally, the feast (or at least a part of it) was celebrated outside (cf. Jg 21: 19-21), and the feast of Ingathering could also be called the feast of the huts (*sukkôth*). Deuteronomy retained the name, and allowed huts to be erected in the orchards, but prescribed that, for the sacrifices, men should go to the central sanctuary, not to the local sanctuaries (Dt 16: 13-15). The last step (a consequence of the centralization of worship) was that similar shelters were eventually erected in Jerusalem itself, and so the 'huts' became an essential part of the feast (Lv 23: 42; Ne 8: 16).

Like the Passover before it, and the feast of Weeks in later times, the feast of Tents became connected with an event in the history of salvation: the Israelites are to live in huts, says the Bible, in memory of the 'huts' (*sukkôth*) in which Yahweh made their fathers live after the Exodus from Egypt (Lv 23: 43). But this cannot be the primary meaning, for the Israelites lived in tents, not huts, during their days in the desert. Huts represent a custom followed among settled populations, and the first time the word is found in the Bible is when Jacob is settling in Canaan after his return from Mesopotamia: 'He built a house and made huts (*sukkôth*) for his cattle; that is how the place came to be called Sukkoth' (Gn 33: 17).

1. Cf. pp. 296-297.

Nevertheless, one recent writer has attempted to justify the connection of the feast of Tents with the desert. He does not deny that it was an agricultural feast, or that it is connected with Canaanite customs; he claims, however, that when the Israelites were living as semi-nomads, they still had a feast of Tents: the regulations in Nb 2, about the arrangement of the camp around the Tent of Re-union, refer, he says, to this. Secondly, Dt 31: 9-13 prescribes that the Law be read out at the feast of Tents: therefore the feast must have been a feast for the renewal of the Covenant, celebrated, at first, at Shechem. It was later modified to correspond with the conditions of a settled life, and, under the influence of Canaanite cults, its connections with nature became the predominant feature; this is how it was celebrated at Shiloh. Once the monarchy was established, and the Temple built, there was no sense in recalling the wanderings in the desert: as Is 33: 20 (a late text, however) says, 'Sion, city of our feasts' is 'a tent which is never moved'. The feast would, therefore, have taken on a new meaning: it commemorated the choice of Jerusalem as Yahweh's home, and the Covenant of Yahweh with the house of David. This argument is not convincing. The ancient texts (down to, and including, Deuteronomy) stress only the agricultural aspect of the feast, and the explanation given in Lv 23: 43 is clearly not the primary one. There is no proof whatever that, in Old Testament times, the feast commemorated the Covenant, and Dt 31: 9-13 connects the reading of the Law primarily with the sabbatical year, and only secondarily with the feast of Tents in that year. And when, in later ages, the Covenant was commemorated on a feast, the feast chosen was not the feast of Tents, but the feast of Weeks.[1]

4. *Was there a New Year feast?*

Among the Jews, the New Year feast, the Rosh ha-Shanah, is one of the great feasts of the year. It was already so in New Testament times and the Mishnah devotes a special treatise to it. The feast was kept on the first of Tishri (the Babylonian name of the seventh month in a calendar beginning in spring);[2] a horn (*shôphar*) was sounded, and hymns of praise were sung.

Under this name, and with these rites, the feast never existed in Old Testament times. There is no mention of it in the liturgical texts, or in the pre-exilic historical texts. Ezechiel dates his vision of the future Temple at the *rôsh hashshanah*, on the 10th of the month (Ez 40: 1), and this is the only biblical text which uses the expression. In later Hebrew, it came to mean the New Year, but it cannot possibly have this meaning in Ezechiel; indeed it is surprising to find so many writers accepting, without the flicker of an eyelid, that New Year's Day was kept on the '10th day' of a month. In this verse, *rôsh hashshanah* means 'the beginning of the year', and, in fact, of a year which commenced in the spring. This is the only kind of dating

1. Cf. pp. 494-495. 2. Cf. pp. 186 and 192-193.

Ezechiel ever uses, and he must therefore be referring to the month of Nisan, not to the month of Tishri, in which the Rosh ha-Shanah was later observed. This reckoning of the year from the spring-time is emphasized by Ex 12: 2, which refers to a change of calendar: 'This month shall come at the head of the others; you shall make it the first month of the year.' In this text, which comes from the Priestly editors, there is no mention of a New Year feast either; it merely tells us that the victim for the Passover was to be chosen on the 10th of this month' (Ex 12: 3). It would be pointless to make the question still more complicated by comparing with the text of Ezechiel that of Lv 25: 9-10 (a late text) fixing the 10th day of the seventh month as the Day of Atonement (cf. Lv 23: 27) and the end of the Jubilee period.

Neither Ezechiel nor the Priests' Code knew of any New Year feast; nor did Esdras. On the 1st day of the seventh month, Esdras read out the Law until mid-day, and those listening wept as they heard him read. Esdras, however, told them rather to rejoice, and they did so (Ne 7: 72—8: 12); surely he would have mentioned the New Year feast, if it had been held on that same day?

This leaves only two texts, both of which belong to the last edition of the Pentateuch, after Esdras. Leviticus (Lv 23: 24-25) prescribes that the 1st day of the seventh month shall be kept as a day of rest, with sacrifices, a cultic assembly and acclamation (*t'rû'ah*).[1] This ruling is given in a more extended form in Nb 29: 1-6, which calls the feast 'The Day of Acclamation', and lays down what sacrifices are to be offered to it. But it is by no means clear that this feast on the 1st of the seventh month, Tishri, is there regarded as a New Year feast; in the calendar of Lv 23, and in the commentary on it in Nb 28-29, the religious year always begins at the Passover. The feast held on the 1st of the seventh month was simply an unusually solemn new moon, the first day of a month which, at that time, was full of feasts (the Day of Atonement on the 10th, and the feast of Tents, from the 15th to the 22nd); perhaps too, this feast perpetuated the memory of the old civil and religious year which used to begin in the autumn, about the time of the feast of Ingathering.

Those apocryphal books of the Old Testament which date from before the Christian era never mention any New Year feast; Josephus does not include it in his list of Jewish feasts; Philo, too (*De special. legibus* II, 188), mentions ten Jewish feasts, among which we find the 1st Tishri, but he merely repeats what is said in Lv 23: 24-25 and Nb 29: 1-6: it is a 'feast of trumpets' at the beginning of the month of the great feasts, which he calls the sacred month (ἱερομηνία), using a Greek liturgical term. The Jewish feast of Rosh ha-Shanah adopted the rite of acclamation prescribed in the Priests' calendar for the new moon of the seventh month, but it is impossible to say at what time or under what influence this New Year feast was

1. Cf. pp. 254 and 259.

instituted. It is unlikely that it was due, as some have said, to the influence of the Syro-Macedonian calendar in which the year began in autumn, for, in their internal affairs, the Jews always kept to the Babylonian system of reckoning, which they had adopted shortly before the Exile.[1]

5. *Was there a feast of the Enthronement of Yahweh?*

NO.

For all this, a considerable number of scholars hold that the New Year feast had its equivalent in ancient times, in the feast of Ingatherings or of Tents. This feast was kept, as we have said, at the turn of the year; it would have provided the framework for a 'New Year feast of Yahweh' or 'a feast of Yahweh's enthronement' or 'a feast of Yahweh's kingship', according to the different ways in which the thesis is proposed. The principal arguments put forward are these:

(1) In Babylon, a New Year feast (Akitu) was celebrated during the first twelve days of the month of Nisan (the beginning of the spring year). The feast commemorated the renewal of creation and the kingship of Marduk. The epic of creation, of Marduk's struggle against chaos, was recited and re-enacted, and the god himself was acclaimed with the words 'Marduk is King!' The same elements, it is claimed, are found in Egypt; we may presume that they existed in Canaan, and we may therefore conclude that a similar drama was enacted at Jerusalem on the feast of Tents at the beginning (or the end) of the (autumnal) year.

(2) Traces of the same cultic customs are then sought for in the Old Testament, especially in the psalms about the reign of Yahweh (which include at least Pss 47, 93 and 96–99). The defenders of this thesis call them 'The Psalms of the Enthronement of Yahweh' and these psalms would have formed part of the liturgy for the feast of Tents.

(3) The two accounts of the transfer of the Ark (2 S 6: 1-23 and 1 K 8: 1-13) would also have been used in worship, during an annual procession at which Yahweh was installed in his sanctuary; this procession is said to have taken place during the feast of Tents (on the basis of 1 K 8: 2).

Working from this information, an ancient feast is reconstructed. It would have included (according to a relatively moderate partisan of this thesis): (a) the celebration of Yahweh's original triumph over the forces of chaos, his enthronement in the assembly of the gods, and the demonstration of his power, not only in the creation of the world, but also in the guidance of history; (b) a dramatic representation of the eschatological 'Day' when Yahweh would assert his power against the rebellious gods, and against the nations of the earth, when he would establish his kingship not only over nature, but also in the moral order; (c) a corresponding representation of the Messiah's (the earthly king's) descent into the lower world and of Yahweh's

1. Cf. p. 192.

deliverance of him from darkness and death; (d) a triumphal procession, in which the Ark, the symbol of Yahweh's presence, and the king, the true Messiah, were led to the Temple for the final act of enthronement, which marked the beginning of a new era. Other scholars are still bolder, and use the Mesopotamian liturgies of Tammuz and the poems of Ras Shamra to add to this already rich ritual the death and resurrection of the god, and the sacred marriage between the god and his consort (the rôle of the god being played, in this liturgical drama, by the deified king).

In spite of the authority of the scholars who put forward these theories, and in spite of the erudition with which they defend them, one cannot help expressing very serious doubts as to whether the theories are true:

(1) The ritual for the New Year feast at Babylon dates from the Neo-Babylonian period. In all likelihood, its origins go back further into history, and Assyrian and Hittite texts from the end of the second millennium B.C. prove that a New Year feast was kept in Assyria and in Asia Minor; this feast included at least a procession of the god, and the fixing of destinies for the year. These texts, however, contain nothing similar to the mythological drama which is drawn out of the Babylonian ritual. If this mythical and cultic scheme is to be extended to the entire Near East, including Israel, further arguments are needed.

(2) In the psalms about the reign of Yahweh, the formula *yhwh malak* does not mean 'Yahweh has become king': it is not a formula of enthronement, for it is impossible to see who, according to Israel's religious concepts, could have enthroned Yahweh, since he himself possesses all power. Secondly, even in the Babylonian texts, and in those Egyptian texts which can be compared with them, the words 'Marduk is King' are not a formula of enthronement either: they are an acclamation, a recognition of Marduk's power: he acts as king. The biblical formula has the same meaning; it too is an acclamation, like the cry 'Long live the king!', which was used at the crowning of kings in Israel; it did not make the man king; it merely acknowledged the royal character of the new Anointed of Yahweh.[1]

These psalms, then, are not 'Enthronement Psalms', but psalms about the kingship of Yahweh. The idea of Yahweh as King certainly existed from early times in Israel, but the Psalms of his Kingship are so closely connected with second Isaias that they must be dependent upon him, and must therefore be post-exilic. They cannot possibly have been composed, or used, for a feast held under the monarchy.

(3) The accounts in 2 S 6 and 1 K 8 are concerned with two different transfers of the Ark: in the first, it is taken to the tent erected by David, and in the second, to the Temple built by Solomon. This entry (or these entries) of Yahweh into his sanctuary are commemorated in Pss 24 and 132,[2] which certainly belong to the Temple liturgy, but we do not know on what

1. Cf. p. 106. 2. Cf. p. 309.

not much validity.

many cannot enthrone YHWH.

long live the king!

Enthronement Ps. one about YHWHs Kingship

occasion they were sung. There are no positive arguments for connecting them with the feast of Tents or with any 'enthronement' of Yahweh.

In addition, there are further objections of a more general kind. This feast of the enthronement of Yahweh is said to have been connected with the feast of Tents; why, then, is there no trace of it either in the liturgical or in the historical texts of the Old Testament? The only plausible argument is the late text of Za 14: 16: 'All the survivors of all nations which have marched against Jerusalem will come, year by year, to bow in adoration before the King, Yahweh Sabaoth, and to celebrate the feast of Tents' (cf. vv. 17-18). The connection between the two terms, however, is merely accidental: the entire passage is devoted to the eschatological triumph, to that 'Day' when Yahweh will be king over the whole earth (v. 9), and the feast of Tents is mentioned only because it was the main feast for pilgrimage to Jerusalem. We have seen too, that the feast of Tents was from the very beginning, and always, remained, an agricultural feast; it is rather paradoxical to say (as some do) that this was not its primary feature, and that it had at first an 'historical' character, *i.e.* the celebration of creation, and of Yahweh's victory over chaos.

Moreover, when the Israelites decided to give an historical meaning to the feasts of Tents, late on in their history, they connected it not with a creation-myth, but with their days in the desert. Here we encounter once again a general characteristic of the Israelite cult;[1] whatever may be said of neighbouring religious, the cult practised in Israel was not the outward expression of myths, but the homage paid by man to a personal God, who had made a Covenant with the people he had saved, and who remained faithful to that Covenant.

1. Cf. p. 272.

CHAPTER EIGHTEEN

THE LATER FEASTS

DURING the last centuries of Old Testament times, several new feasts were introduced into the liturgical calendar.[1] We shall restrict ourselves here to those which are still observed: the Day of Atonement, the Hanukkah and Purim.

1. *The Day of Atonement*

The Yom Kippur is still one of the most solemn feasts of the Jews. In the New Testament times, the *yôm hakkippurîm* or 'Day of Expiations' was already important enough to be called 'The Day', without further qualification, and this is its name in the treatise (*Yomah*) which the Mishnah devotes to it. It has always been observed on the 10th Tishri (September-October).

Before the Babylonian names were adopted for the months of the year, the Day of Atonement was fixed for the same date, i.e. for the 10th of the seventh month (Lv 23: 27-32; Nb 29: 7-11, both late Priestly texts). Details of the ritual are given in Lv 16, which is also a late text.

(a) *The ritual of expiation*. No work whatever was to be done on this day; instead, penance and fasting were enjoined, and there was to be a meeting in the Temple at which special sacrifices were to be offered, to make expiation for the sanctuary, the priests and the people. The ritual outlined in Lv 16 is evidently made up of various strata, for the text has been re-edited several times: there are a number of doublets (vv. 6 and 11, vv. 9*b* and 15, vv. 4 and 32); vv. 2 and 3 do not follow logically, and on the other hand, v. 4 should not come between vv. 3 and 5, etc.; there are two conclusions (vv. 29*a* and 24); and vv. 29*b*-34 are an addition commenting on the preceding rites, which reminds us of Lv 23: 27-32.

This ritual is a combination of two ceremonies which were different both in their spirit and in their origin. First, there is a Levitical ritual: the high priest offered a bull as a sacrifice for his own sinfulness and for that of his 'house', *i.e.* of the Aaronite priesthood; then he entered—the only occasion during the year—behind the veil which shut off the Holy of Holies, to incense the mercy-seat (*kapporeth*)[2] and to sprinkle it with the bull's blood (vv. 11-14). Next he offered a goat for the sin of the people; he took the

1. Cf. pp. 473-474. 2. Cf. pp. 300-301.

blood of the goat, too, behind the veil, where he sprinkled it over the mercy-seat, as he had sprinkled the bull's blood (v. 15). This expiation of the sins of the priesthood and of the people is linked, artificially, it seems, with an expiation for the sanctuary, and more particularly for the altar, which also had blood rubbed and sprinkled upon it (vv. 16–19). The two ceremonies of expiation are combined in the final addition (v. 33), but the order is inverted. This ritual contains those ideas about purity and the expiatory value of blood which are a characteristic of the rulings in Leviticus.[1]

(b) *The goat 'for Azazel'*. Into this ritual, however, another one has been inserted, which is based on other ideas. The community put forward two goats, and lots were cast: one was for Yahweh, and the other 'for Azazel'. The goat for Yahweh was used for the sacrifice for the sins of the people, which has just been described. When this ceremony was over the other goat, still alive, was set 'before Yahweh': the high priest placed his hands on the goat's head and transferred to it all the faults, deliberate and indeliberate, of the Israelites. A man then took this goat off into the desert, and it carried with it the sins of the people (vv. 8–10, 20–22). The man who took the goat away became impure by doing so, and could not rejoin the community until he had washed himself and his clothes (v. 26). Rabbinical tradition says that the goat was taken to Beth Ḥadûdû, or Beth Ḥadûdûn, the modern Khirbeth Khareidan, which overlooks the Kedron valley some three and a half miles away from Jerusalem.

It is interesting to compare with this a Babylonian rite which took place on the 5th day of the New Year feast, *i.e.* the 5th Nisan: a cantor, singing incantations, purified the sanctuaries of Bel and of Nabu with water, oil and perfumes; then someone else beheaded a sheep and rubbed the corpse against the temple of Nabu, to take away the impurities of the temple; the two men then carried the head and the body of the sheep to the Euphrates and threw them into the river; finally, they went off into the country and were not allowed to return to the town until the end of the feast, on the 12th Nisan. No one can deny that there is a marked similarity with the ritual of the 'scape-goat': the animal was taken away, loaded with impurity, and those who perform the ceremony become impure by contact with it. But in Babylon, the animal was killed and was used to purify the sanctuary; the Day of Atonement certainly included this rite, but the 'scapegoat' figured only in order to carry away the sins of the people (a feature which is not mentioned in the Babylonian ritual).

In their researches into primitive civilisation of folklore, scholars have collected evidence of many more or less similar rites about the transferring of guilt, stain or sickness to animals. But there is a very close analogy in the Bible itself: in the ritual for leprosy, a living bird was released in the country to carry the evil away, and the leper was declared clean.[2]

1. Cf. pp. 419 and 460–461.

2. Cf. p. 463.

In the ritual for the Day of Atonement, however, there is something more than this. The name 'scape-goat' is the common translation in our English Bible, but the Septuagint and Vulgate call it the 'goat sent out' (*caper emissarius*). In the Hebrew the goat is destined 'for *'aza'zel*'. One scholar has recently suggested that this is a common noun, as the Greek and Latin versions take it, but that it means 'the precipice' and is the name of the place to which the goat was taken. Whatever be the philological value of this suggestion, it does not really fit the text: the high priest drew lots between the goats, one 'for Yahweh' and the other 'for *'aza'zel*'. The translation 'for the Precipice' does not seem sufficient for a true parallelism, which demands that the second name, like the first, should be the name of a person. It is more probable, therefore, that Azazel is the name of a supernatural being, a devil, and this is how it is interpreted by the Syriac version, the Targum and even the Book of Henoch, which makes Azazel the prince of the devils, banished to the desert. (We may recall that the Israelites looked on desert places as the dwellings of devils: Is 13: 21; 34: 11-14; cf. Tb 8: 3 and Mt 12: 43.)

And yet it is important to remember that the transferring of sins and the expiation which results from it are said to be effective only because the goat is presented before Yahweh (v. 10): Yahweh brought about the transfer, and the expiation. The goat was not sacrificed to Azazel or to Yahweh because, once it had been charged with the sins of the people, it was impure, and therefore could not be used as a victim for sacrifice. The Levitical ritual has therefore incorporated an old custom of unknown origin into its liturgy, but it has at the same time exorcised it.

(c) *When was the feast instituted?* This does not mean, however, that the Day of Atonement and its ritual are of very ancient origin. On the contrary, the opposite would seem to be true, for we have already had occasion to note that the combination of Levitical customs with popular superstitions is a characteristic of the very latest rituals of purification.[1] There is no mention of the feast in any pre-exilic text, either historical or prophetical. Ezechiel foretold that on the 1st and the 7th of the first month[2] a bull would be offered in sacrifice: the blood of the first bull would be used for the purification of the Temple and of the altar, whereas the second would be offered for the indeliberate sins of the people; and the two together would constitute 'the expiation for the Temple' (Ez 45: 18-20). Though the intention is undoubtedly the same, this is not yet the Day of Atonement, for the latter was fixed for the 10th day of the seventh month, and the ceremony of the goat 'for Azazel' is not mentioned.

There is no mention of it in the books of Esdras and of Nehemias, though this raises a further problem which is made still more complicated by difficulties of literary criticism. Esd 3: 1-6 contains no mention of the Day

1. Cf. pp. 461-464. 2. Cf. p. 473.

of Atonement, but only of the feast of Tents, which was observed by the first groups to return from exile. Ne 8 (which is based on Esdras' memorandum, and is the sequel to Esd 8: 36) says that the Law was read out, and then studied, on the 1st and the 2nd of the seventh month; it then goes on to describe the feast of Tents, which must have been held from the 15th to the 22nd;[1] it makes no mention of a Day of Atonement, on the 10th of this month. One suggestion is that in this particular year, the preparation for the celebration of the feast of Tents in a new way (Ne 8: 14–15) led to the omission of the Day of Atonement; this explanation seems hardly satisfactory. On the other hand, Ne 9: 1 (immediately after the account of the feast of Tents) says that on 'the 24th day of this month' there was a fast and a penitential ceremony. It is therefore suggested that this day was the Day of Atonement, and that it was either postponed, in this particular year, to the 24th, or that at this time it was celebrated on the 24th and later put forward to the 10th. Neither of these solutions is convincing, for Ne 9: 1–2 does not form a sequel to the document in Ne 8: modern commentators connect Ne 9: 1–2 either with Esd 10: 17 (the mission of Esdras) or with Ne 10: 1f. (the mission of Nehemias). The reference in Ne 9: 1–2 is therefore useless, and so is the date which it gives: 'the 24th day of *this* month': we do not know to which year or to which month it is referring, and perhaps this feast had no connection at all with the Day of Atonement.

The argument from silence is not, of course, decisive, but it does furnish a presumption that the feast had not yet been instituted in the time of Esdras and Nehemias. We may add, too, that the ritual in Lv 23: 26–32 begins with the words 'And Yahweh spoke', which would indicate an addition; we may also note that this ritual makes no mention of the goat for Azazel, which is a distinctive feature of the celebration of the feast in Lv 16. The only possible conclusion is that the feast was instituted at a late date, though we cannot say precisely either when it was instituted or when the ritual of Lv 16 was first put into practice. The connection in Lv 16: 1 with an episode in the desert (the death of Nadab and Abihu) is quite artificial (cf. Lv 10: 1–6).

2. *The feast of the Hanukkah*

Most modern translations call this feast the feast of the Dedication. Its Greek name, Τὰ Ἐγκαίνια, means the 'inauguration' or 'the renewal', and this is a more literal rendering of the Hebrew *ḥanukkah*, the name which was given to the feast by the Rabbis and by which it is still known among the Jews. Josephus calls it the feast of Lights, after the rite which was its principal feature.

(a) *The origin and history of the feast.* The story of its institution is told in 1 M 4: 36–59. Antiochus Epiphanes, after desecrating the Temple of Jeru-

1. Cf. p. 500.

salem and its altar, erected, over the altar of holocausts, a pagan altar, the Abomination of Desolation (1 M 1: 54; Dn 9: 27; 11: 31), and there offered the first sacrifice to Zeus Olympios, on the 25th Kisleu (December), 167. Three years later, Judas Maccabee, after his first victories, purified the sanctuary, built a new altar and inaugurated it on the 25th Kisleu, 164, the third anniversary of its profanation (2 M 10: 5). It was then decided that the feast should be observed each year (1 M 4: 59).

It is questionable whether the feast could have been regularly observed during the following years, for the Syrians occupied the Citadel and there was fighting in Jerusalem. The situation would have changed once religious freedom was regained, and once Jonathan was appointed high priest, in 152 B.C. The opening verses of the second book of Maccabees (2 M 1: 1-9) contain a letter written to the Jews of Egypt in 124: in this letter, they are recommended to keep the Hanukkah, and reference is made to a previous letter sent in 143. This document bears all the marks of authenticity. It is followed, however, by another letter, for which the same claims cannot be made (2 M 1: 10—2: 18): this second letter is said to have been despatched at the first feast of the Dedication, in 164, and it already contains some legendary features. Like the first, it ends with an invitation to keep the Hanukkah. In the body of the book itself, all the first part (2 M 2: 19—10: 8) is an historical justification of the feast (cf. the author's preface, 2 M 2: 19, and conclusion, 2 M 10: 8). The second part of the book is parallel to the first, and gives the events leading up to the feast of Nicanor, which was held on the 13th Adar in memory of the defeat and death of this Syrian general (2 M 15: 36). The feast of Nicanor was not observed for long, and we shall omit all further mention of it.

The feast of the Hanukkah, however, continued to be observed. It is mentioned in the New Testament (Jn 10: 22), under its Greek name (Τὰ Ἐγκαίνια) and in Josephus (*Ant.* XII, vii, 7), under the name of the feast of Lights. The Mishnah merely alludes to it here and there, but this can be explained by the hostility of orthodox circles to the Hasmoneans; the Rabbis had no desire to bestow their approval on a feast instituted by them. All the same, it remained a popular feast, and later rabbinical treatises give some casuistic solutions and some bizarre explanations of problems connected with it. The feast was originally in memory of the renovation of the Temple, but it survived the destruction of the Temple because the ritual of lights, as we shall see, made it independent of the sanctuary and allowed it to take on a new meaning. Even to-day, it is still one of the great Jewish feasts.

(b) *The rites: the Hanukkah and the feast of Tents.* The celebration of the feast lasted eight days from the 25th Kisleu (December), and it was a most joyful feast (1 M 4: 56-59). Apart from the sacrifices offered in the Temple, thyrsus, green branches and palms were carried around, and hymns were sung (2 M 10: 6-8; cf. 1 M 4: 54). The title of Ps 30 says it was to be sung at the Dedication of the Temple, and it must have been used on this occasion. But the principal psalms sung were the Hallel (Pss 113–118), and the addition of v. 27 in Ps 118 probably refers to a rite of this feast: it can be translated as 'Bring your procession (*or*, your dance, *ḥag*), palms in hand, close to the horns of the altar'.

Apart from this procession with palms and the singing of the Hallel, the feast was characterized by the use of lights (Josephus, as we have said, calls it 'The feast of Lights'). The Mishnah and rabbinical writings tell us that lamps were lit in front of each house, and that the number increased by one a day until the last day of the feast. The oldest texts do not mention this rite explicitly: the lighting of lamps in 1 M 4: 50 refers to the reintroduction of the chandelier into the Temple, not to the inauguration of the altar. Nevertheless, there are allusions to the rite in the first letter of 2 M 1: 8, which quotes a previous letter in the words 'We have lit lamps'; the second letter (2 M 1: 18f.) connects the commemoration of the sacred fire, miraculously preserved, and found by Nehemias, with the feast of the Hanukkah; and Ps 118: 27 has, just before the verse about the palms, 'Yahweh is God, he is our light'.

The second book of Maccabees stresses the similarity between the Hanukkah and the feast of Tents. It was celebrated on the first occasion, 'in the way they kept the feast of Tents' (2 M 10: 6), and the letter of 124 B.C. calls it 'the feast of Tents in the month of Kisleu' (2 M 1: 9). The first book of Maccabees does not make this connection, but the second deliberately underlines its relation to one of the great traditional feasts, in order to secure it a favourable reception in the Egyptian Diaspora. It is, of course, possible that Judas Maccabee himself wanted it to be like the feast of Tents, for this was the date on which Solomon's Temple (1 K 8: 2, 65) and the altar which was erected after the Exile (Esd 3: 4) had been dedicated.

In fact, the two feasts both lasted eight days (if we include the closing day of the feast of Tents, Lv 23: 34–36), and palms were carried both at the Hanukkah and at the feast of Tents (according to the ritual then in force, Lv 23: 40–41). But this is where the resemblances end. Psalms were certainly sung at the feast of Tents, but there is no evidence that it was the Hallel; it seems rather that the Hallel was first sung at the Hanukkah and later extended to the feasts of the Passover, of Pentecost and of Tents. During the Hanukkah, no-one lived in huts, and the lights put out in front of the houses are only remotely connected with the illumination of the Temple on the nights of the feast of Tents. Josephus (*Ant.* XII, vii, 7) says the lights of the Hanukkah symbolized that freedom had 'shone' upon the Jews in a way that could never have been hoped for; in later times, they became the symbol of the Law, which, in Pr 6: 23 and Ps 119: 105, is called a light. We still have to explain, however, why one more lamp was lit on each succeeding day of the feast, and this brings us to the question of pagan influences on the festal rites.

(c) *Was there any pagan influence in the origin or the rites of the Hanukkah?* The Hanukkah is the only Jewish feast whose institution is recorded in a late text, and which is also connected with an undeniable historical event. For some scholars, this seems too simple, and they have tried to show that the feast originated outside Israel. They say it is the Jewish adaptation of a feast of the winter solstice, and that the 'Hanukkah' should be connected with Henoch, who lived 365 years (Gn 5: 23), *i.e.* the number of days in a solar year. Other writers, leaving Henoch aside, have maintained with less improbability that the feast corresponds to that of the *Sol invictus*, which was celebrated at Rome on the 25th December. Others again recall that during the persecution of Antiochus Epiphanes, the Jews were ordered to wear crowns of ivy and to take part in a procession in honour of Bacchus (2 M 6: 7), and that an old man from Athens (2 M 6: 1) was sent by the king to instruct them in the new rites: they add that the assimilation of the Nabatean god Dusares and Bacchus could have made these rites less foreign to the Jews. But they forget to prove (and it cannot be proved) that the Dionysiac rites took place on the 25th Kisleu at Jerusalem: we shall see that the text of 2 M 6: 7 implies rather that they fell at a different time. Lastly, other writers maintain that an extra light was lit each day to symbolize the lengthening of days after the winter solstice.

The objections which can be raised against these theories seems to be decisive. We cannot admit that this Jewish feast was of pagan origin, because all the information we possess about it shows that it was instituted, and thereafter observed, only to commemorate the purification of the Temple after it had been defiled by pagan customs, and the restoration of lawful worship. Further, even if this most unlikely possibility were accepted, it is impossible for a feast of the winter solstice, which is tied to the solar calendar, to be a feast fixed on a definite day of a lunar year, however many corrections one may introduce: the 25th Kisleu would fall on the day of the solstice only on rare occasions.

Nevertheless, there may have been a connection between the Hanukkah and certain pagan usages, but it is an indirect and an adverse connection. Judas Maccabee inaugurated the new altar on the precise anniversary of the profanation of the old one, the 25th Kisleu. Now Antiochus Epiphanes had deliberately chosen this date for the first sacrifice to Zeus Olympios. It has been suggested that in the year 167, the winter solstice fell on the 25th Kisleu, but attempts to prove this by calculation have not yielded any certain results. The texts themselves, however, indicate the answer: according to 2 M 6: 7, the Jews were obliged to take part in the monthly sacrifice, on the king's birthday; according to 1 M 1: 58-59, attacks were made every month on recalcitrant Jews, and on the 25th of each month, a sacrifice was offered on the pagan altar. In this last verse, both the grammar and the context show that the reference is not merely to the sacrifice of 25th Kisleu, 167, but to a sacrifice which was repeated on the 25th of each month, *i.e.* to a monthly sacrifice offered for the king's birthday, as 2 M 6: 7 says. There is evidence of the custom in the Hellenistic East, and it continued in vogue in these same regions until after the establishment of the Roman Empire.

The feasts of Dionysus, in which the Jews were ordered to wear ivy crowns, are distinguished from this monthly sacrifice in 2 M 6: 7 and this is yet another reason for denying that the branches carried at the Hanukkah were connected with the cult of Bacchus. Nevertheless, brandishing these branches in honour of the true God may have been intended to do away with the memory of the pagan rite which faithful Jews had been forced to follow, and which Hellenizing Jews had freely adopted: the custom followed on the feast of Tents would provide a justification. The lighting of lamps in front of the houses could be intended to replace the incense which, under Antiochus Epiphanes, had been burnt at the house-doors and on the squares (1 M 1: 55). Why one more lamp should have been lit each day we do not know: there is no evidence of it in the earliest documents; but neither is there evidence to show that it was connected with the rising of the sun from its solstice. The rite may indicate merely the increasing solemnity of the feast, or it may merely mark its passing from day to day. Popular customs and liturgical rules love these gradations: to take one example in the Jewish ritual, the sacrificial code in Nb 29: 13-32 prescribes that from the first to the seventh day of the feast of Tents, the number of bulls sacrificed should be one less each day, until, on the seventh day, seven victims were offered. If these secondary contacts with pagan customs are well-founded, and if our interpretation of them is valid, then the fundamental character of the Hanukkah is thereby confirmed: it was a feast for the purification of all the defilement contracted under the domination of the wicked (cf. 1 M 4: 36). Hence 2 M 2: 16 and 10: 5 call it simply the day of 'the purification of the Temple'.

3. *The feast of Purim*

(a) *Its date and its rites.* Josephus (*Ant.* XI, vi, 13), writing in the first century of our era, says that the feast of Purim was held on the 14th and 15th Adar, to commemorate the revenge of the Jews of Persia upon their enemies. The ritual is described in rabbinical writings. The feast was preceded by a day's fasting, on the 13th Adar: in the evening, lamps were lit in all the houses, and everyone went to the synagogue. The 14th and 15th were days of rejoicing. Everyone went to the synagogue again, to listen to the reading of the book of Esther; while the story was being read, the congregation would interrupt with curses against Aman and the wicked in general, and the meeting closed with a solemn blessing of Mardochai, of Esther and of the Israelites. Apart from this reading, the feast was an occasion for the distribution of presents and of alms, and pious persons made these gifts with a religious intention; but otherwise, it was an utterly profane feast, taken up with banquets and amusements, and considerable liberty was allowed. The Rabbis allowed that anyone could go on drinking until he could no longer tell the difference between 'Cursed be Aman!' and 'Blessed be Mardochai!' Later, the custom of putting on disguises was introduced, and the feast of Purim became the Jewish carnival.

(b) *Purim and the Book of Esther*. Obviously, the Book of Esther had to be read, for the feast owed both its name and institution to this story. The final note in the Greek translation of the book calls it 'this letter about the Purim' (Est 10: 3). Est 3: 7 (completed with the aid of the Greek) and 9: 24 tell us that these days are called 'Purim' because Aman had cast lots (*pûr*) on the 14th of Adar to exterminate the Jews, and this wicked plot of his had turned against him, and he had been hanged. The word *pûr* is not Hebrew, and in both cases needed to be glossed by the Hebrew *gôral* (lot). Because of the background against which the story is told, attempts have been made to find a Persian etymology, but it is now certain that the word is Akkadian (*pûru* means 'lot' or 'destiny'); we shall return to this point later.

It is curious that this casting of lots does not have a more prominent place in the story, and that there is no reference to it in the feast which bears its name. Moreover, Est 3: 7 breaks the narrative, and the second mention of 'lots' is the section (Est 9: 20-32) which tells how Mardochai wrote to the Jews of the Diaspora telling them to keep the feast; the same passage alludes to a previous letter of Mardochai on the same subject, and ends by saying that Esther herself issued an order confirming what Mardochai had written. It would seem that Est 3: 7 and 9: 20-32 were inserted into the story to spread the feast and to fix its name as Purim.

The body of the book, however, is already a 'legend of a feast'. Everything in the story—Esther's elevation and the intervention of her uncle Mardochai, the hatred of Aman for the Jews, his punishment and the revenge of the Jews, thanks to the esteem in which Esther and Mardochai were held by the king—converges on the feast which took place on the day after the massacre, and the final verses are an attempt to explain why the feast lasted two days (the 14th and 15th Adar), 'amid joy and banquets, amid festivities and the exchange of presents' (Est 9: 16-19). It is quite possible that the story has an historical foundation in some unexpected deliverance of the Jews of Susa from the threat of extermination, but we know nothing of the circumstances, and this historical basis would then have been freely adapted until it became the 'legend' of a feast.

(c) *The origin of the feast*. The origin of this feast is utterly different from that of the Hanukkah. The Book of Esther undertakes to justify the feast of Purim, but it is not an historical book, and the feast which it seeks to justify is quite unlike any of the feasts we have so far examined: it was not a religious feast; it was not held (at least directly) in honour of the God of Israel (whose name is not even mentioned in the Hebrew book of Esther); it was not connected with the ancient history of the Chosen People; and it contained no cultic elements at all. It was a foreign feast, but its origins are obscure.

Attempts have been made to show that it came from Babylonia, and that it should be explained in terms of mythology: Mardochai-Esther would be the divine couple Marduk-Ishtar; Aman-Vashti would be the two Elamite divinities Uman-Mashti (though the present reading of this name is: Parti); and the story would be a symbol of the victory of the god of light over the god of darkness. Vashti's reign lasted one hundred and eighty days (*i.e.* throughout the winter) and Esther came to power with the coming of spring; the feast would then be connected with the New Year feast, in which 'lots' were cast. But there is nothing comparable to the feast of Purim in Babylonia, and to bring in the Persian and Babylonian feast of the Σακαῖα which was (or became) a popular feast in which masters changed place with their servants, and the king with a subject, is merely to add to the confusion: we do not know enough about the history or the meaning of the Σακαῖα to throw further light on the story of Esther.

There is a far more interesting connection with a story related at length by Herodotus (*Hist.* III, 68-79). After the death of Cambyses, the magus Gaumata usurped the throne by passing himself off as Smerdis, the brother of Cambyses, whom the latter had secretly put to death. The Pseudo-Smerdis was unmasked by a certain Otanes, assisted by his daughter, who was one of the royal harem. Gaumata was put to death, and the people turned against all the Magi, and massacred them. The Persians celebrated this event in a great feast called the Massacre of the Magi. The story is very similar to the story of Esther, and cuneiform texts prove that it has an historical basis, for they mention that this Gaumata did actually usurp the throne. But the cuneiform texts do not mention the feast itself. Nevertheless, other texts from Persia show that it had some connection with the New Year.

If we now return to the feast of Purim, the pronounced local colour in the Book of Esther and its correspondence with what we know of the ancient town of Susa and of the customs at the court of Xerxes (Assuerus) give us ground for thinking that the feast is of Persian origin. Nevertheless, there are certain Babylonian features: the name Mardochai=Marduk, and Esther=Ishtar, and the Akkadian word *pûru*, which gave the name to the feast (unless Esther is derived from the ancient Persian *star-*, meaning 'star'). We suggest, therefore, that the origin of the feast is not to be sought in one civilisation alone; but this reconstruction is largely hypothetical.

We can say for certain that the feast originated in the communities of the Eastern Diaspora, perhaps at Susa itself. It probably commemorates a pogrom from which the Jews escaped in a way which seemed to them miraculous; this may have taken place in the fourth century B.C. It is clear, on the other hand, that the feast preserves certain characteristics of a foreign New Year feast (the amusements, the banquets, the New Year gifts, the notion of a change which brings a renovation); it is possible, therefore, that the Jewish feast was modelled on a Persian New Year feast. From Persia, the feast would have spread first to Mesopotamia, and would there have taken on its Babylonian character; in particular, it would have acquired its name (*pûrîm*) from the casting of lots (*pûru*); this would fit in with the Babylonian idea that at the beginning of each year men's destinies were fixed, and it might also be an attempt to explain the Persian name for the first month of the year (Farvadin) by the Akkadian. The feast did not reach Palestine until long afterwards; Ben Sirach, writing about 190 B.C., does not mention Mardochai or Esther in his praise of Israel's ancestors (Si 44–50). The first mention of the feast is in 2 M 15: 36, where it is called the 'Day of Mardochai', and is fixed for the 14th Adar. The Hebrew text of Esther calls it 'the days of the Purim' (in the addition contained in Est 9: 28, 31), and under this name, distorted into φρουραί ('watches' or 'guards') it was introduced into Egypt, from Jerusalem, in 114 B.C. (Est 10: 3, Greek).

It is next mentioned in Josephus (*Ant.* XI, vi, 13), and so makes its definitive entry into history. It was a popular feast, of suspect origin, and we must ask the reader's pardon for so ending our study of the religious institutions of ancient Israel.

BIBLIOGRAPHY

Abbreviations

AASOR	*Annual of the American Schools of Oriental Research.*
AfO	*Archiv für Orientforschung.*
AJSL	*American Journal of Semitic Languages and Literatures.*
BASOR	*Bulletin of the American Schools of Oriental Research.*
BIFAO	*Bulletin de l'Institut Français d'Archéologie Orientale* (Cairo).
BJPES	*Bulletin of the Jewish Palestine Exploration Society.*
BJRL	*Bulletin of the John Rylands Library* (Manchester).
HTR	*Harvard Theological Review.*
HUCA	*Hebrew Union College Annual.*
IEJ	*Israel Exploration Journal.*
JAOS	*Journal of the American Oriental Society.*
JBL	*Journal of Biblical Literature.*
JNES	*Journal of Near Eastern Studies.*
JPOS	*Journal of the Palestine Oriental Society.*
JQR	*Jewish Quarterly Review.*
JTS	*Journal of Theological Studies.*
PEQ	*Palestine Exploration Quarterly.*
PJB	*Palästinajahrbuch.*
RB	*Revue Biblique.*
RHPR	*Revue d'Histoire et de Philosophie Religieuses.*
TLZ	*Theologische Literaturzeitung.*
VT	*Vetus Testamentum.*
ZA	*Zeitschrift für Assyriologie und verwandte Gebiete.*
ZAW	*Zeitschrift für die Alttestamentliche Wissenschaft.*
ZDMG	*Zeitschrift der Deutschen Morgenländischen Gesellschaft.*
ZDPV	*Zeitschrift der Deutschen Palästina-Vereins.*

IV

Religious Institutions

Introductory

See, in addition to works on biblical theology:

W. Zimmerli, 'Das zweite Gebot', in *Festschrift Bertholet*, Tübingen, 1950, 550–63.

S. Mowinckel, *Religion und Kultus*, Göttingen, 1953.
K. H. Bernhardt, *Gott und Bild*, Berlin, 1956.
J. Hempel, *Das Bild in Bibel und Gottesdienst*, Tübingen, 1957.
C. R. North, 'The Essence of Idolatry', in *Von Ugarit nach Qumran* (*Festschrift Eissfeldt*), Berlin, 1958, 151–60.
S. H. Hooke (ed.), *Myth, Ritual and Kingship*, Oxford, 1958, especially the essay by G. Widengren, 'Early Hebrew Myths and their Interpretation', 149–203.
A. S. Herbert, *Worship in Ancient Israel*, London, 1959.

1

Semitic Sanctuaries

On the sacred territory and its privileges:

M.-J. Lagrange, *Études sur les religions sémitiques*[2], Paris, 1905, 180–7.
G. Dalman, 'Der Gilgal der Bibel und die Steinkreise Palästinas', in *PJB*, XV, 1919, 5–30.
M. Gaudefroy-Demombynes, *Le pèlerinage à La Mekke*, Paris, 1923.
T. Canaan, *Mohammedan Saints and Sanctuaries*, London, 1927.
J. d'A. Waechter, 'The Excavations at Wadi Dhobaï', in *JPOS*, XVIII, 1938, p. 174, pl. xliii.

On waters, trees and heights with a sacred character:

W. W. Baudissin, 'Heilige Gewässer, Bäume und Höhen bei den Semiten, insbesondere bei den Hebräern', in his *Studien zur semitischen Religionsgeschichte*, II, Leipzig, 1878, 145–269.
M.-J. Lagrange, *Études sur les religions sémitiques*[2], Paris, 1905, 158–80.
H. Danthine, *Le palmier-dattier et les arbres sacrés dans l'iconographie de l'Asie Occidentale ancienne*, Paris, 1937.
N. Perrot, *Les représentations de l'arbre sacré sur les monuments de Mésopotamie et d'Élam*, Paris, 1937.

On Saphon:

J. Jeremias, *Der Gottesberg*, Gütersloh, 1919.
O. Eissfeldt, *Baal Zaphon, Zeus Casios und der Durchzug der Israeliten durchs Meer*, Halle, 1932.
B. Alfrink, 'Der Versammlungsberg in äussersten Norden', in *Biblica*, XIV, 1933, 41–57.
R. de Langhe, *Les Textes de Ras-Shamra-Ugarit et leurs Rapports avec le Milieu Biblique de l'Ancien Testament*, Gembloux, 1945, II, 217–45.
W. F. Albright, 'Baal-Zaphon', in *Festschrift Bertholet*, Tübingen, 1950, 1–14.

On Hermon:

R. Mouterde, 'Antiquities de l'Hermon et de la Beqa'', in *Mélanges de l'Université S. Joseph* (Beirut), XXIX, 1951–3, 22–37.

On Thabor:

O. Eissfeldt, 'Der Gott Tabor und seine Verbreitung', in *Archiv für Religionswissenschaft*, XXXI, 1934, 14–41.
J. Boehmer, 'Der Gottesberg Tabor', in *Biblische Zeitschrift*, XXIII, 1935–6, 333–41.
J. Lewy, 'Tabor, Tibar, Atabyros', in *HUCA*, XXIII, 1, 1950–1, 357–86.

On Carmel:

R. de Vaux, 'Les prophètes de Baal sur le mont Carmel', in *Bulletin du Musée de Beyrouth*, V, 1941, 7–20.
M. Avi-Yonah, 'Mount Carmel and the God of Baalbek', in *IEJ*, II, 1952, 118–24.
K. Galling, 'Der Gott Karmel und die Ächtung der fremden Götter', in *Geschichte und Altes Testament* (*Festchrift Alt*), Tübingen, 1953, 105–25.
O. Eissfeldt, 'Der Gott Karmel' (*Sitzungsberichte der deutschen Akademie*, Berlin), 1953.
H. H. Rowley, 'Elijah on Mount Carmel', in *BJRL*, XLIII, 1960–1, 190–210.

On ziggurats:

Th. Dombart, 'Der babylonische Turm' (*Der Alte Orient*, XXIX, 2), Leipzig, 1930.
W. Andrae, *Das Gotteshaus und die Urformen des Bauens im Alten Orient*, Berlin, 1930.
H. J. Lenzen, 'Die Entwicklung der Ziggurat von ihren Anfängen bis zur Zeit der II. Dynastie von Ur' (*Ausgrabungen in Uruk-Warka*, IV), Leipzig, 1941.
L.-H. Vincent, 'De la Tour de Babel au Temple', in *RB*, LIII, 1946, 403–40.
A. Parrot, *Ziggurats et Tour de Babel*, Paris, 1949.
A. Parrot, *La Tour de Babel*, Neuchâtel-Paris, 1953.
P. Amiet, 'Ziggurats et culte en hauteur', in *Revue d'Assyriologie*, XLVIII, 1953, 23–33.
R. Ghirshman, 'Cinquième campagne de fouilles à Tchoga-Zanbil, près Suse', in *Comptes Rendus de l'Académie des Inscriptions* (Paris), 1956, 335–44.

On temples:

W. ANDRAE, *Das Gotteshaus und die Urformen des Bauens im Alten Orient*, Berlin, 1930.
W. ANDRAE, 'Kultbau im Alten Orient', in *Mélanges Syriens offerts à M. R. Dussaud*, II, Paris, 1939, 867-71.
H. H. NELSON, L. OPPENHEIM, G. E. WRIGHT, 'The Significance of the Temple in the Ancient Near East', in *The Biblical Archaeologist*, VII, 1944, 41-63, 66-77.
M. AVI-YONAH and S. YEIVIN, *The Antiquities of Israel* (in Hebrew), I, Tel-Aviv, 1955, ch. II: 'Places of Worship and Sanctuaries', 145-204.

On the cult of the 'high places':

H. INGHOLT, 'Le sens du mot ḥammân', in *Mélanges Syriens offerts à M. R. Dussaud*, II, Paris, 1939, 795-802.
K. ELLIGER, 'Chammânim=Masseben?', in *ZAW*, LVII, 1939, 256-65.
W. F. ALBRIGHT, *Archaeology and the Religion of Israel*, Baltimore, 1942, 105-7, 202-4.
K. ELLIGER, 'Der Sinn des Worthes Chammân', in *ZDPV*, LXVI, 1943, 129-39.
G. LOUD, *Megiddo II*, Chicago, 1948, 73-81.
L.-H. VINCENT, 'La notion biblique du haut lieu', in *RB*, LV, 1948, 245-78, 438-45.
D. NEIMAN, 'Pgr, A Canaanite Cult-Object in the Old Testament', in *JBL*, LXVII, 1948, 55-60.
C. C. MCCOWN, 'Hebrew High-Places and Cult Remains', in *JBL*, LXIX, 1950, 205-19.
R. AMIRAN, 'Excavations in the Tumuli West of Jerusalem', in *Bulletin of the Israel Exploration Society*, XVIII, 1954, 44-59 (in Hebrew, with a summary in English).
S. YEIVIN, art. '*bamah*', in *Encyclopaedia Biblica* (in Hebrew), II, Jerusalem, 1954.
F. HVIDBERG, 'The Massebah and the Holy Seed (Is 6: 13)', in *Interpretationes ad Vetus Testamentum pertinentes* (*Festchrift Mowinckel*), Oslo, 1955, 96-9.
M. DOTHAN, 'Excavations at Nahariyah', in *IEJ*, VI, 1956, 14-25.
A. DUPONT-SOMMER, 'Les autels à encens de Lakish', in *Mélanges Isidore Lévy* (*Annuaire de l'Institut de Philologie et d'Histoire Orientales et Slaves*, XIII), 1955, 135-52.
W. F. ALBRIGHT, 'The High Place in Ancient Palestine', in *Volume du Congrès, Strasbourg* (Supplement to VT IV), Leiden, 1957, 242-58.
S. IWRY, 'Maṣṣēbāh and Bāmāh in 1Q Isaiah^A 6: 13', in *JBL*, LXXVI, 1957, 225-32.
R. AMIRAN, 'The Tumuli West of Jerusalem', in *IEJ*, VIII, 1958, 205-27.

2

THE FIRST ISRAELITE SANCTUARIES

Two monographs, both old and insufficient:

A. VON GALL, *Altisraelitische Kultstätten*, Giessen, 1898.
G. WESTPHAL, *Jahwes Wohnstatten nach den Anschauungen der alten Hebraer*, Giessen, 1908.

On Shechem:

A. ALT, 'Die Wallfahrt von Sichem nach Bethel', in his *Kleine Schriften*, I, Munich, 1953, 79-88.
E. NIELSEN, *Shechem, A Traditio-Historical Investigation*, Copenhagen, 1955.
C. A. KELLER, 'Über einige alttestamentliche Heiligtumslegendes, I, A. *Die Legenden um Sichem*', in *ZAW*, LXVII, 1955, 143-54.
W. HARRELSON, B. W. ANDERSON, G. E. WRIGHT, 'Shechem, "Navel of the Land"', in *The Biblical Archaeologist*, XX, 1957, 2-32.
J. T. MILIK, 'Le sanctuaire de Ba'al Berit à Sichem', in *RB*, LXVI, 1959, 560-2.

On Bethel:

O. EISSFELDT, 'Der Gott Bethel', in *Archiv für Religionswissenschaft*, XXVIII, 1930, 1-30.
J. P. HYATT, 'The Deity Bethel and the Old Testament', in *JAOS*, LIX, 1939, 81-98.
K. GALLING, 'Bethel und Gilgal', in *ZDPV*, LXVI, 1943, 140-55; LXVII, 1944-5, 21-45.
C. A. KELLER, 'Über einige alttestamentliche Heilgtumslegendes, I, C. Die Legende von Bethel', in *ZAW*, LXVII, 1955, 162-8.

On Mambre:

R. DE VAUX, art. 'Mambré', in *Dictionnaire de la Bible, Supplément*, V, 1957, 753-8.
E. MADER, *Mambre, Die Ergebnisse der Ausgrabungen im heiligen Bezirk Râmet el Ḫalîl in Südpalästina*, Freiburg i. Breisg., 1957.

On Beersheba:

W. ZIMMERLI, *Geschichte und Tradition von Beerseba im Alten Testament*, Giessen, 1932.

On the Tent and the Ark:

H. Gressmann, *Die Lade Jahves und das Allerheiligste des salomonischen Tempels*, Leipzig, 1920.
H. Lammens, 'Le culte des bétyles et les processions religieuses chez les Arabes pré-islamiques', in *BIFAO*, XVII, 1920, 39-101.
H. Schmidt, 'Kerubenthron und Lade', in *Eucharistèrion Gunkel*, I, Göttingen, 1923, 120-44.
H. G. May, 'The Ark—A Miniature Tempel', in *AJSL*, LII, 1935-6, 215-34.
H. Ingholt, 'Inscriptions and Sculptures from Palmyra', in *Berytus*, III, 1936, 83-8.
H. Danthine, 'L'imagerie des trônes vides et des trônes porteurs de symboles dans le Proche Orient ancien', in *Mélanges Syriens offerts à M. R. Dussaud*, I, Paris, 1939, 857-66.
O. Eissfeldt, 'Lade und Stierbild', in *ZAW*, LVIII, 1940-1, 190-215.
J. Morgenstern, 'The Ark, the Ephod and the "Tent of Meeting"', in *HUCA*, XVII, 1942-3, 153-266; XVIII, 1943-4, 1-52.
F. M. Cross, 'The Tabernacle', in *The Biblical Archaeologist*, X, 1947, 45-68.
A. Bentzen, 'The Cultic Use of the Story of the Ark in Samuel', in *JBL*, LXVII, 1948, 37-53.
A. Kuschke, 'Die Lagervorstellung der priesterlichen Erzählung', in *ZAW*, LXII, 1951, 74-105.
J. Jomier, *Le Mahmal et la caravane égyptienne du pèlerinage de la Mecque*, Le Caire, 1953.
Ch. Picard, 'Le trône vide d'Alexandre dans le cérémonie de Cyinda et le culte du trône vide à travers le monde gréco-romain', in *Cahiers Archéologiques*, VII, 1954, 1-17.
M. Haran, 'The Ark of the Covenant and the Cherubs', in *Eretz-Israel*, V (*Volume Mazar*), 1958, 83-9 (in Hebrew, with a summary in English).
G. von Rad, 'Zelt und Lade', in *Neue Kirchliche Zeitschrift*, XLII, 1931, 476-98 = *Gesammelte Studien zum Alten Testament*, Munich, 1958, 100-29.
M. Haran, 'The Ark and the Cherubim. Their Symbolic Significance in Biblical Ritual', in *IEJ*, IX, 1959, 30-8.
D. W. Gooding, *The Account of the Tabernacle. Translation and Textual Problems of the Greek Exodus*, Cambridge, 1959.
L. Rost, 'Die Wohnstätte des Zeugnisses', in *Festschrift F. Baumgärtel*, Erlangen, 1959, 158-65.
M. Haran, 'The Nature of the *'ōhel mô'ēdh* in Pentateuchal Studies', in *Journal of Semitic Studies*, V, 1960, 50-65.
E. Nielsen, 'Some Reflections on the History of the Ark', in *Congress Volume, Oxford*, 1959 (Supplement VII to *VT*), Leiden, 1960, 61-74.
E. Kutsch, art. 'Lade Jahwes', in *Religion in Geschichte und Gegenwart*[2]', 1960, 197-9.

On Gilgal:

K. Galling, 'Bethel und Gilgal', in *ZDPV*, LXVI, 1943, 140-55; LXVII, 1944-5, 21-5, 34-43.
A. George, 'Les récits de Gilgal en Josué v. 2-15', in *Mémorial Chaine* (Bibliothèque de la Faculté Catholique de Théologie de Lyon, 5), 1950, 159-86.
F. M. Abel, 'Galgala qui est aussi le Dodecalithon', *ibid.*, 29-34.
H. J. Kraus, 'Gilgal, ein Beitrag zur Kultusgeschichte Israels', in *VT*, I, 1951, 181-9.
F. M. Abel, 'L'apparition du chef de l'armée de Yahweh à Josué, Jos. v. 13-15', in *Miscellanea Biblica et Orientalia R. P. A. Miller oblata*, Rome, 1951, 109-13.
C. A. Keller, 'Über einige alttestamentliche Heiligtumslegenden, II, D. Der Hieros Logos von Gilgal', in *ZAW*, LXVIII, 1956, 85-94.

On Shiloh:

O. Eissfeldt, 'Silo und Jerusalem', in *Volume du Congrès, Strasbourg* (Supplement to VT, IV), Leiden, 1957, 138-47.

On Mispah:

H. W. Hertzberg, 'Mizpa', in *ZAW*, XLVII, 1929, 161-96.
J. Muilenburg, in C. C. McCown, *Tell en-Nasbeh*, I, New Haven, 1947, 3-49.

On Gibeon:

A. Bruno, *Gibeon*, Leipzig, 1923.
H. Cazelles, 'David's Monarchy and the Gibeonite Claim, II Sam. XXI 1-14', in *PEQ*, 1956, 155-75.
J. Dus, 'Gibeon, eine Kultstätte des Šmš und die Stadt des benjaminitischen Schicksals', in *VT*, X, 1960, 353-74.

On Ophra:

C. A. Keller, 'Über einige alttestamentliche Heiligtumslegenden, I, B. Die Legenden um Ophra', in *ZAW*, LXVII, 1955, 154-62.
E. Kutsch, 'Gideons Berufung und Altarbau, Jdc 6, 11-24', in *TLZ*, LXXXI, 1956, 75-84.

On Dan:

A. Fernandez, 'El santuario de Dan', in *Biblica*, XV, 1934, 237-64.
A. Murtonen, 'Some Thoughts on Judges XVII sq.', in *VT*, I, 1951, 233-4.

Ch. HAURET, 'Aux origines du sacerdoce danite', in *Mélanges Bibliques . . . A. Robert*, Paris, 1957, 105-13.

On Jerusalem:

H. S. NYBERG, 'Studien zum Religionskampf im Alten Testament', in *Archiv für Religionswissenschaft*, XXXV, 1938, 329-87.
H. H. ROWLEY, 'Zadok and Nehustan', in *JBL*, LVIII, 1939, 113-41.
A. BENTZEN, 'The Cultic Use of the Story of the Ark in Samuel', in *JBL*, LXVII, 1948, 37-53.
M. NOTH, 'Jerusalem und die israelitische Tradition', in *Oudtestamentische Studiën*, VIII, 1950, 28-46= *Gesammelte Studien zum Alten Testament*, Munich, 1958, 172-87.
H. H. ROWLEY, 'Melchizedek and Zadok', in *Festschrift Bertholet*, Tübingen, 1950, 461-72.
L.-H. VINCENT, 'Abraham à Jérusalem', in *RB*, LVIII, 1951, 360-71.
R. PORTER, 'The Interpretation of 2 Samuel VI and Psalm CXXXII', in *JTS*, n.s. V, 1954, 161-73.
H. SCHMIDT, 'Jahwe und die Kulttradition von Jerusalem', in *ZAW*, LXVII, 1955, 147-97.
O. EISSFELDT, 'Silo und Jerusalem', in *Volume du Congrès, Strasbourg* (Supplement to VT, IV), 1957, Leiden, 138-47.
G. AHLSTRÖM, 'Natan och tempelbygget', in *Svensk Exegetisk Årsbok*, XXV, 1960, 5-22.

3

THE TEMPLE AT JERUSALEM

General works:

K. MOEHLENBRINK, *Der Tempel Salomos*, Stuttgart, 1932.
A. PARROT, *Le Temple de Jérusalem*, Neuchâtel-Paris, 1954.
L.-H. VINCENT and A.-M. STEVE, *Jérusalem de l'Ancien Testament*, II-III, Paris 1956, 373-610.

On Solomon's Temple and its plan:

K. GALLING, 'Das Allerheiligste in Salomos Tempel', in *JPOS*, XII, 1932, 43-6.
S. SMITH, 'Timber and Brick or Masonry Construction', in *PEQ*, 1941, 5-17.
L. WATERMAN, 'The Damaged "Blueprints" of the Temple of Solomon', in *JNES*, II, 1943, 284-94.
R. DE VAUX, 'Notes sur le Temple de Salomon', in *Qedem*, II, 1945, 48-58 (in Hebrew).
L. WATERMAN, 'The Treasuries of Solomon's Private Chapel', in *JNES*, VI, 1947, 161-3.
G. E. WRIGHT, 'Dr. Waterman's View concerning the Solomonic Temple', in *JNES*, VII, 1948, 53.
L. WATERMAN, 'A Rebuttal', *ibid.*, 54-5.
P. L. GARBER, 'Reconstructing Solomon's Temple', in *The Biblical Archaeologist*, XIV, 1951, 2-24.
G. E. WRIGHT, 'The Steven's Reconstruction of the Solomonic Temple', in *The Biblical Archaeologist*, XVIII, 1955, 41-4.
P. L. GARBER, 'Reconsidering the Reconstruction of Solomon's Temple', in *JBL*, LXXVII, 1958, 116-29.
W. F. ALBRIGHT and G. E. WRIGHT, 'Comments on Professor Garber's Article', *ibid.*, 129-33.

On the bronze pillars:

R. B. Y. SCOTT, 'The Pillars Jachin and Boaz', in *JBL*, LVIII, 1939, 143-9.
W. F. ALBRIGHT, 'Two Cressets from Marissa and the Pillars of Jachin and Boaz', in *BASOR*, **85**, 1942, 18-27.
H. G. MAY, 'The Two Pillars before the Temple of Solomon', in *BASOR*, **88**, 1942, 19-27.
S. YEIVIN, 'Jachin and Boaz', in *Eretz-Israel*, V (Volume . . . Mazar), 1958, 97-104 (in Hebrew with a summary in English).

For the analogies with, and influences on, Solomon's Temple:

C. W. MCEWAN, 'The Syrian Expedition of the Oriental Institute of the University of Chicago', in *American Journal of Archaeology*, XLI, 1937, 9-13 (Tell Tainat).
A. ALT, 'Verbreitung und Herkunft des syrischen Tempeltypus', in *PJB*, XXXV, 1939, 83-99= *Kleine Schriften*, II, Munich, 1955, 100-15.
L. WOOLEY, *Alalakh, An Account of the Excavations at Tell Atchana*, London, 1955, 82-9.
Y. YADIN, 'Excavations at Hazor, 1957', in *IEJ*, VIII, 1958, 11-14.

On the identification of the site:

The best expositions of the two opposing theses are:

H. SCHMIDT, *Der heilige Fels in Jerusalem*, Tübingen, 1933 (second thesis).
L.-H. VINCENT and A.-M. STEVE, *Jérusalem de l'Ancien Testament*, II-III, Paris, 1956, 587-95 (first thesis).

On the cherubim:

P. DHORME and L.-H. VINCENT, 'Les Chérubins', in *RB*, XXXV, 1926, 328-58, 481-95.

W. F. ALBRIGHT, 'What were the Cherubins?', in *The Biblical Archaeologist*, I, 1938, 1-3.
M. HARAN, 'The Ark of the Covenant and the Cherubs', in *Eretz-Israel*, V (*Volume Mazar*), 1958, 83-90 (in Hebrew, with a summary in English).
J. TRINQUET, art. 'Kerub', in *Dictionnaire de la Bible*, Supplément, V, 1957.
M. HARAN, 'The Ark and the Cherubim', in *IEJ*, IX, 1959, 30-8, 89-94.

On the furnishings:

W. F. ALBRIGHT, *Archaeology and the Religion of Israel*, Baltimore, 1942, 142-55.
L.-H. VINCENT, 'Les bassins roulants du Temple de Salomon', in *Miscellanea Biblica B. Ubach*, Montserrat, 1953, 147-59.

On the character of the Temple:

K. GALLING, 'Königliche und nichtkönigliche Stifter beim Tempel von Jerusalem', in *ZDPV*, LXVIII, 1946-51, 134-42.
L.-H. VINCENT, 'Le caractère du Temple de Salomon', in *Mélanges Bibliques . . . A. Robert*, Paris, 1957, 137-48.
B. MAZAR, 'Jerusalem—"King's Chapel" and "Royal City"', in *Judah and Jerusalem*, Jerusalem, 1957, 25-32 (in Hebrew, with a summary in English).

On the Temple of Ezechiel:

Apart from commentaries on Ezechiel:

A. LODS, 'Les cuisines du Temple de Jérusalem', in *Revue de l'Histoire des Religions*, CXXVII, 1944-A, 30-4.
L.-H. VINCENT, 'L'autel des holocaustes et le caractère du Temple d'Ézéchiel', in *Analecta Bollandiana*, LXVII, 1949 (*Mélanges Paul Peeters*), 7-20.
K. ELLIGER, 'Die grossen Tempelsakristeien im Verfassungsentwurf des Ezechiel', in *Geschichte und Altes Testament* (*Festschrift Alt*), Tübingen, 1953, 79-104.
TH. CHARY, *Les Prophètes et le culte à partir de l'Exil*, Paris-Tournai, 1955, chap. I-III.
H. GESE, *Der Verfassungsentwurf des Ezechiel* (*Kap.* 40-48), Tübingen, 1958.

On the post-exilic Temple:

J. JEREMIAS, 'Hesekieltempel und Serubbabeltempel', in *ZAW*, LII, 1934, 109-12.
R. DE VAUX, 'Les décrets de Cyrus et de Darius sur la reconstruction du Temple', in *RB*, XLVI, 1937, 29-57.
E. BICKERMAN, 'The Edict of Cyrus in Ezra 1', in *JBL*, LXV, 1946, 249-75.
S. SMITH, 'Foundations: Ezra IV, 12; V, 16; VI, 3', in *Essays Presented to J. H. Hertz*, 1946, 385-96.
E. BIKERMAN, 'Une proclamation séleucide relative au Temple de Jérusalem', in *Syria*, XXV, 1946-8, 67-85.
J. BRAND, 'Some Observations on the Second Temple Edifice', in *Tarbiz*, XXIX, 1959-60, 210-17 (in Hebrew).
M. AVI-YONA, *Reply to the Article by J. Brand, ibid.*, 218-221 (in Hebrew).

On the theology of the Temple:

FR. JEREMIAS, 'Das orientalische Heiligtun', in *ΑΓΓΕΛΟΣ*, *Archiv für neutestamentliche Zeitgeschichte*, IV, 1932, 56-69.
W. J. PHYTHIAN-ADAMS, *The People and the Presence*, London, 1942.
J. DANIÉLOU, *Le Signe du Temple ou de la Présence de Dieu*, Paris, 1942.
W. F. ALBRIGHT, *Archaeology and the Religion of Israel*, Baltimore, 1942, 142-55.
R. PATAI, *Man and Temple in Ancient Jewish Myth and Ritual*, London, 1947.
M. SCHMIDT, *Prophet und Tempel. Eine Studie zum Problem der Gottesnähe im Alten Testament*, Zollikon-Zürich, 1948.
G. FOHRER, 'Jeremias Tempelwort, 7, 1-15', in *Theologische Zeitschrift*, V, 1949, 401-17.
M. SIMON, 'La prophétie de Nathan et le Temple', in *RHPR*, XXXII, 1952, 41-58.
J. DANIÉLOU, 'Le symbolisme cosmique du Temple de Jérusalem', in *Symbolisme cosmique et Monuments religieux*, Paris, 1953, 61-4.
TH. CHARY, *Les Prophètes et le culte à partir de l'Exil*, Paris-Tournai, 1955.
M. J. CONGAR, *Le Mystère du Temple ou l'Économie de la Présence de Dieu à sa créature, de la Genèse à l'Apocalypse*, Paris, 1958.
E. L. EHRLICH, *Kultsymbolik im Alten Testament und im nachbiblischen Judeutum*, Stuttgart, 1959, 24-33.
G. WIDENGREN, 'Aspetti simbolici dei templi e luoghi di culto nel Vicino Oriente Antico', in *Numen*, VII, 1960, 1-25.

4

THE CENTRALIZATION OF THE CULT

On Jeroboam's schism, and Bethel:

O. EISSFELDT, 'Lade und Stierbild', in *ZAW*, LVIII, 1940-1, 190-215.

R. DE VAUX, 'Le schisme religieux de Jéroboam Ier', in *Angelicum*, XX, 1943=*Biblica et Orientalia R. P. Vosté dicata*, 77-91.
M. BIČ, 'Bet'el. Le sanctuaire du roi', in *Archiv Orientální*, XVII, 1, 1949, 46-63.

On the reforms of Ezechias and Josias, and Deuteronomy:

F. HORST, 'Die Kultusreform des Königs Josia', in *ZDMG*, LXXVII, 1923, 220-38.
K. BUDDE, 'Das Deuteronomium und die Reform König Josias', in *ZAW*, XLIV, 1926, 177-224.
A. C. WELCH, *The Work of the Chronicler*, London, 1939, ch. v.: 'Hezekiah's Reform'.
G. VON RAD, *Deuteronomium-Studien*², Göttingen, 1948.
H. H. ROWLEY, 'The Prophet Jeremiah and the Book of Deuteronomy', in *Studies in Old Testament Prophecy presented to Th. H. Robinson*, Edinburgh, 1950, 157-74.
H. CAZELLES, 'Jérémie et le Deutéronome', in *Recherches de Science Religieuse*, XXXVIII, 1951, 5-36.
H. JUNKER, 'Die Entstehungszeit des Ps 78 und das Deuteronomium', in *Biblica*, XXXIV, 1953, 487-500.
A. ALT, 'Die Heimat des Deuteronomiums', in *Kleine Schriften*, II, Munich, 1953, 250-75.
V. MAAG, 'Erwägungen zur deuteronomischen Kultzentralisation', in *VT*, VI, 1956, 10-18.
F. DUMERMUTH, 'Zur deuteronomischen Kulttheologie', in *ZAW*, LXX, 1958, 59-98.
A. JEPSEN, 'Die Reform des Josia', in *Festschrift F. Baumgärtel*, Erlangen, 1959, 97-108.

On the temple at Elephantine:

A. VINCENT, *La religion des judéo-araméens d'Éléphantine*, Paris, 1937, ch. VII.
E. G. KRAELING, *The Brooklyn Museum Aramaic Papyri*, New Haven, 1953, 76-119.
C. H. GORDON, 'The Origin of the Jews in Elephantine', in *JNES*, XIV, 1955, 56-8.
P. GRELOT, 'Le papyrus pascal d'Éléphantine et le problème du Pentateuque', in *VT*, V, 1955, 250-65.

On the temple at Leontopolis:

E. SCHÜRER, *Geschichte des jüdischen Volkes zur Zeit Jesu Christi*, III, Leipzig, 1909, 144-8.
M.-J. LAGRANGE, *Le Judaïsme avant Jésus-Christ*, Paris, 1931, 490-3.
A. FEUILLET, 'L'oracle d'Isaïe XIX (vv. 16-25) sur la conversion de l'Égypte', in *Recherches de Science religieuse*, XXXIX (*Mélanges Lebreton*, I), 1951, 65-87.
V. A. TCHERIKOVER and A. FUKS, *Corpus Papyrorum Judaicarum*, I, Jerusalem, 1957, 44-6.
A. BARUCQ, art. 'Léontopolis', in *Dictionnaire de la Bible, Supplément*, V, 1957, 359-72.

On the Samaritan temple:

E. BIKERMAN, 'Un document relatif à la persécution d'Antiochus IV Épiphane', in *Revue de l'Histoire des Religions*, CXV, 1937-A, 188-223.
P. ANTOINE, art. 'Garizim', in *Dictionnaire de la Bible, Supplément*, III, Paris, 1938, 535-61.
H. H. ROWLEY, 'Sanballat and the Samaritan Temple', in *BJRL*, XXXVIII, 1955-6, 166-98.

On the origin of synagogues:

K. GALLING, 'Erwägungen zur antiken Synagoge', in *ZDPV*, LXXII, 1956, 163-78.
J. MORGENSTERN, 'The Origin of the Synagogue', in *Studi Orientalistici in onore di G. Levi Della Vida*, II, Rome, 1956, 192-201.
V. A. TCHERIKOVER and A. FUKS, *Corpus Papyrorum Judaicarum*, I, Jerusalem, 1957, especially pp. 7-8.
E. L. EHRLICH, *Die Kultsymbolik im Alten Testament und im nachbiblischen Judentum*, Stuttgart, 1959, 85-96.

5

THE PRIESTLY OFFICE

On the priesthood in general:

There are no great modern works, but the following must still be consulted:

W. W. VON BAUDISSIN, *Die Geschichte des alttestamentlichen Priesterthums*, Leipzig, 1889.
A. VAN HOONACKER, *Le sacerdoce lévitique dans la loi et dans l'histoire des Hébreux*, London-Louvain, 1899.
G. HÖLSCHER, art. 'Levi', in PAULY-WISSOWA, *Real-Encyclopädie . . .*, XII 2, Stuttgart, 1925, 2155-208.
G. B. GRAY, *Sacrifice in the Old Testament. Its Theory and Practice*, Oxford, 1925, 179-270.

On the assumption of office:

E. LOHSE, *Die Ordination in Spätjudentum und in Neuen Testament*, Göttingen, 1951.
M. NOTH, *Amt und Berufung im Alten Testament*, Bonn, 1958.

On priests and divine oracles in general:

F. KÜCHLER, 'Das priesterliche Orakel in Israel und Juda', in *Abhandlungen zur semitischen Religionskunde und Sprachwissenschaft* (*Festschrift Baudissin*), Giessen, 1918, 285-301.

J. DÖLLER, *Die Wahrsagerei im Alten Testament*, Münster i. W., 1923.
J. BEGRICH, 'Das priesterliche Heilsorakel', in *ZAW*, LII, 1934, 81-92.

On the ephod:

E. SELLIN, 'Das israelitische Ephod', in *Orientalische Studien Th. Nöldeke . . .*, II, Giessen, 1906, 699-717.
W. R. ARNOLD, *Ephod and Ark* (Harvard Theological Studies, 3), Cambridge, Mass., 1917.
K. BUDDE, 'Ephod und Lade', in *ZAW*, XXXIX, 1921, 1-42.
J. GABRIEL, *Untersuchungen über das alttestamentliche Priestertum, mit besonderer Berücksichtigung des hohenpriesterlichen Ornates*, Vienna, 1933, 44-70.
E. SELLIN, 'Ephod und Terafim', in *JPOS*, XIV, 1934, 185-94.
H. THIERSCH, *Ependytes und Ephod. Gottesbild und Priesterkleid im Alten Vorderasien*, Stuttgart, 1936.
E. SELLIN, 'Zu Efod und Terafim', in *ZAW*, LV, 1937, 296-8.
H. G. MAY, 'Ephod and Ariel', in *AJSL*, LVI, 1939, 44-52.
W. F. ALBRIGHT, 'Are Ephod and Terafim mentioned in the Ras Shamra Texts?', in *BASOR*, **83**, 1941, 39-42.
J. MORGANSTERN, 'The Ark, the Ephod and the Tent of Meeting', in *HUCA*, XVIII, 1943-4, 1-17.
M. HARAN, 'L'éphod d'après les sources bibliques' (in Hebrew), in *Tarbiz*, XXIV, 1955, 381-91.
K. ELLIGER, 'Ephod und Choschen', in *VT*, VIII, 1958, 19-35.

On the Urim and Thummim:

R. PRESS, 'Das Ordal im Alten Testament', II, in *ZAW*, LI, 1933, 227-31.
A. JIRKU, 'Die Mimation in den nordsemitischen Sprachen und einige Bezeichnungen der altisraelitischen Mantik', in *Biblica*, XXXIX, 1953, 78-80.
J. LINDBLÖM, 'Lottdragning och Lottkastning i Gammeltestamentliga Texter', in *Septentrionalia et Orientalia Studia B. Karlgren dedicata*, Lund, 1960, 262-9.

On priests and teaching:

J. BEGRICH, 'Die priesterliche Tora', in *Werden und Wesen des Alten Testaments*, Berlin, 1936, 63-88.
G. ÖSTBORN, *Tora in the Old Testament*, Lund, 1945.
O. PLÖGER, 'Priester und Prophet', in *ZAW*, LXIII, 1951, 157-92.
H. W. WOLFF, '"Wissen um Gott" bei Hosea als Urform von Theologie', in *Evangelische Theologie*, XII, 1952-3, 533-54.

On priests and sacrifice:

L. GAUTIER, 'Pretre ou sacrificateur?' in *Études sur la religion d'Israël*, Lausanne, 1927, 247-76.
A. E. J. RAWLINSON, 'Priesthood and Sacrifice in Judaism and Christianity', in *Expository Times*, LX, 1949, 115-21.

On the priest as mediator:

A. ROBERT, art. 'Médiation dans l'Ancien Testament', in *Dictionnaire de la Bible, Supplément*, V, Paris, 1957, 1004-8.

6

THE LEVITES

Etymology:

Apart from the classical dictionaries (with references), see:

M. NOTH, 'Remarks on the Sixth Volume of Mari Texts', in *Journal of Semitic Studies*, I, 1956, 327.
L. KOPF, 'Arabische Etymologien und Parallelen zum Bibelwörterbuch', in *VT*, VIII, 1958, 181-2.

On the Levitical tradition:

G. HÖLSCHER, art. 'Levi', in PAULY-WISSOWA, *Real-Encyclopädie . . .*, XII 2, 1925, 2155-208.
K. MÖHLENBRINK, 'Die levitischen Überlieferungen des Alten Testaments', in *ZAW*, LII, 1934, 184-231.
A. LEFÈVRE, 'Notes d'exégèse sur les généalogies des Qehatites', in *Recherches de Science religieuse*, XXXVII, 1950, 287-92.

On the historical development:

J. GOETTESBERGER, 'Das alttestamentliche Priestertum und Ezechiel', in *Episcopus, Festgabe Faulhaber*, Regensburg, 1949, 1-19.
M. GREENBERG, 'A New Approach to the History of the Israelite Priesthood', in *JAOS*, LXX, 1950, 41-6.
G. E. WRIGHT, 'The Levites in Deuteronomy', in *VT*, IV, 1954, 325-30.
E. NIELSEN, *Shechem. A Traditio-Historical Investigation*, Copenhagen, 1955, 264-86.
CH. HAURET, 'Aux origines du sacerdoce danite, à propos de Jud. 18, 30-1', in *Mélanges Bibliques . . . A. Robert*, Paris, 1957, 105-13.

On Levitical towns:

W. F. ALBRIGHT, 'The List of Levitic Cities', in *Louis Ginzberg Jubilee Volume*, I, New York, 1945, 49-73.
A. ALT, 'Bemerkungen zu einigen judäischen Ortslisten des Alten Testaments', in *Beiträge zur biblischen Landes- und Altertumskunde* (=*ZDPV*), LXVII, 1951, 193-210=*Kleine Schriften*, II, Munich, 1953, 289-305.
A. ALT, 'Festungen und Levitenorte im Lande Juda', in *Kleine Schriften*, II, Munich, 1953, 306-15.
M. HARAN, 'The Levitical Cities: Utopia and Historical Reality', in *Tarbiz*, XXVII, 1957-8, 421-39 (in Hebrew, with a summary in English).
B. MAZAR, 'The Cities of the Priests and Levites', in *Congress Volume, Oxford*, 1959 (Supplement VII to *VT*), Leiden, 1960, 193-205.

On the origin of the Levites:

H. GRIMME, 'Der südarabische Levitismus und sein Verhältnis zum Levitismus in Israel', in *Museon*, XXXVII, 1924, 169-99.
L. WATERMAN, 'Some Determining Factors in the Northward Progress of Levi', in *JAOS*, LVII, 1937, 375-80.
TH. J. MEEK, 'Moses and the Levites', in *AJSL*, LVI, 1939, 113-20.
H. H. ROWLEY, 'Early Levite History and the Question of the Exodus', in *JNES*, III, 1944, 73-8.
S. YEIVIN, 'The Exodus', in *Tarbiz*, XXX, 1960-1, 1-7 (in Hebrew).

7

THE PRIESTHOOD OF JERUSALEM UNDER THE MONARCHY

On Sadoq and the Sadoqites:

TH. MEEK, 'Aaron and the Sadocides', *AJSL*, XLV, 1928-9, 149-66.
E. AUERBACH, 'Die Herkunft der Sadokiden', in *ZAW*, XLIX, 1931, 327-8.
A. BENTZEN, *Studier over det Zadokidiske Praesterkabs historie*, Copenhagen, 1931.
A. BENTZEN, 'Zur Geschichte der Ṣadoiḳden', in *ZAW*, LI, 1933, 173-6.
K. BUDDE, 'Die Herkunft Ṣadok's', in *ZAW*, LII, 1934, 42-50, cf. 160.
H. H. ROWLEY, 'Zadok and Nehustan', in *JBL*, LVIII, 1939, 113-41.
H. H. ROWLEY, 'Melchizedek and Zadok', in *Festschrift Bertholet*, Tübingen, 1950, 461-72.

On the priestly hierarchy:

J. MORGENSTERN, 'A Chapter in the History of the High Priesthood', in *AJSL*, LV, 1938, 1-24, 183-97, 360-77.

On the revenues of the priests:

O. EISSFELDT, *Erstlinge und Zehnten*, Leipzig, 1917.

On the lower-ranking staff:

M. LÖHR, *Die Stellung des Weibes zu Yahwe-Religion und -Kult*, Leipzig, 1908.
G. B. GRAY, *Sacrifice in the Old Testament. Its Theory and Practice*, Oxford, 1925, 184-93.
B. D. EERDMANS, 'Thoda-Songs and Temple-Singers', in *Oudtestamentische Studiën*, I 2, 1942, 162-75.
W. F. ALBRIGHT, *Archaeology and the Religion Of Israel*, Baltimore, 1942, 125-8.
M. HARAN, 'The Gibeonites, the Nethinim and the Servants of Salomon', in *Judah and Israel*, Jerusalem, 1957, 37-45 (in Hebrew, with a summary in English).

On the cult prostitutes:

B. S. BROOKS, 'Fertility Cult Functionaries in the Old Testament', in *JBL*, LX, 1941, 227-53.
J. P. ASMUSSEN, 'Bemerkungen zur sakralen Prostitution im Alten Testament', in *Studia Theologica*, XI, 1957, 167-92.

On cultic prophets:

S. MOWINCKEL, *Psalmenstudien* III: *Kultprophetie und prophetische Psalmen*, Kristiania (Oslo), 1923.
A. R. JOHNSON, *The Cultic Prophet in Ancient Israel*, Cardiff, 1944.
A. HALDAR, *Associations of Cult Prophets among the Ancient Semites*, Uppsala, 1945.
N. W. PORTEOUS, 'Prophet and Priest in Israel', in *Expository Times*, LXII, 1950-1, 4-9.
O. PLÖGER, 'Priester und Prophet', in *ZAW*, LXIII, 1951, 157-92.
E. WURTHWEIN, 'Ursprung der prophetischen Gerichtsrede', in *Zeitschrift für Theologie und Kirche*, XLIX, 1952, 1-16.
F. HESSE, 'Wurzelt die prophetische Gerichtsrede im israelitischen Kult?', in *ZAW*, LXV, 1953, 45-53.
R. HENTSCHKE, *Die Stellung der vorexilischen Schriftpropheten zum Kultus*, Berlin, 1957.
H. H. ROWLEY, 'Ritual and the Hebrew Prophets', in S. H. HOOKE (ed.), *Myth, Ritual and Kingship*, Oxford, 1958, 236-60.

8

The Priesthood after the Exile

On the priests and the Levites:

G. von Rad, *Das Geschichtsbild des chronistischen Werkes*, Stuttgart, 1930.

R. Meyer, 'Levitische Emancipazionsbestrebungen in nach-exilischen Zeit', in *Orientalistische Literaturzeitung*, XLI, 1938, 721-8.

A. C. Welch, *The Work of the Chronicler, Its Purpose and its Date*, London, 1939.

A. Alt, 'Bemerkungen zu einigen judäischen Ortslisten des Alten Testaments', in *Beiträge zur biblischen Landes- und Altertumskunde* (= *ZDVP*), LXVIII, 1951, 193-210=*Kleine Schriften*, II, Munich, 1953, 289-305.

On the line of Aaron and the line of Sadoq:

M. Noth, *Überlieferungsgeschichte des Pentateuch*, Stuttgart, 1948, 195-9.

F. S. North, 'Aaron's Rise in Prestige', in *ZAW*, LXVI, 1954, 191-9.

H. G. Judge, 'Zadok and Abiathar', in *JTS*, n.s. VII, 1956, 70-4.

On the high priest:

J. Gabriel, *Untersuchungen über das alttestamentliche Hohepriestertum*, Vienna, 1933.

J. Morgenstern, 'A Chapter in the History of the High Priesthood', in *AJSL*, LV, 1938, 16-24; 183-97; 360-77.

F. Stummer, 'Gedanken über die Stellung des Hohenpriesters in der alttestamentlichen Gemeinde', in *Episcopus, Festgabe Faulhaber*, Regensburg, 1949, 19-49.

A. De Buck, 'La fleur au front du Grand Prêtre', in *Oudtestamentische Studiën*, IX, 1951, 18-29.

S. Zeitlin, 'The Titles High Priest and the Nasi of the Sanhedrin', in *JQR*, XLVIII, 1957-8, 1-5.

M. Noth, *Amt und Berufung im Alten Testament*, Bonn, 1958, 11-16.

J. Jeremias, *Jerusalem zur Zeit Jesu*², Stuttgart, 1958 (almost exactly the same as the 1923 edition). See especially B 3-59.

E. Cothenet, art. 'Onction', in *Dictionnaire de la Bible, Supplément*, VI, Paris, 1959, 701-32.

On the revenues of the clergy:

There is no modern monograph, but the following should still be consulted:

E. Schurer, *Geschichte des jüdischen Volkes im Zeitalter Jesu-Christi*, II, Leipzig, 1907, 297-317.

O. Eissfeldt, *Erstlinge und Zehnten im Alten Testament*, Leipzig, 1917.

M. A. Beek, 'Hasidic Conceptions of Kingship in the Maccabean Period', in *The Sacral Kingship* (Supplement IV to *Numen*), Leiden, 1959, 349-55.

9

Altars

J. de Groot, *Die Altäre des salomonischen Tempelhofes*, Stuttgart, 1924.

K. Galling, *Der Altar in den Kulturen des Alten Orients*, Berlin, 1924.

G. B. Gray, *Sacrifice in the Old Testament. Its Theory and Practice*, Oxford, 1925, 96-178.

H. M. Wiener, *The Altars of the Old Testament*, Leipzig, 1927.

M. Löhr, *Das Räucheropfer im Alten Testament. Eine archäologische Untersuchung*, Halle, 1927.

W. F. Albright, *Archaeology and the Religion of Israel*², Baltimore, 1946, 150-2.

L.-H. Vincent, 'L'autel des holocaustes et le caractère du Temple d'Ézéchiel', in *Analecta Bollandiana*, LXVII, 1949 (*Mélanges Paul Peeters*), 7-20.

R. De Langhe, *Het gouden altaar in de Israëlitische eredienst*, Brussels, 1952.

A. Parrot, 'Autels et installations cultuelles à Mari', in *Congress Volume, Copenhagen* (Supplement to *VT*, I), Leiden, 1953, 112-19.

R. De Langhe, 'L'autel d'or du temple de Jérusalem', in *Studia Biblica et Orientalia*, I. *Vetus Testamentum*, Rome, 1959, 342-60=*Biblica*, XL, 1959, 476-94.

10

The Ritual of Sacrifice

On sacrifices in general:

G. B. Gray, *Sacrifice in the Old Testament. Its Theory and Practice*, Oxford, 1925.

A. Wendel, *Das Opfer in der altisraelitischen Religion*, Leipzig, 1927.

W. O. E. Oesterley, *Sacrifices in Ancient Israel. The Origin, Purposes and Development*, London, 1937.

On certain particular rites:

A. Vincent, 'Les rites de balancement (tenoûphâh) et de prélèvement (teroûmâh) dans le sacrifice de communion de l'Ancien Testament', in *Mélanges Syriens offerts à M. R. Dussaud*, I, Paris, 1939, 267–72.

W. B. Stevenson, 'Hebrew 'olah and zebach Sacrifices', in *Festschrift Bertholet*, Tübingen, 1950, 109–18.

G. R. Driver, 'Three Technical Terms in the Pentateuch' (for 'azkârah and t^{e}nûphah), in *Journal of Semitic Studies*, I, 1956, 97–105.

N. H. Snaith, 'Sacrifices in the Old Testament' (for zèbaḥ, minḥah, ḥaṭṭa'th), in *VT*, VII, 1957, 308–17.

L. Moraldi, 'Terminologia cultuale israelitica', in *Rivista degli Studi Orientali*, XXXII, 1957 (*Scritti in onore di Giuseppe Furlani*, I), 321–37.

L. Rost, 'Erwägungen zum israelitischen Brandopfer', in *Von Ugarit nach Qumran* (*Festschrift Eissfeldt*), Berlin, 1958, 177–83.

A. Charbel, 'Virtus sanguinis non expiatoria in sacrificiis *š^{e}lamîm*', in *Sacra Pagina, I* (*Vetus Testamentum*), Gembloux, 1959, 366–76.

On expiatory sacrifices:

D. Schötz, *Schuld- und Sündopfer im Alten Testament*, Breslau, 1930.

P. Saydon, 'Sin-Offering and Trespass-Offering', in *Catholic Biblical Quarterly*, VIII, 1946, 393–9.

L. Moraldi, *Espiazione sacrificiale e riti espiatori nell'ambiente biblico e nell'Antico Testamento*, Rome, 1956.

On incense-offerings:

M. Löhr, *Das Räuchopfer im Alten Testament. Eine archäologische Untersuchung*, Halle, 1927.

A. Vincent, *La religion des judéo-araméens d'Éléphantine*, Paris, 1937, 212–23.

M. Haran, 'The Use of Incense in the Ancient Israelite Ritual', in *VT*, X, 1960, 113–29.

11

The History of Sacrifice in Israel

The bibliography is the same as for the preceding chapter, but add:

R. Hentschke, *Die Stellung der vorexilischen Schriftpropheten zum Kultus*, Berlin, 1957.

G. W. van Beck and A. Jamme, 'An Inscribed South Arabian Clay Stamp from Bethel', in *BASOR*, **151**, 1958, 9–16.

12

The Origin of Israelite Ritual

On sacrifice among the Assyrians and Babylonians:

G. Furlani, *Il sacrificio nella religione dei Semiti di Babilonia e Assiria*, Rome, 1932.

E. Dhorme, 'Le sacrifice accadien à propos d'un ouvrage récent', in *Revue de l'Histoire des Religions*, CVI, 1932-A, 107–25.

F. Blome, *Die Opfermaterie in Babylonien und Israel*, Rome, 1934.

G. Furlani, *Riti babilonesi e assiri*, Udine, 1940.

E. Dhorme, 'Les religions de Babylonie et d'Assyrie', in *Mana. Introduction à l'Histoire des Religions*, I II, Paris, 1945, 220–33.

R. Labat, 'Le sort des substituts royaux en Assyrie au temps des Sargonides', in *Revue d'Assyriologie*, XL, 1945–6, 123–42.

G. Goossens, 'Les substituts royaux en Babylonie', in *Ephemerides Theologicae Lovanienses*, XXV, 1949, 383–400.

J. Gray, 'Royal Substitutes in the Ancient Near East', in *PEQ*, 1955, 180–2.

W. von Soden, 'Beiträge zum Verständnis der assyrischen Briefe über die Ersatzkönigsriten', in *Festschrift V. Christian*, Vienna, 1956, 100–7.

W. G. Lambert, 'A Part of the Ritual of the Substitute King', in *AfO*, XVIII, 1, 1957, 109–12.

On sacrifice among the ancient Arabs:

J. Wellhausen, *Reste arabischen Heidenthums*[2], Berlin, 1897.

J. Henninger, 'Das Opfer in den altsüdarabischen Hochkulturen', in *Anthropos*, XXXVII–XL, 1942–4, 779–810.

J. Henninger, 'Le sacrifice chez les Arabes', in *Ethnos* (Stockholm), XII, 1948, 1–16.

G. Ryckmans, 'Le sacrifice DBH dans les inscriptions safaïtiques', in *HUCA*, XXXIII 1, 1950–1, 431–8.
G. Ryckmans, *Les religions arabes préislamiques*[2], Louvain, 1951.
J. Henninger, 'Ist der sogenannte Nilus-Bericht eine brauchbare religionsgeschichtliche Quelle?', in *Anthropos*, L, 1955, 81–148.
J. Chelhod, *Le sacrifice chez les Arabes*, Paris, 1955.
J. Henninger, 'Zur Frage des Haaropfers bei den Semiten', in *Die Wiener Schule der Völkerkunde, Festschrift zum 25jährigen Bestand, 1929–1954*, Vienna, 1956, 359–68.

On Canaanite sacrifice:

Th. H. Gaster, 'The Service of the Sanctuary: a Study in Hebrew Survivals', in *Mélanges Syriens offerts à M. R. Dussaud*, II, Paris, 1939, 577–82.
R. Dussaud, *Les origines cananéennes du sacrifice israélite*[2], Paris, 1941.
R. Dussaud, *Les découvertes de Ras Shamra et l'Ancien Testament*[2], Paris, 1941.
D. M. L. Urie, 'Sacrifice among the West Semites', in *PEQ*, 1949, 67–82.
J. Gray, 'Cultic Affinities between Israel and Ras Shamra', in *ZAW*, LXII, 1949–50, 207–20.
A. De Guglielmo, 'Sacrifices in the Ugaritic Texts', in *Catholic Biblical Quarterly*, XVII, 1955, 76–96.
J. G. Février, 'Le vocabulaire sacrificiel punique', in *Journal Asiatique*, CCXLIII, 1955, 49–63.
J. Gray, 'The Legacy of Canaan' (Supplement to *VT*, V), Leiden, 1957.
J. G. Février, 'Remarques sur le grand tarif dit de Marseilles', in *Cahiers de Byrsa*, VIII, 1958–9, 35–40.

On connections with Greek sacrifice:

R. K. Yerkes, *Sacrifice in Greek and Roman Religions and Early Judaism*, New York, 1952.
L. Rost, 'Erwägungen zum israelitischen Brandopfer', in *Von Ugarit nach Qumran* (*Festschrift Eissfeldt*), Berlin, 1958, 177–83.

On human sacrifice:

A. George, 'Le sacrifice d'Abraham', in *Études de Critique et d'Histoire Religieuses* (*Mélanges Vaganay*), Lyons, 1948, 99–110.
F. M. Th. Böhl, 'Das Menschenopfer bei den alten Sumerern', in his *Opera Minora*, Groningen, 1953, 162–73, 488–90.
H. Cazelles, 'David's Monarchy and the Gibeonite Claim, II Sam. XXI, 1–14', in *PEQ*, 1955, 165–75.
A. S. Kapelrud, 'King and Fertility, A Discussion of II Sam. 21: 1–14', in *Interpretationes ad Vetus Testamentum pertinentes S. Mowinckel . . . missae*, Oslo, 1955, 113–22.
J. Henninger, 'Menschenopfer bei den Arabern', in *Anthropos*, LIII, 1958, 721s, 776s.

On 'sacrifice to Moloch':

O. Eissfeldt, *Molk als Opferbegriff im Punischen und Hebräischen und das Ende des Gottes Moloch*, Halle a. Saale, 1935.
R. Dussaud, 'Précisions épigraphiques touchant les sacrifices puniques d'enfants', in *Comptes Rendus de l'Académie des Inscriptions et Belles-Lettres* (Paris), 1946, 371–87.
W. Kornfeld, 'Der Moloch, eine Untersuchung zur Theorie O. Eissfeldts', in *Wiener Zeitschrift für die Kunde des Morgenlandes*, LI, 1952, 287–313.
J. G. Février, 'Molchomor', in *Revue de l'Histoire des Religions*, CXLIII, 1953–A, 8–18.
R. Charlier, 'La nouvelle série des stèles puniques de Constantine et la question des sacrifices dits "molchomor" en relation avec l'expression "bšrm btm"', in *Karthago*, VI, 1953, 3–48.
J. G. Février, 'Le vocabulaire sacrificiel punique', in *Journal Asiatique*, CCXLIII, 1955, 49–63.
J. G. Février, 'Un sacrifice d'enfants chez les Numides', in *Annuaire de l'Institut de Philologie et d'Histoire Orientales et Slaves*, XIII (*Mélanges Isidore Lévy*), Brussels, 1955, 161–71.
E. Dhorme, 'Le dieu Baal et le dieu Moloch dans la tradition biblique', in *Anatolian Studies*, VI, 1956, 57–61.
H. Cazelles, art. 'Molok', in *Dictionnaire de la Bible, Supplément*, V, Paris, 1957, 1337–46.
J. Hoftijzer, 'Eine Notiz zum punischen Kinderopfer', in *VT*, VIII, 1958, 288–92.

13

The Religious Value of Sacrifice

For the general bibliography, see chapter X. In addition:

A. Bertholet, 'Zum Verständnis des alttestamentlichen Opfergedankens', in *JBL*, XLIX, 1930, 218–33.
A. Metzinger, 'Die Substitutionstheorie und das alttestamentliche Opfer', in *Biblica*, XXI, 1940, 159–87; 247–72; 353–77.
J. E. Coleran, 'Origins of the Old Testament Sacrifice', in *Catholic Biblical Quarterly*, II, 1940, 130–44.
R. Dussaud, *Les origines cananéennes du sacrifice israélite*[2], Paris, 1941.
H. Wheeler Robinson, 'Hebrew Sacrifice and Prophetic Symbolism', in *JTS*, XLVIII, 1942, 129–39.
A. Bertholet, 'Der Sinn des kultischen Opfers', in *Abhandlungen der preussischen Akademie der Wissenschaften*, 1942, Phil.-hist. Klasse, 2, Berlin, 1942.

H. H. Rowley, 'The Meaning of Sacrifice in the Old Testament', in *BJRL*, XXXIII, 1950–1, 74–110.
G. Van der Leeuw, *Phänomenologie der Religion*², Tübingen, 1956, 393–406.
W. Herrmann, 'Götterspeise und Göttertrank in Ugarit und Israel', in *ZAW*, LXXII, 1960, 205–16.

On polemic against sacrifice:

P. Volz, 'Die radikale Ablehnung der Kultreligion durch die alttestamentlichen Propheten', in *Zeitschrift für systematische Theologie*, XIV, 1937, 63–85.
C. Lattey, 'The Prophets and Sacrifice: a Study in Biblical Relativity', in *JTS*, XLII, 1941, 155–65.
J. E. Coleran, 'The Prophets and Sacrifice', in *Theological Studies*, V, 1944, 411–38.
N. H. Snaith, 'The Prophets and Sacrifice and Salvation', in *Expository Times*, LVIII, 1946–7, 152–3
H. H. Rowley, 'The Prophets and Sacrifice', in *Expository Times*, LVIII, 1946–7, 305–7.
H. W. Hertzberg, 'Die prophetische Kritik am Kult', in *TLZ*, LXXV, 1950, 219–26.
J. M. Baumgartner, 'Sacrifice and Worship among the Jewish Sectarians of the Dead Sea (Qumrân) Scrolls', in *Harvard Theological Review*, XLVI, 1953, 141–59.
H. Kruse, 'Die "dialektische Negation" als semitisches Idiom', in *VT*, IV, 1954, 385–400.
Th. Chary, *Les prophètes et le culte à partir de l'Exil*, Paris–Tournai, 1955.
J. Carmignac, 'L'utilité ou l'inutilité des sacrifices sanglants dans la "Règle de la Communauté" de Qumrân', in *RB*, LXIII, 1956, 524–32.
R. Hentschke, *Die Stellung der vorexilischen Schriftpropheten zum Kultus*, Berlin, 1957.
R. Press, 'Die Gerichtspredigt der vorexilischen Propheten und der Versuch einer Steigerung der kultischen Leistung', in *ZAW*, LXX, 1958, 181–4.
R. Dobbie, 'Deuteronomy and the Prophetic Attitude to Sacrifice', in *Scottish Journal of Theology*, XII, 1959, 68–82.

14

Secondary Acts of the Cult

On prayer:

N. Johansson, *Parakletoi, Vorstellungen von Fürsprechern*, Lund, 1940.
P. A. H. De Boer, *De vorbeede in het Oud Testament=Oudtestamentische Studiën*, III, 1943.
E. Peterson, 'Die geschichtliche Bedeutung der jüdischen Gebetsrichtung', in *Theologische Zeitschrift*, III, 1947, 1–15=*Frühkirche, Judentum und Gnosis*, Rome–Freiburg, 1959, 1–14.
N. B. Johnson, 'Prayer in the Apocrypha and Pseudepigrapha: a Study of the Jewish Concept of God' (*JBL*, Monograph Series, III), Philadelphia, 1948.
D. R. Ap-Thomas, 'Notes on Some Terms Relating to Prayer', in *VT*, VI, 1956, 225–41.

On rites of purification and consecration:

J. Döller, *Die Reinheits- und Speisegesetze des Alten Testaments*, Münster i. W., 1917.
J. Scheftelowitz, 'Das Opfer der roten Kuh (Num 19)', in *ZAW*, XXXIX, 1922, 113–23.
W. H. Gipsen, 'Clean and Unclean', in *Oudtestamentische Studiën*, V, 1948, 190–7.
L. Koehler, 'Aussatz', in *ZAW*, LXVII, 1955, 290–1.
J. Bowman, 'Did the Qumran Sect burn the Red Heifer?', in *Revue de Qumrân*, I, 1958, 73–84.
P. Reymond, 'L'eau, sa vie et sa signification dans l'Ancien Testament' (*Supplement to VT*, VI), Leiden, 1958.

On vows and the Nazirites:

M. Jastrow, 'The "nazir" Legislation', in *JBL*, XXXIII, 1914, 265–85.
H. Salmanowitch, *Das Naziräat in Bibel und Talmud*, Wilna, 1931.
A. Wendel, *Das israelitisch-jüdische Gelübde*, Berlin, 1932.
J. Pedersen, *Israel, its Life and Culture*, III–IV, London, 1947, 264–6.
J. Henninger, 'Zur Frage des Haaropfers bei den Semiten', in *Die Wiener Schule der Völkerkunde, Festschrift zur 25jährigen Beistand 1929–1954*, Vienna, 1956, 359–68.

15

The Liturgical Calendar

On the ordinary services in the Temple:

E. Schürer, *Geschichte des jüdischen Volkes im Zeitalter Jesu-Christi*, II⁴, Leipzig, 1907, 336–57.

On the liturgical calendars:

No one has yet made a comparative study of the liturgical calendars. We can only refer to the bibliography given in later chapters for the different feasts, and to general studies of Israelite feasts, in particular:

I. ELBOGEN, 'Die Feier der drei Wallfahrtsfeste im zweiten Tempel', in *46. Bericht der Hochschule für die Wissenschaft des Judentums in Berlin*, Berlin, 1929, 25-46.

I. ELBOGEN, *Der jüdische Gottesdienst in seiner geschichtlichen Entwicklung*, Leipzig, 1931, 107-54.

E. AUERBACH, 'Die Feste im alten Israel', in *VT*, VIII, 1958, 1-18.

E. KUTSCH, 'Feste und Feiern. II, in Israel', in *Die Religion in Geschichte und Gegenwart*³, II, Leipzig, 1958, 910-17.

E. L. EHRLICH, *Kultsymbolik im Alten Testament und im nachbiblischen Judentum*, Stuttgart, 1959, 52-82.

J. VAN GOUDOEVER, *Biblical Calendars*, Leiden, 1959.

16

THE SABBATH DAY

J. MEINHOLD, *Sabbat und Woche im Alten Testament*, Göttingen, 1905.

J. HEHN, 'Siebenzahl und Sabbat' (*Leipziger semitische Studien*, II 5), Leipzig, 1907.

J. MEINHOLD, 'Die Entstehung des Sabbats', in *ZAW*, XXIX, 1909, 81-112.

J. MEINHOLD, 'Zur Sabbatfrage', in *ZAW*, XXXVI, 1916, 108-10.

T. J. MEEK, 'The Sabbath in the Old Testament', in *JBL*, XXXIII, 1914, 201-12.

B. B. Eerdmans, 'Der Sabbat', in *Vom Alten Testament* (*Festschrift Marti*), Giessen, 1925, 79-83.

K. BUDDE, 'The Sabbath and the Week', in *JTS*, XXX, 1929, 1-15.

J. MEINHOLD and K. BUDDE, 'Zur Sabbatfrage', in *ZAW*, XLVIII, 1930, 121-45.

W. W. CANNON, 'The Weekly Sabbath', in *ZAW*, XLIX, 1931, 325-7.

E. J. KRAELING, 'The Present Status of the Sabbath Question', in *AJSL*, XLIX, 1932-3, 218-28.

S. LANGDON, *Babylonian Menologies and the Semitic Calendars*, London, 1935.

G. SCHRENK, 'Sabbat oder Sonntag?', in *Judaica*, II, 1946-7, 169-89.

H. M. FÉRET, 'Les sources bibliques', in *Le Jour du Seigneur* (Congrès de Pastorale Liturgique, Lyon), Paris, 1948, 41-404.

N. H. TUR-SINAI, 'Sabbat und Woche', in *Bibliotheca Orientalis*, VIII, 1951, 14-24.

H. H. ROWLEY, 'Moses and the Decalogue', in *BJRL*, XXXIV, 1951-2, 81-118.

G. J. BOTTERWECK, 'Der Sabbat im Alten Testament', in *Theologische Quartalschrift*, CXXXIV, 1954, 134-47; 448-57.

TH. H. GASTER, 'Le jour du repos', in *Évidences*, 43, Nov. 1954, 43-8.

R. NORTH, 'The Derivation of Sabbath', in *Biblica*, XXXVI, 1955, 182-201.

E. JENNI, *Die theologische Begründung des Sabbatgebotes im Alten Testament*, Zürich, 1956.

E. VOGT, 'Hat "sabbat" im AT den Sinn von "Woche"?', in *Biblica*, XL, 1959, 1008-11.

D. GILAT, 'The Thirty-nine Classes of Work forbidden on the Sabbath', in *Tarbiz*, XXIX, 1959-60, 222-8 (in Hebrew).

E. LOHSE, art. 'Σάβαττον' in *Theologisches Wörterbuch zum Neuen Testament*, VII, 1960, 1-34.

A. CAQUOT, 'Remarques sur la fête de la "néoménie" dans l'ancien Israël', in *Revue de l'Histoire des Religions*, CLVIII, 1960-ii, 1-28.

17

THE ANCIENT FEASTS OF ISRAEL

On the Passover and the feast of Unleavened Bread:

G. BEER, *Pesachim* (*Die Mischna . . .*, II, 3), Giessen, 1912.

F. HORST, *Das Privilegrecht Yahves. Rechtsgeschichtliche Untersuchungen zum Deuteronomium*, Göttingen, 1930.

J. JEREMIAS, *Die Passahfeier der Samaritaner und ihre Bedeutung für das Vertständnis der altt. Passahüberlieferung*, Giessen, 1932.

J. PEDERSEN, 'Passahfest und Passahlegende', in *ZAW*, LII, 1934, 161-75.

J. PEDERSEN, *Israel. Its Life and Culture, III-IV*, London, 1940. Appendix I: 'The Crossing of the Dead Sea and the Paschal Legend', 728-37.

L. ROST, 'Weidewechsel und altisraelitischer Festkalendar', in *ZDPV*, LXVI, 1943, 205-16.

A. DUPONT-SOMMER, 'Sur la fête de Pâque dans les documents araméens d'Éléphantine', in *Revue des Études Juives*, CVII, 1946-7, 39-51.

TH. H. GASTER, *Passover. Its History and Traditions*, New York, 1949.

J. HENNINGER, 'Les fêtes du printemps chez les Arabes et leurs implications historiques', in *Revista do Museu Paulista* (São Paulo); IV, 1950, 389-432.

H. J. KRAUS, 'Gilgal', in *VT*, I, 1951, 181-99.

S. Mowinckel, 'Die vermeintliche "Passahlegende", Ex 1-15', in *Studia Theologica*, V, 1951, 66-88.
I. Engnell, 'Paesaḥ-Maṣṣot and the Problem of "Patternism"', in *Orientalia Suecana*, I, 1952, 39-50.
P. Grelot, 'Études sur le "Papyrus Pascal" d'Éléphantine', in *VT*, IV, 1954, 348-84.
H. Haag, 'Ursprung und Sinn der alttestamentlichen Paschafeier', in *Luzerner Theologische Studien*, I, 1954, 17-46.
P. Grelot, 'Le Paphyrus Pascal d'Éléphantine et le problème du Pentateuque', in *VT*, V, 1955, 250-65.
B. Couroyer, 'L'origine égyptienne du mot "Pâque"', in *RB*, LXII, 1955, 481-96.
J. Henninger, 'Zum Verbot des Knochenzerbrechens bei den Semitern', in *Studi Orientalistici in onore di G. Levi della Vida*, I, Rome, 1956, 448-58.
H. J. Kraus, 'Zur Geschichte des Passah-Massot-Festes im Alten Testament,' in *Evangelische Theologie*, XVIII, 1958, 47-67.
E. Kutsch, 'Erwägungen zur Geschichte der Passahfeier und des Massotfestes', in *Zeitschrift für Theologie und Kirche*, LV, 1958, 1-35.
H. Haag, art. 'Pâque', in *Dictionnaire de la Bible, Supplement*, VI, 1960, 1120-49.

On the feast of Weeks:

E. Brögelmann, 'Pfingsten in Altisrael', in *Monatschrift für Gottesdienst und kirchliche Kunst*, XLIV, 1939, 119-28.
K. H. Rengstorf, 'Christliches und jüdisches Pfingstfest', in *Monatschrift für Gottesdienst und kirchliche Kunst*, XLV, 1940, 75-8.
E. Lohse, '*Πεντηκοστή*', in *Theologisches Wörterbuch zum Neuen Testament*, VI, 1954, 45-9.

On the feast of Tents:

R. Kittel, 'Osirismysterien und Laudhüttenfest', in *Orientalistische Literaturzeitung*, XXVII, 1924, 385-91.
J. A. Wensinck, 'Arabic New Year and the Feast of Tabernacles' (*Verhandelungen d. kon. Akad. v. Wetenskap, Letterkunde, N.R.*, XXV, 2), Leyden, 1925, 1-41.
L. I. Pap, *Das israelitische Neujahrfest*, Kampen, 933, 1933, 33-47.
H. Bornhäusen, *Sukka* (*Die Mischna* . . ., II, 6), Berlin, 1935.
J. Morgenstern, 'Amos Studies, II', in *HUCA*, XII-XIII, 1937-8, 20-34.
G. von Rad, *Das formgeschichtliche Problem des Hexateuchs*, Stuttgart, 1938, 30-7=*Gesammelte Studien zum Alten Testament*, Munich, 1958, 41-8.
R. de Vaux, 'Le schisme religieux de Jéroboam Ier', in *Angelicum*, XX, 1943=*Biblica et Orientalia R. P. Vosté dicata*, 77-91.
A. Alt, 'Zelte und Hütten', in *Alttestamentliche Studien* (*Festschrift Nötscher*), Bonn, 1950, 16-25.
H. J. Kraus, *Gottesdienst in Israel. Studien zur Geschichte des Laubhüttenfest*, Munich, 1954.
S. Talmon, 'Divergences in Calendar-Reckoning in Ephraim and Juda', in *VT*, VIII, 1958, 48-74.
G. W. MacRae, 'The Meaning and Evolution of the Feast of Tabernacles', in *Catholic Biblical Quarterly*, XXII, 1960, 251-76.

See also the bibliography for the next two paragraphs.

On the New Year and the feast of Yahweh's enthronement:

Since the two problems are often treated together, we have combined the bibliography for the two paragraphs into one:

P. Volz, *Das Neujahrfest Yahwes*, Tübingen, 1912.
P. Fiebig, 'Rosch ha-schana' (*Die Mischna* . . ., II, 8), Giessen, 1914.
F. Thureau-Dangin, *Rituels akkadiens*, Paris, 1921.
S. Mowinckel, *Psalmenstudien*, II. *Das Thronbesteigungsfest Jahwäs und der Ursprung der Eschatologie*, Kristiania, 1922.
H. Schmidt, *Die Thronfahrt Jahves am Fest der Jahreswende im Alten Testament*, Tübingen, 1927.
L. I. Pap, *Das israelitische Neujahrsfest*, Kampen, 1933.
S. H. Hooke (ed.), *Myth and Ritual*, Oxford, 1933.
N. H. Snaith, *The Jewish New Year Festival. Its Origin and Development*, London, 1947.
A. Bentzen, 'The Cultic Use of the Story of the Ark in Samuel', in *JBL*, LXVII, 1948, 37-53.
R. Pettazzoni, 'Der babylonische Ritus des Akītu und das Gedicht der Weltschöpfung', in *Eranos-Jahrbuch*, XIX, 1950, 403-30.
H. J. Kraus, *Die Königsherrschaft Gottes im Alten Testament. Untersuchungen zu den Liedern von Jahwes Thronbesteigung*, Tübingen, 1951.
A. Feuillet, 'Les Psaumes eschatologiques du Règne de Yahvé', in *Nouvelle Revue Théologique*, LXX, 1951, 244-60; 352-63.
F. Köcher, 'Ein mittelassyrisches Ritualfragment', in *ZA*, L, 1952, 192-202.
S. Mowinckel, *Zum israelitischen Neujahr und zur Deutung der Thronbesteigungspsalmen*, Oslo, 1952.
J. de Fraine, *L'aspect religieux de la royauté israélite*, Rome, 1954.
A. R. Johnson, *Sacral Kingship in Ancient Israel*, Cardiff, 1955.
G. Widengren, *Sakrales Königtum im Alten Testament und im Judentum*, Stuttgart, 1955.
S. Mowinckel, *He that Cometh*, Oxford, 1956.
D. Michel, 'Studien zu den sogenannten Thronbesteigungspsalmen', in *VT*, VI, 1956, 40-68.

H. OTTEN, 'Ein Text zum Neujahrsfest aus Boğazköy', in *Orientalistische Literaturzeitung*, LI, 1956, 101-5.
H. GROSS, 'Lässt sich in den Psalmen ein "Thronbesteigungsfest Gottes" nachweisen?' in *Trier theologische Zeitschrift*, LXV, 1956, 24-40.
E. AUERBACH, 'Neujahr- und Versöhnungs-Fest in den biblischen Quellen', in *VT*, VIII, 1958, 337-43.
S. H. HOOKE, ed., *Myth, Ritual and Kingship*, Oxford, 1958.
H. CAZELLES, 'Nouvel An en Israël', in *Dictionnaire de la Bible, Supplément*, VI, Paris, 1959, 620-45.

18

THE LATER FEASTS

On the Day of Atonement:

J. G. FRAZER, *The Scapegoat*, London, 1913.
J. MEINHOLD, 'Joma' (*Die Mischna* . . ., II, 5), Giessen, 1913.
S. LANDERSDORFER, *Studien zum biblischen Versöhnungstag*, Münster i. W., 1924.
M. LÖHR, *Das Ritual von Lev. 16*, Berlin, 1925.
H. KAUPEL, *Die Dämonen im Alten Testament*, Augsburg, 1930, 81-91.
I. SCHUR, 'Versöhnungstag und Sündenbock' (*Soc. scient. Fennica, Comm. Hum. Litt.*, VI, 3), Helsingfors, 1934.
G. ORMANN, *Das Sündenbekenntnis des Versöhnungstag*, Bonn, 1935.
L. ROST, 'Weidewechsel und altisraelitischer Festkalendar', in *ZDPV*, LXVI, 1943, 205-16.
TH. C. VRIEZEN, 'The Term *hizza*: Lustration and Consecration', in *Oudtestamentische Studiën*, VII, 1950, 201-35.
J. MORGENSTERN, 'Two Prophecies from the Fourth Century B.C. and the Evolution of Yom Kippur', in *HUCA*, XXIV, 1952-3, 1-74.
G. R. DRIVER, 'Three Technical Terms in the Pentateuch' (for Azazel), in *Journal of Semitic Studies*, I, 1956, 97-8.
E. AUERBACH, 'Neujahrs- und Versöhnungs-Fest in den biblischen Quellen', in *VT*, VIII, 1958, 337-43.

On the Hanukkah:

H. HÖPFL, 'Das Chanukafest', in *Biblica*, II, 1922, 165-79.
O. S. RANKIN, *The Origins of the Festival of Hanukkah*, Edinburgh, 1930.
E. BICKERMANN, 'Ein jüdischer Brief vom Jahre 124 v. Chr. (II Macc. 1: 1-9)', in *Zeitschrift für die neutestamentliche Wissenschaft*, XXXII, 1933, 233-54.
O. S. RANKIN, 'The Festival of Hanukkah', in S. H. HOOKE (ed.), *The Labyrinth*, London, 1935, 159-209.
F.-M. ABEL, 'La fête de la Hanoucca', in *RB*, LIII, 1946, 538-46.
J. MORGENSTERN, 'The Chanukkah Festival and the Calendar of Ancient Israel', in *HUCA*, XX, 1947, 1-136; XXI, 1948, 365-496.
TH. H. GASTER, *Festivals of the Jewish Year*², New York, 1955.

On the feast of Purim:

In addition to commentaries on the book of Esther, see:

N. S. DONIACH, *Purim, or the Feast of Esther. An Historical Study*, Philadelphia, 1933.
J. LEWY, 'The Feast of the 14th Day of Adar', in *HUCA*, XIV, 1939, 127-51.
V. CHRISTIAN, 'Zur Herkunft des Purim-Festes', in *Alttestamentliche Studien* (*Festschrift Nötscher*), Bonn, 1950, 33-7.
J. LEWY, 'Old Assyrian *puru'um* and *pūrum*', in *Revue Hittite et Asianique*, V, 1939, 117-24.
A. BEA, 'De origine vocis *pûr*', in *Biblica*, XXI, 1940, 198-9.
Th. H. GASTER, *Purim and Hanukkah in Custom and Tradition*, New York, 1950.
H. RINGGREN, 'Esther and Purim', in *Svensk Exegetisk Årsbok*, XX, 1955, 5-24.

GENERAL INDEX

In this first index, the most important page-references are given first, and the sub-headings are arranged, as far as possible, in a logical order (*e.g.* historically).

INDEX TO PROPER NAMES

1. *Jabesh, etc. For words beginning with J not listed here, see Y.*

INDEX OF SEMITIC FORMS

(including a few Egyptian words)

INDEX OF BIBLICAL REFERENCES

List of Abbreviations of Biblical References

Ab — Abdias
Ac — Acts of the Apostles
Ag — Aggaeus
Am — Amos
Ap — Apocalypse
Ba — Baruch
1 Ch — 1 Chronicles
2 Ch — 2 Chronicles
1 Co — 1 Corinthians
2 Co — 2 Corinthians
Col — Colossians
Ct — Canticle
Dn — Daniel
Dt — Deuteronomy
Eph — Ephesians
Esd — Esdras
Est — Esther
Ex — Exodus
Ez — Ezechiel
Gal — Galatians
Gn — Genesis
Ha — Habaquq
He — Hebrews
Is — Isaias
Jb — Job
Jdt — Judith
Jg — Judges
Jl — Joel
Jn — John
Jon — Jonas
Jos — Josue
Jr — Jeremias
1 K — 1 Kings
2 K — 2 Kings
Lk — Luke
Lm — Lamentations
Lv — Leviticus
1 M — 1 Maccabees
2 M — 2 Maccabees
Mi — Micheas
Mk — Mark
Ml — Malachi
Mt — Matthew
Na — Nahum
Nb — Numbers
Ne — Nehemias
Os — Osee
Pr — Proverbs
Ps — Psalms
Qo — Qoheleth (Ecclesiastes)
Rom, Ro — Romans
Rt — Ruth
1 S — 1 Samuel
2 S — 2 Samuel
Si — Sirach (Ecclesiasticus)
So — Sophonias
Tb — Tobias
Za — Zacharias